BRAIN-BASED LEARNING

BRAIN-BASED LEARNING

Eric Jensen

Printed in the United States of America
Published by The Brain Store
San Diego, CA USA

Brain-Based Learning
Eric Jensen

Printed in the United States of America
Published by The Brain Store
San Diego, CA USA

Brain-Based Learning
Eric Jensen
©1995
©2000 Revised

Dedicated to my wife Diane
Illustrations: Tracy Sciacca and Eric Jensen
Layout: Tracy Sciacca
Editing: Karen Markowitz

Printed in the United States of America
Published by The Brain Store Publishing
San Diego, CA, USA

ISBN # 1-890460-05-2

For additional copies or
bulk discounts, contact:
The Brain Store
San Diego, CA USA
Phone (858) 546-7555 or (800) 325-4769
Fax (858) 546-7560

In a gentle way you can shake the world.

—*Gandhi*

Table of Contents

6 Preparing the Learner 73

7 The Brain, Gender, and Learning 91

8 The Nonconscious Learning Climate 101

9 Attentional States 121

10   *Uniqueness and the Brain*

11   *Enriching the Brain*

12   *The Role of Movement and Exercise*

13   *Enhancing Cognition*

14 Driven by Emotions 197

15 Memory and Recall 215

16 Stress and Threat 229

17 Music with a Purpose 243

Preface

Keeping pace with the explosion of brain research over the past two decades has proved challenging, but astute educators are applying the findings with astonishing success. The result is a learning approach that is more aligned with how the brain naturally learns best. This dramatic new paradigm, known as brain-compatible or brain-based learning, has emerged with spellbinding implications for teachers and learners worldwide. Based on research from the disciplines of neuroscience, biology, and psychology, our understanding of the relationship between learning and the brain now encompasses the role of emotions, patterns, meaningfulness, environments, body rhythms, attitudes, stress, trauma, assessment, music, movement, gender, and enrichment. By integrating what we now know about the brain with standard education practices, *Brain-Based Learning* suggests ways that our schools can be transformed into complete learning organizations.

As many of our conventional educational models have been shattered like glass, many are saying, "it's about time." The visionary author-scientist H. G. Wells said, "Civilization is a race between education and catastrophe." Indeed, there is an urgency to our planet that we've never before collectively known. At both the local and global level, we lack the luxury of being able to weather a continued "Dark Age" in learning. Too much is at risk: We must act on the problems facing us now.

> *Present problems cannot be solved with the same level of thinking or with the same tools that created them.*

This book calls for the initiation of a fundamental shift in thinking. Shortsighted priorities, outdated teacher-education programs, visionless leaders, "program-of-the-week" mentalities, clumsy systems, budgetary bottlenecks, hierarchical infighting, and professional jealousy all contribute to the problem; and they've got to stop. Furthermore, we need to quit playing "victim" and arm ourselves with change strategies that work. We can affect the changes called for if we collectively make it important enough to do so. Each brain-based strategy outlined in this book can be achieved by any one of us at little or no expense.

The first step, however, is to make an important distinction between core problems and symptoms. While solving core problems provides a twenty to fifty-fold return on our investment of resources, solving mere symptoms creates a net loss. When an organization is antagonistic to the natural and effortless way the brain learns, it faces a mind-boggling array of symptoms that result in ever greater challenges. This means that for every *symptom* you "solve," you not only miss the real problem, but you wear down an already overburdened staff and ultimately drain valuable resources. Every new program that has come and gone over the past thirty years was brain-antagonistic. Schools must open their collective doors to the simple and fundamental questions that science is now answering for us: "How does the brain learn best?" And, "How do we create successful learning organizations with the brain in mind?"

Why is now the time for a shift in thinking? The research on what works is both compelling and comprehensive. We are all great natural learners. Failing children and failing schools are an indication of a faulty system, not a faulty brain; and our schools have taken enough of a beating! When students are provided with a learning environment that is optimal for learning, graduation rates increase, learning difficulties and discipline problems decrease, a love of learning flourishes, administrators focus on the real issues, and learning organization thrive. In short, creating an organization around the way the brain naturally learns best may be the simplest and most critical educational reform ever initiated. In fact, of all the reforms, nothing provides a better return on your investment of time, energy, and money than developing a brain-based approach to learning.

Now is the time to expand the research-to make it school-tested and classroom-proven. And that is up to us as educators. As such, it's imperative that we share our knowledge and experiences with others.

> *As in most change efforts,*
> *the first thing we face from others is indifference*
> *followed by ridicule and opposition...*
> *and then, finally, respect.*

Even as you read this, learning organizations across the globe, determined individuals, cooperating teams, and whole communities have successfully implemented brilliant, innovative, low-cost, brain-based learning solutions. Thus, it's no longer a question of "Can we?" We know we can provide learners with brain-compatible environments and curriculums that support their natural learning abilities. The question now is, "Will we?"

Brain-based learning is a way of thinking about the learning process.
It is not a panacea; nor is it the solution to all of our problems.
It is not a program, dogma, or recipe for teachers.
And it is not a trend or gimmick.
It is, however, a set of principles; and a base of knowledge and skills
upon which we can make better decisions about the learning process.

People who teach and train others make a vital contribution to the preservation of humanity. We must become a world of learners and begin to value learning as much as freedom, liberty, justice, shelter and good health. We are obliged to take this assignment seriously-our collective future, in fact, depends on it. I invite you to start now. If you can't do it by yourself, ask for support: Start a network. Determined people everywhere have done it. They've simply said, "Let's get all of these people talking to each other and see what comes of it." As they shared what works for them, they realized a success rate that exceeded the norm.

You can make a significant difference. You are a once-in-forever biological event. This planet gets only one opportunity to experience your unique and powerful contributions, so share all that you are capable of at this moment. Can you step up to the challenge and accept your historical role? Go on, join the learning revolution: You've got nothing to lose and everything to gain. Find other like-minded people and organize yourselves for greater impact. As Margaret Mead once said:

> *"Never doubt that a small group of*
> *concerned citizens can change the world.*
> *It is, indeed, the only thing that ever has."*

Isn't how the brain learns fundamental to all that we do? This book is written for those who want to know not only *what* works, but *why* it works, and *how* to incorporate the methods. It is written in non-technical terms for the new, as well as veteran teacher or trainer. When positive habits are formed early, the job of teaching becomes significantly easier. When what we know intuitively works is validated, we are rewarded with great satisfaction. So everyone will benefit-no matter what your level of experience. By picking up this book, you've already taken the first step. Turn the page and take the next. If not now, when? If not you, who? Carpe diem.

Rethinking
the Brain

It's a Jungle in There

How Things Are Changing

Is Behaviorism Outdated?

What Is Brain-Based Learning?

Critics of the Brain-Based Movement

Rethinking the Brain

It's a Jungle in There!

For centuries scientists have tried to decipher the inner workings of the human brain. They've mapped the circulation, noted the electrical activity, exposed glucose metabolism, measured and probed its parts, and even traced neuronal growth. Still, the vast complexity of our "thinking organ" has left scholars short of an efficient explanation of how it works. Over the years, however, a few metaphors have emerged to aid the process. The brain has been compared to a hydraulic system, a telephone switchboard, a massive city, and a high-powered computer with each subsequent analogy reflecting the most current technological innovation of the time.

Although metaphors provide a valuable mental and visual framework for understanding complex subjects, when left unqualified, they can also perpetuate gross generalizations. Therefore, we acknowledge the newest brain metaphor of the rain forest jungle as a useful starting point in our discussions, but warn against the inherent risk of oversimplification. Keeping this in mind, let's consider how this fantastic three-pound universe we call the human brain has been compared to a jungle.

The jungle, like the brain, is active at times, quiet at others, but always teeming with life. Both the jungle and the brain are equipped with their own internal clocks which are influenced by light and weather patterns. The jungle thrives in its own distinctive ecosystem where elements such as soil, air, streams, ground cover, low-lying plants, shrubs, and the forest canopy are interdependent. The brain also has distinctive regions that handle various mental functions, such as thinking, sexuality, memory, survival, emotions, breathing, and creativity. While the jungle changes over time, one constant remains true: The law of the jungle is survival and no one creature is ultimately in charge! A jungle has no "teacher" or "trainer." It is simply a rich, evolving system that is as complex as it is fascinating to explore.

Just as no creature (not even The Lion King or Tarzan!) runs the jungle, no individual region of the brain is equipped to run the whole show either. It is a symbiotic relationship: Everyone and everything participates to make the "jungle production" happen. In fact, it is a messy, overlapping, and inefficient process in many ways. Rather than one distinct pathway, there are many channels that feed information into the brain and subsequently many pathways to access it. A plant may not directly communicate with a bird or a monkey, but it, nevertheless, makes an essential contribution to its neighbors' survival, perhaps providing food or shelter.

The jungle has no short- or long-term goals with one exception, the genetic goal of survival. It simply does everything it can, systematically and ecologically, to survive and thrive. The brain is also best at learning what it needs to learn to survive—socially, economically, emotionally, and physically. Both our brain forest and the rain forest are constantly evolving in response to stimulation—becoming more complex with age and experience. Both are capable of weathering extremes in the environment and adapting to change. This resilience allows us to grow stronger over time. When we consider the amazing complexity of the human brain forest, it is extraordinary to think that today we know with impunity, *how our brain naturally learns best.*

Why is our newfound knowledge about the brain important to classroom teachers? For years educators threw out a wide net merely *hoping* to "catch" the largest "school" of learners. Today, by simply applying the principles of brain-based learning, we can guarantee most learners will get hooked most of the time.

Here's an example how contributions from neuroscience and developmental psychology are informing teaching and learning: If the brain's primary need is survival, the approach we take with an abused or neglected student will be different that used to motivate learners who feel safe and academically affirmed at home. Learning multiplication tables, for instance, is likely to be a much lower priority for the abused child than others well cared for; whereas, being street smart may be a much lower priority for the nurtured child. Brain-based learning considers what is natural to our brain; and how the brain is impacted by circumstances and experiences.

How Things are Changing

Brain-based learning emerged in the 1980s as a whole new breed of science was quietly developing. By the 1990s, it had exploded into dozens of mindboggling subdisciplines. Suddenly, seemingly unrelated disciplines were being mentioned in the same science journals. Readers found immunology, physics, genes, emotions, and pharmacology seamlessly woven into articles on learning and brain theory. The voices that we were hearing were those of biochemists, cognitive scientists, neuroscientists, psychologists, and educational researchers with names such as Alkon, Gage, Gazzaniga, Greenough, Kosslyn, LeDoux, Crick, Rose, Damasio, Calvin, Herbert, Pert, Sachs, and Edelman. From this broad multi-disciplinary body of research about the brain came a new way of thinking about learning.

> *The brain is poorly designed for formal instruction.*
> *In fact, it is not at all designed for efficiency or order.*
> *Rather, it develops best through selection and survival.*

This means that if you want to maximize learning, you'll first want to discover how "nature's engine" runs. This singular realization alone has fueled a massive and urgent movement worldwide to redesign learning. What we thought was critical in the past may, in fact, not be very important at all. Perhaps, our instructional methods of the past really emerged because they were "measurable." Think about this though: You can have the most efficient net in the world, and if you're fishing in the wrong place, you're still not going to go home with a big catch.

Is Behaviorism Outdated?

The importance of this paradigm to those who teach or train is stunning: It's no less than the destruction of our old Skinnerian model of instruction that proposed the best means for molding individuals was operant conditioning (through rewards and punishment). This basic tenet of behaviorism, which was popularized in the 1950s by B. F. Skinner and John Watson, continues to rear its short-sighted head half a century later. Adamant policy-makers still insist that achieving the highest possible rank in test scores (instead of producing happy, well-adjusted human beings who can think, care about others, and innovate) should be the top priority in our school-systems.

But human beings are not rats; and to account for our unique condition, which includes our propensity to be creative, depressed, oppositional, motivated, and to make conscious choices, a bit more sophistication is required. Consideration must be given to these factors and the diversity of our experience and backgrounds. How then would you integrate a simple reward/punishment system with such diverse human learners? Shouldn't the student who is living with abuse, rage, brain insults, or distress, for instance, be evaluated on an individual basis? How can educators possibly account for all of these differences? The answer is that we can't—at least, not with a simple model that uses either a carrot or stick to impose learning. The vast range of learners in today's school environment are subjected typically to one of the following three models:

1. *Survival of the Fittest*

"You can lead a horse to water, but you can't make it drink." This old adage reflects the thinking of some educators that their responsibility ends at leading the horse to water. Thus, if the child doesn't learn to read in the standard program provided, they are deficient. The thinking is that "if the student can't cut it (or doesn't want to) that's their problem." This model reduces the teacher's accountability and allows many learners to drop through the cracks.

2. *Determined Behaviorist*

"With enough punishment and rewards, you can get any behavior you wish." This model basically views learners as rats to be manipulated by the whims of the establishment. If scores are too low, the thinking is bribe them to achieve higher ones. If there's violence, the thinking is put in more guards and metal detectors. This model manipulates learners and reduces the classroom to a place where students have little voice or choice.

3. *Brain-based Naturalist*

"How can we make the horse thirsty so that it will *want* to drink from the trough?" This shift in thinking reflects the approach of brain-based educators. A teacher following the brain-based model would think, how can I discover the learner's natural impediments and built-in motivators so that desired behavior emerges as a natural consequence?

Each of these models is played out through a series of overt or covert suppositions. Can you think of colleagues' whose styles match the modes of thinking described? Most organizations end up with a variety of models represented because an official model has not been declared; and because not all involved parties have been trained and brought on board. This inconsistency in approaches and philosophies is hard on the staff, parents, and students alike. Many school districts and organizations have come to realize this important concern in recent years and have begun to make a concerted effort to get unified.

But how can you design optimal education practices and policies if you don't understand the brain? You can't. While it's easy to see which of the models above makes more sense when spelled out like this, the fundamental reason why the third choice makes more sense is:

> *Nature's biological imperative is simple:*
> *No intelligence or ability will unfold until, or unless,*
> *it is given the appropriate model environment.*

In short, our students are bringing a survival-oriented genetic blueprint to "work" each day. It's up to us to create the conditions whereby their brain will "choose" or "select" the learning that will best enhance their chances of survival. After all, that's what happens anyway. When we are talking about survival on a larger "systems" (school or work) level, all processes are instructive. When we are talking about instruction (in the classroom), all processes are simply selective mechanisms. In other words, nature is evolving the best brains through natural selection. The "jungle" has no "special education" programs for plants that need extra fertilizer or for birds that sing poorly. They survive or they don't.

Now you might be thinking, "That's cruel. Schools ought to help all children learn"; and that is true. We no longer live in the jungle; and hopefully we are a bit more caring, sophisticated, and culturally advanced than a jungle population. But from a biological perspective, the fact that our brain, like our immune system, is designed solely for survival, is important information. Students will do what they need to do to survive in the "schoolyard jungle." The "negative" behaviors they learn—putdowns, deceit, attacking, avoidance, and peer pressure—are to be expected as long as students perceive their survival is at stake. This precept calls for dramatic changes in the way we organize formal teaching and training. As you continue to read this book, keep in mind this basic brain-based principle: "*The brain is designed for survival, not formal instruction.*"

What This Means to You

We must begin to think of teaching as "learning to get out of the way of the learner." The brain is trying to learn, in order to survive. This is why it makes so much sense to design your approach so that it is centered on the needs of the learner. The learner's own goals, when encouraged to be identified, may include social, economic, and personal considerations that you were unaware of as important to this individual. Support and expand programs that already incorporate survival learning. Such programs include life-skills classes, community service opportunities, mentoring, tutoring, sports, apprenticeships, music, after-school clubs, and the arts. Perceived learner survival encourages learning on many levels.

 Having said that the brain operates naturally on a selection principle, can it still learn through instruction? Of course, it can. And it can learn optimally in an environment that is conducive to how it learns best. Every day learners worldwide are developing new skills and knowledge based on a brain-compatible model of instruction. But it is an instructional model that integrates some simple discoveries about what facilitates accelerated learning, enrichment, and reorganization of our cognitive system. The following chapters are devoted to the exploration of these discoveries, applications to the classroom or training environment, and strategies for implementing what we've learned about learning.

What is Brain-Based Learning?

Since all learning is connected to the brain in some way, what is meant by a "brain-based approach"? It is learning in accordance with the way the brain is naturally designed to learn. It is a multidisciplinary approach that is built on the fundamental question, "What is good for the brain?" It crosses and draws from multiple disciplines, such as chemistry, neurology, psychology, sociology, genetics, biology, and computational neurobiology. It is a way of thinking about learning. It is a way of thinking about your job. It is not a discipline on its own; nor is it a prescribed format or dogma. In fact, a "formula" for it would be in direct opposition to the principles of brain-based learning. Although a brain-based approach doesn't provide a recipe for you to follow, it does encourage you to consider the nature of the brain in your decision-making. By using what we know about the brain, we can make better decisions; and we can reach more learners, more often, with less misses. Quite simply, it is learning with the brain in mind.

Critics of the Brain-Based Movement

Anything that threatens an existing system will draw its share of critics. No matter what the event, the discovery, or the insight, critics will emerge: It's human nature. While it's important to consider the concerns of opponents, it is also helpful to think about their frame of reference or mode of thinking. The critics of brain-based learning generally fall into one of the following three categories:

1. *"Been there, done that"*

These are the people that think, "There's nothing new under the sun; or everything that can be invented has already been invented." They see the brain-based movement as a recycling of the Madeline Hunter approach or just plain good teaching that we've known about for fifty years. Their limited thinking reflects that of C. Duell, the Director of the U.S. Patent Office, who upon his retirement in 1899 said, "Nothing else of importance is left to be invented or discovered." Cynics can have a tendency to lack vision and to foresee and acknowledge the value of emerging paradigms that challenge old notions. The past decade has been full of new discoveries that have serious, practical implications for education worldwide. In fact, it is overwhelming to keep up with them. Dozens of new journals (electronic, as well as traditional print) are introduced each year to keep up with the dissemination of new information: To ignore what's new or dismiss it, is to stop growing and improving the systems in which we work and live.

2. *Recycled Behaviorists*

Some people worship the "god of high test scores." They think nothing shows good learning better than an improvement from one test to the next. They see arts, music, physical education, emotional-social skill learning, and recess as "fluff." They promote a "stick to the basics" approach. They want better reading, writing, and arithmetic performance; and believe that the best way to achieve this is by manipulating learners with rewards and punishment. Their thinking is, "If kids don't like it, bribe or reward them until they fall in line; and if they don't perform to expectation, punish them with poor grades." This thinking is a throwback to a 1950s mentality when the "3Rs" were determined to be what kids needed to master to cope in the world.

Beyond this, recycled behaviorists are convinced that there's a causal relationship between test scores and success. Even though high reading scores may be a good indicator of better learning, high overall test scores do not translate to personal success. The world is not run by "A" students; rather most of the intellectual leaders we admire today were considered average students. Bill Gates, for example, was a college dropout and Thomas Edison only went to the eighth grade. There are no studies that support the claim that higher test scores on standardized national grade-level tests or college-entrance exams have a causal relationship to success in life. Test scores don't necessarily correlate to happiness, productive employment, social contributions, loving relationships, personal empowerment, good health, or successful child-rearing practices. And what aspects of life are more important than these?

3. *Prove it to me!*

This group of critics is more skeptical than cynical. They want to know precisely what brain-based learning *proves*. But you can't have it both ways; while you can't empirically "prove" that understanding a particular structure or function of the brain always leads to better instruction, you also can't "prove" nearly anything empirically in education. There are simply too many variables. Prove to me that cooperative learning always works; prove to me that greeting kids at the door always works; prove to me that direct instruction phonics always works. There's no "proof" for anything in education. It's all based on complex, biased assumptions about learning; the social and economic constraints of the moment; and the individual experiences of those with whom we're working.

Having said that, it is also important to acknowledge that some proponents of brain-based learning have gone too far in their interpretations of the literature. While it's true, for example, that we have critical periods for learning (emotional, musical, language, etc.), it's also true that the human brain is highly adaptive. We continue to learn throughout our lives, even if our peak of learning ripeness for a particular type of learning may have passed.

We do have a responsibility to be accurate in translating the research; and to make unsubstantiated leaps from neurons to social policy is just not good practice. For example, although it makes the best sense to offer second language instruction between the ages of five and ten, that does not necessarily mean it should be mandated at every school. However, if you're going to include the learning of a second language in your K-12 curriculum, introducing it in the early grades makes more sense than initiating it in the later grades.

As we deepen our study of brain-based learning, it's healthy to take stock of not only our students' needs, but our own learning needs, as well. In this way, the meaningfulness we speak of as important in brain-based learning gets integrated into our own learning. This journey we're taking together offers lifelong learning opportunities. Keep your feet on the ground and reach for the stars!

Reflection Questions

1. What from this chapter was novel, fresh, or new to you? What was familiar or "old hat"?

2. In what ways, do you already apply the information in this chapter?

3. What three questions might you now generate about this material?

4. How did you react emotionally to the information in this chapter?

5. How did you react cognitively to the information? Do you agree or disagree with the author's point of view? Why?

6. In what ways might you translate the principles presented in this chapter into practical everyday useful ideas?

7. If these things are, in fact, true about the brain, what should we do differently? What resources of time, people, and money could be redirected? In what ways might you suggest we start doing this?

8. What were the most interesting insights you gained from this material?

9. If you were to plan your next step for making your curriculum more brain-based, what would that be?

10. What obstacles might you encounter? How might you realistically deal with them?

Discovering Our Brain

Complex, Multi-Path Learning

Every Brain is Unique

Revisiting Left/Right-Brain Dialogue

Our Asymmetrical Brain

The Paradox of Left-Brain Creativity

The Paradox of Right-Brain Logic

Handedness and Learning

Discovering Our Brain

Learners are far more capable than previously imagined. In fact, each successive study of the brain's potential has documented that earlier predictions were far too modest. The brain is the most complex organ we possess. It contains about one hundred billion (100,000,000,000) cells! For the sake of comparison, consider that a monkey has about ten billion brain cells or 10 percent of human capacity; a mouse has about five million brain cells, and a fruit fly has about one hundred thousand (see figure 2.1).

When linked together, the number of connections our brain cells can make is estimated to be from one hundred trillion to as much as ten followed by millions of zeroes (more than the estimated number of atoms in the known universe). These numbers provide a picture of the theoretical capacity of the human brain; but what about the practical capacity? When on earth would

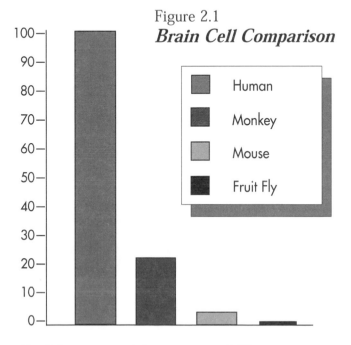

Figure 2.1
Brain Cell Comparison

you have the time to pursue all of these potential connections? The answer is none of us has that kind of time. Sure we could increase our knowledge, skills, and brain connections by 10, 20, or even 50 percent; but realistically, there are not enough hours in the day to fully utilize our brain's potential. We do, after all, have a life to live!

Some researchers say that our brain begins to lose cells starting at birth. Others say, cell deterioration begins about age twelve. This discussion is not very significant, however, when you consider the magnitude of brain cells we are born with: We can afford to lose a few million cells. More significant, is the fact that the brain's plasticity continues as we age. This means that although we may have fewer brain cells, we are still increasing the connections between the cells. Some evidence, in fact, suggests that brain volume increases slightly in subjects aged twenty-five to thirty-nine-years old. We never have to stop learning. Thus, our brain's capacity is more a matter of time, exposure, and motivation, than it is of innate design.

 ## What This Means to You

Most of us underestimate the capacity of our learners (and ourselves as learners). Consider the innate potential of the human brain; and then, reevaluate your expectations. Regardless of what you might perceive as evidence to the contrary, keep in mind that your learners are capable beyond your wildest dreams. Teach to many different learning styles so that the potential of every learner is tapped. Use alternative forms of assessment to provide avenues for those who learn differently. Provide a climate where every learner is respected and affirmed. Encourage cooperative learning with multi-status and multi-age groupings and dyads.

Complex, Multi-Path Learning Is Natural

The brain simultaneously operates on many levels of consciousness, processing all at once a world of colors, movements, emotions, shapes, smells, sounds, tastes, feelings, and more. It assembles patterns, composes meaning, and sorts daily life experiences from an extraordinary number of clues. It is so efficient at processing information that nothing in the living or man-made world comes close to matching human learning potential. Knowing this, perhaps, it is easier to conceive how this amazing multi-processor, called our brain, is undernourished, if not starved in the typical classroom. Many educators unknowingly inhibit the brain's learning ability by teaching in a ultra-linear, structured, and predictable fashion. The result is bored or frustrated learners who then perpetuate the underachievement cycle.

Even though it seems that we think sequentially—one thought after another—this illusion is far from the reality of our brain's true operating system. Biologically, physically, intellectually, and emotionally, we are doing many things at once. In fact, the brain can't do less than multi-process! It is constantly registering perceptions (over 36,000 visual cues per hour), monitoring our vital signs (heart, hormone levels, breathing, digestion, etc.), and continually updating our reality (matching new learning with representations from the past). In addition, the brain is attaching emotions to each event and thought, forming patterns of meaning to construct the larger picture, and inferring conclusions about the information acquired.

Retired University of Oregon professor Robert Sylwester compares our brain's multi-processing capabilities to that of a jazz quartet: "...Members of a jazz quartet communicate with one another as each improvises on a simple theme, blending individual efforts into a unified song" (1995). The four separate areas or lobes of the cerebrum blend like four different musician's instruments without overt communication; yet, they make great music together. Much of our learning happens in random, personalized, often complex patterns that defy description except in the most reductionist terms. In fact, the brain thrives on multi-path, multi-modal experiences. Any teacher who thinks they can inspire great learning by teaching with a singular approach is going to be sadly disappointed.

Some scientists say that there is very little learning that the brain does best in an orderly, sequential fashion. In fact, Nobel Prize winning scientist and co-discoverer of DNA's double-helix formation, Francis Crick, says that the functions of the brain are massively parallel (1994). Our brain uses parallel-processing methods in rapid, serial, visual presentation tasks. What this means to learning is that we understand complex topics better when we experience them with rich sensory input, as opposed to merely reading or hearing about the subject. For example, consider how you learned about the city you live in. Did you learn about it from a guidebook? Or did you learn about it from walking its streets, visiting its attractions, tasting its foods, experiencing its traditions, and interacting with its people? It would be absurd to think that you truly had your finger on the pulse of your community after reading a book on the subject or watching a TV program about it.

As children we learned about our neighborhoods from scattered, random input that was messy at times and left room for exploration and manipulation. Most of what we learned, in fact, as children was imprinted in our memory in this chaotic sort of way. We certainly didn't get lessons from a "how to" book on how to crawl or talk—acts that require complex sequences of precise movements. We figured it out by trial and error.

Even something as simple as crossing the street safely requires the interplay of five different areas of the brain. Without even a brief conscious effort, separate mechanisms in our brain interpret visual patterns, movement, shape, velocity, sounds, and feelings to form a unified perception. Even as demanding as this task may seem on the brain, it is
mundane processing for a fifteen-year-old. If we expect to challenge young people, we need to start doubling or tripling the input and stimulation we provide. The result you can expect is more motivated learners with fewer behavior problems.

The brain is concerned primarily with survival, not formal instruction. In other words, the brain will concentrate on instruction that is only if perceived as meaningful and only if the brain's primary survival needs have been satisfied. For many students, traditional teaching approaches ignore their individual life circumstances and therefore, the needs of their brain. When we throw the net out, many of them are left outside the catch. Psychologist Leslie Hart (1983) says:

> *Any group instruction that has been tightly, logically planned will have been wrongly planned for most of the group, and will inevitably inhibit, prevent, or distort learning.*

Meaningful instruction is, thus, the key. And of course you're thinking, "how can teachers possibly individualize their curriculum for each learner?" We can't possibly achieve this goal every time, but we can get a whole lot closer to the mark. And the way we can do this is to use individualized approaches and reduce traditional group instruction. Lock-step, sequenced teaching ignores the real complexity of the brain.

 ## What This Means to You

Provide complex, multi-sensory immersion environments. Reduce or avoid lock-step whole class instruction. Offer options for learning. For example, a video may be playing in one part of the room. In another, there is a reading area, in another, a discussion group or study session. Make the room rich with colorful posters, pictures, charts, mobiles, and mind-maps. Use mastery learning centers or groupings by common interests. Play some low volume music; and encourage projects with multi-status, multi-age cooperative groups. We learn the most from rich, multi-modal influences such as field trips, simulations, excursions, discussions, real-life projects, and personalized activities. Enrich the environment.

Every Brain Is Unique

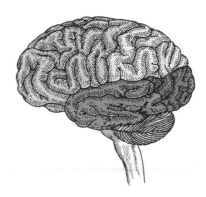

Scientists have verified that like your thumbprint, your brain is unique in the world. The variability of a learner's brain reflects many factors, including genetic and environmental influences. The connections between cells that are made as a result of our experiences form our personal cognitive maps. Our retinotectal maps (thinking and perception) are highly variable; and show major fluctuations in the borders over time. In our visual system alone, we have more than thirty interconnected brain centers, each with its own map. Learning occurs when these maps or neural networks talk to each other. The more connected they are, the greater the "meaning" one derives from the learning. Each of these connections may have from 50 to 100,000 neurons in them. They represent life as we know it. In fact, if you don't have a representative neural network for something out there in the real world, it simply doesn't exist. That is why totally new concepts are so difficult to grasp at first: Existing networks need to expand to support the new associations.

Brain size and weight vary among humans as well. While the founder of relativity, Albert Einstein, had an average-size brain, the French writer Honore de Balzac, had a 40 percent larger than average brain. Our brain's internal wiring is distinct, too. Consider how two people at the scene of the same accident can have such different eyewitness reports. Our perceptions are very personal translations of stimuli based on our neural networks, which act as filters. This is why stereotypes and biases are so persistent: They are embedded in our neural networks. In short, our genetics, as well as our life experiences, sculpt our brains into distinctly unique organs.

> *Lock-step, assembly-line learning violates*
> *a critical finding about the human brain:*
> *Each brain is not only unique, it is*
> *expanding at its own pace.*

In addition to the experience-based differences in physiology, neural wiring, and biochemical balance, every brain is on a different timetable of development. For some brains, the "normal" time to learn to read is age six. For another, the "normal" time may be age three. Completely normal development can differ by a spread of three years between learners (Healy 1987). This finding has dramatic implications for the organization of learning worldwide.

All five year olds should not be expected to perform academically, physically, or socially at the same level. Statewide curriculums and frameworks which include specific grade-level performance standards are biologically inappropriate. While a few exceptional learners are ready, most thirteen-year-olds may not be neurologically ready for algebra or geometry. The human brain is capable of an enormous amount, *if* the neurological groundwork (environmental exposure) has been laid or the teacher has extraordinary flexibility. Glen Doman (1965) showed the world he could teach most babies under three to read, while others from around the world (especially Japan) claimed similar achievements. On the other hand, when the groundwork is not laid, a typical learner will be sabotaged by frustration. Many learners simply conclude they're stupid and give up.

 ## What This Means to You

Provide for differences in learning. Lobby against rigid age-based assessments. Add more variety, choice, and complexity to the learning process. Give students an opportunity to express themselves and interact with each other. Encourage learning with music, mind-maps, role plays, journals, model building, movement, community projects, theater, and art. Special projects can provide learners with more meaning. Reduce whole-class instructional practices. Incorporate "learning stations," partner-oriented learning, and individualized mastery learning. If you enforce learning in a particular way, the learner's brain may resist. Talk to learners: As you inquire about their process, they'll become more aware of how they learn best (meta-cognition). It is difficult, of course, to please all learners at the same time; however, small localized learning groups can go a long way in serving individual needs without compromising organization and structure.

Revisiting the Left/Right-Brain Dialogue

Is there more to our brain than the simple left-side, right-side split? Yes. Even though it is this lateral dichotomy we hear about the most, the energy in our brain moves up and down on a vertical axis—from the brain stem to the cortex and back down again—as well. Our brain is designed to process spatially from left to right hemisphere, but we process time (past to future) from back to front; and neuropeptides circulating through the blood also influence our thinking, behaviors, and reactions. Our brain is, indeed, a micro-universe.

Contrary to what some would lead you to believe, there is no such thing as right-brain learning or left-brain learning. There are only preferences where *more* of one hemisphere is activated than another. There is no learning taking place *only* in the upper cortex or *only* in the brain stem. Our brain is highly interactive.

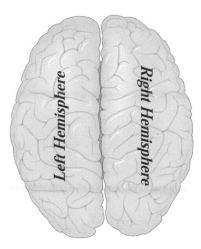

Much of the original work of Nobel Prize Laureate Roger Sperry, PhD. who discovered the functioning differences between left- and right-brain hemispheres, remains valid today. The challenge, however, has been keeping the finding in perspective. Some have oversimplified the conclusions or taken them to an extreme, creating a "split" in thinking that is unwarranted by the literature. Some books have even appeared that draw up battle lines over the "old left-brain way" and the "updated right-brain approach." It is an oversimplification to say that an individual is "left brained" or "right brained." We are all whole brained. Each area of the brain senses what is needed and interacts with other areas in a symbiotic micro-second. What we can safely say about each brain hemisphere is this:

> **The left hemisphere processes "parts" (sequentially):**
> **The right side processes "wholes" (randomly).**

Follow-up research by Jerry Levy, PhD. (1983, 1985) of the University of Chicago has confirmed that both sides of the brain are involved in nearly every human activity; and timing and degree of involvement are important factors. Events occurring in one hemisphere can influence developmental events occurring at the same time at very remote parts of the other hemisphere. It is best to consider brain side specificity in a more metaphorical sense. It may help us understand how we process information, but to pigeon-hole all behaviors into a blueprint of right-left hemispheric behaviors leads to faulty interpretation.

Here's an example of how complex brain side specificity can be. Listening to someone speak may seem like a left-hemisphere activity since the left side processes words, definitions, and language. Contrary to this, however, evidence suggests that the right hemisphere processes the inflection, tonality, tempo, and volume of the communication—elements that are actually more critical to the meaning of a conversation than the words themselves. Further, the female brain processes both language and feelings at the same time far more efficiently than the male brain. Thus, gender may be a factor, as well. James Iaccino, PhD. (1993) suggests that although each hemisphere does have some clear-cut specialization, each side "still requires the other to complement its overall functioning."

Figure 2.2
Corpus Callosum

Top View
Front

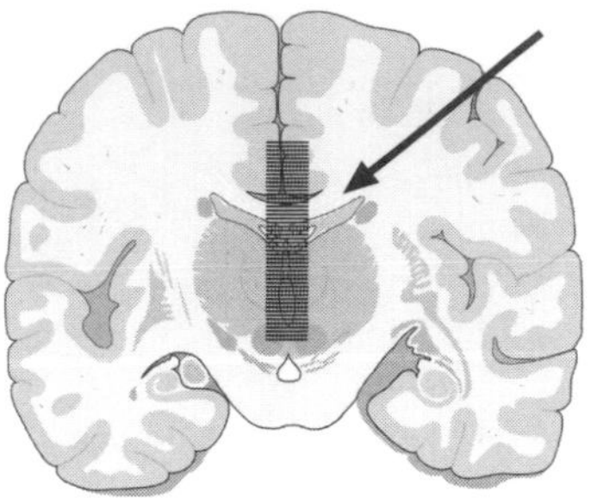

Back

The corpus callosum is the larger
of the two bundles of nerve fibers
that connect the left and right brain.

The corpus callosum (see figure 2.2)—the largest of the hemisphere's interconnecting nerve fibers, which also includes the anterior commissure—develops at a slow rate, causing the two hemispheres to develop unequally. While some researchers, such as Dr. Levy, believe the corpus callosum copies the messages from one side to another, Stanford University scientist Karl Pribram (1979, 1971) believes the brain operates through patches or pocket holograms called neural fields. Others describe the role as topological inhibition, meaning an excited neuron on one side sends a generalized contextual message to the other. The message then simply calls on related programs to prompt further understanding. This model provides some explanation for how ideas are "turned on" and how the "ahaa effect" may occur.

In short, we are using both sides of the brain, most of the time. In fact, it's impossible to shut them off. Even when we come up with the appropriate answer to a question, the brain continues to process alternative responses and explanations nonconsciously. It literally practices thinking while you're not even aware of it! So much of our brain's work is, indeed, outside of our conscious awareness.

Our Asymmetrical Brain

Originally it was thought that the left brain controlled the right 50 percent of the body; and the right brain controlled the other 50 percent. But researchers now know that our brain is asymmetrical. Dr. Iaccino asserts that the left brain is "in charge in a majority of cases, regardless of body side." Considering how much else in the body is asymmetrical, it is no surprise that we have functional preferences for handedness, eyedness, and earedness. Oddly, even maladies like tumors (in the breast, kidney, nasal, ovary, and testes areas) are reported more often on the left-side of the body.

The common biological preference to right-handedness may be related to the greater number of motor fibers in the nerve pathways from the left hemisphere to the right side of the body. The right hemisphere's frontal and central regions are wider, as are the left brain's co-occipital lobes. The major lateral groove, the sylvian fissure, is longer on the left side. The left temporal planum is also larger than the right, as is the parietal operculum. In the prefrontal area, the left areas are smaller then the right side, but more hemispheric "folding" may compensate. Blood flow is unequally distributed, depending on which appendages are in use.

Many educators have applied the left- and right-brain learning model in their classrooms to help them understand their students' individual learning styles. As long as we keep in mind that this division is not cut and dry, it can help us plan more inclusive and global lesson plans.

Left-brain dominant learners, more often than not, may:

- ▼ Prefer things in sequence
- ▼ Learn best from parts to wholes
- ▼ Prefer a phonetic reading system
- ▼ Like words, symbols, and letters
- ▼ Rather read about a subject first
- ▼ Want to gather related factual information
- ▼ Prefer detailed orderly instructions
- ▼ Experience more internal focus
- ▼ Want structure and predictability

Right-brain dominant learners, more often than not, may:

- ▼ Be more comfortable with randomness
- ▼ Learn best from wholes to parts
- ▼ Prefer a whole-language reading system
- ▼ Like pictures, graphs, and charts
- ▼ Rather see it or experience a subject first
- ▼ Want to gather information about relationships among things
- ▼ Prefer spontaneous, go with the flow, learning environments
- ▼ Experience more external focus
- ▼ Want open-ended approaches, novelty, and surprises

The Paradox of Left-Brain Creativity

The notion that one side of the brain is logical and the other side is creative is outdated. We can become very creative by following and using logical sequences, patterns, and variations. The work of Edward DeBono on lateral thinking (1970) reminds us that one can use "left-brain systems" to be creative. For years he has articulated processes to arrive at creative solutions through sequential methods. Is music a right-brain experience? Think again! Researchers discovered that musicians process music to a greater degree in the left hemisphere, while non-musicians process it more in the right hemisphere. This paradox points to the complexity of our brain functions. In this case, since musicians tend to analyze music more than the novice, their left brain is engaged to a greater degree.

PET (positron emission tomography) scans provide researchers with a look at what specific brain locations are engaged during particular activities, moods, or thinking tasks. For example, we can see that the right side of the brain is more activated when the learner is feeling depressed or stressed. But when the learner is feeling a healthy optimism about life and the future, the left hemisphere is more engaged. A "Pollyanna" view of reality (defined by an overestimated sense of good feelings and a denial of negative ones), however, is linked to right-hemisphere activity.

When learners are taught effective ways to process negative moods or events, their learning time is optimized. Model good decision-making processes and critical thinking, for example. Optimism comes from mastering conflict-resolution as well as from experiencing a sense of belonging and acceptance. Engage learners in visualization and goal-setting activities, decision-making scenarios, case studies, and exercises that require logical thinking, brainstorming, and mind-mapping.

The Paradox of Right-Brain Logic

The right side of the brain can intuit many logical things. Drawing, composing, and painting may seem like a right-hemisphere activity, yet artists show bilateral activity. In the planning of artwork, they follow their own logic and rules about shapes, colors, and sounds. An artist can express anything they wish on canvas, clay, glass, metal, or paper; but to be acceptable to the masses, very specific (though unwritten) rules of proportionality, color, balance, and order must be considered. The right brain, it seems, prefers its own kind of holistic *order*.

In the 1970s and 80s, an emphasis on teaching more to the "right-brained learner" occurred. Current brain research tells us that we generally use both sides of the brain, most of the time. Nevertheless, the right-brain emphasis produced the proverbial "pendulum swing," which resulted in a hyper-awareness of the brain's lateral processing tendencies.

> *The prevailing research in neuroscience*
> *avoids the definitive left-right brain labels.*
> *Scientists now use the term "relative lateralization."*

What we can say with impunity is that at a given time, there will be more activity in one hemisphere over the other. However, to say that music is a right-brained activity would be an oversimplification. To ensure optimal learning, we must facilitate learning activities that include the strengths of both hemispheres. Ideally, our efforts ought to be focused on "whole-brained" learning.

 ## What This Means to You

Both parts and wholes are important to learning. Neither should be emphasized at the expense of the other. Those who advocate "right-brain thinking" are better off promoting "whole-brain thinking." Provide learners with global overviews, as well as step-by-step instructions. Show students how you will proceed. If you have access to an overhead projector, create transparencies that represent the learning plan. Present first a transparency depicting the big picture followed by more detailed transparencies representing the subtopics. Alternate between the "big picture" and the details. Validate that we are "whole-brain learners."

Handedness and Learning

Researchers have yet to determine conclusively the cause or explanation for handedness—a functional preference for one side of the body over the other. However, it does appear that most early tools were made for the right hand. Among Americans, 90 percent are right-handed, 8 percent are left-handed, and the remaining are ambidextrous. Hand-preference surveys and handedness inventories have made it possible for us to determine degrees of handedness; but it is still unclear how the preference is triggered. Is it inherited? Probably not. Most left-handers have two right-handed parents. And, among identical twins, 25 percent of pairs had both preferences represented.

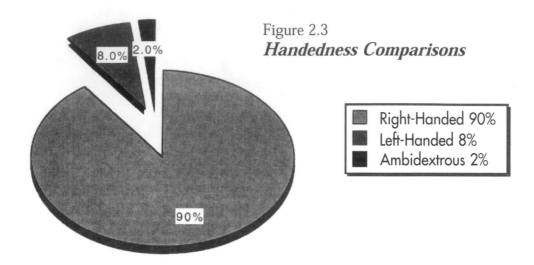

Figure 2.3
Handedness Comparisons

Right-Handed 90%
Left-Handed 8%
Ambidextrous 2%

It seems that it's a right-hander's world: Left-handers are five times as likely to die of accident-related injuries than right-handers. One study (Coren 1992) which examined life span using 5,147 subjects showed a complete and total absence of left-handers over age eighty! Could the life stresses associated with being left-handed be a factor? It is possible. Think about it: Schools, books, pens, jobs, tools, appliances are all designed primarily for right-handers. Among the left-handed population, spatial processing is more often impaired and deficits in both visuo-spatial and verbal tasks are more common. Left-handers, too, are represented in greater numbers among clinical pathological populations. Other problems among left-handed samples include a greater incidence of dyslexia, a weaker immune system, and more maturational delays (Iaccino 1993).

It's not all bad for left-handers though. On a more positive note, left-handers exhibit superiority in listening tasks and may have less lateralized ear superiority, giving both ears the ability to process instructions well (ibid). This can be of benefit in attentional areas. Left-handers exhibit less head turning when asked to solve verbal or spatial problems and longer attentional sets. While most right-handers process language to a greater degree in the left brain and show a consistent right-ear comprehension superiority, some left-handers use both sides of the brain equally for processing language.

Although the brain is the most complex organ in the human body, we are acquiring knowledge about it at an unprecedented rate. The result is that teaching and learning can now be approached in a way that is aligned with how the brain naturally learns best. In view of the science that supports our work as educators, we can't afford to do things the way we've always done them. Now is the time to rethink and rediscover this awesome responsibility we have and to work with our brain, rather than against it.

Reflection Questions

1. What from this chapter was novel, fresh, or new to you? What was familiar or "old hat"?

2. In what ways, do you already apply the information in this chapter?

3. What three questions might you now generate about this material?

4. How did you react emotionally to the information in this chapter?

5. How did you react cognitively to the information? Do you agree or disagree with the author's point of view? Why?

6. In what ways might you translate the principles presented in this chapter into practical everyday useful ideas?

7. If these things are, in fact, true about the brain, what should we do differently? What resources of time, people, and money could be redirected? In what ways might you suggest we start doing this?

8. What were the most interesting insights you gained from this material?

9. If you were to plan your next step for making your curriculum more brain-based, what would that be?

10. What obstacles might you encounter? How might you realistically deal with them?

How the Brain Learns

3

How the Brain Learns

As we learn to teach in a way that is natural to the brain, it is helpful to have a basic understanding of the brain's anatomy. While the process of learning involves the whole body, the brain acts as a way station for incoming stimuli. All sensory input gets sorted, prioritized, processed, stored, or dumped on a subconscious level as it is processed by the brain. Every second a neuron can register and transmit between 250 and 2,500 impulses. When you multiply this transmission ability by the number of neurons we're estimated to have (approximately 100 billion), you can begin to fathom just how unfathomable our human learning potential is.

Basic Brain Anatomy

There are a few distinguishing features of the human brain. Compared to other mammals, we have relatively large brains for our body weight. The adult human brain weighs about three pounds (1300-1400 gms.). By comparison, a sperm whale brain weighs about seventeen pounds (7,800 grams)! A dolphin brain weighs about four pounds; and a gorilla brain weighs about one pound. Your pet dog's brain weighs about seventy-two grams or 6 percent of your own brain's total weight. Comparable in size to a large grapefruit, this three-pound wonder of ours is made up of mostly water (78%), a little fat (10%), and even less protein (8%). The largest, most highly developed portion of the brain (80%) is called the cerebrum. The cerebrum is made up of billions of nerve cells and is divided into two hemispheres. The right side of the cerebrum controls the left side of the body, and vice versa. It is the cerebrum that is responsible for higher-order thinking and decision-making functions.

A normal living human brain is flesh colored and soft enough that it can be cut with a butter knife. Distinguishing the outer surface of our brain, the cerebral cortex (Latin for bark or rind), appears as folds or wrinkles about the thickness of an orange peel. Rich in brain cells, this tissue covering would be about the size of an unfolded sheet of newspaper if stretched out flat. Its importance is highlighted by the fact that the cortex constitutes about 70 percent of the nervous system: Its nerve cells or neurons are connected by nearly *one million miles* of nerve fibers. The human brain has the largest area of uncommitted cortex (no particular required function) of any species on earth. This gives humans extraordinary flexibility and capacity for learning.

The Brain's Four Lobes

The cerebrum is made up of four primary areas called lobes: They are the occipital, frontal, parietal, and temporal lobes (see figure 3.1). The occipital lobe is located in the middle back of the brain and is primarily responsible for vision. The frontal lobe is located in the area around your forehead and is involved with purposeful acts like judgment, creativity, problem-solving, and planning. The parietal lobe is located at the top back portion of your brain: Its duties include processing higher sensory and

Figure 3.1
Lobes of the Human Brain

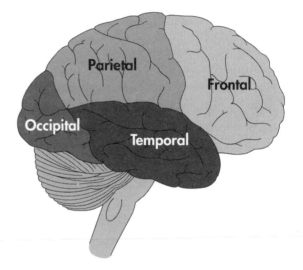

language functions. The temporal lobes (left and right side) are above and around your ears. These areas are primarily responsible for hearing, memory, meaning, and language, although there is some overlap in functions between lobes.

Figure 3.2
Medial View of the Brain

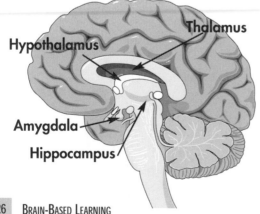

The Mid-Brain Area

The territory in the middle of the brain or core (sometimes referred to as the mid-brain or limbic system) includes the hippocampus, thalamus, hypothalamus, and amygdala (see figure 3.2). This area, which constitutes about 20 percent of the brain by volume, is responsible for sleep, emotions, attention, body regulation, hormones, sexuality, smell, and the production of most of the brain's chemicals.

The part of your brain that is "you"—that is, the part you know as your inner self or the conscious thinker—is not totally clear. It is possible that our consciousness is dispersed throughout the cortex; or it may be located near the reticular formation atop the brain stem. Some scientists, however, believe that the seat of consciousness is in the front-left hemisphere or the orbitofrontal cortex (see figure 3.3).

The sensory cortex (monitoring your skin receptors) and the motor cortex (needed for movement) are narrow bands located across the top middle of the brain in the parietal lobe. In the back lower area of the brain is the cerebellum (Latin for "little brain"), which is primarily responsible for some aspects of balance, posture, motor movement, music, and cognition.

Figure 3.3
Potential Areas of Consciousness

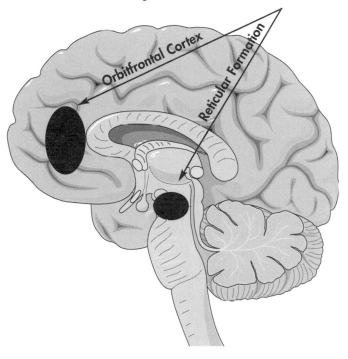

Learning begins on a microscopic cellular level. The basic functional unit of the nervous system, the neuron (Greek for "bowstring"), is responsible for information processing which it accomplishes through the conversion of chemical signals to electrical signals and back again. For the sake of comparison, a fruit fly has one hundred thousand neurons; a mouse has five million; and a monkey has ten billion. You have about one hundred *billion* neurons. Adults have about half the number of neurons found in the brain of a two-year-old. A single cubic millimeter (1/16,000th of an inch) of brain tissue has over one million neurons, each about fifty microns in diameter.

Are we losing our minds? All of us are losing some brain cells all the time as a result of attrition, decay, and disuse. Scientists estimate that our loss of neurons, in fact, is about eighteen million per year from the age of about twenty to seventy. This, however, is not a problem for two reasons: First, even if we were to lose a half-million neurons per day, at this rate, it would still take centuries to "lose our mind." And second, in spite of this naturally occurring pruning process, new research suggests (Eriksson, et al. 1998) that we can also grow new brain cells, at least in one area of the brain called the hippocampus (refer back to figure 3.2).

Figure 3.4
Neuron

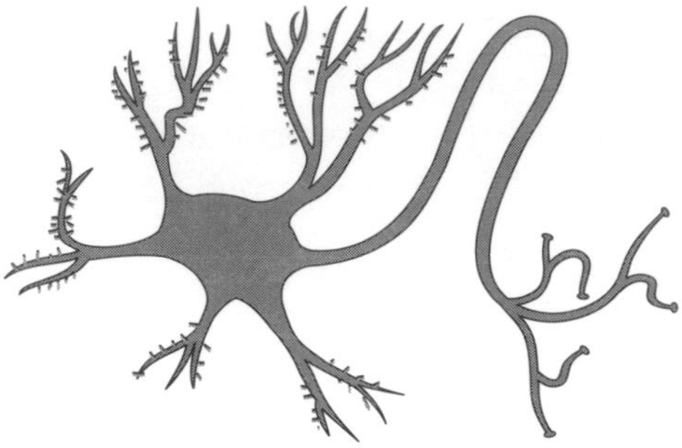

Neuronal growth in the hippocampus may be a result of "exercise"—that is both physical and participating in complex thinking activities, and/or intense mental stimulation. In fact, animal experiments suggest (van Praag, et al. 1999) that with proper enrichment, neurons in the hippocampus can increase 25 to 40 percent in quantity! Thus, the question to ask yourself at the end of the day may not be, "How many cells did I lose today, but how many did I grow?"

Brain Cells

We possess two types of brain cells—glial cells (see figure 3.5) and neurons (see figure 3.4). Glial cells (Greek for "glue"), also known as interneurons, have no cell body and are about ten times more concentrated in our brain than their neuronal

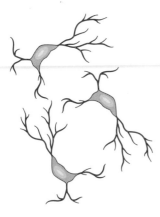

Figure 3.5
Glial Cells

counterparts. A number this large is difficult to conceive, but it means that at birth we have as many as one thousand billion glial cells—that is, one hundred times the number of stars known in the Milky Way. An autopsy of Einstein's brain revealed that, although it was of average size, a greater than average number of glial cells was apparent. However, more recent research has revealed other atypical features of the genius's brain, as well. (Witelson, et al. 1999). The roles assigned glial cells seem to be multifaceted and likely include the production of myelin for the axons, structural support for the blood-brain barrier, the transportation of nutrients, and regulation of the immune system.

A normal functioning neuron continuously fires, integrates, and generates information across microscopic gaps called synapses, thereby linking one cell to another. No neuron is an end point in itself. Rather, they act as conduits for information: Always busy, neurons generate a hotbed of activity. In fact, a single neuron may connect with one thousand to ten thousand other cells. The more connections your cells make, the better. The sum total of all the synaptic reactions arriving from all the dendrites (see figure 3.6) to the cell body at any given moment determines whether that cell will, in fact, fire. In other words, learning involves groups or networks of neurons.

Although the cell body has the capacity to move, most adult neurons stay put and simply extend their single axon outward. Some axonal migration is genetically programmed, while some is a result of environmental stimulation. Although each neuron has only one axon, it has numerous fibers, called dendrites, that also extend from the cell. Axons normally only talk to dendrites; and dendrites normally only talk to axons. When an axon (which is a thinner, leg-like extension) meets up with a dendrite from a neighboring cell, "Ah-ha!", learning has happened.

Figure 3.6
Axon and Dendrite Model

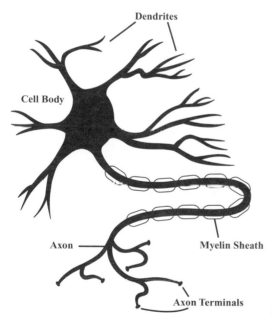

Remember, axons only connect with dendrites; dendrites don't connect with each other. To connect with thousands of other cells, the axon repeatedly subdivides itself and branches out. Neurons serve to pass along information which flows in one direction only. The dendrites are receiving input from other axons and they transmit the information to their cell body. Then it moves out to the axon, which communicates it to another cell through its dendritic branches.

An axon has two essential functions: to conduct information in the form of electrical stimulation and to transport chemical substances. They vary in size with the longer specimens stretching to about one meter. The thicker the axon, the faster it conducts electricity (and information). Myelin, a fatty lipid substance that forms around well-used axons, is present around all axons to some degree. Myelination seems to not only speed the electrical transmission (up to twelve-fold), but also reduces interference from other nearby reactions. Nodes along the axons, along with myelination, can boost electrical impulses to speeds of 120 meters per second or 200 miles per hour. The smallest axon probably receives no advantage from myelination.

Learning Insights

Learning physically changes the brain. That's right: Every new experience we encounter actually alters our electrochemical wiring. Although scientists aren't precisely sure how this happens, we do know that when the brain receives a stimulus of any kind, the process of cell-to-cell communication is activated. The more novel and challenging the stimuli (up to a point), the more likely it will be to activate a new pathway. If the stimuli is not considered meaningful to the brain, however, the information will be given less priority and will leave only a weak trace. If the brain deems something important enough to commit it to long-term memory, a memory potential occurs. Called long-term potentiation (LTP), this electrochemical signaling process is what scientists say constitutes memory.

The consensus today is that our cognitive maps aren't purely a result of nature or nurture, but a dynamic interplay of both—a theory called "emergentism." At each stage of development, particular genes are affected by particular environmental factors. Recent research has focused on what has been called "windows of opportunity," referring to a period of heightened readiness for learning. It is thought that exposure to appropriate stimuli during these peak times can optimize a child's natural appetite for learning—especially learning related to language, music, and motor development. Genes are not templates for learning; they do, however, represent enhanced risk or opportunity. Thus, if a child is born with the genes of a genius, but is raised in a non-enriched environment, the chances of him/her actually becoming a genius are low. A child with average genes, on the other hand, raised in a supportive and intellectually stimulating environment, may achieve greatness by virtue of his/her enriched environment.

Learning Factors

A typical learner arrives not with a "blank slate," but with a highly customized brain bank of experience. Their cognitive map is already a reflection of much more than just previous grade coursework and test scores. This, in fact, is only a small sliver of the neural pie. Even by pre-school age, a learner's brain has already been shaped by a multitude of influences including home environment, siblings, extended family, playmates, genes, trauma, stress, injuries, violence, cultural rituals and expectations, enrichment opportunities, primary attachments, diet, and lifestyle (see figure 3.7). Even a seemingly trivial incident like a bump on the head can have a lifelong impact on learning ability. If, for example, the fragile temporal lobes (or other key brain areas) are injured, a child may experience emotional, processing, and/or memory function problems. Likely the association of the head injury to the learner's challenges will never be made. This example illustrates the complexity of issues educators face.

Prolonged distress is another factor that negatively impacts brain function. Our body releases stress hormones (glucocorticoids) in response to danger. This is what generates the "fight or flight" rush of adrenaline that supports our survival when faced with endangerment. This, of course, is a positive response when it saves our life; however, when our body releases glucocorticoids frequently in response to chronic stress and worry, the mechanism meant to save our lives becomes overused and leaves us in a state of persistent heightened alert. Over time, the result is a toxic effect on neurons and impaired memory. Enjoyable experiences, on the other hand, stimulate the release of chemicals (neurotransmitters) which have been shown to enhance the learning experience. Later chapters will discuss these findings in more detail.

Figure 3.7
7 Learning Influencers

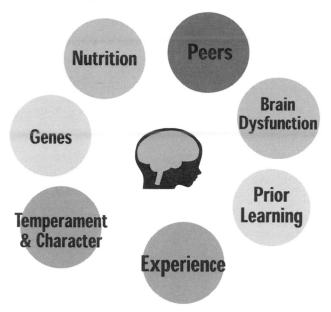

The Stages of Learning

Optimal learning occurs in a predictable sequence. This sequence includes five stages (see figure 3.8). First, the pre-exposure or preparation stage provides a framework for the new learning and primes the learner's brain with possible connections. This stage may include an overview of the subject and a visual representation of related topics. The more background a learner has in the subject, the faster they will absorb and process the new information. The second stage, acquisition, can be achieved through either direct means—as in providing handouts—or indirect means—as in putting up related visuals. Both approaches can work; and they actually complement each other. The elaboration or third stage explores the interconnectedness of topics and encourages depth of understanding. The fourth stage, memory formation, cements the learning, so that what was learned on Monday is retrievable on Tuesday. And, finally, the fifth stage, functional integration, reminds us to use the new learning so that it is further reinforced and expanded upon.

Ultimately, learning is the development of goal-oriented neural networks: Remember, single neurons aren't smart, but integrated groups of neurons that fire together, on cue, are very smart. This orchestrated neural symphony is what learning is all about. Elaborate neural networks are developed over time through the process of: making connections; developing the right connections; and strengthening the connections. In a nutshell, the three most critical aspects of learning are acquisition, elaboration, and memory formation, which are described in detail below.

Acquisition

The first stage of learning is receiving sensory input; does that mean you've learned? In considering what's constitutes learning let's say, for example, that you just heard a very funny joke. You laugh out loud and make a mental note to share it with your colleagues tomorrow in the lunch room. But when the time comes, you've forgotten the joke. If, however, you can't remember the joke, did you ever really learn it? Before you answer, think about this: If you were given five choices from which to choose the joke you heard, would you recognize it? Probably, right? Than perhaps you did actually learn it! The connection, however, might have been weak and so it deteriorated rapidly. Now let's say that more time passes and you aren't even able to recognize the joke anymore. Is your answer to the question still the same? How can you say you learned something if you can't even recognize the joke anymore?

This little enigma reflects a fundamental question in education. When, in fact, has a student learned something? Is it when they experience that great "Ah-ha" moment of discovery or insight? Maybe, but just as the "Ah-ha" or "Ha-ha" moment can be weakened overnight, so might this student's learning if the input is not reinforced. A moment of insight does

Figure 3.8
5 Stages of Optimal Learning

Preparation
(Priming & Pre-Exposure)

Acquisition
(Direct & Indirect Learning)

Elaboration
(Error correction & Depth)

Memory Formation
(Rest, emotions, associations encode learning)

Functional Integration
(Extended Usage)

AH-HA!
is the same neurological event from the point of view of how we learn and remember as is:

HA-HA!
Both are moments of insight which trigger chemical releases, but unless processed for depth, meaning, and storage, they weaken.

Remember, making connections is not enough. We still need to elaborate on them make the right ones, strengthen them, and integrate them into other learning.

not necessarily translate to learning, but it is clearly a vital step in the learning process. So you see that making connections between cells is one thing; retaining them is quite another. And maintaining accurate connections is yet another. The point here is a critical one: Never confuse a moment of insight with learning. "Ha-ha" and "ah-ha" have the same impact on the brain. To remember something, however, elaboration is necessary. As the Chinese saying reminds us: *Learning is not a singular event; it is the process of using it over time.*

The neurological definition of *acquisition* is the formation of new synaptic connections. The cell body of a neuron has spindly branches called dendrites and a single longer projection called an axon (refer back to figure 3.6). The single axon of a cell reaches out to connect with the multiple dendrites on other cells. These connections are formed when the experiences are both novel and coherent. Quite simply, if the input is incoherent, only weak connections (if any) will be made. However, if the input is familiar, existing connections get strengthened and learning results.

Thus, the acquisition stage is the making of connections or neurons "talking" to one another. The sources for acquisition are endless. They may include discussion, lecture, visual tools, environmental stimuli, hands-on experiences, role modeling, reading, manipulatives, videos, reflection, group projects, and pair-share activities. Remember, however, that this first step of

Figure 3.9
Neurons Connecting

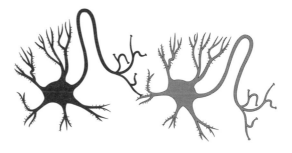

making a connection is highly dependent on prior knowledge. A joke isn't funny unless you have the prior knowledge to make the necessary connections.

Here's an example: A head rolls into a bar and asks the bartender for a drink. The bartender gives him one and amazingly, the head grows the rest of a body and becomes a human. The head is very happy now with a body. The head then asks for another drink and the bartender obliges. But this time, the body melts away and the head is back to where it started. That prompts the bartender to say, "You should have quit when you were a head." This joke (or attempt at one) only makes sense if you possess the prior knowledge and understanding of the idiom "to quit while you're ahead." If you laugh (or even smile at the joke), a connection was made. The "take home" message here is: the greater the prior knowledge, the greater the likelihood of an "ah-ha" or "ha-ha" experience.

What This Means to You

Pre-exposure provides learners with a foundation upon which to build connections. The more background you provide, the better and faster learning will occur. Let your learners be surprised by the process, rather than the content. Post a summary of what will be learned a month in advance and suggest to learners that they start exploring the subject with video previews, museum visits, library exploration, or TV viewing. The more they know before they get to you, the better off they'll be, and the more fun you'll have together. Pre-exposure is a strategy that has been used at the college level for some time. University students often review the texts their professors will be using before the first day of class.

One best way for students to learn something does not exist, but the old adage that "students who do the most talking and doing, do the most learning," still applies. Although formal methods of instruction are still the most commonly used in schools, more teachers are realizing how the traditional "stand and deliver" approach is brain antagonistic. The brain is not very good at absorbing countless bits of semantic (factual) information. What feeds the brain more is meaningful exposure to larger models, patterns, and experiences. From this rich diet, the learner's brain will extract for itself the information it deems important.

Figure 3.10

Explicit and Implicit Learning

Explicit Learning	Implicit Learning
• Discussion	• Simulations
• Reading	• Theater Projects
• Listening	• Field Trips
• Spelling	• Role Play
• Math Facts	• Complex Games
• Q & A	• Model-making
• Work Sheets	• Life Experiences
• Lectures	

The larger pattern or model is just as important (or more) than the data itself.

If during a given day, a teacher yells at a student for running in the hallways, gripes at them for aberrant behavior, and then nags them for homework failures, some learning may be accomplished; however, the chances that the student learned to 1) walk in the hallway; 2) be less disruptive; and 3) do their homework, are pretty slim. Instead, what they probably extracted from the experience was to avoid being caught running in the hallway and other undesirable responses that are aligned with the learner's personal needs. The brain experiences a condition and forms a generalized rule that is adaptive for the learner. What the student learned in this case was certainly not what the teacher intended. And, this is the scenario that happens over and over again in our classrooms and schools.

This is why it makes good brain sense to facilitate a variety of experiences from which students can extract their own learning. The proportion of time that learners ought to be doing and talking, rather than sitting and listening, is a function of several variables. These include learner background, content complexity, and accountability. In general, however, a sound practice is to plan about half of your time for input and half for processing the new learning. Most teachers set aside far too little time for learners to adequately manipulate, experiment, discuss, and revisit new content learning; and the result is we do an enormous amount of reteaching. Education standards typically push for more in-depth understanding, critical thinking, and a wider span of content, but paradoxically, you can go deeper or wider (but not both), without expanding your time frame.

Elaboration

As illustrated by the joke example presented earlier in this chapter, a synaptic connection can be made temporarily, and then lost. Neural space is expensive real estate and the brain is most concerned with saving that which is important for survival. To ensure that the brain maintains the synaptic connections made from new learning, additional intention through elaboration is usually necessary.

An enormous gap exists between what a teacher explains and what a learner understands. To reduce this gap, teachers need to engage students for deeper understanding and feedback with implicit and explicit learning strategies (see figure 3.10). If you don't know what they didn't get, how can you elaborate effectively? Making corrections as we go along is a critical approach for teaching with the brain in mind. Once a learner is lost, the brain somehow switches off. Experienced brain-based instructors adjust their course before this happens.

 What This Means to You

Implicit and explicit approaches are useful in the elaboration stage. Explicit strategies such as answer keys, peer editing, debriefing, or videotaping provide valuable student feedback; but learner feedback can also be provided in a more subtle or nonconscious fashion with implicit strategies, such as simulations, role playing, role modeling, field trips, complex games, and real-life experiences. Elaboration gives the brain a chance to sort, sift, analyze, test, and deepen the learning. To really know something, one must know they know it. An old adage that reflects this rule is, "If you want to *really* learn something, teach it." I may pick up some valuable information by reading a book about horseback riding, but until I actually ride a horse, I won't deeply relate to that learning. The elaboration stage ensures that what gets taken home, is not only "owned" by the students, but is also accurate.

Neural networks are developed through trial and error. The more experimentation and feedback, the better the quality of the neural networks. Smarter humans don't always get the answers first; and they don't always get them right. But they do eliminate wrong answers better than their peers. And this ability to avoid "bad" choices is developed through trial and error. It isn't developed by someone else telling us the right answer and then having us repeat it back to them. This type of rote learning may produce high scores on a standardized test, but it does not produce high-level thinking.

The old paradigm for student feedback was to pass out tests then pass out scores. Many educators still live by this credo. And some mistakenly still believe they are the only ones who can provide their learners with effective feedback. The brain thrives on feedback; and it is less important from whence it comes. If we rely on only one teacher to provide feedback for twenty or more students, the numbers don't add up. There's not enough time in the day. If students are to receive adequate feedback, other sources must be engaged.

Figure 3.11
Model of Neural Networks

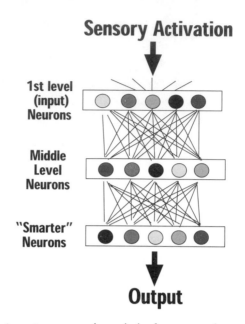

Learning occurs through the formation of neural networks. However, this is only a model of a learning network. Instead of a simple three-layer network, (as depicted here) each neuron commonly interacts with thousands of others.

 What This Means to You

Providing learners with sufficient feedback doesn't require hiring a team of teacher's aides. Good alternatives include incorporating peer reviews, group processes, student-generated rubrics, answer sheets, pair shares, video or audiotaped sessions, self-evaluations, journaling, classroom volunteers or aides, reference materials, and project or portfolio results. When multiple sources of feedback are engaged, students not only learn more, and more accurately, but their intrinsic motivation is deepened, as well.

The bonus students get in this process is that they learn to review and evaluate their own and others' work and receive constructive feedback in a way that is productive. The elaboration process is the step that ensures learners aren't merely regurgitating rote facts, but are developing complex neural pathways in their brain that connect subjects in meaningful ways. This stage is a precursor to remembering.

Memory Formation

After incorporating the elaboration strategies described above, you'd think the learner's brain would have permanently encoded the day's learning. Unfortunately, it's not quite this simple. Sometimes even after the learner is provided with plenty of opportunity for experimentation and interaction, the memory trace is still not strong enough to be activated at test time. Additional factors that contribute to the issue of retrievability include adequate rest, emotional intensity, context, nutrition, quality and quantity of associations, stage of development, learner states, and prior learning. All of these encoding factors play a vital role in the depth of processing and learning that occurs. As you make your way through the following chapters, these factors will be addressed in more detail.

Rest (and especially REM sleep time) is vital to learning, as this is the time when much of the information we are processing is consolidated. Intense emotions also strengthen learning, as emotional responses trigger the release of neurotransmitters, thereby, biologically marking the event as significant. Nutrition plays a role because the foods we eat provide the raw materials needed to produce these all-important "memory chemicals". In short, there are many ways that learning is either strengthened or simply released depending on the strength of the memory formation.

Figure 3.12
Synapse and Neurotransmitters

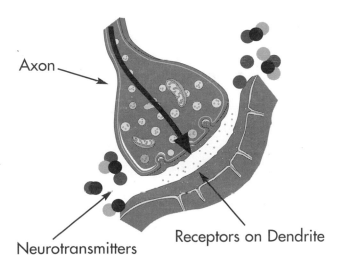

Axon

Neurotransmitters

Receptors on Dendrite

In figure 3.12 you see the basic physiological process for learning: An electrical impulse travels down the axon where it triggers the release of neurotransmitters into the synaptic gap. In a process that takes a micro-second, the chemicals travel across the gap (about 50 microns) and are absorbed into receptor sites on the surface of the receiving dendrite. The neurotransmitters are released, absorbed, and reabsorbed via the thousands of rapid fire impulses activated each second.

Neurotransmitters influence the synaptic reactions and result in either learning impairment, enhancement, or no affect. For example, a low level of the stress hormone cortisol during a learning session has no known effect. Moderate levels, however, enhance synaptic efficiency; and high levels impair learning. On the other hand, the neurotransmitter noradrenaline seems to have the opposite effect. Low levels have no effect, but high levels seem to enhance learning and memory. Progesterone, testosterone and dozens of other hormones also impact learning. Some neurotransmitters can be influenced by the teacher—for example, adrenaline is increased by competition—but other levels are not easily modified.

> *Get it, get it right, and strengthen it. This is the basic learning process that builds intricate neural networks and makes them uniquely our own.*

But there's more to learning than this synaptic focal point. Most of the communication in the brain takes place outside the axon-to-synapse-to-dendrite connection. In spite of the time we invest in learning about the physical structure of the brain, it's the processes that are the workhorses of communication. Trillions of bits of information are stored in chained protein molecules called peptides. These peptides circulate throughout the brain (and body) transmitting their knowledge to available receptor sites on each and every cell in the body. Miles Herkenham of the National Institute of Health (Pert 1997) estimates that this parasynaptic communication system, composed of peptides, is responsible for about 98 percent of the brain's communication. The remaining 2 percent, he believes, is synaptic, representing the traditional axon-to-synapse-to-dendrite system.

Bottom line? Learning is complex: It's more than neurons getting electrocuted while holding hands. The development of neural networks made up of cells that have fired together often enough to "wire together," are activated by complex interactions between genes and our environment, and are modulated by countless biochemicals. Remember that to truly understand new content, we must move from the micro to the macro and back to the micro world. In this process, information may become oversimplified and out of context, but as elaboration occurs, the pieces of the puzzle reunite to form an accurate picture that results in accurate learning. Now, that you are armed with the basics of how the brain learns, let's elaborate on how this knowledge informs our profession.

Reflection Questions

1. What from this chapter was novel, fresh, or new to you? What was familiar or "old hat"?

2. In what ways, do you already apply the information in this chapter?

3. What three questions might you now generate about this material?

4. How did you react emotionally to the information in this chapter?

5. How did you react cognitively to the information? Do you agree or disagree with the author's point of view? Why?

6. In what ways might you translate the principles presented in this chapter into practical everyday useful ideas?

7. If these things are, in fact, true about the brain, what should we do differently? What resources of time, people, and money could be redirected? In what ways might you suggest we start doing this?

8. What were the most interesting insights you gained from this material?

9. If you were to plan your next step for making your curriculum more brain-based, what would that be?

10. What obstacles might you encounter? How might you realistically deal with them?

Bio-Cognitive Cycles

Your Brain's Time Clock

Dual Cycles Run Our Learning Brain

Even Memory Varies by the Clock

Relax-to-Energize Learning Cycle

"Pulse" Style of Learning Best for Brain

Gender Learning Cycles

Our Brain Needs Deep Rest

Sleep Time Assists Long-Term Memory

Bio-Cognitive Cycles

Your Brain's Time Clock

Most neuroscientists agree that we are far from a "learning machine." Instead, our performance is dramatically affected by our biological rhythms (Brewer and Campbell 1991; Koulack 1997; Rossi and Nimmons 1991; Rossi and Rossi 1980; Webb 1982). These rhythms are regulated primarily by the hypothalamus, the supra chiasmatic nucleus (SCN), and the pineal gland, which are, in turn, influenced by our genes, sunlight exposure, and other environmental factors.

Our body's own circadian rhythms correspond to the twenty-four-hour solar and the twenty-five-hour lunar cycles. Generally, the human circadian rhythm leans closer to twenty-five hours, so as learners our efficiency is bumped ahead an hour each day. For example, if we are at our peak of efficiency at 3 p.m. today, it will probably be 4 p.m. tomorrow. This means it isn't always easy to stay "in sync."

Further complicating matters, we also have a seven-day cycle, as do rats and other animals, and unicellular organisms. This cycle may explain why organ transplant patients have the highest rejection episodes seven days after surgery, and then at multiples of seven days, thereafter. The physiological functions that are impacted by our biorhythms include pulse rate, blood pressure, neurotransmitter levels, and cell division. Psychological responses include changes in mood, concentration level, and learning—hence, the name bio-cognitive cycles. In addition, these cycles influence memory, accident rate, immunology, physical growth, reaction time, and pain tolerance.

In studying bio-cognitive cycles, we've learned that overall physical strength and body temperature are at their zenith in the afternoon; and that sleep and alert cycles are predictable. One's peak of nighttime sleep and daytime drowsiness, for instance, follows a regular twelve-hour cycle. Every two hours hormones released into our blood-stream can dramatically alter our mood, which we know, impacts learning. Some research suggests, for example, that women learn better in the two weeks following menstruation as opposed to the two weeks before it (Kimura 1989, 1990, 1992).

Even our breathing happens in predictable cycles through the day and night. On average, we breathe through one nostril for about three hours until the tissue becomes slightly engorged; then we switch to the other side. The nostril we breath through affects which brain hemisphere we use. When our breathing is left-side dominant, our learning will be right-brain dominant, and vice versa.

Based on measurements of psychomotor tasks, intellectual tasks, affective state tasks, and physiological function tasks during various times of the day, research reveals that overall intellectual performance (thinking, problem-solving, debating) peaks in the late afternoon (Brewer and Campbell 1991). Although comprehension increases as the day progresses, reading speed decreases.

Researchers have also discovered that mineral, vitamin, glucose, and hormone levels can vary as much as 500 percent in a given day. This fluctuation can profoundly affect the brain's efficiency and learning effectiveness. In general, our short-term memory is *best* in the morning and *least effective* in the afternoon, as opposed to our long-term memory which is generally *best* in the afternoon.

All of us have different internal rhythms or "chronomes" which we must be cognizant of to perform and learn at peak efficiency. This personal knowledge can influence, not only *what* you do, but *when* you do it. For example, the potency of medications one takes varies depending on the time of day. For maximum effect, a person should plan to take them two hours before their daily blood-pressure rhythm peaks. When medication is maintained on this schedule, lower doses can achieve the same effect as higher doses taken during a low point or drop in blood pressure.

> ***We may be underestimating the ability of students***
> ***if we test them at the "wrong" times of the day.***

You may have noticed that you have natural attentional highs and lows throughout the day. One of our brain's key cycles is about ninety minutes. This means we have about sixteen cycle revolutions every twenty-four-hour period. The odd thing is that while we are used to "light and deep" sleep rhythms, we rarely connect this with the typical high and low arousal-rest cycles we experience during the day. Some students who are consistently drowsy in class may be at the bottom of their attentional cycle.

Movements such as stretching or marching can help refocus their attention. Students should be encouraged to stand and stretch (without attracting undue attention) if they feel drowsy.

As this ninety-minute high/low bio-cognitive cycle alters our blood flow and breathing, our brain alternates between more efficient verbal and spatial processing abilities (Khalsa, et al. 1986). The differences are significant. One study exhibited a verbal task score increase on average from 165 to 215 correct answers; and a simultaneous downswing of 125 to 108 correct answers on spatial tasks (Klein and Armitage 1979). This oscillation suggests that we will get lower scores if we test students at the wrong time. Giving learners choice, however, in the assessment process may reduce this inherent discrepancy. The nature of our bio-cognitive cycles and how they impact learning, as well as assessment, makes a good case for alternative assessment measurements, such as portfolios. A portfolio, which reflects learning over a span of time, may prove to be a more accurate analysis of learning. Not only do they provide a more inclusive means for assessing performance and improvement, they better accommodate the highs and lows of our bio-cognitive rhythms.

The message our brain receives at each low end of our cycle is, "take it easy." In fact, some research suggests that in congruence with our bio-cognitive cycles, productivity increases when learners are given mental breaks several times a day (Rossi and Nimmons 1991). Instead of fighting the lack of energy or alertness, take advantage of it. Pierce Howard, PhD., author of *The Owner's Manual for the Brain* (1994), says that in general, workers need five- to ten-minute breaks every hour and a half. This recommendation aligns itself well with the bottom of our 90-minute cycle. Students need brain breaks, too. And running from one classroom to another between periods does not necessarily constitute "down time." Based on what we know about bio-cognitive cycles, an argument for block scheduling at the secondary level can be made. If classes lasted longer, the teacher would be able to provide students with time to stretch or relax quietly for ten minutes each ninety-minute period.

Figure 4.1
The Brain's High-Low Cycles

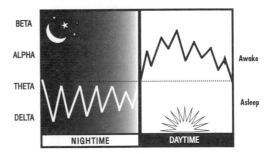

The brain's right and left hemispheres alternate cycles of efficiency—from high spatial, low verbal to high verbal, low spatial—every ninety to one hundred minutes. In other words, learners switch from right-brain to left-brain dominance sixteen times throughout the day. Naturally, teachers will get more cooperation and understanding when they work with students at the peak of their cycle. The students' natural "low" period often coincides with the teacher's low time which can be good or bad depending on whether the teacher is aware of the situation or not.

Another of our bio-cognitive cycles called ultradian rhythm or the "B-R-A-C" cycle (Basic Rest-Activity Cycle), corresponds to our REM (rapid-eye-movement) state of sleep. REM, which makes up most of our dream time, alternates with non-REM rest periods throughout the night. This cycle continues through the daytime, as well.

Carol Orlock, author of *Know Your Body Clock* (1998), suggests that our ultradian rhythms coincide with the periodic release of hormones into the bloodstream; and also regulate our hunger and attention span. She cites experiments where subjects consistently headed for the refrigerator or the coffee pot about every ninety minutes. Sensitivity to pain, appetite, and learning varies with the cycle. She also notes that hemispheric-dominance oscillations that also occur every 90 minutes seem to impact thinking, reasoning, and spatial skills test results.

Some assert that this ninety-minute cycle may be the perfect time for suggestion and affirmation. Why? The changeover may be a time when the body is switching gears and entering a neutral time that is highly receptive to change and healing.

At the Hermann Center for Chronobiology and Chronotherapy in Houston, Texas, the staff helps patients track their biorhythms as an aid to treatments. One patient who had a twenty-six-hour daily cycle and experienced great agitation was re-synchronized with solar therapy. An elderly woman's daily rhythm was entirely redesigned by exposing her to four extra hours of bright light each day for one week, says Researcher C. A. Czeisler (1986). Her temperature and cortisol rhythms were actually reset as a result.

 ## What This Means to You

Brain-based learning considers how the brain learns best. The brain does not learn "on demand" by a school's rigid inflexible schedule. It has its own rhythms. Problems in learning, in some cases, might be a result of lateralization. Learners who are at the peak of their right- or left-hemisphere dominance may need cross-lateral activation to "unstick" them. Proponents of cross-lateral physical activity, like Carla Hannaford, PhD. author of *Smart Moves* (1995), suggest that exercises which encourage limb movement across the body's lateral center can stimulate both sides of the brain and energize thinking. Providing options for assessment at varied times of the day is important for accuracy in measuring learner performance. Also, vary your presentation/lecture times and other scheduled activities. Provide learners with choice and a diverse menu of activities to suit their bio-cognitive cycles and learning styles.

Dual Cycles Run Our Learning Brain

Our brains consistently run on two learning cycles, says R. Thayer (1989). The first is a low-to-high-energy cycle and the second is a relaxation-to-tension cycle. These two cycles dramatically affect our learning and perception of ourselves, he says. Learners often focus better in the late morning and early evening, and are more pessimistic in the middle to late afternoon. Our thinking can get unrealistically negative at certain low times, yet swing to the positive side during high cycles. These patterns, or "rhythms of learning," coincide with the ultradian cycles described by many researchers.

Can these patterns be modified; and are they consistent? The answer is yes to both questions. Learners can be taught to modify the rhythms by varying their sleep, exercise, diet, and exposure to sunlight, says Dr. Thayer. Personality differences also influence pattern variations. For example, introverts report higher tension during the first two-thirds of the day, while extroverts report greater tension during the last two-thirds.

 ## What This Means to You

We may have greater influence over the quality of our learning than previously thought. By understanding bio-patterns and fluctuations, we can better learn to take preventive action. Help your learners to become aware of their own best times for learning. Emphasize the importance of repetition and investing effort at various times of the day. Discuss how nutrition, rest, and activity impact learning, as well.

Even Memory Varies by the Clock

University of Sussex researcher J. Oakhill (1988) conducted experiments to discover whether the time of day affects memory. She found that we incorporate two different types of memory in learning: literal (facts, names, numbers, formulas, etc.) and inferential (poetry, fiction, conversations, etc.). In the morning we seem to favor literal memory and in the afternoon our brain is better at integrating new information with prior learning, she concluded.

The authors of *Rhythms of Learning*, C. Brewer and D. Campbell (1991), offer the following time frame recommendations. They suggest that from 9 to 11 a.m., the brain is 15 percent more efficient for short-term memory tasks; and that from 9 a.m. to 12 noon, learning tasks that require rote learning, spelling, problem-solving, test review, report writing, math, theory, and science will be most efficiently learned.

Noon to 2 p.m. is best for movement-oriented tasks, paperwork, manipulatives, music, computer work, singing, and art, they say. And 2 to 5 p.m. is best for studying literature and history; and for doing sports, music, theater, and manual-dexterity tasks. Because some of us are "morning people" and others are "night people," there is a two- to four-hour variance among learners for optimal timing.

Research conducted by Cynthia May of Duke University (1993) set out to determine how recall relates to age and time of day. Her findings suggest that young adults do best on memory recall in the afternoon or evenings, while older individuals performed significantly better in the morning.

Given all of the variations in personality types, no matter when you present a particular topic, it is likely to be out of sync, or the wrong time, for about one-third of your learners. However, when adolescents are allowed to learn subjects at their preferred time of day, their motivation, behavior, and scores in mathematics improved, cites Dr. May (ibid).

> *The question then arises: "If we know what time of the day learning is optimized, what can we do about it?*

Of course it is impossible to accommodate every learner's individual time clock; however, there are numerous practices that help make the classroom more accommodating to learners' variations. For example, if a standardized test is always given after lunch, some students will consistently underperform. And, if test reviews are regularly scheduled early in the day, learners may better remember semantic material, such as names, places, dates, and facts, but, more meaningful connections would be better grasped in the afternoon.

What This Means to You

Since it seems that literal memory declines across the day, rather than forcing learners to pay closer attention in the afternoon, relate learning at this time to personal experience. Present new information in the morning, while using the afternoon to integrate it with prior learning. For example, schedule reading, listening, and watching activities in the morning, and role-playing, projects, and simulations in the afternoon.

The Relax-to-Energize Learning Cycle

Researcher and educator Georgi Lozanov of Bulgaria says (1991) that the activation and suppression of cerebral/limbic structures is a key aspect of accelerated teaching and learning practices. He says the relaxing effects of a positively suggestive learning climate are critical in "reducing the vigilance intensity, activating the serotonin-energetic systems and suppressing the catecholaminegetic systems." Translated, this means the best teachers take advantage of the brain's alert/relaxed periods for feeding new information, and reduce content during anxious/low periods.

Dr. Lozanov adds that the whole brain is a system that needs to be simultaneously satisfied. By purposely activating both the more structured, sequential educational content and the more emotionally satisfying experiences (left and right hemisphere, cerebral, and limbic areas of the brain), learning is accelerated at all levels. In fact, Lozanov believes that by satisfying the "optimum functional needs of the central nervous system... [teaching and training can become] a factor in the accelerated development of the personality." In other words, the richer the learning experience, the more developmental benefits there are to the learner aside from the intended content.

 ## What This Means to You

Any teaching process which is primarily lecture (or for that matter, primarily any *one* type of methodology) is going to lead some students to failure. Rather, provide as many methodology approaches as possible. A simulation/role-play followed by a discussion would fit the activity-rest cycle in learning. Many students who are not succeeding now may be impaired by the methodology used. Make sure that your facilitation is sequenced to appeal to the abstract/cerebral and emotional/limbic parts of the brain. Alternating formats of activity and rest, instruction and discussion, or exploration and debriefing makes the most sense to the brain and our bio-cognitive cycles.

"Pulse" Style of Learning Is Best for Brain

Allan Hobson of Harvard University (1989) reports that the ability to maintain learning attentiveness is affected by normal fluctuations in brain chemistry. These fluctuations occur in cycles of approximately ninety minutes throughout the day and night. At night we all experience periods of deep sleep, REM time, and light sleep. During the daytime, these cycles continue, but at a level of greater awareness. Even animals exhibit this cycle of basic rest and activity—a natural learning pulse.

> *Learning is best when focused, diffused, then focused again. Constant focused learning is increasingly inefficient. In fact, the whole notion of "time on task" is in conflict both biologically and educationally with the way the brain naturally learns.*

Requiring learners to be attentive for a long period of time is counterproductive, since much of what we learn cannot be processed consciously: It just happens too fast. Internal time is needed to process it and create meaning, as meaningfulness is a process generated within each individual. This "down time" after each new learning experience will also reinforce the "imprint" on our memory.

Breaks can be structured. They don't have to just be "free time." They can consist of a diffusion activity, a content break, or an alternate form of learning, such as a peer teaching session, mind-mapping session, or project work. Deep breathing and physical relaxation are useful strategies for sustaining energy through the break/rest cycle. The following pie charts represent the variables related to optimal content/rest cycle periods:

Figure 4.2
High Content Background

Figure 4.3
Low Content Background

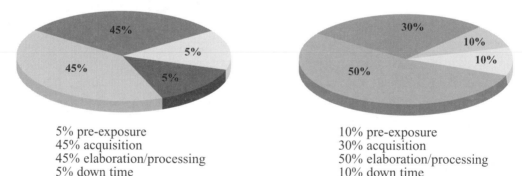

5% pre-exposure
45% acquisition
45% elaboration/processing
5% down time

10% pre-exposure
30% acquisition
50% elaboration/processing
10% down time

Our visual capacity, measured by bits per second and carried by the optical nerve, is in the tens of millions—far too much to process consciously or continuously. In order to integrate the data, learners must focus their attention inward. If external input continues beyond a point, our brain will unconsciously turn itself off. After completely new learning takes place, teachers should consider short, divergent activities like a ball toss or a walk. Encourage learners to discuss their learning in a relaxed state. This is when many of our best ideas seem to "pop out of the blue." As educators, we must allow for this creative time if we want deep and lasting learning to occur.

In scheduling time for content acquisition and processing, how do you know what will be optimal for most learners? Two critical variables need to be taken into account. First, the *novelty and complexity* of the material: High complexity and novelty means more processing time is needed. Second, *learner background* is critical: Low background on the content being learned means more time is needed and of course, high background means less time is needed.

 ## What This Means to You

In working with young learners, limit content, lectures, and cognitive activities to periods of five to ten minutes each. In working with adolescents, limit content sessions to ten to fifteen minutes each; and with adults, no more than twenty-five minute content sessions are recommended. After each focused learning period, conduct an elaboration activity, such as mind-mapping, pair-shares, or model building. Provide down time with activities such as walking, stretching, deep breathing, clean up, or recess.

Gender Learning Cycles

According to some research on hormonal influences on the brain (Hampson 1990), a woman's menstrual cycle may influence learning efficiency throughout the month. Higher levels of estrogen, it seems, translates to better verbal fluency and fine motor skills.

If estrogen, in fact, promotes more active brain cells, increases sensory awareness, and increases brain alertness, then it would make sense that a woman may learn more efficiently in the first half of her cycle when estrogen levels are higher (see figure 4.4). The brain, when flooded with this hormone, experiences feelings of pleasure, sexual arousal, well being, enthusiasm, and self-esteem. What better time for optimal learning?

During the second half of the cycle, however, progesterone is present with the estrogen. Progesterone induces a reduction in cerebral blood flow, oxygen, and glucose consumption; and produces sluggish, unmotivated behavior. It is also responsible for a sense of calm and acceptance. But in the five final days before menstruation, both levels drop: Without significant estrogen to promote well-being and without progesterone to calm anxious moods, learning may be negatively affected (Kimura 1999). Females who do not experience such fluctuations may have more hemispheric laterality and higher levels of testosterone, Kimura reports.

Figure 4.4
Levels of Estrogen and Progesterone

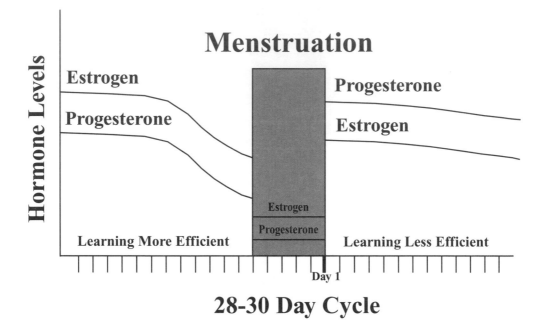

For women (and men), it's not uncommon to feel like you're learning at a high-performance level one week and the next week you've gone "brain dead." Spatial ability is higher when testosterone is lower; as is musical ability. Interestingly, the variations of women's hormone levels are matched in men (Kimura 1999). Margaret Henderson, a research physiologist and endocrinologist (ibid), says that men appear to have a temperature cycle that is synchronous with the menstrual cycle of their cohabiting partner; and temperature changes, like a woman's hormonal fluctuations, are known to affect sexuality, attention, immunity, and learning, as well.

 ## What This Means to You

Hormonal differences in males and females may account for some learning differences; and certainly impact mood and motivation. Of course *equal* opportunity for both sexes is critical, but the *same* treatment may be inappropriate. In spite of all of today's awareness about gender equality, boys and girls still develop at different speeds and with more variance across genders than within gender groups. Let's acknowledge differences; and work with boys and girls in ways that best match their own developmental and learning needs.

Our Brain Needs Deep Rest

Surprisingly, the brain may become more easily fatigued when conditions for learning are less than optimal. To get the brain's best performance, it needs deep physiological rest—the kind in which you are "dead to the world." Students living in abusive or highly stressed families, areas of high crime or poverty, or impacted by trauma, are much more likely to be sleep deprived.

Learners who live under stress, anxiety,
or a constant threat of some kind don't receive the
all-important brain rest needed for optimal functioning:
Without it, learning and thinking are impaired.

How dramatic is the impairment? At the Three-Mile Island nuclear power plant, sleep loss and exhaustion were blamed for the failure to recognize a coolant leak, which in turn led to a near catastrophic melt-down of the reactor. Sleep loss was also a contributing factor in the faulty decision-making that led to the Challenger explosion and the disastrous Chernobyl accident. At its most extreme, sleep deprivation can be lethal; to a lesser extreme, inadequate sleep impairs new learning.

How much sleep is enough? This varies from individual to individual; however, we do know that it is the REM period (the dream state) of sleep that is most crucial. While some adults will require eight to ten hours of sleep per night, others seem to function perfectly well on four to six hours. Learners who are short on sleep may perform well on short quizzes requiring rote memorization, but not as well on extended performance testing that requires stamina, creativity, and higher-level problem solving.

Sleep Time Assists Long-Term Memory

Researcher Bob Stickgold at Harvard University (1997) suggests that sleep time may affect the previous day's learning. By cutting nighttime sleep by as little as two hours, your ability to recall may be impaired the next day. The more complicated and complex the material is, the more important sleep is to the learning of it. It is believed that sleep gives your brain time to do its "housekeeping"—to rearrange circuits, clean out extraneous mental debris, and process emotional events.

One researcher (Freeman 1995) suggests that the real reason for this may be a concept called "unlearning." Using complex mathematical and computer modeling, he discovered that neural networks can become much more efficient when certain memories are "unlearned"—much like your computer "cleaning up the desktop."

By eliminating unnecessary information (usually during sleep time), the brain becomes more efficient. The fact that you have trouble remembering dreams may indicate how effective your brain is at "cleaning up" your cerebral "house."

What This Means to You

Many of your learners may either need more sleep or better quality sleep. Discuss the importance of physical rest and dreaming; and encourage your learners to get adequate rest at night. Also provide learners with some down time during the day for optimal brain performance. The Latin tradition of an afternoon "siesta" from 12 to 2 p.m. may have a useful biological basis to it. Give learners the opportunity to move around, stretch, drink some water, or change their focus periodically as their cycles impact their energy level.

Based on what we know about the brain and learning today, it is appropriate to ask a different set of questions. Where we used to ask, how can we make sure students learn what's expected of their grade level, we are now asking:

▼ **What is the optimal environment for learning?**

▼ **What learning strategies have the highest impact at the lowest cost?**

▼ **How can we interest staff in making changes?**

▼ **How can we find the necessary resources to support these changes?**

▼ **What one simple step can I take immediately to improve learning?**

In short, the answer to all of these questions is to get proactive and use more brain-based learning strategies. Although you don't have control of everything, you do have control of a lot. Brain-based learning is an approach that doesn't require you to fly to the moon and back. Rather, you can begin implementing the simple strategies outlined in this book tomorrow. In addition to having lasting and powerful effects on learners, brain-based teaching will also reward you in numerous ways as you build your own knowledge base and enjoy the fruits of your labor.

Reflection Questions

1. What from this chapter was novel, fresh, or new to you? What was familiar or "old hat"?

2. In what ways, do you already apply the information in this chapter?

3. What three questions might you now generate about this material?

4. How did you react emotionally to the information in this chapter?

5. How did you react cognitively to the information? Do you agree or disagree with the author's point of view? Why?

6. In what ways might you translate the principles presented in this chapter into practical everyday useful ideas?

7. If these things are, in fact, true about the brain, what should we do differently? What resources of time, people, and money could be redirected? In what ways might you suggest we start doing this?

8. What were the most interesting insights you gained from this material?

9. If you were to plan your next step for making your curriculum more brain-based, what would that be?

10. What obstacles might you encounter? How might you realistically deal with them?

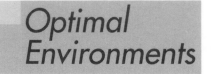

Optimal Environments

The Psychological Environment

The Visual Environment

Color in the Environment

Concrete Vivid Images

The Impact of Peripherals

Light in the Environment

Seasons Can Impact Learning

Optimal Temperature for Learning

Dehydration Hurts Learning

Can Plants Affect Learning?

Aromas May Boost Attention & Learning

Impact of Negative Ionization

Music & Noise in the Environment

Optimal Environments

The Psychological Environment

The facilitator-learner relationship is of critical importance to the training and learning environment. Unless this relationship is characterized by trust, safety, and mutual respect, the learning process will be stilted. Walk into any classroom or training facility and you can very quickly sense the impact of the emotional, intellectual, and social climate. As a teacher or facilitator, our primary responsibility is to provide a positive psychological and physical climate in which to orchestrate learning. The focus of this chapter is how we can optimally accomplish this comprehensive task, based on what we now know about the brain.

The Visual Environment

One of the critical factors of an enriched environment is one which is mostly taken for granted, the visual climate. Our eyes are capable of registering 36,000 visual messages per hour—a huge number when you stop to think about it. Imagine 36,000 monetary bills (from all different parts of the world) laid out on the floor and your brain has the capacity to register each one. Between 80 and 90 percent of all information that is absorbed by our brain is visual. In fact, the retina accounts for 40 percent of all nerve fibers connected to the brain. With this enormous capacity, it is important to be aware of the environmental factors that influence how we see and process information.

The essential elements enabling our eyes to actually compose meaning from our visual field are contrast, tilt, curvature, line ends, color, and size. These elements, perceived even before the learner consciously understands what they've seen, can inform teaching practice and provide a framework for attracting learner attention.

While optimal learning involves far more than getting and keeping students' attention, the principles of brain-based attention-getting are useful.

> **Quite simply, attract the brain with movement, contrast, and color changes.**

Our brain's attention priority is to wavelengths of color, light, darkness, motion, form, and depth; thus, these elements can provide a basis for attracting your learners' attention. There are many ways to access the brain's inherently fast response to these properties. For example, when speaking to a group, move around the room and increase and decrease your distance from the audience. Turn the lights off for a moment of group introspection. Pass an object around for learners to touch and feel. Color code boxes of student materials for easy access. And, turn standard black and white overhead transparencies into colorful images with marking pens or a color printer.

Color in the Environment

Color is a truly powerful medium; and one that is generally underestimated. A recent study (Vuontela, et al. 1999) measured the relative value of verbal cues versus color cues in learning and memory. In testing memory for verbs and memory for colors, learners better recalled color. And when objects were tested against color, once again, color memory was stronger. Even an intention to remember did not affect the outcome of the experiment.

You might wonder, "Why does color have such an impact on our brain?" Consider this: Color is part of the spectrum of electromagnetic radiation. Other electromagnetic radiation forms include x-rays, infrared, heat, and microwaves—pretty powerful mediums. Color is no different. In his book, *The Power of Color* (1991), Morton Walker cites research conducted by Robert Gerard, PhD. of University of California, Los Angeles who studied the physiological affects of color on anxiety, pulse, arousal and blood flow. His findings suggest that every color has a wavelength; and every wavelength, from ultraviolet to infrared (or red to blue) affects our body and brain differently. How a color affects you depends on your personality and state of mind at the moment. If you are highly anxious and stressed, for example, red can trigger more aggressiveness. But if you're relaxed, it can trigger engagement and positive emotions. Walker presents the following synopsis of "the power of color" (ibid):

The Power of Color

Red is an engaging and emotive color. Best for restaurants. It is considered more disturbing by anxious subjects, and more exciting to calm subjects. Triggers the pituitary and adrenal glands and releases adrenaline. May increase blood pressure and breathing, and stimulate appetite and sense of smell.

Yellow is the first color a person distinguishes in the brain. Associated with stress, caution, and apprehension, yet it stimulates an overall sense of optimism, hope, and balance. Excellent for use in classrooms.

Orange has the characteristics halfway between red and yellow. It is one the best colors for stimulating learning.

Blue is the most tranquilizing color. It calms tense subjects and increases feelings of well-being. When you see blue, your brain releases eleven neurotransmitters that relax the body, and may result in a reduction of temperature, perspiration, and appetite. Blue may be a bit too calming for most learning environments.

Green is also a calming color. In response blood histamine levels may rise resulting in reduced sensitivity to food allergies. Antigens may be stimulated for overall better immune system healing.

Dark Colors lower stress and increase feelings of peacefulness.

Brown promotes a sense of security, relaxation, and reduces fatigue.

Bright Colors such as red, orange, and yellow spark energy and creativity. They can also increase aggressive and nervous behavior.

Gray is the most neutral color.

For optimal learning, choose yellow, light orange, beige, or off-white. Those colors seem to stimulate positive feelings.

Source: Walker, Morton. 1991. *The Power of Color.*

Our color preferences may say a great deal about us; and they may be innate. You might, for example, walk into a room and immediately feel uncomfortable, while another room makes you feel happy and inspired, and another makes you feel drained and depressed. It is very possible that the prevailing colors of the room are impacting your mood more than you realize. Even in everyday language, it is obvious how strongly color influences us. We often identify people by the color of their skin or by the color of their clothing. In general, we remember colors first and content second.

 ## What This Means to You

> We may be underutilizing the potential of color in the learning environment. Use color handouts and overhead transparencies. Consciously choose the colors you use in the classroom; hang colorful posters; and encourage the use of color in mind-maps, painting, projects, and posters.

Concrete Vivid Images

What is the best way to convey information? Is it through discussion, reading material, or computers? Neither of these mediums, say researchers (Fiske and Taylor 1984). *Concrete* vivid images are most influential. Neuroscientists theorize this is because 1) the brain has an attentional bias for high contrast and novelty; 2) 90 percent of the brain's sensory input is from visual sources; and 3) the brain has an immediate and primitive response to symbols, icons, and other simple images.

Savvy advertisers and political strategists have known this for years. Consider, for example, how many people quite vividly recall images of the John F. Kennedy assassination, the CNN shots of the SCUD missile attacks in the 1990 Gulf War, and famines around the world. Images like these are powerful enough to mold public opinion. Footage of starving children, for example, rallied the U.S. to send relief aid to Somalia in 1992; and the sight of an American soldier beaten and dragged through the streets of Mogadishu was a prime motivator for American policy changes.

The brain is wired to identify objects more quickly when they differ from a group of similar objects. These differences are analyzed in parallel by the brain so that while the learner may be observing location, the brain may also be processing property differences, such as color, form, weight, etc. This evolutionary tendency of the brain provides humans with an edge that has ensured our survival. Thus, in the learning environment, working models, project-based assignments, a variety of information mediums (i.e., computers, videos, books, cameras, writing equipment, etc.) and an array of art supplies, make for productive learning and a happy brain. We remember best concrete visuals that we can touch and manipulate.

 ## What This Means to You

We may be underutilizing the value of our brain's visual system. The more visuals you can incorporate, the better. The visual environment can be positively impacted by providing changes in location and learning stations. Visuals are an important key to remembering content. Make lectures or presentations more compelling to the brain with objects, photographs, graphics, charts, graphs, slides, video segments, bulletin board displays, and color. For maximum impact, change mediums frequently—from inspiring videos and vivid posters, to mindmaps, drawings, and symbols. Bring in things to show and tell. Challenge students to generate evocative images, either through visualization or in the form of artwork, posters, or murals. Why not produce a class photo, collage, or movie?

The Impact of Peripherals

The brain absorbs information from surrounding peripherals on a conscious and unconscious level. Although many of us commonly use peripherals (or items of visual interest in the environment), they may support learning even more than we realize. Since colors, decorative elements, sounds, smells, and other stimuli are processed by the brain on a priority basis, these elements should be considered important in the planning of optimal learning environments. Peripherals in the form of positive affirmations, learner- generated work, and images depicting change, growth, and beauty can be powerful vehicles of expression.

Figure 5.1 reflects the difference in learner retention of new material over a fourteen-day period when direct instruction only versus direct instruction combined with peripherals is incorporated.

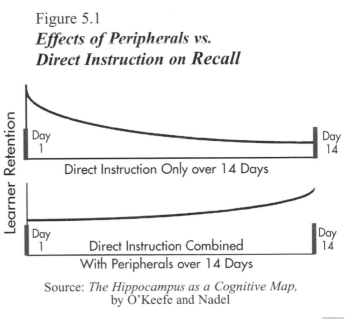

Figure 5.1

Effects of Peripherals vs. Direct Instruction on Recall

Source: *The Hippocampus as a Cognitive Map,* by O'Keefe and Nadel

> *With direct instruction only (lecture) , audience recall drops quickly; but with the addition of peripherals, effortless, subject-specific, longer-lasting recall is generated.*

What This Means to You

A purposeful plan should be made for positively influencing the learner in ways aside from the traditional lesson. Assess what factors may be influencing your learning space currently. Consider influences like posters on the wall, room color, concrete visuals, and bulletin board items. What is the feeling one gets when they walk into your room? Do they respond positively? Do both children and adults feel comfortable in the space? How might you improve the physical climate? How about the emotional climate? A passive approach to surroundings can actually detract from the learning. Make an effort to enhance your visual environment. Add interesting collections, photos, objects, and bulletin boards.

Light in the Environment

Lighting strongly influences our vision, which strongly influences learning. Thus, anything we can do to make our eyes more comfortable in the classroom contributes to optimal learning. Wayne London's experiments (1988) caught worldwide attention when the Vermont psychiatrist studied the affects of lighting in three elementary school classrooms. During the December holiday break, London swapped the standard fluorescent lighting for Vitalite full-spectrum lighting (simulating natural light); and then compared before and after illness absentee rates. Students in the classrooms with full-spectrum lighting missed 65 percent fewer days than students in the fluorescent lit classrooms. Dr. London explained the results this way: "Ordinary fluorescent light has been shown to raise the cortisol level in the blood, a change likely to suppress the immune system." Although we are rarely consciously aware of it, fluorescent lights have a flickering quality and barely audible hum which can have a very powerful impact on our central nervous system. Apparently the brain reacts to this visual-auditory stimulus by raising the cortisol levels in the blood (indications of stress) and blinking excessively.

There's some evidence that lengthy computer or TV/video viewing may also stress the eyes. Young eyeballs are especially impacted, as they are soft and easily distorted by the continual near focusing which is much harder on the eyes than the more relaxed distant vision. Neurophysiologist Dee Coulter (1993) says, the task of keeping the eyes focused on a flat backlit screen is stressful. Many children spend up to five hours a day watching television, playing video games, or using a computer; and we're seeing an earlier increase in adolescent corrective lenses, she says.

Researcher D. B. Harmon, PhD. (1991) in a study of 160,000 school-age children determined that lighting was a major contributor to student health and learning. By the time the children in his study were in sixth grade, more than 50 percent had developed deficiencies related to classroom lighting! Subsequent changes to lighting in the learning environment reversed the results. The same children six months later experienced a 65 percent reduction in visual problems, a 55 percent reduction in fatigue, a 43 percent reduction in infections, and a 25 percent reduction in posture problems. In addition, they exhibited an increase in academic achievement, the study noted.

> *The positive impact of a quality learning environment with strong natural lighting is both dramatic and lasting.*

Dr. Harmon's experiments have since been repeated with similar results. But even if students didn't show an increase in achievement related to lighting, just the fact that many students relax and focus better in low-light situations is reason enough to reduce the use of fluorescent lighting, says learning styles experts Rita Dunn, PhD and associates (1985). Bright lights (especially fluorescent) create restless, fidgety learners, while low-level lights have a calming effect, especially at the younger ages. Which effect would you prefer as a teacher in a classroom with thirty third graders?

 ## What This Means to You

Many learners may be underperforming simply because the lighting is difficult on their eyes or hard on their nervous system. Soft, natural lighting is best for learning. Provide a variety of lighting types in your room; and give learners say in their seating choices.

Seasons Can Impact Learning

Can sunlight affect our learning? Definitely, says Carol Orlock (1993). The length and brightness of daylight affects our body's melatonin and hormone levels and influences the release of neurotransmitters. A portion of the hypothalamus (located in the mid-brain area), which scientists call the SCN (suprachiasmatic nucleus), gets direct information from the eyes and sets our bodies' time clocks. This affects our concentration, energy, and moods. And anything that affects our mental state, in turn, impacts our learning.

A specific condition, known as Seasonal Affective Disorder (SAD), in fact, was recorded in 1987 by the American Psychiatric Association. This officially recognized biomedical problem is caused by a lack of exposure to sunlight during the winter months. Women, it seems, are more inclined to be affected by the condition which results in depression; and, therefore, negatively impacts learning.

Residents who live closer to the equator face less than a 2 percent chance of being affected by SAD, but those farthest from the equator face up to a 25 percent chance, say scientists. The *best time* for learning (Liberman 1991) is when the hours of the day are longest—from June to August in the Northern Hemisphere and December to February in the Southern Hemisphere. In contrast, however, these are the times when most schools break for the summer and the holidays.

A small amount of artificial or sunlight therapy can alleviate the symptoms of SAD if the dosage of light is strong enough, says Dr. Liberman (ibid). Phototherapists measure light in lux units. Typical outdoor light measures between 10,000-80,000 lux units. Successful light therapy requires 2,500 lux to be effective. To put this in perspective, a typical indoor light has 500-700 lux. Treatment sessions can last from thirty minutes to four hours a day. The good news is that 85 percent of SAD sufferers who participate in light therapy are relieved of the symptoms of anxiety depression.

 ## What This Means to You

We may be able to improve learning simply by improving the lighting during the darker winter months. Explore your options for improving the lighting in your environment during periods of low sunlight. Ask others if they have witnessed symptoms of SAD among their students. Seek the help of your medical provider if you think you may be suffering from the condition yourself.

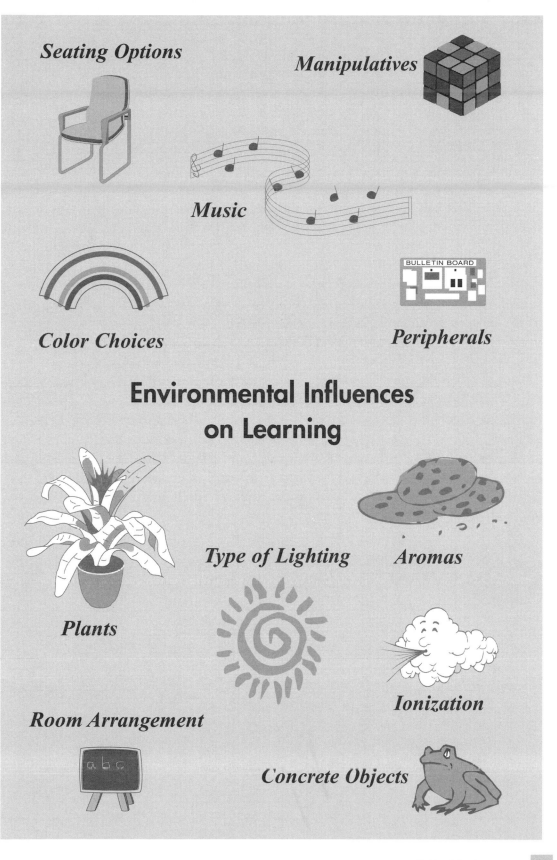

Seating Options

Manipulatives

Music

Color Choices

Peripherals

BULLETIN BOARD

Environmental Influences
on Learning

Type of Lighting

Aromas

Plants

Room Arrangement

Ionization

Concrete Objects

Optimal Temperature for Learning

In U.S. Defense Department studies, H. L. Taylor and J. Orlansky (1993) reported that heat stress dramatically lowered scores in both intellectual and physical tasks. In combat tests where special protective clothing was worn, Taylor found that high temperatures were responsible for decreases in performance requiring accuracy, speed, dexterity, and physical acuity. While many types of obstacles are known to impair learning, heat stress is one of the most preventable.

Stanford professor Robert Ornstein, PhD. (1991) speculates that the evolutionary benefit of humans standing upright and walking was related to the brain's temperature needs. The further our heads are from the ground, (where the temperature is higher) the less likely we are to get overheated. "Even a rise of only 1 to 3 degrees centigrade in brain temperature above normal is enough to disturb brain functions," says Ornstein. In fact, as brain size has increased over the last two million years, one of the most important adaptations has been the cooling mechanisms. Our very survival is vested in maintaining normal brain temperature.

Choice may be the most important variable when it comes to classroom temperature. There is a wide variety of perceptions as to what constitutes a warm or cool room, say Rita and Kenneth Dunn (1992). The optimal is not always 68 to 72 degrees Fahrenheit for all learners, says P. G. Murrain (1982). Preference differences exist among individuals in and across the same age groups; and they can change from day to day depending on mood, weather, and numerous other factors. Having said that, however, 70 degrees (give or take a few degrees) is still a good baseline for optimal temperature in the learning environment.

 ## What This Means to You

We may be creating learning environments that are too rigid. Do your learners have the option to sit where it feels best for them? Can you easily adjust your room temperature? Comfort is important in the process of optimal learning. It's better to be too cool than too warm; but it is best to be neither of these. Provide learners with choice; and be responsive to their temperature needs.

Dehydration Hurts Learning

Neurophysiologist Carla Hannaford, PhD. (1995) asserts that the average learner is often dehydrated which leads to poor learning performance. Hospitals have reported patient improvement when up to twenty glasses of water per day are consumed. Athletes know the importance of increasing water consumption for peak performance. Theaters performers keep a pitcher of water nearby; and an increasing number of educators are realizing the learning benefits of drinking plenty of pure water, as well.

Learning specialists recommend eight to fifteen glasses of water per day depending on the individual's body size and activity level and the climate. Nutritionists recommend pure water to ensure that it is free of contaminants. Water is better for the body than coffee, tea, soft drinks, or fruit juices, as it is free of diuretic or sugar agents that can throw your body's natural rhythm off. Many teachers have found that when they encourage their students to drink water as often as needed, behavior improves, as well as performance.

 What This Means to You

Students who are bored, listless, drowsy, and lacking concentration may, in fact, be dehydrated. Talk to your students about the consequences of dehydration and the value of water. Remind learners to drink water on their breaks and at recess. Allow learners to bring water bottles into the classroom. If you teach sessions that last more than 45 minutes, it is especially important to see that students have access to water.

Can Plants Affect Learning?

Scientists at the National Aeronautics and Space Administration have discovered that the use of plants creates a better learning and thinking environment for astronauts (Wolverton 1996). Could this research also apply to other indoor learning environments? Dr. Wolverton, who headed up NASA's Environmental Research Laboratory in the 1980s, says that certain plants have improved life for the astronauts (and he adds, his own personal life at home) by removing pollutants from the air, increasing the negative ionization in the atmosphere, and charging the indoor air with oxygen. In fact, Federal Clean Air Council studies (ibid) found that plants raised indoor oxygen levels and increased productivity by 10 percent. A single plant may impact 100 square feet of space.

Have you ever taken a class or workshop in a stark classroom or conference room and felt totally unresponsive? Consider whether you may have perked up in an environment filled with plants. Plants not only make the air cleaner and richer, they enhance the aesthetic environment. Most of us use only 10 to 25 percent of our lung's capacity with each breath we take. This is bad because stale air starves the brain. For optimal learning, provide your learners with fresh, uncontaminated, highly oxygenated air. The ideal humidity level is between 35 and 65 percent. Encourage your students to breathe deeply; and don't forget to do so yourself, especially when you're feeling stressed or pressured.

According to Dr. Wolverton, the best plants for optimal air cleansing and oxygen enhancing indoor learning environments are areca palms, lady palms, bamboo palms, rubber plants, gerbera daisies, yellow chrysanthemums, ficus benjamina, philodendrons, dracena deremensis, and peace lilies.

 ## What This Means to You

We often don't realize the impact of the air we breathe; and the pollutants around us go unnoticed. These factors are, however, important to creating an optimal brain-friendly environment for learners. Include four to eight plants in your classroom if it's of typical size (approximately 900 square feet), and more if it's larger.

Aromas May Boost Attention and Learning

A direct link between the olfactory glands and our nervous system sets up a vital connection that can aid learning. Smells in our environment can influence our moods and levels of anxiety, fear, hunger, depression and sexuality. Some research (Weiner and Brown 1993) reports that certain aromas even inspire individuals to set higher goals for themselves, take on greater challenges, and get along better with others.

In rat experiments, Sullivan and associates (1991) found that conditioned odor stimulation and tactile stimulation "are addictive in their effects on learning." The positive learning effects came from a peppermint odor injected into various norepinephrine receptor blockers, a procedure which allowed researchers to rule out other causes for the change.

Alan Hirsch, a Chicago neurologist, found (1993) that certain floral odors increase the ability to learn, create, and think. Working with recovering patients, he used thinking and creative puzzles with control groups and with those exposed to a flowery scent. Those with the scent consistently solved the puzzles 30 percent faster.

Lewis Thomas, PhD., President Emeritus of the Sloan-Kettering Cancer Center in Ohio says (Lavabre 1990), "The act of smelling something, anything, is remarkably like the act of thinking: You can feel the mind going to work.... Particular scents may even be effective in re-triggering specific optimal learning states." And, Harry Walter, former Chairman of International Flavors and Fragrances, says (ibid), "Brain inputs from smell and taste receptors are known to affect vital brain functions that influence reproductive behavior, learning, memory, and emotional states." Eugene Grisante, PhD., also a Chairman at the organization, suggests aromas may be potent enough to "boost learning, decrease food intake, increase productivity, and aid relaxation." Certainly, we've all used scents to inspire desire and calm our nerves, at the very least.

The olfactory regions are also rich receptors for endorphins, which generate feelings of pleasure and well-being. The human brain's ability to detect changes in the environment are well documented. People can distinguish odors with tiny variations in the chemical structures of the odor molecule. Try experimenting with various aromas in your own classroom or training environment. Ask learners what they think. Do they feel energized and more alert after a whiff of peppermint? How do they feel when surrounded with the aroma of chocolate chip cookies, a pumpkin scented candle, or fresh baked bread? If nothing else, you'll enjoy watching your learners' eyes light up when they walk into the room.

 ## What This Means to You

Smell is an important sense that we have underutilized in the learning environment. An awareness of aromas, and what's been coined aromatherapy, can give you a very powerful edge in reaching learners and optimal learning states. Start simple. Research suggests that peppermint, basil, lemon, cinnamon, and rosemary enhance mental alertness, while lavender, chamomile, orange, and rose calm nerves and encourage relaxation.

Impact of Negative Ionization

Have you ever heard of negative air? In spite of its label, this is a desirable thing. The air around us is electrically charged by many environmental factors, including cosmic rays, friction caused by air movement, radioactive dust, ultraviolet radiation, and atmospheric pressure changes. In areas of higher population, the atmosphere's healthy balance of positive to negative ions can be disrupted. Human activity, it seems, destroys negative ions and ultimately reduces the amount of oxygen in the air. Smoke, dust, smog, pollutants, electrical emissions, heating systems, coolers and traffic exhaust are all culprits. The air can become too highly electrified (too many positive ions) and the humans reaction is counterproductive to learning.

When it comes to air, the more negatively charged it is, the better. When the electrical charge in the air is too positive, it can cause you to feel groggy, lethargic, sleepy or depressed. Have you ever noticed that when you stand in front of a waterfall, or step outdoors just after a rain, or stand atop a mountain, or just get out of a shower, you feel fresh and energized. You may be enjoying the benefits of negative ionization.

Just for the sake of comparison, a stuffy classroom may have an ionization count of say +1000, while that spot in front of the waterfall has an ionization level of say 100 times that amount (-100,000). This difference can have a powerful effect on learning. Some estimates claim that 57 to 85 percent of the population may benefit from more negative ions. Ion levels have been studied for their ability to speed recovery in burn or asthma patients, to stabilize alpha rhythms, positively impact our reactions to sensory stimuli, and to impact serotonin levels in the bloodstream. Higher levels of alertness and improved sense of well-being are definite learning enhancers; and with evidence pointing to air quality as an important factor, it should not be ignored.

Music and Noise in the Environment

Twenty years ago you could hardly find a teacher who complemented learning with music, unless they were a music or nursery school teacher. Now, it is common practice to include music within the curriculum, as well as extracurricularly. However, music programs have faced recent attacks as budget cuts threaten to reduce us "back to the basics." Ironically, at the same time that critics call music a "right-brained frill," a surge of recent research supports the positive benefits of listening to, and playing, music. Since, learning to play an instrument is normally done outside of class, this section addresses how any teacher can derive learning benefits from music in the classroom.

At the very least music can enhance the learning environment by calming our nervous systems; but recent studies are suggesting that music can also improve memory, cognition, concentration, and creativity. Although a subsequent chapter has been devoted entirely to "music and learning" (Chapter 17), this chapter on "optimal learning environments" would not be complete were we to leave out this important subject. So, we have provided a summary here that will hopefully get you excited about "eating the whole enchilada" shortly hereafter.

There are numerous ways to incorporate music purposefully.  Simply playing baroque in the background on low volume can evoke a relaxed and optimal learning state. Depending on the type of music played, you can also use it to help learners cool down, warm up, relax, mark an important moment or occasion, or to get energized. Beyond influencing mood, some educators use music to carry positive messages and content to learners unconsciously. At its most elemental, frequent music playing will increase the pleasure of learners and give them the feeling that their classroom is a happy, pleasant place to be.

Learner preference is an important consideration when incorporating music in your lesson plans. Like room temperature, preference differences among learners are high. For some, low-level background music (such as Baroque, in a major key) will be ideal; while others will get a better response from nature sounds or popular tunes with inspirational lyrics. Variables include learner's cultural background, learning style preferences, personality type, and prior exposure. Volume level, music type, and instruments featured are other important factors. The best results will be achieved by experimenting with your particular group of learners. Some individuals learn best in a noisy, busy environment, while others need total silence. In one study, one-fifth (20%) of elementary-school-age learners preferred a noisy environment to a quiet one (Carbo, et al. 1986). On the other hand, some students need so much silence that only earplugs may suit their needs.

Extraneous noise in the environment can be an obstacle for these learners. Researchers at the University of Evansville found (Sutter 1991) that VDTs (video display terminals) produce a barely audible high-frequency tone that induces stress and impairs learning. Women in the study were especially impacted by the noise. Researchers reported an 8 percent loss of productivity in some cases. The noise may be more detrimental to women due to their better hearing, report researchers. The tones emitted are at about a 16 k Hz level: Men rarely hear above 15 k Hz.

In conclusion, imagine that you are walking into a classroom or training facility that incorporates the principals of a brain-based environment. What does it feel like? What does it look like? What does it sound like? What does it smell like? Remember, if you can visualize it, you can accomplish it.

Tips for Incorporating Music in the Classroom

▼ **Discuss the value of music with learners. Explain the various benefits and approaches (i.e., stress reduction, memory enhancement, concentration, creativity, energy, etc.)**

▼ **Listen to music selections carefully before playing in class; choose them purposefully and exclude any that are not gentle on the nerves. Do not use selections where lyrics are questionable or not easily interpreted.**

▼ **Involve learners in the choice and control of the music. Ask for a volunteer to be the "disc jockey" for the day; and be open to student suggestions for selections that will complement the learning goals.**

▼ **Create custom cassettes or CDs for various learning purposes (see song suggestions on page 250).**

▼ **Involve students in a classroom study that focuses on determining for themselves what learning benefits might be derived from music.**

▼ **In dealing with differences, preferences, and complaints, do not disregard anyone's opinion. It is very important to accommodate the needs of all learners, as much as possible.**

▼ **Be careful not to overuse or saturate the environment with too much music. A basic rule is to limit its use to 30 percent of total class time.**

What This Means to You

We may be accidentally driving our learners crazy by stressing uniformity in the environment. Many lethargic or underperforming learners may simply be very highly susceptible to air quality, noise, lighting, and/or room temperature. We are better off offering choices to learners and/or rotating the use of various learning stations and settings in and out of the classroom. Many of our learners are underperforming due to restrictive classroom policies that conflict with their preferred learning style. Provide for diversity in aptitudes and styles; and acknowledge developmental differences within age groups. Provide a variety of lighting and music choices; maintain a quiet corner with earplugs available for students who prefer silence; and encourage cooperative learning, as well as individual learning.

Reflection Questions

1. What from this chapter was novel, fresh, or new to you? What was familiar or "old hat"?

2. In what ways, do you already apply the information in this chapter?

3. What three questions might you now generate about this material?

4. How did you react emotionally to the information in this chapter?

5. How did you react cognitively to the information? Do you agree or disagree with the author's point of view? Why?

6. In what ways might you translate the principles presented in this chapter into practical everyday useful ideas?

7. If these things are, in fact, true about the brain, what should we do differently? What resources of time, people, and money could be redirected? In what ways might you suggest we start doing this?

8. What were the most interesting insights you gained from this material?

9. If you were to plan your next step for making your curriculum more brain-based, what would that be?

10. What obstacles might you encounter? How might you realistically deal with them?

Preparing the Learner

Factors that Influence Attitude

The Role of Nutrition in Learning

Nutrition Boosts Learning

Nutrition Tips for Teachers

Learning-to-Learn Skills

Faster Learning with Pre-Exposure

How Mind-Mapping Aids Learning

Learning Boosted with Prior Knowledge

Goal-Setting Increases Performance

Personal Agency Beliefs

Pre-visualization Boosts Learning

Relaxation Boosts Learning

6

Preparing the Learner

What a person believes about him or herself impacts learning in a very powerful way. If a student feels empowered, their beliefs tend to be more positive. A positive attitude has a tsunami-like quality: It builds upon itself and ultimately aids learning. A negative attitude on the other hand, has a whirlpool-like quality: The descent can be fast and crippling. If a child believes he or she is smart, funny, and quick-witted, their performance will reflect this; If a child, however, believes he or she is dumb, lazy, or inadequate, their performance will reflect *this* belief and learning will suffer. Our internal beliefs about ourselves and our environment are the primary influencers of our external attitude. Our attitude is also impacted by numerous other factors, including the following influences:

Factors that Influence Attitude

Biological-Medical-Developmental Considerations

Over the past decade, scientists have discovered greater than fifty different neurotransmitters that act as chemical messengers in our brain. Neurotransmitter levels can impact energy, mood, concentration, and many other learning factors. Scientists are just beginning to understand how our neurotransmitters are also impacted by such factors as nutrition, sunlight exposure, illness, disease, hormones, biorhythms, medications, drugs, and stimulants, etc.

Developmental differences between girls and boys (i.e., girls develop language and reading skills earlier than boys) and between individuals within the same age and gender groups can vary by up to three years. Thus, it is quite normal for a six year old to be reading at the same level as a nine year old. This wide discrepancy, as you can imagine, has a powerful influence on learners' self-confidence levels and beliefs about themselves.

Beyond this, you can expect that children who are labeled ADHD (Attention-Deficit Hyperactivity Disorder), SED (Severely Emotionally Disturbed), LD (Learning Disabled), "slow learners", or "handicapped" in any other way are also apt to experience self-esteem issues.

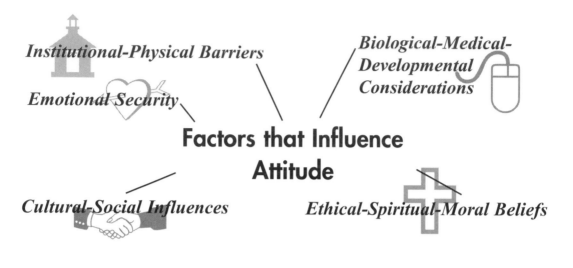

Institutional-Physical Barriers

Biological-Medical-Developmental Considerations

Emotional Security

Factors that Influence Attitude

Cultural-Social Influences

Ethical-Spiritual-Moral Beliefs

Emotional Security

Our fears, concerns, and emotions largely impact our attitudes. Shy learners may worry about feeling embarrassed, looking stupid, calling attention to themselves, not succeeding, or *even* succeeding. Such worrying, of course, induces stress which inhibits learning.

The extrovert on the other hand, may try out many new behaviors and approaches; and is therefore more likely to find the "right" answer. They are also generally more adept at making friends, which can further enhance their feelings of popularity and adequacy. Although some introverts may gain confidence from receiving high marks and performing at an accelerated level, what about the shy learner who *doesn't* accelerate in their studies or have many friends? This learner is in double jeopardy for developing poor self-esteem. The sooner an intervention can be initiated, the better. The best intervention is helping the student find something at which they can excel—something that makes their heart sing. Perhaps that something will be a love of art, sports, music, skateboarding, poetry writing, dancing, singing, reading, model building, martial arts, or performing. Whatever that passion is, encourage them to pursue it for as long as it brings them pleasure and a healthy sense of challenge.

When authority figures of any kind make a statement about a child, the child is apt to accept it as true, whether it's close to the truth or as far away from it as the moon. Children do not have the brain development for reasoning until about the age of ten or twelve. By this time, they have built up a whole set of capability beliefs, many erroneously, that are already shaping their future success. A capability belief is likely to be formed when even a well-meaning parent, relative, or teacher blurts out in a moment of frustration, "Why don't you understand this simple concept?" Or worse, "You'll never learn what you need to at this rate!" Such false statements serve as the catalyst for many poor attitudes; and their impact can be a lifetime of learning paralysis.

Ethical-Spiritual-Moral Beliefs

The ethical, spiritual, and moral values that a child's family holds is going to impact what, when, how, and why a child does or doesn't learn something. Many families hold beliefs which deter rapid effortless learning. We've all heard people say, "Learning only happens with struggle; no one is successful overnight." What does this message convey to the child who happens to understand a concept in ten minutes, while others grasp it only after days? It is quite possible that they will discount their own learning.

On the other hand, positive messages conveyed by a family's moral values can give learners a feeling of empowerment, internal reward, and self control. "You can make of yourself whatever you can envision," for example, is an affirmation that serves learners well. Or, "We are confident you will succeed." These statements feed and nurture learners to persevere through the inevitable rough periods that we all face.

Cultural-Social Influences

The cultural and social messages we hear impact us on the deepest level—from gender-role expectations, popular opinion, and ethnic traditions, to learning-style differences, peer pressure, and cultural norms. A whole set of behaviors are born of these influences. From a pure cultural standpoint, consider how many Asians are expected to study and excel in school and what consequences they face for not achieving the expected standard. Consider how many first-generation college graduates are both held up by their families as a model of success and simultaneously shunned for their departure from the norm. Consider how girls traditionally have not been pushed to succeed in math and science. Consider how it is more acceptable for boys to express anti-social behavior. Consider how stereotypes and prejudice have impacted learners over the decades and centuries. Consider how peer pressure may have encouraged or discouraged you or others you know from achieving the highest level of excellence. Even some individuals with a particular learning style preference, such as kinesthetic (tactile) learners, may experience a significant disadvantage as misguided educators shift their instructional approach to a lecture format (especially common at the higher grades).

Institutional-Physical Barriers

Barriers of access, including discrimination, financial limitations, accessibility, and authority restrictions, influence learning more than many of us would like to believe. When money, politics, and power are at stake, learners who are different in some way from the status quo are bound to face discrimination. Groups that are often disenfranchised from our learning institutions include the poor, disabled, ill, pregnant, or elderly, just to name a few. Fortunately as awareness increases and economic disparity decreases, the barriers to learning are slowly lessening.

What This Means to You

Instead of judging a learner's potential by their outward attitudes or behavior, assess what invisible barriers may be impacting their attitude. Many learners underperform when seemingly faced with "immovable" obstacles. How can you help learners successfully penetrate or negotiate these challenges? Are there things you can do to counter the effects of the negative barriers. Consider using positive posters, oral affirmations, and immediate hands-on learner successes.

The Role of Nutrition in Learning

Good nutrition promotes healthy functioning of neurons—the essential building blocks of mental performance. Your brain's most critical need is for oxygen and glucose; and the only way to provide this fuel is to consume foods rich in the necessary nutrients. Second, it needs water—pure water—every day for optimal learning. The brain is composed of 80 percent water and is highly sensitive to variances in pH levels. The actual transmission of neurons is dependent upon the polarity of each cell and that's influenced by calcium, potassium, and water. Typically thirsty learners drink coffee, tea, or soft drinks; but these drinks are diuretics and are processed as foods rather than water. The sugars bind to the water and the beneficial effect of the liquid is, therefore, lost.

As with all animals, we have a "consumatory" prowling behavior that emerges when water is absent or restricted. This behavior increases our stress hormones (cortisol) and increases responses to novelty (overreactions). But within five minutes of consuming water, there is a marked drop in stress hormones and our behaviors become more predictable.

Beyond oxygen and water, Judith Wurtman, PhD. of MIT (1986) says that amino acids set the stage for learning—either positively or negatively. The ingredients in protein are critical to the brain. Tyrosine and tryptophan are two examples. The first enhances thinking; the latter has a calming effect.

Your brain uses tyrosine to make the neurotransmitters dopamine and norepineph-rine. These two electrically-charged chemical messengers are critical to alertness, quick thinking, and fast reactions; and help you perform calculations, maintain atten-tion span, and increase conscious awareness. Tyrosine is found in protein-rich foods, such as milk products, meats, fish, eggs, and tofu.

The consumption of protein can partially counteract the negative effects of sugar, Dr. Wurtman says. "Eating protein either alone or with some carbohydrate can increase the alertness chemicals dopamine and norepinephrine if your brain's supply is low," she adds. Is more protein better? No, it's not. Obviously, if your brain already has enough, too much is just an overkill and has no beneficial effect. But how much is enough? It depends on your weight, age, and activity levels, but 15 to 30 grams per day is sufficient, say most experts.

Unfortunately, many low-income learners typically have carbohydrates for breakfast (toast, breads, cereals); and this may not provide the boost to thinking that a break-fast of eggs, bacon, and cottage cheese would.

 ## What This Means to You

Ensure that learners have access to water during class time. Allow them to bring water bottles into the learning area, or to be excused momentarily without embarrassment or hassle. Explain to your students the value of water versus other beverages, such as soda, juice, coffee, etc. Remind them to rehydrate often. Also discuss the relationship between good nutrition and good brain power. Encourage learners to eat "close to the earth"—fresh fruits and vegeta-bles—and to eat regular frequent meals including good protein and fiber.

Nutrition Boosts Learning

How much does what we eat (or don't eat) affect our brain and thinking? Researchers say, "Plenty!" Vitamins and other nutrients are essential to brain development, neur-al maintenance, and brain metabolism. Glucose, a blood sugar, for example, is the sole source of fuel for our brain cells, yet many learners skip breakfast—our first opportunity to refuel after overnight glucose depletion. And, in spite of the fact that our alertness, memory, visuospatial ability, attention and planning/organizational skills are directly impacted by critical vitamins (such as vitamins A, C, E, and most of the Bs, as well as folic acid, lecithin, magnesium, sodium, potassium, zinc, iron, boron, and selenium), many learners are deficient in these nutrients (LaRue, et al. 1997; Ramakrishna 1999).

Research supports the importance of taking a daily vitamin supplement in addition to eating your spinach, oranges, bran cereal, seafood, chicken, and vitamin-packed foods. Researchers in one study (Benton and Roberts 1988), measured visual acuity, reaction time, and intelligence among a group of ninety twelve- and thirteen-year-olds, some of whom were given a multivitamin supplement and some of whom were given a placebo. The experiment group showed a significant increase in all scores over the control group.

> ### *It's time to take learner nutrition more seriously: An important step is to enhance school lunch menus and provide healthy vending-machine snacks.*

Figure 6.1
Brain Foods

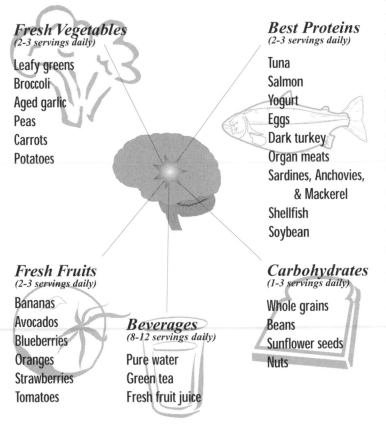

Fresh Vegetables
(2-3 servings daily)

Leafy greens
Broccoli
Aged garlic
Peas
Carrots
Potatoes

Best Proteins
(2-3 servings daily)

Tuna
Salmon
Yogurt
Eggs
Dark turkey
Organ meats
Sardines, Anchovies,
& Mackerel
Shellfish
Soybean

Fresh Fruits
(2-3 servings daily)

Bananas
Avocados
Blueberries
Oranges
Strawberries
Tomatoes

Beverages
(8-12 servings daily)

Pure water
Green tea
Fresh fruit juice

Carbohydrates
(1-3 servings daily)

Whole grains
Beans
Sunflower seeds
Nuts

Vitamin deficiencies as an obstacle to learning remain a serious concern to educators, especially among those who work with low-income schoolchildren. Although low-income schoolchildren are most prone to nutritional deficiencies, J. Minninger reports (1984) that any diet under 2,100 calories per day is deficient in some vitamin, mineral, or trace element, unless tailored by a physician for a patient. After three months on a low-calorie diet, people exhibit faulty memory, increased error rates, clumsiness, panic, anxiety, and hostility, he found. Thus, even minor vitamin deficiencies can impact learning performance.

For instance, a research team led by Asenath LaRue (1997) concluded that vitamin supplements can yield cognitive benefits even if the person is already eating smart. The study followed 137 elderly, healthy participants for six years and found that the vast majority of the participants improved their performance on memory, visuospacial, and abstraction tests (initially given six years earlier) after taking supplements of vitamins C, E, A, B-6, B-12, and folic acid while routinely eating well-balanced meals.

In a study by Karen Riggs and colleagues (1996) on the cognitive effects of B-12, B-6, and folic acid, it was found that those persons with the highest levels of these vitamins in their blood performed significantly better on a battery of memory and spatial copying tests than those subjects with lower bloodlevels of these vitamins. Vitamin B-12 is found abundantly in shellfish; B-6 is found in chicken, fish, and whole wheat products; and folic acid (or folate) is contained in fortified cereals and leafy green vegetables.

A recent study published in the *Journal of the American Medical Association* examined the breakfast-eating habits of 1,151 low-income second- and fifth-graders in schools without federally-funded breakfast programs. The research team led by Amy Sampson found (1995) that on any given day, 12 to 26 percent of the students attended school without having eaten anything. At least 36 percent of the students were obese, and a significantly greater portion of the students consumed less than 50 percent of the required daily allowance for vitamins A, E, B-6, and folate. And, one-fourth of the students were found deficient in vitamin C, calcium, and iron.

Nutrition Tips for Teachers

▼ Vitamin and mineral deficiencies result from either insufficient food intake or inadequate nutrient absorption by the body. Either can cause fatigue, loss of appetite, poor concentration, failing memory, hostility, depression and insomnia. If you suspect a problem among your learners, seek advice from the health/medical consultant at your school. Vitamin and mineral deficiency can be determined by a simple blood test.

▼ If your school is located in a predominantly poor area, there is an increased chance that many students are not eating properly. Initiate steps to begin a federally-funded breakfast and lunch program at your school, if one is not already in place.

▼ Monitor the menu of your existing cafeteria lunch program and make suggestions for additional vitamin-nutritious meals.

▼ Instruct your students on the relationship between a nutritious diet and cognition and well-being.

▼ Megadoses of vitamins have no benefits and can be toxic. Stay within the required or suggested dosage.

▼ Vitamin supplements are best absorbed when taken with other foods. However, caffeinated beverages, alcohol, nicotine, aspirin, and other medications obstruct absorption. (Note: Since high levels of caffeine are known to block vitamin absorption, perhaps school district contracts that promote the increased presence of beverage vending machines on campus may be adversely affecting student nutrition and learning.)

 ## What This Means to You

You or your learners may be underperforming due to dietary deficiencies. To boost your alertness and mental performance, include a vitamin supplement in your diet. The best foods for protein are eggs, fish, turkey, tofu, pork, chicken, and yogurt. Eat just three to four ounces, since eating more than this does not further increase alertness. Keep saturated fats low and iron levels normal. Eat a "nibbling" diet of many meals a day, if possible. Too much time in between eating can cause loss of concentration and decreased alertness. Allow for appropriate foods in the classroom. Make sure your learners are given several opportunities to eat nutritious snacks throughout the day. Talk to your learners about the positive role nutrition can play in performance, thinking and testing. Many important nutrients are often not found in your typical learner's diet.

Learning-to-Learn Skills

When learners are instructed in learning-to-learn skills, their ability to process new information can rise substantially (Weinstein and Mayer 1986). Futurist and business guru Peter Drucker says, "We can predict with confidence that we will redefine what it means to be an educated person...[(it)] will be somebody who has learned how to learn and who continues to learn..." If we fail to teach these skills to our students, who will prepare them for a fast-changing global society? What are the key ingredients for study skills mastery? Most sources suggest that learners:

▼ **Get proper nutrition and enough sleep.**
▼ **Set goals; develop a purpose.**
▼ **Browse the material; learn how to identify key concepts and build "perceptual maps."**
▼ **Develop mind-maps that reflect your thoughts, questions, concerns, and connections to prior learning.**
▼ **Read with a highlighter pen in hand; make notes in the margins.**
▼ **Summarize what's been learned; reflect on it; ask questions.**
▼ **Act on the learning, make tapes, build models, do projects, etc.**

What This Means to You

Among the many benefits of study skills programs, they 1) help students to incorporate their preferred learning style; 2) improve student's confidence in learning; thus, improving self esteem; and 3) encourage students to become more proactive—to take control of their learning. Ensuring your learners have the study skills necessary to succeed is a worthwhile investment of teaching time.

Faster Learning With Pre-Exposure

What is pre-exposure; and how does it accelerate learning? Robert Ornstein, PhD. of Stanford says (1984) that pre-exposure to information (or exposure to information on a non-conscious level), sometimes called priming, makes subsequent learning proceed more quickly. The greater the amount of "priming" stimulus, the more the brain extracts and "compartmentalizes" (lateralizes) the information (Gratton, et al. 1992). He thinks the brain has a way of putting information and ideas into a "buffer zone" or "cognitive waiting room" for rapid access. If the information is not utilized over time, it simply lays unconnected and random. But if the other parts of the puzzle are offered, the understanding and extraction of meaning is rapid.

Michael Gazzaniga, PhD. (1992) reports that in experiments done at Stanford, prior exposure to a presentation of questions led to quicker responses. Learning and recall also increased when a pattern is provided prior to exposing learners to new material (Bower and Mann 1992). Providing "post-organizing clues" is also useful as a framework for recall (Bower, et al. 1990).

In my own workshops, participants are asked to recount, as part of an exercise, all of the forms of pre-exposure they encountered before or during the training. They usually come up with the following sources:

▼ **Course description mailed out prior to attending**
▼ **The opportunity to talk to past participants**
▼ **Reading books on the subject**
▼ **Watching a "what to expect" video about the course**
▼ **Colorful peripherals in the training room**
▼ **Transparencies previewed at the beginning of the course**
▼ **The workbook provided**
▼ **My own specific "previews of coming attractions"**

One of the key characteristics of the cortex is the ability to detect and create patterns of meaning. This process involves deciphering cues, recognizing relationships, and indexing information. The clues best assembled by the brain are those presented in a Gestalt format, rather than a sequential, linear format. Of course, the majority of teachers mistakenly learned that teaching must be sequential and linear to be effective. The result of this traditional approach is bored and frustrated learners.

> *The brain's capacity to elicit patterns of meaning is one of the key principles of brain-based learning.*

Pattern recognition depends heavily on what experience one brings to a situation. Our neural patterns are continually revised as new experiences provide us with additional information, insights, and corrections. In fact, learning is the extraction of meaningful patterns from confusion. In other words, figuring things out *in your own way*. As young children, our cognitive understanding is limited by our ability (or lack of) to create personal metaphors or models for the information. This point is quite important about the brain, so here it is again:

> *We never really cognitively understand something until we can create a model or metaphor that is derived from our unique personal world.*

Many teachers know that comprehension increases when readers create a mental model for the material while reading it. Making connections between the characters' actions and the learners' own goals or values, for example, creates a mental marker in the learner's neural map. Activating these kinds of personal connections results in increased reader recall and comprehension.

Generally speaking, learning results from the operation of neural linkages between global mappings and value centers. Learning is achieved when behavior leads to synaptic changes in global mappings that satisfy set points. In other words, we are learning when we can relate the knowledge from one area to another, then personalize it. Three essentials of higher brain functions are categorization, memory, and learning. The last depends on the first two; the second depends on the first. Perceptual categorization is essential for memory. The value centers are located in the hypothalamus and mid brain.

Consider this example: When you arrive in a new city, you not only need to know how to get where you want to go, but where you are in relation to your destination. In other words, the spatial, contextual relationships are the patterns which help you understand and get around in the world. You might link up information such as, where are the hotels, entertainment, and McDonald's with personal meanings, such as why am I here; or where should I eat dinner?

What This Means to You

Knowing facts may provide answers at test time, but it is pattern detection that helps learners become thinking adults. Before beginning a new topic, ask your students to discuss it orally, or to represent it graphically in a mind-map; then post it. This gives the brain an "address" or a visual storage space for the new information. Reduce the amount of "piecemeal" learning. During a course, continually have students make maps, story boards, graphic organizers, paintings, models, or other artistic renderings of the material. At the end of the course, ask them to make a video, a play, or a larger, mural-sized map of their learning. The key is getting students to relate the learning to their own personal life, and increasing the contexts surrounding it.

How Mind-Mapping Aids Learning

Did you know that hanging a poster-sized graphic organizer or mind-map on the wall in your classroom can improve learning? It's true! The process of creating a mind-map—a graphic visual display of a subject depicting key relationships with symbols, colors, and buzz words—creates meaning for the learner.

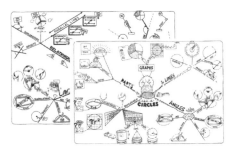

The research of M. O. Weil and J. Murphy (1982) suggests that the use of some kind of pre-exposure is very powerful. They say, "Advance organizers are especially effective for helping students learn the key concepts or principles of a subject area and the detailed facts and bits of information within these concept areas [the advance organizer idea]... is a highly effective instructional strategy for all subject areas where the objective is meaningful assimilation...."

J. Luiten and associates (1980) reviewed 135 studies examining acquisition and retention effects of advance stimulation and organizers on learning. His conclusions were that some form of "advanced organizers" are consistently positive. Mapping our ideas gives learners a way to conceptualize ideas, shape their thinking, and better understand what they do know (and don't know). But most importantly, when we produce mind-maps, it helps us feel like the learning is really "ours."

> ## *Consistent pre-exposure will encourage quicker and deeper learning.*

Georgi Lozanov, the founder of accelerated learning, used pre-exposure with positive visual suggestion by color-coding key items. He reports (1979) that five hundred subjects exposed to this technique exhibited better recall than subjects who did not get the color-coded material. By preparing the mind, it learns naturally. This is the essence of "ownership."

Mind-mapping is an excellent method for pre-exposing learners to a topic. Through the use of color, movement, drawing, contrast, and organization decisions, information becomes encoded in our mental maps. Once they are created, learners can subsequently share them with others, thus, further reinforcing the learning.

 ## What This Means to You

Many students who seem like slow learners may simply need pre-exposure to lay the foundation for better comprehension and recall. Pre-expose learners to your topic before officially starting it. You might want to first expose them to the topic with mentions of the subject prior to exposure; then post mind-maps two weeks before beginning the topic; then preview the texts to be used; then provide handouts. You can also get them ready with oral previews, music, personal examples, storytelling, and metaphors. Kinesthetically, you can facilitate role plays, create simulation situations, or play games that expose learners to the new learning in a subconscious manner.

Learning Boosted With Prior Knowledge

When prior learning is activated, the brain is much more likely to makes connections to the new material, therefore increasing comprehension and meaning. The research of R. C. Anderson and P. D. Pearson (1984) revealed that the importance of discovering and relating to previously learned material is much greater than earlier thought. "It is a better predictor of comprehension than is an intelligence test score....," the researchers suggest.

Let's say you're a student attending a new class and the instructor immediately starts in on the new material. You're lost and overwhelmed in the first ten minutes. By the end of the first class, you're already worried about how you'll do. Wouldn't it have helped to first find out what you already know, and tie that into the course material?

What This Means to You

Many learners who should do well in a subject actually underperform because the new material seems irrelevant. Unless connections are made to students' prior learning, comprehension and meaning may be dramatically lessened. Before starting a new topic, ask students to discuss what they already know about the subject; do role plays or skits; make mind-maps; and brainstorm its potential value.

Goal-Setting Increases Performance

Teachers maintain many types of goals for their students. Some are directed by a governmental entity (standards for outcome-based learning, for example). Others may be your own goals: "I want them to develop a real love of learning." And yet others may be determined by a particular learner's situation: "Johnny's going to learn to read this year." But most critical to a brain-based learning approach is the learner's goals for him or herself. The best goals are student-generated goals.

Two researchers, E. A. Locke and G. P. Latham (1990), reviewed 400 studies examining goals for motivation, and the results were definitive. They found that specific, difficult goals lead to better performance than easy, vague ones. The results, based on studies conducted in the U.S. and seven other countries, included more than forty thousand subjects, eighty-eight different tasks, time spans ranging from one minute to three years, and many different performance criteria, including behavior change, quantity and quality outcomes, and costs.

However, a few other criteria are important for effective goal setting, says Martin Ford, author of *Motivating Humans* (1992). First, the target has to be at an optimal level of difficulty—challenging, but attainable. In addition, learners need to have 1) ample feedback to make corrections; 2) capability beliefs to help them persevere in the face of negative feedback; 3) the actual skills needed to complete the task; and 4) an environment conducive to success. The three keys to learner goal acquisition, says Ford, are the learner's beliefs, the learner's emotions, and the goals themselves.

However, if goals are given too much attention, they can be counter-productive, says to R. F. Baumeister (1984). When the pressure is too great, learners report feelings of self-consciousness and the tendency to make simple mistakes and "choke" on material they know that they know, but can't remember in the pressure of the moment.

Personal Agency Beliefs

Personal agency beliefs (PABs)—a term used to describe a person's capability beliefs about him or herself—are activated once a goal is set and are influenced by the context of the moment. For example, a student's belief upon being accepted to a university might be, "Wow, I think I can do well and graduate from this university in four years." However, once the student is attending classes, she may begin thinking, "Gee, with a full load at school and working part time, getting good grades is harder than I thought."

In a long-term study of 250 students, ages twelve to fifteen, researcher J. L. Meece and associates (1990) found that the single best predictor of success in mathematics was *the student's expectancy* of future math success. Once these students were in the classes, the best predictor of their likelihood of continuing in math classes was *its importance* to them.

Although an instructional leader isn't always privy to a learners ever-evolving PABs, when it is obvious that the student is lacking strong capability beliefs, there is a solution. Co-establish, with significant student input, "controllable short-term goals," say R. C. Barden and M. E. Ford (1990). By doing this, the long-term outcomes may still be in doubt, but the short-term successes can positively impact the PABs of the underconfident learner.

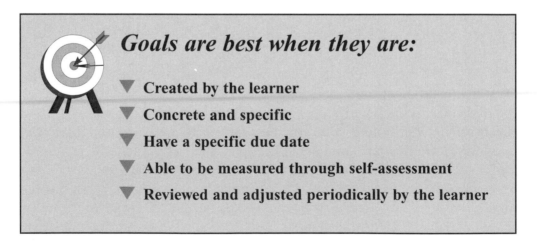

Goals are best when they are:

▼ Created by the learner

▼ Concrete and specific

▼ Have a specific due date

▼ Able to be measured through self-assessment

▼ Reviewed and adjusted periodically by the learner

The beliefs or PABs the instructional leader holds about their students—both individually and collectively—also impact the learner in powerful ways. Researchers R. Rosenthal and L. Jacobsen in their famous experiment and subsequent book, *Pygmalion in the Classroom* (1968), presented a compelling argument for why teachers and trainers should maintain high expectations of learners. Results of the study, you may remember, suggest that students will perform, not coincidentally, as well as you expect them to.

Some learners may get sufficiently engaged with simple goals, such as "Here's what we can get done today," while others may require more challenging goals, such as "Let's design a better health-care system and see if we can get it picked up by the local news."

 ## What This Means to You

Goal setting is an important aspect of the learning process. Let students generate their own goals. Have them discover whether their own beliefs can support them. Ask them about the learning environment. Do they feel it supports them in achieving their goals? Do they have the resources they need to reach their goals? Most learners who want to succeed are capable of succeeding, though often they lack the beliefs to do so. Ask learners to set immediate short-term goals for the day in addition to longer term goals. Make sure the goals are positive, measurable, and obtainable. For example, the goal could be as simple as wanting to learn two new interesting things today. You then need to provide the resources, learning climate, and feedback to help your learners reach their goals. Hold them accountable. Check back later to assess results and celebrate, if appropriate. If necessary, help learners reassess their goals or approach to achieving them. Celebrate each step to success.

Pre-Visualization Boosts Learning

An Oxford University study (Drake 1996) found that visualization before a learning activity improved learning. A group of elementary school children were asked to practice visualization, imagery, and make believe before being tested, while the control group only took the test. The group that did the visualization first scored higher.

Before you went to your last job interview, chances are you rehearsed the interview in your mind a few times over. This kind of practicing help you access important information, and, in a sense, "pre-exposes" your mind to pertinent data.

What This Means to You

In some cases, your learners may not be unmotivated, they may just need mental warm-ups. A few minutes invested early in the class can produce a big payoff later. Create a daily routine for learners. Before you start, have them do some physical stretching and mental warm-ups, such as role-playing, generating questions, visualizing a scene, solving a problem, or brainstorming.

Relaxation Boosts Learning

The work of J. O'Keefe and L. Nadel (1978) and more recently Robert Sapolsky (1996, 1999) reminds us of the powerful effects of distress on the brain. They use descriptors like "rigidity of behavior," "stereotyped behavior," and "repeated use of particular responses." In other words, prolonged stress or distress produces an uptight learner—not a student who loves to learn.

Most teachers have seen this over and over. The more the distress, the more students tighten up and underperform. Authors M. Murphy and S. Donovan (1988) say that lowered learner distress through meditation may reduce the release of hormones linked with threat, while maintaining those linked with the ability to meet a challenge. In other words, a relaxed nervous system is best for learning.

Physical changes begin to occur in the hippocampus, a brain region important to learning and memory, in response to a major stressor or prolonged exposure to elevated cortisol levels from major depression, post-traumatic stress disorder, or a physiological malfunction. These physical changes may interfere with the ability to induce long-term potentiation in the hippocampus: The result is memory failure (LeDoux 1996; Sapolsky 1996, 1999).

What This Means to You

Take the time before beginning each session to facilitate a few moments of relaxation for students. Here are some of the best ways to encourage a relaxed state for optimal learning: 1) slow stretching; 2) laughter and humor; 3) music; 4) games and activities; 5) unstructured discussion and sharing; 6) low-stress rituals; and 7) visualization.

Reflection Questions

1. What from this chapter was novel, fresh, or new to you? What was familiar or "old hat"?

2. In what ways, do you already apply the information in this chapter?

3. What three questions might you now generate about this material?

4. How did you react emotionally to the information in this chapter?

5. How did you react cognitively to the information? Do you agree or disagree with the author's point of view? Why?

6. In what ways might you translate the principles presented in this chapter into practical everyday useful ideas?

7. If these things are, in fact, true about the brain, what should we do differently? What resources of time, people, and money could be redirected? In what ways might you suggest we start doing this?

8. What were the most interesting insights you gained from this material?

9. If you were to plan your next step for making your curriculum more brain-based, what would that be?

10. What obstacles might you encounter? How might you realistically deal with them?

The Brain, Gender, and Learning

Socially-Conditioned Differences

Biological Differences

Functional Differences

Gender Tips for Teachers

The Brain, Gender, and Learning

Gender issues are extremely complex. The variations within gender groups are as great as those found between genders. This does not negate the fact, however, that in general a variety of social and biological differences between men and women exist and they impact learning.

When we start to talk about differences, immediately the tendency is to point out the exceptions to the rule. There will always be exceptions—many, in fact. Although the average woman in America is 5'5" tall, for example, and the average man is 5'9" tall, many of us fall outside of this norm. So to point out that the tallest woman in the world, as of this writing, is 7'4" and the shortest is 4' tall, does not contribute to the discourse. The purpose of this chapter is to examine gender differences through generalized profiles, rather than accounting for the inevitable exceptions.

A difficult question arises when we begin to study gender: Are the differences a result of biological or social conditions? Although some studies have been designed to reduce or eliminate social variables by studying infants, for instance, in the first few days of life or students who have only attended same-sex schools, identifying purely biological differences has proven a difficult task. Nevertheless, some studies using high-tech brain imaging devices, as well as animal models, have drawn some general conclusions about anatomical differences. First, let's take a look at the differences that are most likely socially derived.

Socially-Conditioned Differences

Researchers have documented (Shaw 1995; Sheridan and Henning-Stout 1994) pervasive demotivating influences on females in academics and subsequent career pursuits in technology, mathematics, science, and computer-related fields. The most common solutions are often one-dimensional (such as single-sex schools). But I. T. Miura (1987) says the problem of under-representation of females in this fields requires more complex and integrated solutions. Gender inequities are largely influenced by social expectations which may be expressed in the following ways:

▼ **Boys and girls (women and men) may set different goals.**

▼ **Their emotional responses may be different.**

▼ **Their capability beliefs may be different.**

▼ **Their context issues may be different.**

Figure 7.1
Male/Female Brains

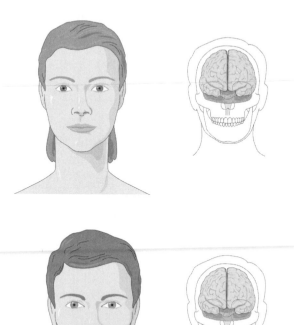

Even though changing social policy reflects a more liberal attitude towards strict gender-type scripting and sex-role expectations, issues of access and support for equity in education are still present. A thirteen-to-one ratio of males to females in higher-level math classes, for example, still exists today. Martin Ford (1992) suggests that the rate of progress to reduce such discrepancies could be greatly enhanced by a more comprehensive program. He says, "Interventions designed to address just one aspect of the inequity problem will probably yield disappointing results." For example, encouraging girls to take up a math, science, or technology fields is a great idea; but unless you address the issue of peer pressure, capability beliefs, context beliefs, and emotions, there's little chance for large-scale success.

What This Means to You

If women are to gain equal representation in fields traditionally dominated by men, we must address the less obvious underlying problems: Differing beliefs, emotions, and goals. Examine your own beliefs about gender roles and expectations. Interview your students. Find out what interests them, what would encourage them to pursue studies in fields traditionally pursued by the opposite sex and what support they might need to maintain their interest. Encourage all learners to pursue that which interests them most, regardless of their gender. Combat the stereotypes that may hinder anyone from achieving their goals, however far from the "norm" they may seem to be. Boys can make great teachers and nurses, just as girls can make great scientists and computer programmers.

Biological Differences

After years of research, dozens of eminent scientists (Kimura 1989-1999; Butler 1988, Burton and Levy 1989; McGuiness 1976; Allen and Gorski 1991; Ankey 1992; Driesen and Raz 1995; Pakenberg and Gundersen 1997) have noted physical differences between the male and female brain. These structural differences may account for behavioral, developmental, and cognitive processing differences between males and females.

For starters, males have a 10 to 15 percent larger brain than females in general. When a control is set up for body size, studies still indicate that male brains average 100 grams heavier (Ankey 1992). In addition, men have about four billion more cortical neurons than women (Pakenberg and Gundersen 1997). Other areas of the brain are different, too. In the hypothalamus, some areas are smaller in women (INAH region) and others are larger (SCN), the former area plays a key role in sexuality, the latter a role in biological rhythms. The hippocampus is larger in male rats, but at this point, there's no human evidence of such a difference.

The corpus callosum was originally thought to be much thicker in females than in males; however, recent research

Figure 7.2

Interhemispheric Connections

In females, the anterior commissure is generally larger and carries more interhemispheric neural traffic

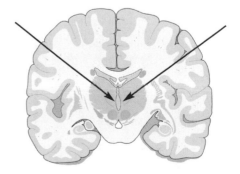

has debunked the earlier studies (Driesen and Raz 1995). Another lesser known bundle of interhemispheric fibers, called the anterior commissure (see figure 7.2), however, is clearly larger in female brains (Allen and Gorski 1991). This advantage may allow females to tie together verbal and nonverbal information more efficiently. Variances within the same gender group do exist, but certainly not to the same extent as those found between the sexes.

Developmental neuroanatomists have found that in the early years, brain growth rates vary from a few months to five years both within and across gender groups, as well. Some believe this may be the reason boys generally outperform girls on spatial task measures, and girls outperform boys in verbal and reading skills early in life. Other functional differences show up as well.

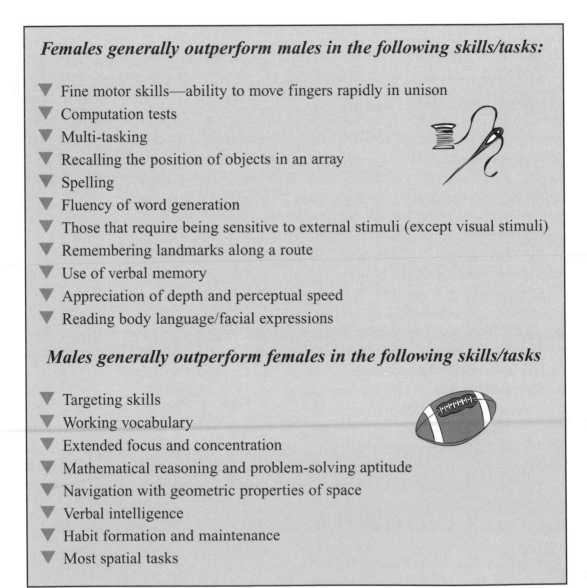

Females generally outperform males in the following skills/tasks:

▼ Fine motor skills—ability to move fingers rapidly in unison
▼ Computation tests
▼ Multi-tasking
▼ Recalling the position of objects in an array
▼ Spelling
▼ Fluency of word generation
▼ Those that require being sensitive to external stimuli (except visual stimuli)
▼ Remembering landmarks along a route
▼ Use of verbal memory
▼ Appreciation of depth and perceptual speed
▼ Reading body language/facial expressions

Males generally outperform females in the following skills/tasks

▼ Targeting skills
▼ Working vocabulary
▼ Extended focus and concentration
▼ Mathematical reasoning and problem-solving aptitude
▼ Navigation with geometric properties of space
▼ Verbal intelligence
▼ Habit formation and maintenance
▼ Most spatial tasks

Functional Differences

Although we can acknowledge the physiological differences between the genders and note performance variances overall, additional research is necessary before we can draw more definitive conclusions. Additional functional differences that impact learners of both sexes are outlined in the next couple of pages. Be aware, however, that these are general differences and not absolute.

Hearing:
The female ear is better able to pick up nuances of voice, music, and other sounds. In addition, females retain better hearing longer in life. At 85 decibels, females perceive the volume twice as loud as males. Females have greater vocal clarity and are one-sixth as likely as males to be monotone. They learn to speak earlier and learn languages more quickly. Three-quarters of university students majoring in foreign languages are female. Women excel at verbal memory and process language faster and more accurately. Infant girls are comforted by singing and speech to a greater degree than males. In contrast to this summary of research, however, N. Klutky (1990) says females show no significant auditory advantage in his own studies.

Vision:
Males have better distance vision and depth perception; while females excel at peripheral vision. Men see better in brighter light; while women's eyesight is superior at night. Females are more sensitive to the red end of the spectrum; they excel at visual memory; are superior at interpreting facial clues and context; and exhibit greater ability to recognize faces and remember names. In repeated studies, women were able to store more random and irrelevant visual information than men (Williams and Anderson 1997; Velle 1992).

Figure 7.3
Male/Female Testing Differences

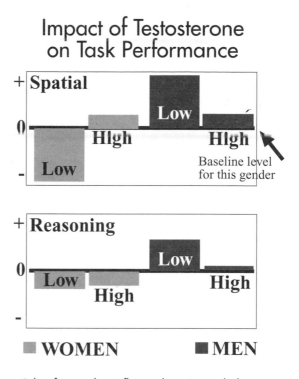

Other factors that influence learning include maturation, motivation, context, and hormones. Females excel in other tasks (ie. language, etc.)

Touch:

Females have a more diffused and sensitive sense of touch. They react faster and more acutely to pain, yet can withstand pain over a longer duration than males. Males react more to extremes of temperature. Females have greater sensitivity in fingers and hands. They are superior in performing new motor combinations, and in fine motor dexterity.

Activity:

Male infants play more with objects, more often, than females. Females are more responsive to playmates. The directional choice, called "circling behavior," is opposite for men and women. In other words, when right-handed males walk over to a table to pick up an object, they are more likely to return by turning to their right. Right-handed females are more likely to return by circling around to their left.

Smell and Taste:

Women have a stronger sense of smell and are much more responsive to aromas, odors and subtle changes in smell. They are more sensitive to bitter flavors and prefer sweet flavors. A "significant advantage" in olfactory memory was found by N. Klutky (1990). Differences in the brain also relate to the effects of contaminants from beauty products. By using neuroraudiological imaging to assess brain shrinkage, C. Harper and J. Kril (1990) found that women are more susceptible to the damaging effects of alcohol than males.

Problem-Solving:

Researchers D. Kimura and E. Hampson (1990) say that males and females have very different ways of approaching and solving problems. Dr. Kimura has been a pioneer for decades on the anatomical and functional differences between the sexes. Here is a summary of the research on differences in problem-solving, broken down by gender.

But what does this tell us about learning? Although there are some documented functional differences between the genders, there are also cultural and social biases that begin impacting us at birth. While some parents and administrators have opted for same-sex schools to better meet their child's needs, the effectiveness of such an intervention on cognition and social skills is unknown. There are some things, however, educators can do in the co-educational school setting to support gender differences in the learning environment.

Gender Tips for Teachers

▼ **Be aware of how gender differences may impact learners.**

▼ **Be patient with learners who may not show the same brain development that others do (especially with boys who usually learn language skills one to two years later than girls; or girls who are not as skilled in the spatial or physical tasks as early).**

▼ **Respect differences and appreciate each learner's uniqueness. Use differences as an opportunity to teach about respecting our own and others developmental timelines. Refrain from labeling students "slow learners" or "hyperactive."**

We should not confuse equality of opportunity with equality of outcome. Often the most objective criteria for a standardized test (like the SAT or LSAT) may result in higher male or higher female scores due to general differences. Some advocate altering aptitude tests so that scores don't waver widely across genders, calling that the true "unbiased" 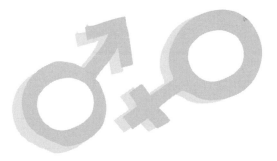 measure. The PSAT adopted a policy which, instead of weighting the math and verbal scores evenly, used an index called "two times the verbal score plus the math" to try to raise girl's scores. Adding a writing skills subtest to the PSAT has also been tried. These alterations, however, have still not offset boys' generally higher scores in math (Arenson 1998).

What This Means to You

Becoming familiar with gender differences and their potential impact on learners is a good way to move towards meeting the gender-specific needs of all learners.Equal education does not mean that everything should be done the same; it means providing equal opportunity. There are real, physical differences between the sexes. Many male-female behaviors make much more sense when considered in the context of brain development. Eliminate groupings by age or grade. They tend to cause feelings of inadequacy. Learners are being measured against those with developmental advantages instead of by effort. Change expectations. Keep students in age clusters, such as ages 2-4, 5-7, 8-10, 11-13, and 14-17. Become informed. Learn the differences between culturally-reinforced stereotypes and real physical differences. Keep expectations high and avoid stereotyping. Many problems may not be problems at all. They may simply be an expression of the "natural" timeline along which one's developmental process is unfolding.

Reflection Questions

1. What from this chapter was novel, fresh, or new to you? What was familiar or "old hat"?

2. In what ways, do you already apply the information in this chapter?

3. What three questions might you now generate about this material?

4. How did you react emotionally to the information in this chapter?

5. How did you react cognitively to the information? Do you agree or disagree with the author's point of view? Why?

6. In what ways might you translate the principles presented in this chapter into practical everyday useful ideas?

7. If these things are, in fact, true about the brain, what should we do differently? What resources of time, people, and money could be redirected? In what ways might you suggest we start doing this?

8. What were the most interesting insights you gained from this material?

9. If you were to plan your next step for making your curriculum more brain-based, what would that be?

10. What obstacles might you encounter? How might you realistically deal with them?

The Non-conscious Learning Climate

8

The Nonconscious Learning Climate

As revealed in previous chapters, so much of what impacts learning is not in a teacher's lesson plan at all. Rather, it is the hundreds of micro-variables present in every learning environment. From instructor appearance to personal belief systems, the brain is bombarded by stimuli from all directions and there's no way anyone can be conscious of it all. Nevertheless, our brain has mechanisms that allow information to be taken in without our conscious awareness. Consequently we are influenced by things beyond our will moment by moment, day by day. Let's explore some of these influences.

Some Learning Is Automatic

Your nonconscious mind acts before your conscious one does! In fact, as early as two seconds prior to an actual activity or movement, our brain has already decided what body parts to activate and which side of the brain to use. This means that we are already acting on a thought before we're even aware of it.

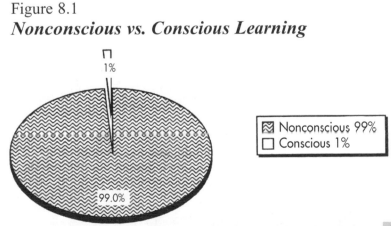

Figure 8.1
Nonconscious vs. Conscious Learning

▨ Nonconscious 99%	
☐ Conscious 1%	

1%

99.0%

Emanual Donchin, PhD. at the Champaign-Urbana campus of the University of Illinois and colleagues has documented a profound statistic (Coles, Donchin, and Porges 1986). He says that more than 99 percent of all learning is nonconscious. This means that the majority of what you and your students are learning—a quantity of stimuli that far exceeds that derived from traditionally delivered content or what's outlined in a lesson plan—was never consciously intended. From visual cues, sounds, experiences, aromas, and feelings, you are a walking, talking sponge.

> *Most of what's learned in your class is* **not** *in your lesson plan; in other words, there's a documented, enormous, and profound differential between teaching and learning.*

To illustrate this perspective, consider that you have just driven from one city to another. You arrive safely and check into a motel or stay with a friend. Someone asks you about something, and you can't quite recall it. But then they mention the company's name and suddenly a light goes on. "Yes," you say, "I *have* heard of that company. I think I saw their billboard advertisement somewhere on the road. Oh, yes, now I remember. They are the ones who... "You actually learned this information hours ago, but at the time, you were not conscious of it.

For a more classroom pertinent example, let's say your students are working on a group project in cooperative teams. In their view, they are learning the content, but they are also learning about each other and acquiring collaboration skills. In fact, this may constitute the majority of their learning. Simply absorbing an experience is valuable to our learning process as our brain expands its perceptual maps. We are all learning all the time: The question really is, what are we learning and are we consciously aware of it?

What Are We Learning?

If so much learning happens on a nonconscious level, how might subliminal messages impact the brain. Some research suggests (Parker 1982; Taylor 1988; Yahnke 1989; Urban 1992) that *when* presented in the appropriate medium, using the right message, and aligned with the subject's belief systems, subliminals can, indeed, affect behavior.

A subliminal is defined as a stimulus perceived *below* the threshold of awareness. In other words, the auditory or visual trigger must be detectable, but at a level that does not require conscious attention or analysis. For example, a whisper a block away is well below your threshold of perception unless you're equipped with some electronic spy device. This does *not* represent a subliminal message because no neural activity is triggered. A poster placed on a classroom wall out of normal awareness (off to the side, in the back of the room) also does not represent a subliminal message because at any time you can turn and read it. So then, what does represent a subliminal?

Visual subliminals usually (but not always) fall into one of three categories: 1) Altered light levels; 2) High-speed flash projection; or 3) Variable insertion. Altered light levels is a technique whereby a lower wattage message may be shown on a screen continuously during the time a brighter message is being consciously perceived. The second technique, high-speed flash projection, also used continuously, incorporates images via a movie camera at such rapid speeds (1/100th to 1/3000th of a second) that the eye can't consciously register them. And the third technique, variable insertion, might be compared to adding a "flashcard" to a deck of cards and flipping it like an old-time motion picture. Although it is not likely that you would add these subliminal techniques to your bag of teaching tricks (nor do we suggest that you should), they may remind you how important it is to imbue your teaching practice with a positive, affirming, and expectant attitude.

The Power of Nonconscious Learning

The power of nonconscious learning was one of the fundamental concepts explored by the notable Bulgarian researcher Georgi Lozanov, PhD. (1979). His impressive success at teaching foreign languages (often 500 words a day with a 90 percent recall rate weeks later) was established on the basis of three key principles:

1. **The enormous capacity of a receptive mind.**
    Lozanov says that everything suggests something to our complex minds and we cannot *not* suggest. All communications and activities are occurring on a conscious *and* nonconscious level at the same time. It is critical, therefore, to train teachers to make the most of non-verbal messages and replace negative implications with affirming impressions.

2. **The value of visuals, music, stories, myth, metaphor, and movement.**
    All stimuli to the brain is coded, symbolized, generalized, and is multiprocessed in ways we have yet to fully understand.

3. **Our perceptions, biases, and barriers must be addressed before learning can be accelerated.**
    Once we recognize our strengths and weaknesses, we can achieve dramatic results.

Because of the nearly unlimited capacity of the human brain, and it's natural predisposition to sort, label, and code things, all the so-called "unimportant influences" turn out to be very important. Lozanov's success in the area of suggestopedia (or accelerated learning) suggests that in a well-orchestrated, positively suggestive learning environment, student learning can be dramatically improved.

What This Means to You

Create a learning environment rich with positive suggestions. Set high standards for yourself and the environment in which you teach. Involve your learners in setting and achieving agreed upon standards, as well. Remember that even though you may be focusing on content, learners are absorbing much more than just what you're saying. While you put up an overhead transparency, for example, they are also listening to your utterings and observing your facial expressions. In fact, they may be hearing more of what you're *not* saying than what you are saying. Thus, it is important that you be aware of your non-verbal messages and that they are congruent with what you intend to impart. Practice your presentation in front of a mirror or with a colleague to ensure that your words are congruent with your body language. Or videotape your presentation and critique yourself. Most importantly, check your attitude: You can be assured your learners have; and it does influence them.

The bottom line is this: Your students are *learning* much more than you're *teaching*. How you treat them, what you say, how you say it, what you don't say, your sensitivity to their needs, your attitude about your own work, your feelings about your environment and life, how well you listen or don't—all of these assorted impressions— influence your students, whether they (and you) realize it consciously or not.

The following strategies reflect a positive approach to "subliminal" or nonconscious learning. Such techniques can go a long way in reversing paralyzing learner beliefs and attitudes.

Teaching Tips for Optimizing Nonconscious Learning

▼ Model a positive attitude and your enjoyment of learning.

▼ Post affirming posters and peripherals in the room.

▼ Highlight positive role models, idols, guest speakers, etc.

▼ Cite experts in a subject area.

▼ Incorporate videos, CDs, slides, and photographs on topics.

▼ Tell stories about prior students who have persevered and succeeded.

▼ Create a contemporary spin on the topic or subject, so that it is perceived as "cool" and relevant.

▼ Counter negative stereotypes and myths with positives.

continued...

continued...

▼ **Focus on skill-building and problem-solving so that learners who want to succeed can learn how.**

▼ **Open a new subject or topic with a celebration.**

▼ **Hold student discussions; and encourage learners to talk about their fears, feelings, and concerns about learning.**

▼ **Provide sufficient resources; and enable students to learn in the style that is most natural to them.**

▼ **Encourage learners to find personal meaning in their studies and projects.**

▼ **Always be receptive to students' questions and comments.**

▼ **Provide an atmosphere of physical and emotional safety, where students feel accepted, respected, and welcomed to class.**

Teacher Authority and Credibility

The more "positive authority" and credibility the teacher has with the students, the stronger the learning. Lozanov's research on the power of "teacher authority" was extensive (1979). His studies indicated that a great deal of learning took place simply because of the teacher's prestige and authority in the subject taught. Some might call this a variation on the "placebo effect"—that is, if you believe a particular treatment will help you, it's more likely to work.

Although Lozanov's orientation was Eastern European (stronger respect, male dominated and authoritative cultural positioning of the teacher role), much can be learned from his insights. In light of the fact that a student's opinion of their teacher is critical in the learning process, the prudent path for teachers is to be more attentive to the factors that influence their credibility. Although it is clear that students don't *automatically* respect a teacher's authority today just by virtue of their position, many teachers have learned how to earn the respect of their students year after year. Generally, these teachers view themselves as "role models" for students.

While traditional "authority," which was based on using a "heavy hand," may have worked in the past, the more appropriate approach for today's students is recognizing their rights, offering them some choices, and instilling in them the desire to cooperate. The defining question educational leaders of today are asking is, "Is my approach to teaching worthy of respect?" Some of the defining characteristics of a strong educational leader are strength of character, integrity, purpose, presence, charisma, confidence, and competency.

Teachers today don't have the luxury of gaining immediate respect by virtue of donning a uniform. Your credibility will rather be determined by your ability to "win over" your learners' respect. They will judge your actions, as well as your content message. If you're successful, they will *want* to do what you ask them to because they believe and trust you.

What This Means to You

Become more aware of the things you do, or can do, to increase your credibility. Here are some specific examples:

- Model respect. Respect your learners and they will be more respectful of you.
- Share your experience: How long you've been in the profession; How you developed your specialty knowledge or area of expertise; Personal experiences that have been instrumental in your growth.
- Talk about your mentors and role models.
- Volunteer to work on district, state, or national projects or committees.
- Become known as your organization's spokesperson on a particular subject—preferably your area of expertise.
- Attend continuing education courses, conferences, and workshops. Present at them if possible.
- Keep your promises and commitments.
- Use positive language—never vulgarity or profanity. Interrupt all racist or sexist remarks made by anyone in your presence.
- Contribute articles to periodicals, anthologies, or scholarly journals for publication consideration.

Figure 8.2
Impact of Teacher Communication Types

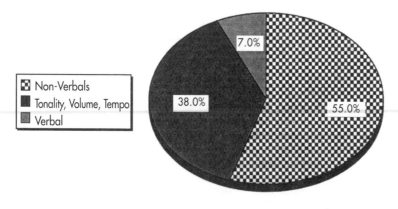

- Non-Verbals
- Tonality, Volume, Tempo
- Verbal

7.0%
38.0%
55.0%

Teacher Congruency

Although we are only able to consciously process one incoming sensory message at a time, our subconscious works overtime translating all the other sensory data. While, for example, you are *watching* a movie, what you are *hearing* is being registered on a subconscious level; and while you are *listening* to a concert, what you are *seeing* takes a back seat to the music. Thus, it is critical to ensure that what you're saying is congruent with your body language. Lozanov describes teacher and trainer congruency as "dual plane messages," messages that are received by your learners on two levels, the conscious and the paraconscious. Your learners are aware of both your verbal and non-verbal communication. Thus, they are being influenced by messages that you, the presenter, may not even be aware you are sending.

Let's say, for example, that you verbalize to your students the following: "I'm very happy to be here today." But actually, your head is shaking from side to side as if to say, "I'd rather be elsewhere." While both messages are being received, the second one will have the most impact.

 ## What This Means to You

We all convey mixed messages at times, which can undermine the goal of our communication and reduce our credibility. You may want to practice your non-verbals. Videotape yourself for review. Identify two or three areas where you might improve your congruency and delivery. Seek feedback from others. And be sure that what you're trying to convey is accurate and true to your real position on the matter.

Teacher Appearance

As we learned from the Pygmalion experiments (Rosenthal and Jacobsen 1968), teacher expectations of a learner's ability affects learning outcomes; but does this theory work in reverse? Do students' expectations of teachers affect performance? According to clothing consultant John Malloy, yes. In his book *Dress for Success* (1975), Malloy summarizes the results of his study to determine the impact of teacher dress on student learning.

> *"The clothing worn by the teachers substantially affected the work and attitudes of the pupils"*
>
> —John Malloy

Malloy reports that better dressed teachers experienced fewer student discipline problems and better work habits. He also found that socio-economic background influenced the type of clothing students best responded to. Some educators attribute the results of Malloy's study to the "placebo effect"—that is, teacher credibility positively influences believability, which positively influences the treatment results.

Let's say, for example, that you attend a conference and the presenter is wearing something very outdated or sloppy. Your first impression will be different than if she/he is wearing a suit or other business apparel. Like the patient who believes his doctor knows best, the student who believes her teacher knows best, will likely have better results. Whatever credibility edge one can obtain by dressing presentably, is one that ought not be overlooked.

What This Means to You

Your clothing conveys powerful messages about your attitude, your values, and your personality. Make the effort to dress professionally. Take pride in your appearance, as you would want your students to do. We may not like it, but nevertheless, human nature is to judge others based on their appearance—unconsciously, if not consciously. When it comes to credibility, image plays a key role.

The Value of a Positive Climate

Learners in a positive, joyful environment are likely to experience enhanced learning, memory, and feelings of self-esteem, report researchers (Mills 1987; Levinthal 1988; Rosenthal and Jacobsen 1968; Sylwester 1995). This finding may not be too surprising; but did you know that sarcasm, criticism and put-downs increase abnormalities in heart rate? Alan Rozanski, PhD. (1988) reports in *The New England Journal of Medicine* that these aberrations are as significant and measurable as those from heavy workouts or pre-attack myocardial chest pains.

> *The fact that negative comments may pose a health risk to students is stunning new evidence that speaks to the importance of positive teacher attitude.*

But how do teacher attitudes impact learning? Researcher R. C. Mills (1987) says that learners pick up on the particular emotional state of the instructor, which either enhances or interferes with cognition. Teachers who smile, use humor, have a joyful demeanor, and take genuine pleasure in their work generally have high-performing learners. This may help explain why when you're in a good mood, your learners seem to mirror it back to you.

Noted researchers Rosenthal and Jacobsen (1968) report that the single greatest influence on learners is the classroom climate; and there is a biological explanation for this. In a classroom climate typified by positive challenge and joy, the body releases endorphins—the peptide molecules that elevate our feelings and cause us to feel good. Research by C. Levinthal (1988) and Robert Sylwester (1995) suggest that a "positive learning climate" promotes better problem-solvers and higher quality learning. In short, when we feel good, we learn better!

> *Learners in positive, joyful environments*
> *are likely to experience enhanced learning,*
> *memory, and feelings of self-esteem.*

As teachers, our beliefs and attitudes are inextricably intertwined with how we teach. Moment by moment we offer suggestions about learning through our unconscious attitudes. We may, for example, "suggest" that learning is hard or easy, homework is valuable or not, schools are happy places that we enjoy, or merely places we have to go. We also suggest that a student may find a subject easy, fun, and challenging or hard, boring, and frustrating. Your smile, or lack of it, communicates more to your students than the words you verbalize. The tone of your conversations, your appearance, your organization, and effort, all contribute to the "collective whole.

What This Means to You

Your attitude each day is as important to learning as the material you present. Take the time to get centered and positive. Do whatever ritual or activity is necessary for you to be at your best. More important than *how* it works, we know that a positive attitude *does* work. Teachers who are happier and more pleasant to be around bring out the best in their learners. Take a few minutes each day to destress and regroup. Listen to music that enhances your mood; eat well; exercise if that grounds you; and post affirming or humorous reminders around your home and teaching area. Making the conscious effort to get into a good teaching state before you start the day will go a long way towards creating a successful learning environment.

Learner Expectations

Researcher G. Gratton and associates (1992) were interested in finding out when, why, and how the learner's brain responds to new visual and auditory information. The results of the study suggest that an important factor in processing new data is whether the learner *thinks* the material is going to be useful to them. In other words, "expectancies about the relative utility of the information was *the key determiner* of how successfully they responded."

Just as we don't conduct research in a vacuum, we don't learn or teach in a vacuum either. Rather, our expectancy of the future must be acknowledged as a factor if we are to move towards the goal of objectivity. Philosopher Karl Popper points out that the supposed "science" of scientific reasoning is staged with a backdrop of prior beliefs, presuppositions, and prejudices, which can certainly influence what is, or is not, discovered. His lecturing ploy which made the point beautifully, was to ask the audience to please "observe." Their reply was typically, "Observe what?" To which he said, "Exactly my point." Observation does not occur in a vacuum; it is strongly influenced by what we are looking for. Perhaps, the teaching tip here is to acknowledge that our predictions and our projections indeed influence results.

 ## What This Means to You

Because your so-called "top" learners often expect to get the most out of a class, they usually do. The proverbial snowball effect seems to apply here: The more often students practice learning, the more they learn. You can positively influence your learners' expectations regarding your class by consciously embedding positive suggestions into materials, your presentation, and the learning environment. How much learners get may be affected profoundly by how motivated they become, how much relevance the material has for them, and how much they think they will learn. Some suggestions for generating positive expectancy include: sending home positive notes about the course content; asking students to describe their hopes, expectations, and desires for the class; encouraging excitement and celebration over new learning; and, providing learners with a time for "showing off" to peers and parents.

Forced Silence and Class Inactivity

Many learners are asked to remain in their seats and to remain quiet by teachers who believe a controlled and quiet environment is best for learning. But research by J. Della Valle and associates (1986, 1984) suggests that this may not be a good idea. Among adolescents studied, 50 percent of them needed "extensive mobility while learning." Of the remaining 50 percent, half of those (25%) needed occasional mobility and the remaining subjects needed minimal movement opportunities. We've all been in the situation of addressing a group and some of the listeners appear to be tired, drowsy, or listless. Is this your fault or the audience's? It doesn't matter; let them get up and move around!

Figure 8.3
Learner Mobility Needs in the Classroom

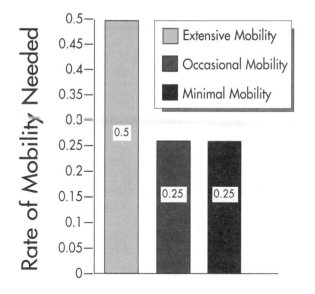

The work of James Asher (1986), which resulted in the TPR (Total Physical Response) approach to learning reminds us that actions and movement can play a powerful role in the learning and recall of new information. While it's true that much learning can occur without ever leaving a seat, it's also true that most of what you think is important in your life that you "really know" you have learned through experience, from doing something, not from a chalkboard or textbook. In addition, the research on the power of physiological states is conclusive: The body remembers as well as the mind: In many cases, it remembers better!

 ## What This Means to You

If learners seem lacking in attention, energy, or curiosity, they may need more permission to move around. Provide more active-learning opportunities and kinesthetic/tactile stimulation. What may seem like a boring topic or a bad time of day may simply be a product of learners who are restless and need some activity. Schedule a stand-up-and-stretch break every twenty minutes or so. Include cross-lateral movements and deep breathing. Provide a diversity of activities so that learners can choose what appeals to them. Offer team and partner learning, excursions outside the classroom, frequent water breaks, and simple movement activities that get the circulation going and keep active learners happy.

Thinking Skills

The old model of teaching, analogous to "filling an empty container," is long outdated. We all have a brain with unlimited potential; and it's a disgrace to treat it like a wheelbarrow. The brain's most important work is thinking and problem-solving. Learning is an interactive process that occurs on many levels. The learning has to be input, filtered, associated, processed, evaluated and stored to be useful. Learning to think is an evolutionary process. The more learning is generalized, contextualized, and reframed, the more the learner "owns" it. Deep learning requires usage and feedback. Over time the meaning of the material expands; and eventually the learner develops a level of expertise. The new model of teaching, analogous to offering substance for the learner to fill his/her own container, reframes the teacher as more of a learning coach.

Tight Teacher Control

In *Making Connections*, authors Renate and Geoffrey Caine (1994) report that excessive control by teachers actually reduces learning. They say that "learners must have choice and variety." If students are to be predominately self-motivated, they must be given the opportunity to focus on their own areas of interest and to participate in activities they find interesting.

Unless learners are stakeholders in the learning process—that is, they have some influence over it—it will be forced, rote, mechanical, short-lived and, eventually, distasteful. As William Glasser notes in his book *Choice Theory* (1999), the more learners feel controlled, the more resentful they get. And resentment, whether expressed (and manifested as frustration, rebellion, and anger) or suppressed (and manifested as detachment, sabotage, and apathy), detracts from learning. Researcher S. Harter (1982) suggests that students who lack perceived control on an assigned task will hold back and give less than their best efforts. It makes sense. If you feel like you lack control over your own destiny, why would you want to invest in someone else's?

The SAT Method

Overall, there are seven basic auditory forms that are universally used to alter a learner's behavior. SAT is an acronym which stands for the first three characteristics of this method. Your role as a teacher is to determine which is the best approach for a particular learner, as a means of motivating *without manipulating or controlling them*. A short description of each follows:

Generally Most Effective Communication Methods

1. *Suggest:* You make a request that illuminates the preferred options. This approach   provides a strong perceived choice. If you like the options you're likely to choose one. "You might like to use your colored pens for taking notes."

2. *Ask:* You make the request in a way that encourages one to follow. This approach provides some perceived choice. "Would you please use your colored pens for taking notes?"

continued...

continued...

3. **Tell:** Primarily used to provide instructional directions. You simply give learners a directed statement in an expectant tone. This approach provides minimal perceived choice. "Using your colored pens, please write this down..."

Generally Less Effective Communication Methods

4. **Hope:** This request is not verbalized; rather it is simply assumed that the learner will comply. The thought is actually outside the awareness of the learners. Since the learner doesn't know about it, there is no perceived choice.

5. **Imply:** This request is never made; rather it is talked around in the hope that the learner will infer from the implication. Because there is no overt recommendation made, there's minimal perceived choice.

6. **Demand/Threat:** This is an order, delivered in a way that learners have minimal or *no* perceived choice. This method should be reserved for occasions where a person's safety is in danger.

7. **Force:** This approach is to be used only in an emergency. Learners have *no* perceived choice; no other option is available to them. This is unacceptable unless lives or property are at stake.

The ideal rapport consists of sometimes suggesting, sometimes asking, and sometimes telling. Too much of any one approach, however, can create problems. The teachers who have the toughest time with discipline or motivation are consistently the ones who underutilize the SAT approach; or don't balance out their use of the first three (SAT) approaches. If you are always telling learners what to do or hoping they do what you want them to, they will begin to resist and resent your leadership.

 ## What This Means to You

Even the best laid lesson plans can fail if you are too controlling. Control strategies may seem effective in the short run, but inevitably they will backfire. Learners who feel controlled and manipulated will eventually begin performing below their abilities. They will feel resentful; and begin to associate learning with work. It is far more effective to elicit learner cooperation and personal responsibility. Involve your students in decisions about the classroom environment, music, goals, assessment approaches, and learning activities. Provide choices whenever possible. Facilitate discussion groups about classroom rules and performance expectations. Encourage student input. Utilize suggestion boxes, teams, group work, and expression areas. Students buy into and take pride in doing activities that they have helped to define and over which they have some control.

What a teacher wears, what the environment is like, how the material is presented, and hundreds of other simple acts are all couched in suggestion. The most important concept in this chapter is this:

> **Suggestion is everything and everything is suggestion: In fact, you cannot not suggest. The question is, What are you now suggesting to learners? And is this what you want to suggest?**

Bulgarian-born educator Georgi Lozanov was the first teacher who studied the purposeful organization of suggestion. His suggestion approaches included peripherals, positive verbal affirmations about a student's learning ability, and overall group suggestion. It worked. How? While conscious, directed content learning drops off over time, the use of suggestion actually increases learning over time. In the book *Super Memory* (1991), authors Shiela Ostrander and Lynn Schroeder report that on the tenth day after exposing learners to Lozanov's positive suggestion, student recall was five times better than the first day!

Since suggestions affect the biases, beliefs, limiting thoughts, and attitudes of the learner, there can be no suggestion without desuggestion. In other words, all positive suggestions are simply a "counter" to some negative belief. In that sense, we are continually countering prior negative conditioning with current positive conditioning. If negative suggestions suddenly stopped existing tomorrow, there would be no need to pump learners back up with positive suggestions.

> **"There is no suggestion without desuggestion, without freeing the paraconscious from the inertia of something old."**
> —Georgi Lozanov

Consider how the following destructive suggestions can easily be made more constructive and positive, as exhibited by the second sentence:

a) If the instructions are not clear to you, start paying more attention.
b) Let me repeat the instructions, then I'll check back with you to make sure I've presented them clearly.

a) What part of the word 'No' do you not understand?
b) Let's check for meaning. Tell me what you heard.

a) While I don't expect to make scientists out of you, I do expect to provide you with the basics.

b) You might be surprised how interesting science can be; many students ask me to give them more resources.

a) Don't forget to do your homework.

b) Be sure to remember to do the word problems tonight at home. We'll go over your answers tomorrow.

a) Have a Merry Christmas everyone!

b) Happy holidays everyone! (Always be inclusive and consider diversity)

a) Forget about Spanish and enjoy your holiday break.

b) Be sure to use your Spanish on your break—especially when you eat out at a Mexican restaurant. Adios and buena suerte!

a) Hey, guess what? There's only 45 days left until school's out!

b) Bummer, only 45 days are left for us to be together in this classroom. The good news though is there's only 153 days until school starts again; and you'll be a grade higher.

a) If you do not complete any of the four basic requirements, you can expect to fail this course; and there are no exceptions.

b) Complete all four requirements for this course, and you can expect to pass. Anything less, however, means a no pass grade.

a) I know you feel nervous about the upcoming test, but don't worry, you won't fail.

b) Relax, if you've prepared well, you'll do well.

a) I hope you will gain an appreciation for the power, simplicity, and elegance of this material.

b) What do you think? Is a change needed here?

The pioneering work of Lozanov reminds us that suggestion in many forms is always operating. Suggestion is operating at both the conscious and nonconscious level. It is also the single greatest untapped influence you have with your learners, because:

▼ **If the learner is confident, learning increases.**

▼ **If the learner believes in the teacher, learning increases.**

▼ **If the learner thinks the subject is important, learning increases.**

▼ **If the learner believes it will be fun and valuable, learning goes up!**

How do you get the learner to believe these things? Use the power to influence through the artful application of positive suggestion. You can influence (but not control) what your students believe about themselves, you, the topic, learning, etc. And, in fact, you already influence them in those areas. You simply may have underestimated the power of that influence. You could say, "This upcoming chapter is the hardest in the book, so everyone bear down!" Or, you could say, "This upcoming chapter is my favorite, so get ready for a great experience."

As an authority figure, the teacher carries the potential for vast influence. It is common to have had a teacher tell us that we were "bad" in math or spelling or writing. Naturally, that subject became nearly impossible to master. Such a bias can be carried with a student for the rest of their learning life.

All learning is affected by our own personal history: We have a lifetime of experiences, beliefs, values, and attitudes about each subject and our probability of learning it. Lozanov calls these "biases." If all learning is heavily influenced by our biases, should we try to change these, or simply "teach?" You may have guessed the answer. The overwhelming evidence is that the teachers who influence learner biases are much more successful. In other words, we can change the behaviors in the classroom, or we can change the biases (or both).

> *The shortest route to learner success is not simply to change learner biases, but to change the behaviors* **and** *biases simultaneously. In fact, changing biases will eventually and automatically change learner behavior.*

 ## What This Means to You

Positive suggestion is a powerful and ethical method for motivating learners. Post affirming messages on doors and bulletin boards that read, for example, "My success is absolutely assured." Suggest to your learners how interesting they might find the material. Communicate to them that learning is fun, easy, and creative. Suggest that they might enjoy further study on their own. Suggest that new ideas might start popping into their mind as their learning increases. Aim for orchestrating at least twenty positive messages per hour.

The Best Seat in the House

Two researchers, T. C. Shea (1983) and H. Hodges (1985), studied how "formal" classroom seating (hard-backed chairs that face the front of the room) and "informal" classroom seating (pillows, lounge chairs, floor—by student preference) impacted learning. Shea found that students who preferred "informal" seating arrangements performed "significantly" better on English comprehension tests when provided with their seating of choice. Another group scored much higher in mathematics when they were taught and tested in their preferred seating type. These studies speak to the importance of choice in the learning process. They also suggest that seating can influence learning.

Educators Rita and Kenneth Dunn (1978) say that at least 20 percent of learners are significantly affected, positively or negatively, by seating options or lack of them. Some students prefer the floor, a couch, or beanbag furniture, while others will be at their best in a "formal" or traditional seating structure.

In addition to type of seating, location in the room is also a factor in learning effectiveness. How are seats arranged in your teaching environment? Most teachers stick with what they learned in school—that is, chairs (and desks) lined up in straight rows facing the front of the room. Educator R. Wlodlowski (1985) however, says that circles, U shapes, and V shapes are best. When given a choice, good spellers tend to sit on the right side of the classroom. This may be related to handedness (hemispheric dominance), or left-brain-right field of vision, or the fact that visual creativity is dominant on the upper left side of the eye pattern range. Some environmental researchers (Della Valle 1984; Hodges 1985; Shea 1983; and Kroon 1985) have found that the environment (seating choices, comfort levels, and lighting) and learning styles (global, sequential, concrete, abstract, etc.) are all significant factors in student success.

 What This Means to You

---

We may be inadvertently reducing student motivation and learning by maintaining strict seating patterns. Allow learners to change seats often. Provide choice in type of seating and be open to restructuring chair and desk arrangements to improve the environment.

Inspiring Optimal Motivation

Martin Ford (1992) researched optimal environments for motivation and found that four factors were critical to what he calls "context beliefs." These are the functional elements that are "in vitro," meaning embedded within the learner's situation. According to Ford, all of the following must be present to create an optimal environment:

▼ **The environment must be consistent with an individual's personal goals. This means that the learning environment must be a place in which the learner can reach his or her own personal goals.**

▼ **The environment must be congruent with the learner's bio-social and cognitive styles. This means that if abstract learning is taking place in a crowded, competitive room with fluorescent lighting, it will be a problem for a concrete learner who needs space and prefers to work cooperatively.**

▼ **The environment must offer the learner the resources needed. In addition to materials, advice, tools, transportation and supplies, learners need to be provided with adequate time, support, and access.**

▼ **The environment must provide a supportive and positive emotional climate. A sense of trust, warmth, safety, and peer acceptance is critical.**

As a child, did you find yourself naturally and effortlessly engaged in learning? Why or why not? Were the qualities described above inherent in your learning environment? How inherent are they in the learning environment you provide learners today?

 ## What This Means to You

Many students you consider to be unmotivated, may be very motivated, if they are provided the right conditions. Make a big poster featuring the conditions for optimal learning; and post it in your classroom and/or office. Let it be your guide for how to motivate learners and yourself.

Reflection Questions

1. What from this chapter was novel, fresh, or new to you? What was familiar or "old hat"?

2. In what ways, do you already apply the information in this chapter?

3. What three questions might you now generate about this material?

4. How did you react emotionally to the information in this chapter?

5. How did you react cognitively to the information? Do you agree or disagree with the author's point of view? Why?

6. In what ways might you translate the principles presented in this chapter into practical everyday useful ideas?

7. If these things are, in fact, true about the brain, what should we do differently? What resources of time, people, and money could be redirected? In what ways might you suggest we start doing this?

8. What were the most interesting insights you gained from this material?

9. If you were to plan your next step for making your curriculum more brain-based, what would that be?

10. What obstacles might you encounter? How might you realistically deal with them?

Attentional States

9

Attentional States

T he level of attention we are able to apply to a learning situation is limited by our perception of its value. Remember that the brain is most alert to information that helps ensure our survival. In fact, this is the state that elicits maximum attention—a state that thankfully isn't often experienced in a classroom or training environment. Since the survival state is reserved for issues of life and limb, we can't hope, as teachers, for our students' complete attention in the classroom; nor would it even be healthy. We can, however, create an environment where learners have the flexibility to focus on aspects of learning that are personally meaningful to them.

Consider, for example, how your brain kicks into action when viewing a commercial that's advertising something you need versus something you don't. This chapter explores the mechanisms and boundaries of our brain's attentional system and how we can best manage students' attention for optimal learning.

How to Hook the Brain's Attention

The brain has a built-in bias for certain types of stimuli. Since our brain isn't designed to consciously attend to *all* types of incoming data, it sorts out that which is less critical to our survival. A natural prioritization process is occurring all the time, consciously and unconsciously. To the brain, contrast and emotion win hands down. In addition, novelty is a strong third.

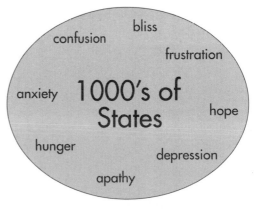

"Giant Two Headed Baby Born to Siamese Dwarf," screams the tabloid headlines. And, "Double murder in our own community with a shocking twist...News at eleven," teases a broadcaster. In a world inundated with insignificant data, novel statements, such as these, are what grab our attention. Advertisers know how to play to our brain's attentional biases; shouldn't we? They are easy to identify. Consider how a passing glance over a crowd of people draws your eye to that which is different—a sudden movement, an unusual color or scene, a familiar face or voice you didn't expect, or something that evokes your emotions.

> *Any stimuli introduced into our immediate environment, which is either new (novel) or of sufficiently strong emotional intensity (high contrast), will immediately gain our attention.*

Learners today are often on stimuli overload—jaded or "over-shocked" by television and tabloid news. As a result, in a sedate learning environment, they may feel bored, listless, and detached. Teachers who know how to capitalize on the brain's attentional biases, however, can get and keep their students' attention longer. This is only half the battle though. The other half is learning how to engage students in meaningful learning, so that the learner begins to drive their own attention and learning process. In this sense, the teacher becomes less of the "show," and the learners, themselves, become more of the show. Maintaining learner attention, thus, becomes a non-issue.

 ## What This Means to You

Give learners more control (and accountability). Engage them in creating classroom rituals, projects, rules, procedures, and consequences. Provide them with choices in the curriculum; and ensure their learning environment reflects a sense of freedom, individual expression, and choice. Encourage students to pursue interesting life-like projects that will engage their curiosity and natural passions. Incorporate field trips and guest speakers. Acknowledge individual learning differences and diverse lifestyles. Capitalize on the brain's bias for high contrast: Be outrageous, funny, or different. But also facilitate learner-generated projects so that you don't have to be a shock-show to spark attention. Encourage groupwork: The novelty and variation provided by other learners, can increase learner momentum and relevance.

What Influences Attention

We know that attention level is determined by the interaction of various factors, such as: 1) the particular sensory input (i.e., textbook, video, fieldtrip); 2) the data's intensity or perceived importance (i.e., threat, opportunity, or pain); and 3) the brain's chemical "flavor of the moment" (i.e., hormone, peptide, and neurotransmitter levels). The sequence of elements in the attentional process are: 1) initial alarm or notice (i.e., "Hey, something's happening here"); 2) orientation (i.e., "Where?"); 3) identification (i.e., "What is it?"); and 4) decision (i.e., "This is what I need to do."). The answer to the "what" question will determine how much and how long attention will be focused. When sophisticated imaging devices are used to observe what happens in the brain at various attention levels, scientists see a greater flow of energy to specific areas at high attention levels. In short, when specialized brain activity is up, attention is up.

So, how does your brain know what specifically to pay attention to in the moment? The secret is that our visual system (which is responsible for about 80 to 90 percent of incoming information in non-impaired learners) is not a one-way street. Information flows both ways, back and forth, from our eyes to the thalamus, to the visual cortex, and back again. This feedback is the mechanism which "shapes" our attention so that we can focus on one particular thing, like a teacher or book. Amazingly, our "attention headquarters" gets feedback from the cortex at nearly six times the amount that originated from the retina. Somehow, the brain corrects incoming images to help you stay attentive, but once it's reached its immediate capacity, it demands the filtering out of incoming stimuli. In other words, the brain has an intrinsic mechanism for shutting down input when it needs to.

Too Much Attention

We absorb so much information nonconsciously that downtime is absolutely necessary to process it all. If it seems that students have "stopped paying attention," consider that they may be doing something just as important to their learning process—reflecting. Down time, in fact, is absolutely necessary for the learning to become imbued with personal meaning. The amount of information an individual can take in before they reach "overwhelm" varies from person to person, but everyone eventually must "go internal" if the new learning is to become imprinted on the brain. In our role as educators, we can offset problems by paying more attention to this basic need. Plan downtime activities after each new learning session. Such activities might include a partner walk, music session, ball-toss time, stretching session, or a few minutes to make a mind-map.

Making Meaning

Humans are natural meaning-seeking organisms. But while the search is innate, the end result is not automatic. Since meaning is generated internally, excessive input can conflict with the process. An important principle to remember is that you can either have your learner's attention or they can be making meaning, but never both at the same time. Facilitate a small group discussion after new material is introduced to sort it out, generate questions, and play "what if" scenarios. Encourage learners to find personal meaning in their new learning. Explain to them how the brain naturally prioritizes information moment by moment.

During this necessary period of incubation, the brain filters out new incoming stimuli. It begins to sift through its full plate of information, looking for links, associations, uses, and procedures as it sorts and stores. "This association and consolidation process can only occur during downtime," says Harvard faculty member Alan Hobson, PhD. (1989). Some kind of reflection time—writing in journals or small group discussion—makes good sense for the brain after new material is presented.

 ## What This Means to You

Provide "settling time." Just as a cake needs to settle after baking, our brain's neural connections need time to solidify and settle after learning. The best type of reflection time is not seatwork or homework, but rather a walk, stretching, rote classroom chores (i.e., clearing the bulletin board or hanging art), doodling, or merely resting. Breaks, recess, lunch, and going home can also be considered downtime. Ideally, "brain-breaks" ought to be built into your lesson plans every twenty minutes or so. The more intense the new learning, the more reflection time is necessary.

The Chemistry of Attention

The chemicals that are produced in our brain are the life blood of our attentional system. These chemicals include neurotransmitters, hormones, and peptides. Acetylcholine is a neurotransmitter that seems to induce drowsiness. In general, its levels are higher in the late afternoon and evening. Researchers suspect that of all the chemicals, norepinephrine is the most involved in attention. Studies indicate (Penny, et. al 1996) that when we are drowsy or "out of it" our norepinephrine levels are usually low and when we are too "hyper" and stressed, our norepinephrine levels are too high.

When an individual is under stress or threat, cortisol, vasopressin, and endorphins are released. The body's response to this flooding of chemicals is immediate and specific. If, for example, a student is called into the principal's office, their pulse rate will likely rise; their skin will become flushed, and a feeling of being "on edge" takes over the body. A change in chemicals means a likely change in behaviors. For example, to prepare students for a creative endeavor, you may have already discovered that it works to get them out of a stressed state with a movement, music, humor, or story-telling session.

All learning is state-dependent. The physiological, emotional, postural, and psychological state that your learners are in will mediate content. The learner's state or neurochemical environment can be influenced in the classroom with simple interventions. Once the proper state is elicited, then the learning process will be less taxing on both learner and teacher.

What This Means to You

Induce calm states (marked by an increase in serotonin) with predictable ritual activities like openings, closings, greetings, etc. To energize or motivate action, induce a surprise state (marked by an increase in cortisol or adrenaline) with novelty or an unexpected change. The ideal state for learning attention is a balance of high serotonin and cortisol/adrenaline. Within a structured context, induce plenty of novelty. In this way, your learners will get the best of both worlds.

Role of Laughter

William Fry, PhD. of Stanford University (1997) and associates have studied how the body reacts biochemically to laughing. The researchers inserted catheters into the veins of medical students to measure if any changes occurred in blood chemistry while viewing a comedy performance. An increase in white-blood-cell activity was noted, among other chemical changes. Some suggest that this response to laughter may boost the body's production of neurotransmitters critical for alertness and memory.

This makes sense. We've always recognized that a good laugh can lower stress; and a low stress brain and body makes for a better learner. In his book *Anatomy of an Illness...*, Norman Cousins, PhD. (1981) cites that laughter therapy was instrumental in his personal battle with cancer. But do we know for certain how laughing changes the chemistry of the brain. Author Stone, PhD. at the State University of New York and colleagues (1987) say that "having fun and pleasant experiences improve the functioning of the body's immune system for three days—the day of the event and two days after."

What This Means to You

Encourage learners to experience pleasure in their work. Celebrate new learning. Have an arsenal of tasteful and appropriate jokes on hand to spice up a dull period. Encourage learners to see the funny side of life; and to share their own humor with the class when appropriate. Provide occasional joke sessions to relieve stress; post a funny cartoon on the bulletin board; and provide appropriately funny reading material.

The Chemistry of Physical Activity

Most of us would say we feel better when we are healthy, exercise a bit, or work out. But are our brains actually better off? K. R. Isaacs, PhD. and associates (1992) report that in a study with rats, vigorous physical activity increased blood flow to the brain.

Carla Hannaford, PhD. (1995) suggests that the use of cross-lateral repatterning motions can have dramatic effects on learning. Cross laterals are arm and leg movements that cross over from one side of the body to the other (i.e., touching the right shoulder with your left hand). Since the left side of the brain controls the right side of the body and vice versa, engaging the arms and legs in such a way forces the brain to "talk to itself." A brain which is fully engaged is far more efficient and effective. For students who are "stuck" or at a standstill, cross-lateral movements can be the perfect, simple antidote for engaging both sides of the brain to full advantage. This is particularly effective for students who are sleepy, overwhelmed, frustrated, or experiencing a learning block.

What This Means to You

When you go for a brisk walk or work out before starting your day, you feel better. This is no coincidence. An active body enhances an active mind. Learners who are active tend to be more alert. Building physical activities into your daily schedule models good learning practice. Take two minutes when you start your class to activate your learners. A short stretching session, a brisk walk, some cross-lateral movements, will all go a long way in activating learning. Also provide brain breaks throughout the day. They don't have to be long, just well-timed. When attention spans start to fade, you know it's time.

Attention Shifts

Our brain's E-I (external-internal) shift is frequent and automatic. This shifting of focus seems to be a critical element in: 1) maintaining understanding; 2) updating long-term memories; and 3) strengthening our neural networks. The brain needs time to "go inside" and link up the present with the past and the future. Without it, learning drops dramatically.

> *When we consider current findings in brain research, it becomes clear that the whole concept of "on task" or "off task" is irrelevant.*

The two critical factors for determining the amount of processing time a person needs are the learner's background in the subject or how much prior knowledge and skill they have; and the intensity or complexity of the new material. High novelty and complexity with low learner background means more processing time will be necessary. The reverse is also true: High learner background with low novelty and complexity (i.e., a review) means less learner settling time is necessary.

Some students need equal external and internal time while others may need a 5-to-1 ratio—meaning they have a longer attention span. When you see a good student in class not paying attention, it is a mistake to automatically assume they are goofing around. It may be that something has triggered their memory or shifted their focus inward.

What This Means to You

It may be that our notion of staying "on-task" is really inappropriate, and in fact, a counterproductive way to measure learning. Keeping students' attention 100 percent of the time is a bad idea. The learner whom you are assuming is not focused, may simply be re-thinking things in light of new information. Build reflection time into each day, as well as group or partner processing time. Avoid long lectures; give frequent breaks; and pay attention to individual and collective states of learners.

How We Listen

A number of researchers (Gordon 1978; Mills and Rollman 1980; Schwartz and Talall 1980) have focused on listening and perception issues in learning. From this body of work, it has been suggested that the right ear is superior for listening. In fact, the more complex the listening, the better the right ear is, as access to the left brain (more capable of processing the internal structure of very complex tones) is achieved through the right ear.

Researcher A. Asbjornsen, PhD. and associates (1990) conducted research with forty right-handed females undergoing thirty-six trials with four different instructions to determine if hearing side mattered in direction following. He varied head and eye turns (together and separate) for both left and right sides, and he varied directions toward and away from the source of the voice. The results were a significant and clear right ear advantage in all groups during all conditions.

Alfred Tomatis, PhD. one of the pioneers of sound, acoustics, and hearing says (1983) that our right ear is the best ear for listening, learning, and language. In fact, his studies show that normal readers became dyslexic when they could only listen with their left ear. Conversely, he has successfully treated thousands of dyslexics by using sound therapy to improve their ability to hear high frequencies.

Music pioneer Don Campbell (1983, 1992) says that "half the people in the world change their voice response depending on which ear receives the information." He adds that if you have sequential, detailed information for your learners, position yourself so that you can address their right ear and the superior path to the left side of the brain.

What This Means to You

Watch your learners. You may notice that some of them consistently turn their head to one side or the other in an effort to "hear" better. They may be unconsciously appealing to the side of their brain that will provide them the best understanding. Just as there are right and left handers, there are also ear dominances—unrelated, however, to handedness. Some listeners will do better by changing positions or "cupping" their dominant listening ear. As you present material, keep in mind that you can ensure you reach all learners effectively by frequently changing your position in the room. Move around the room as you speak; and consider redefining the "front" of the room. Have students move into groups each day; and allow them to sit in different locations each week so that no one is consistently disadvantaged.

Optimal States for Learning

Very little learning happens when students are stressed out, despondent, or in other distracted states. When they are prompted, however, into a positive state for learning, they naturally do better. Noted University of Chicago psychologist Mihaly Csikszentmihalyi and Isabella Csikszentmihalyi (1990) report in their book *Flow: The Psychology of Optimal Experience* that a state of consciousness known as "flow" is the primary criteria for optimal learning. Although it is impossible to merely will this uninterrupted state of concentration into existence, it happens when a person "loses themselves" in an activity. That is,

Intelligence Building States

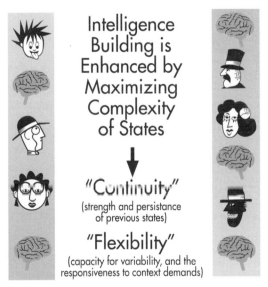

Intelligence Building is Enhanced by Maximizing Complexity of States

↓

"Continuity"
(strength and persistance of previous states)

"Flexibility"
(capacity for variability, and the responsiveness to context demands)

all self consciousness and awareness of time fades; and what is left is a pure pleasure-producing absorption into the experience. Children, teenagers, and athletes find themselves in this state more often than the average adult.

The Csikzentmihalyis define flow as a pattern of activity in which individual or group goals emerge (as opposed to being mandated) as a result of a pleasurable activity and interaction with the environment. When your skills, attention, environment, and will are all aligned, the flow state is more likely to occur. Creativity and learning emerge in an accelerated fashion when learners are encouraged to "go with the flow" while enjoying themselves and defining and refining their own learning challenges. This philosophy allows learners to take responsibility for their learning in a relaxed state.

The flow state is most likely to emerge when the balance of challenge and mastery is equal. Let's say, for example, that you've decided to learn to play the saxophone (or speak a foreign language, ice skate, golf, jog, surf the Web, etc.). At first, the practice takes a lot of effort; but over time, it mysteriously gets easier and before you know it, you're actually having fun! Time passes without your awareness, your skills improve, and you seem to be improving without struggle. You have reached the perfect balance. Your skill level matches the challenge. Watch a child play in the snow, or at the beach or lake. They become totally engrossed; time fades, and before they know it, it's time for dinner. They have also learned a great deal.

The Best State for Learning

▼ **Intrinsically challenged with material that is not too easy, not too hard (best if learner chooses it, so that it is personally relevant).**
▼ **Low-to-moderate stress; general relaxation (this does not mean *no* stress).**
▼ **Immersed "flow" state where attention is focused on learning and doing (rather than self-conscious or evaluative).**
▼ **Curiosity and anticipation (when a learner discovers an interest in a particular subject, build on it).**
▼ **Confusion (can be a motivator, if it's brief and doesn't continue).**

Matching Challenge and Mastery

As viewed by sophisticated imaging devices, brain activity increases when mental tasks are increased in complexity and difficulty, reports the National Institute of Mental Health. Even when learners are unsuccessful at very challenging experiments, the brain continues to be actively engaged. You play much better tennis, for example, when your opponent provides a good challenge for you. If they, however, are at a different skill level than you (either better or worse) you will likely lose interest quite quickly.

The Csikszentmihalyis further contend that we can get into the "magical state" of flow every day. When the challenge is greater than your skills, that's anxiety; and when your skills exceed the challenge, that's boredom. But when the challenge and skill level are matched up, whammo! You've hit the Jackpot! It is fairly easy to get learners into optimal learning states if you remember what gets *you* into that state.

What This Means to You

Teaching in a way that encourages students to reach a flow state may be one of the most important roles you have. In this state learners are highly internally motivated and learning becomes enjoyable. Assist your learners to reach a flow state by setting up favorable conditions for it. Mandated, step-by-step instruction can work well in the initial stages of learning (by instilling focus, confidence, and motivation), but once beyond this, learners will likely be stifled by a rigid structure. Keep challenge high, but stress low. Let learners set the pace, while you provide the support. Have them design a complex project that is personally relevant; and then vary the resources to keep the task appropriate to their ability levels. Make it exciting; use teams, simulations, technology, and deadlines, while maintaining appropriate levels of guidance and control.

What Brainwaves Can Tell Us

Another way to view states is by considering brainwave patterns. EEG (electroencephalogram) readings provide us with a measure of brain activity for identified categories. This is done by observing chemical reactions which produce electrical fields that have a quantifiable CPS (cycles per second). Brainwave patterns are defined by the following categories:

Brainwave Patterns

Delta	0 to 4Hz	**Deep sleep/no outer awareness**
Theta	4 to 8Hz	**Twilight/light sleep/meditative**
Alpha	8 to 12Hz	**Aware/relaxed/calm/attentive**
Beta	12 to 16Hz	**Normal waking consciousness**
High Beta	16 to 30Hz	**Intense outer-directed focus**
K Complex	30 to 35Hz	**The "Ah-ha!" experience**
Super Beta	35 to 150Hz	**Extreme states (i.e., psychic or out-of-body)**

So, which state is best for learning? It all depends on *what type* of learning and for *how long*; but here's a general synopsis: *Delta* is useless for any type of learning, as far as researchers know. Theta is the state that we all go into and out of right before falling asleep and waking up. It can be great for "sleep learning" and free association of creative ideas; however it's too passive for direct instruction. *Alpha* is an alert state for listening and watching, but it is still fairly passive. *Beta* is great for typical thinking, asking questions, and problem solving; but *High Beta* is ideal for intense states such as debating and performing. *K Complex* is difficult to orchestrate, but you can set up the circumstances for it and if it happens, great. And finally, *Super Beta* is such an intense state, it isn't appropriate for schools, classrooms, and formal education. Obviously, can't use an EEG to measure brainwave activity in the classroom, but some simple observations about states can still be made. Here are a few examples of corresponding emotions and body language that may reflect a learner's state:

What Learner Feels	What You Might See
Fear	Restricted breathing; tightened muscles; and closed body posture
Anticipation	Eyes wide open; body leaning forward; and breath held
Curiosity	Hand to head; bright facial expression; and head turned or tilted
Apathy	Relaxed shoulders/posture; slow breathing; and no eye contact
Frustration	Fidgeting and anxious movements; tightened muscles; and shortened breaths
Self-convincer	Breathing shifts; and body rocks, tilts, or rolls

If you observe a student struggling with an unproductive learning state, you have a decision to make: Either let it go; or facilitate a change. Since all behaviors are dependent upon a state, if you help move the learner into an optimal state, you'll get optimal results. If you allow learners to linger, however, in unproductive states, a negative association may develop and eventually impact learning on a very deep-rooted level.

For example, if a learner's state is curiosity, but the task at hand is overly challenging, they can quickly move into confusion. At this point, if the confusion is not resolved, frustration is likely to follow. An aware educator may catch the confusion before it turns to frustration, or worse, anger or apathy. The stages of confusion and frustration only last a short time, so timing is important. You may only have a few minutes to observe the problem and react. If you ignore it, a bigger problem is sure to follow.

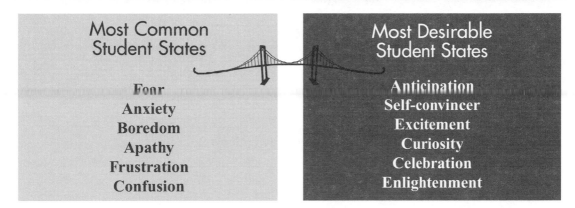

Most Common Student States	Most Desirable Student States
Fear	Anticipation
Anxiety	Self-convincer
Boredom	Excitement
Apathy	Curiosity
Frustration	Celebration
Confusion	Enlightenment

Students go in and out of countless states every day, just as you do. Learning is *not* all in our heads: It's a mind-body experience. How you feel and how they feel is important. It influences every single learning experience. Some strategies for managing learning states productively follow:

1. **Activities:** Facilitate a change from one to another; intensify learner involvement; lead a stretching session or energizing game; shift from individual to group work; move locations; or do something novel.

2. **Environment:** Create an energy shift with a lighting, seating, or temperature change; use aromas, sound, ionizers, plants, or color. Provide an emotionally safe environment.

3. **Multi-Media Sources:** Incorporate a video, computer program, overhead projection system, music, or slides.

4. **People:** Change speakers or shift learners' visual focus; have the students teach each other. Shift to groups or buddy-study.

5. **Tone:** Provide a shift in theme, schedule, timeframe, goals, resources, rules, or opinions.

6. **Focusing:** Facilitate breathing exercises (inhale and exhale slowly through the nose); incorporate visualization and imagery.

7. **Choice:** Provide learners with choices; ask for their input. Student motivation increases as you increase their control and accountability. Provide a safe environment, frequent feedback, positive social bonding opportunities, and adequate nutrition and water. Engage multiple learning styles.

Every day, you'll get more adept at reading states and managing them productively. Always ask yourself, "What's the target state for this learning activity?" If the answer is a reflective state, facilitate a stress reducing exercise; then play some slow music. If the activity calls for an active state, have students stand up and take a few deep breaths; then play some fast music. In any case, be respectful of your learners' processes. Sometimes, a student's state may be reflective of a deep-seeded problem that shouldn't be dismissed. If a problematic state continues for more than a couple of days with an individual student, it may be a good idea to seek additional help from a school psychologist or other mental health professional.

 ## What This Means to You

The most effective instructional leaders know how to recognize and manage learning states; and ultimately teach others how to do this for themselves. As learners begin to recognize their own attentional rhythms, the reward is fewer classroom disturbances and more empowered learners. To move learners from nonproductive states to productive learning states, provide them with some choice, suggest a change of activities, shift your voice or approach to a problem, provide a change of location, alter lighting, facilitate a movement game or activity, play some music, or construct a class art project. Hundreds of other possibilities exist, of course. The bottom line is to give learners some control over their environment and facilitate a shift from a mental or cognitive activity to a physical, creative, or reflection activity.

Reflection Questions

1. What from this chapter was novel, fresh, or new to you? What was familiar or "old hat"?

2. In what ways, do you already apply the information in this chapter?

3. What three questions might you now generate about this material?

4. How did you react emotionally to the information in this chapter?

5. How did you react cognitively to the information? Do you agree or disagree with the author's point of view? Why?

6. In what ways might you translate the principles presented in this chapter into practical everyday useful ideas?

7. If these things are, in fact, true about the brain, what should we do differently? What resources of time, people, and money could be redirected? In what ways might you suggest we start doing this?

8. What were the most interesting insights you gained from this material?

9. If you were to plan your next step for making your curriculum more brain-based, what would that be?

10. What obstacles might you encounter? How might you realistically deal with them?

Uniqueness and the Brain

Honoring Learning Style Differences

Learning Style Characteristics

Context Variables

Input Preferences

Processing Formats

Response Filters

Flexibility of Learning Styles

Learning Styles Warning

10

Uniqueness and the Brain

Every human brain develops uniquely: Even brains of identical twins are different. The most amazing thing is that all of us virtually share the same DNA in 99.5 percent of our bodies, but the .5 percent that is unique makes us each different. One of the goals of a brain-compatible learning environment is to recognize this fact and account for it. We can do this by respecting and encouraging differences between learners. It would not only be a boring world if everyone learned the same, and along the same timeline, but it would be a bad sign for species preservation. Diversity in the gene pool makes for a more resilient population. A superb way to honor uniqueness and diversity is to consider learning styles.

Honoring Learning Style Differences

While many developers of learning styles profiles and formats claim their model is "brain-based," the fact is that learning styles were around long before the current wave of brain research. Learning styles are based on observed behaviors or psychology rather than on neurobiology, so there is no "basis" in the brain for learning styles. Having said this, however, it should also be noted that the models *are* very compatible with our understanding of learner differences and uniqueness. This makes them "compatible" with, but not "based" on brain science.

There is no way today to definitively prove that incorporating specific learning styles, or cooperative learning approaches, or multiple intelligence models is any better for the brain. But, it would be irresponsible to discount the use of these models simply because the data that supports them is psychological and social, rather than biological in nature.

Countless studies have verified learner preferences for different kinds of input, styles of processing, and follow up activities. And we now know, that *the way we learn* affects the very structure of our brain. The fact that we all seem to have favorite ways of learning does not make a learning styles approach "brain-based." However, providing choice and multiple approaches in the learning environment is compatible with the brain's needs.

While there is a substantial body of research that defines and justifies the variety of ways we learn, what is the evidence from neuroscience about learning styles? Gerald Edelman, PhD. (1992) says that activating different parts of the brain can automatically activate other parts of the brain. And, Richard Restak, PhD. (1994) says that "The dynamic interplay of neural activity *within and between systems* is the very essence of brain function." Karl Pribram, PhD. (1979) says that the brain has "holographic tendencies between functions, including sensory input, which *work in parallel concert.*" As such, our brains are multi-processors; and though a learner may have preferences for a particular learning style, brain research suggests that the brain processes information on many levels and from multiple sources.

> *The whole notion of learning styles becomes irrelevant when we consider how much variety the brain thrives on.*

For example, while most of us were taught in our teaching preparation courses to present a lesson in a logical, sequential fashion, this is the "kiss of death" for many learners. Why?

> *Seventy-five percent of teachers have learned to be sequential, analytic presenters, and that's how their lessons are organized; yet 100 percent of their students are multi-processors.*

For some students a learning styles approach will enhance school success, but others will be set back. Derek Blackman and associates (1982) reports that the learners who are field-independent and have a reflective cognitive style are far more likely to succeed in a traditional school context. In order to reach *both* global and sequential type learners, start with a global overview and proceed to the details.

Learning Style Characteristics

There are many learning style profiles available today. Each of them has their strong points. The reason that they are so different is that they are assessing different things. Like the story of the six blind men and the elephant, each has a different opinion of what they are holding. Some are assessing the input process, others the cognitive filters, others the processing, and still others the response styles. The simplest approach to the learning style debate is this: *Simply provide variety and choice.*

The human brain does *not* have a single preference or "learning style." We are far more complex than this. What may be more instructive than considering all of the individual learning style models is to consider some common characteristics of them. The following four categories comprise a realistic and global view of learning styles which can be used in any learning setting to maximize receptivity in spite of diverse preferences and learner uniqueness:

1. Context

The circumstances surrounding the learning provide important clues about what will happen during the learning. For example, how do your learners feel about the learning environment, social conditions, and level of content difficulty? A learning style profile that approaches learning styles this way was developed by educators Rita and Kenneth Dunn (1978).

2. Input

Learners require sensory input for any learning to happen. Since we only have five senses, that input will be either visual, auditory, kinesthetic, olfactory, or gustatory. Although all two-month-old babies are gustatory learners, less than 1 percent of all other learners find gustatory input their preferred (or dependent) source (or style) of learning. Just as one preference can be dominant at a particular stage of life, and another at some later stage, sensory input preferences can change from moment to moment. One moment a learner may prefer external input (from an outside source) and the next internal (created in the mind).

Robert Samples, author of *Open Mind/Whole Mind* (1987) says that our additional sensing systems include vestibular (repetitious movement), magnetic (ferromagnetic orientation) , ionic (electrostatic atmospheric charges), geogravimetric (sensing mass differences), and proximal (physical closeness). He suggests that infants may actually possess all of these senses, but early conditioning defines which ones are "socially acceptable" or "culturally appropriate." Other societies, perhaps, use a wider range of sensory perception mechanisms. The learning styles model that is the most useful for incorporating this information is the Bandler-Grinder model (Bandler 1988).

3. Processing

At this stage of the learning process, the learner manipulates data collected by the senses, either globally or analytically, in a concrete fashion or abstractly, and in a multi-task or single-task environment. Relative hemispheric dominance plays a role here. The left hemisphere, for example, specializes in speech, language, and numerical calculations, while the right hemisphere specializes in the senses and pattern recognition. The two models that deal most with *how* learning is processed are Ned Herrmann's Brain Dominance model (1988), and the Gregorc/Butler model (Gregorc 1979).

4. Responses

Once learners have processed the information, they'll respond intuitively based on factors, such as time, risk assessment, internal or external referencing points, and personality traits. The models drawn from here are the 4-MAT (McCarthy 1990) and Meyers-Briggs (Briggs-Meyers 1995).

Context Variables
(Circumstances)
Field Dependent/Independent
Flexible Environment
Structured Environment
Independent/Dependent
Interdependent
Relationship Driven
Content Driven

Input Preferences
(Source)
Visual-External
Visual-Internal
Auditory-External
Auditory-Internal
Kinesthetic-Tactile
Kinesthetic-Internal

How Do We Learn?

Processing Formats
(How)
Contextual-Global
Sequential-Detailed/Linear
Content (What)
Conceptual (Abstract)
Concrete (Objects & Feelings)

Response Filters
(Results)
Externally Referenced
Internally Referenced
Matcher/Mismatcher
Impulsive-Experimental
Analytical-Reflective

To teach to all learning styles, simply provide as many different learning opportunities as possible. The following provides a summary of learning style factors, characteristics, and examples of relevant activities:

Context Variables

Field Dependent

This preference is for contextual cues; learning presented in natural contexts like field trips, experiments, and real-life situations. This learner might be referred to as "street smart." They like to absorb their environment by interacting with it, exploring, touching, and observing. For example, science comes alive for this learner on a field trip to a museum, or when the class conducts an outdoor experiment.

Field Independent

This style learner can find meaning in "artificial" contexts. For example, they are quite content to learn with computers, textbooks, videos, audio tapes, and books. They are likely good readers. They excel in the classroom environment, enjoy libraries, and are quite comfortable with second-hand learning.

Flexible Environment

This style learner does well in a variety of different environmental conditions. The variables include: lighting, music, temperature, furniture design, seating, noise level, structure level, and people.

Structured Environment

This style learner prefers a more structured environment. They have very particular needs for learning and minimal tolerance for variation. They require more certainty and structure. Emphasize rules, conformity, and authority.

Independent

This style learner prefers to learn alone. They can learn with others, but generally not as effectively.

Dependent

This style learner prefers to work in pairs, groups, and teams. They can learn alone, but generally not as effectively. They are most focused in a busy, interactive environment, in which interpersonal relationships are valued and encouraged.

Interdependent

This style learner likes to help others learn *and* works well alone. Their feeling of success is linked to the success of the group.

Relationship Driven

This style learner needs to *like* the presenter. *Who* delivers the information is more important than *what* is presented. This learner needs to develop a relationship of trust, credibility, and respect with the instructor *before* learning is maximized.

Content Driven

This style learner prefers valuable content. *What* is presented is more important than *who* delivers it. Even if the learner dislikes the teacher, learning continues.

Input Preferences

Visual External

This style learner prefers visual input to auditory input. They generally maintain eye contact with the teacher; their posture is upright; they create mental pictures, talk quickly and in monotone, and like handouts. They tend to use visual terminology like, "*See* what I mean?" A visual learner is usually a good speller; they would rather read than be read to; they enjoy writing, prefer neatness; and they are organized, alert, and, less distracted by noise. They have a "personal space" they protect around them. As aesthetic beings, they love handouts, books, computers, overheads, art, and photos. If asked, "Are you hungry?" They might check their watch to "see" if it's time for them to be hungry! They are good at visualization and have trouble with verbal instructions.

Visual Internal

This style learner prefers to "see it" in the mind's eye first. They visualize a mental picture of the subject to understand it. They tend to daydream, imagine, and visualize internally.

Auditory External

This style learner prefers auditory input over visual. They talk constantly to themselves or others. They are easily distracted; they memorize by steps and procedures; they exhibit head bobs, side-to-side eye movement, and greater awareness of tempo, tonality, pitch, and volume. They like to answer rhetorical questions; they want test questions to be sequenced in the order they were learned; they can mimic voices well; they talk to themselves at night and before they get up in the morning; and they often replay conversations in their head. Math and writing is more difficult for auditory external learners. They speak rhythmically, like class discussions, dislike spelling, like to read aloud, enjoy storytelling, remember what was discussed, and often mimic tone, pitch, tempo, and pace of the teacher. They like social occasions more than others and often are better at recalling jokes and conversations.

Auditory Internal

This style learner carries on internal dialogues with themselves. What do I know? What do I think about this? What does this mean to me? They tend to have difficulty making up their minds. They are also very strong in metacognition.

Kinesthetic Tactile

This style learner prefers physical input. They learn best by doing. They're a "hands-on" try it first, jump in and give it a go kind of learner. They are in touch with their feelings; they're active and physical; they exhibit minimal facial expression; talk less frequently; speak in measured words with pauses; have slower breathing; and like action novels. They use language like, this "*feels* good," or let's "get a handle" on this. They are more likely to be big eaters, relatively right-hemisphere dominant, and are impacted by personal attention and close proximity. This means learning by doing the task is more interesting to them than reading about it or hearing about it.

Kinesthetic Internal

This style learner prefers inferential, intuitive input, such as storytelling and movies. Stories with a great deal of "heart" and feeling in them impact them the most. Strong non-verbal communication is valued (including tonality, tempo, posture, expression, and gestures). They place greater emphasis on *how* something is said than on *what* is said. This learner needs to have positive feelings about the task before they can get totally engaged. Kinesthetic internal learners are less verbally expressive, more physically expressive, and less likely to be the first to raise their hand in class, as they need to go "internal" to check out their answers before offering them. They prefer to experience feelings about a topic before learning about it.

Processing Formats

Contextual Global

This holistic, gestalt learner prefers the big picture. They want an overview of key concepts before they begin processing details; they like relevance, thematic vision, and purpose; and are more likely to prefer multi-tasking, which means they like to work on many problems or tasks at once. They are more likely to be intuitive and able to infer meaning; they probably rely on kinesthetic internal cues to relate; they prefer simple and quick approximation to exact measures; they ask a lot of questions; and they often have a "feeling" for the information. This style, often referred to as a "right-brain" learner, processes in pictures, symbols, icons, and themes. They have external focus tendencies, with a high degree of distractibility. Thus, they are sometimes mislabeled "at-risk" learners. In truth, this learner simply needs to be reached with increased multi-tasking, non-verbals, global overviews, and a stronger instructor/student relationship.

Sequential Detailed/Linear

This style learner prefers a sequenced, step-by-step, menu, or formula approach to learning. They are more likely to be single task learners, preferring to stay focused on one problem at a time. They tend to be analytical. They like measuring, analyzing, asking questions, and comparing and contrasting. They want to fully understand something before diving in completely. They are very word based, and will hold others accountable for what they say, word for word. This learner is often referred to as left-hemisphere dominant. They prefer the world of the written word; they want clear, detailed instructions; and they learn best with structured lessons. They tend to focus internally, which makes them lower in distractibility. They are oriented for the long term and prefer to know what the schedule is. These learners excel in math, language, computers, and other sequential work.

Conceptual (Abstract)

This style learner prefers the world of books, words, computers, ideas, and conversations. They enjoy talking and thinking, but not as much as they like doing. Some

might say of this learner that they are very much "inside their head." They generally lean towards more abstract professions, such as writing, teaching (college
professor), or accounting.

Concrete (Objects & Feelings)

This style learner prefers the world of the concrete—things that can be touched,
jumped over, held, and manipulated. They like specific examples; and learn best with
hands-on, experiential approaches. They prefer physical activities, action, games,
and movement. They generally lean towards professions that allow them to use their
hands or bodies, such as dancing, sculpting, acting, building trades, or truck driving.

Response Filters

Externally Referenced

This style learner responds to life based primarily upon what others think. The question they often ask is, "What do others expect me to act like, think, or say?" They are
responsive to society's norms and rules. They are usually very conscious of etiquette,
dogma, policies, laws, and family expectations.

Internally Referenced

This style learner responds to life based primarily on his or her own judgment and
their own set of rules, which may or may not be the norm of society. This learner is
very independent because they are the sole judge.

Matcher

This style learner responds by noting similarities. They agree easily; they like con-
sistencies; they look for similarities in relationships; and they prefer things that
belong or go together well. This learner will more likely approve of something that
has been done before, that fits into an overall plan, and that is generally consistent
with the rest of the learning.

Mismatcher

This style learner responds by noting differences. They notice what is off, missing,
wrong, or inconsistent. They tend to ask, "But why not?" or, "What if?" They find
flaws in arguments and prefer variety and change. They are not necessarily negative,
just simply contrary. Since mismatchers tend to discover exceptions to the rule, rules
and laws are less significant; and "testing" or bending the rules is more common.
Mismatchers are skeptical of words like, *always*, *everyone*, *all*, *never*, and *no one*.
Hence, you'll hear more responses like, "Yes, *but*... " This learner wants more variety, enjoys experimenting, and abhors traditional lesson plans, predictability, and
doing what everyone else is doing.

Impulsive Experimental

This style learner responds best with immediate action. They prefer learning by trial and error and experiential approaches. Their thought pattern is *do it, then keep doing it until you figure it out*. This learner is more likely to be present oriented.

Analytical Reflective

This style learner responds internally to new learning. They take in information, process it reflectively, and consider all the alternatives before diving in completely. They are pragmatists by nature and tend to keep more distance between themselves and others. They like to stand back and watch; and are more likely to be past or future referenced.

Flexibility of Learning Styles

In experiments by researchers P. Torrance and O. Ball (1978), student learning styles were assessed prior to exposure to an intensive training course where other learning style methods were introduced. Through exposure to right-hemisphere, non-linear learning strategies (imagery, intuition, brainstorming, metaphors, etc.), the learners were able to make more use of their existing capabilities and extend into new areas. The results also showed that the students were able to "change their preferred styles of learning and thinking through brief but intensive training." All of us have altered our own learning style(s) in cases where we simply had to in order to learn. While our dependent input would stay the same, we can increase our tolerance and effectiveness for learning outside of our preferred style(s).

Learning style preference, remember, can change from one day to the next and even from hour to hour. In a study by the University of Sussex in England, researchers (Brewer and Campbell 1991) found that detailed and literal learning was better achieved in the morning, while global, inferential, and contextual learning was better achieved in the afternoon. Most of us are comfortable using several styles, even though our preferred (or dependent) style is likely to remain intact over our lifetime. Why? It seems that our preferred learning style may be the one we needed for survival as an infant. Thus, in situations of stress, threat, or suspense, we revert to our priority learning style.

1. **Look for exits and others in need**

2. **Yell "Fire" or give directions**

3. **Run for exits grabbing others in need**

Consider this example: A fire breaks out in your home. Your immediate reaction will be one of the following: 1) visual—you quickly size up the situation, looking for exits, others in need, etc; 2) auditory—you start yelling "Fire" or giving directions; or 3) kinesthetic—you start running for the exits or grabbing others who need help. While you may eventually respond in all of these ways, one will tend to be an instinctual first reaction. This would be your dominant or dependent input preference.

About 40 percent of learners develop into visual learners by secondary school age. Those learners who remain primarily kinesthetic often fall behind in instruction or get labeled "developmentally delayed" or "hyperactive." More often than not, however, their brain is *not* delayed; there's simply a wide range of what is normal development.

 ## What This Means to You

Many learners who seem apathetic will become more enthusiastic when the learning is offered in their preferred style. Provide continual variety and expose learners to many styles. This exposure will help them become flexible learners. Most importantly, create options for learners so that they are empowered to learn effectively and efficiently in the style they prefer.

Learning Styles Warning

Many teachers and trainers have delighted in grouping their learners by one profile or another. The trouble with this is that groupings always play down individual differences; and we are really much more complex as learners than any one grouping can encompass. Grouping learners does not solve learning problems. Working with individuals based on learning style norms or characteristics, however, will move learners forward. The two most important things to remember for building a successful brain-based learning styles approach is: 1) Provide a variety of approaches; and 2) Offer choices.

> *As learners we don't have a genetically determined or single definitive learning style. Most of the brain is involved in most every act of learning.*

Learning style profiles and formats offer a useful framework for working with learner differences and understanding the importance of variety and choice. Rather than trying to figure out who is what kind of learner, the framework is most valuable in its ability to help you determine if your teaching approaches and methodologies cover the broad spectrum of learner types.

Reflection Questions

1. What from this chapter was novel, fresh, or new to you? What was familiar or "old hat"?

2. In what ways, do you already apply the information in this chapter?

3. What three questions might you now generate about this material?

4. How did you react emotionally to the information in this chapter?

5. How did you react cognitively to the information? Do you agree or disagree with the author's point of view? Why?

6. In what ways might you translate the principles presented in this chapter into practical everyday useful ideas?

7. If these things are, in fact, true about the brain, what should we do differently? What resources of time, people, and money could be redirected? In what ways might you suggest we start doing this?

8. What were the most interesting insights you gained from this material?

9. If you were to plan your next step for making your curriculum more brain-based, what would that be?

10. What obstacles might you encounter? How might you realistically deal with them?

Enriching
the Brain

Human Neurogenesis Is Possible!

The Five Keys to Enrichment

What's So Novel About Novelty?

Feedback Spurs Learning

Activating More of the Brain

Enriching the Brain

U ntil recently, the accepted thinking in the scientific community was that a natural degeneration process of our brain begins at birth and progresses through the lifespan. Thus, the answer to the question, Can we grow a better brain, seemed to be "no." That is until 1964 when Mark Rosenzweig, PhD. of University of California, Berkeley led a research team that revealed rats in an enriched environment indeed "grow better" brains than those in an impoverished environment (Bennett, et. al 1964; Rosenzweig, et. al 1968). The evidence that an enriched environment could enhance brain development was supported further in groundbreaking research by University of California, Berkeley pioneer Marion Diamond, PhD. and, separately, by University of Illinois researcher William Greenough, PhD. (Greenough and Anderson 1991). Based on these pioneering studies, and many subsequent to them, we now know that the human brain actually maintains an amazing plasticity throughout life. We can literally grow new neural connections with stimulation, even as we age. This fact means nearly any learner can increase their intelligence, without limits, using proper enrichment.

Initial studies with rats were eventually extended to human subjects. The animal studies suggested that when exposed to an enriched environment, the number of connections in the brain increased by 25 percent. Dr. Diamond summarized the data from her studies as follows:

> *With increasing amounts of environmental enrichment, we see brains that are larger and heavier with increased dendritic branching. This means those nerve cells can communicate better with each other. With the enriched environment, we also get more support cells because the nerve cells are getting bigger. Not only that, but the junction between the cells, the synapse, also increases in dimension. These are highly significant effects of differential experience.*

Figure 11.1
Enrichment: How the Brain Changes

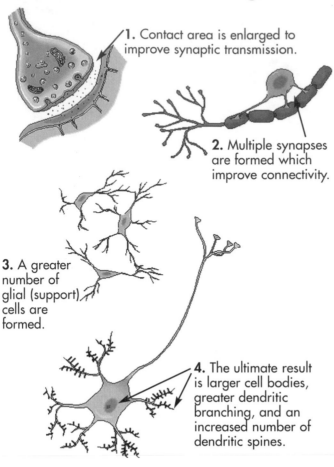

1. Contact area is enlarged to improve synaptic transmission.

2. Multiple synapses are formed which improve connectivity.

3. A greater number of glial (support) cells are formed.

4. The ultimate result is larger cell bodies, greater dendritic branching, and an increased number of dendritic spines.

Eventually we learned that in addition to increased dendritic branching, synaptic plasticity was evident in enriched environments. We now know *how* the brain modifies itself structurally; and that it is dependent on the type and amount of usage. Synaptic growth varies depending on the complexity and type of activity one regularly engages in. For example, when we engage in *novel* motor learning, new synapses are generated in our cerebellular cortex. And when we engage in repeated motor learning (or exercise), our brain develops greater density of blood vessels in the molecular layer.

An area of the mid-brain, the superior colliculus, which is involved in attentional processing grew 5 to 6 percent more in an enriched environment. Using fMRI technology, researchers at the University of Pennsylvania (Ackerman, et. al 1998) discovered that our brain has areas that are only stimulated by letters, not words or symbols. This suggests that new experiences (like reading) can get wired into the malleable brain. In other words, as we vary the type of environment, the brain varies the way it develops.

Our brain changes itself in several ways. First, intrinsic forces, otherwise known as genetic or "pre-wiring," create a template for processes that drive change in the brain. Second, "experience expectant" processes create massive overproduction of synapses prior to (not after) demand. This occurs when: 1) the learning is commonly needed by *all* members of that species; 2) certain events will reliably occur; and 3) the timing is relatively critical. And third, the brain responds to "experience dependent" processes triggered by environmental stimuli.

When scientists extended enrichment studies to human subjects, they found definite correlates. University of California, Los Angeles neuroscientist Robert Jacobs, PhD. and colleagues found (1993) in autopsy studies that graduate students had 40 percent more neural connections than those of high-school dropouts. The graduate students, who were presumably involved in challenging mental activities, also exhibited 25 percent more overall "brain growth" than the control group. Yet education alone was not the only differential. The learning experiences, it was found, needed to be frequent and challenging for the effect to occur. Graduate students who "coasted" through school exhibited fewer connections than those who challenged themselves daily. Dr. Jacob's research on cortical dendrite systems in twenty neurologically normal right-handed humans (half male and half female) evaluated the following variables:

▼ **Total dendritic length**

▼ **Mean dendritic length**

▼ **Dendritic segment count**

▼ **Proximal versus ontogenetically later developing distal branching**

These variables are known to relate to the complexity of the brain, the ability to solve problems, and overall intelligence. Dr. Jacob's measurements investigated several independent variables, as well, including: gender, hemisphere, and education. The results of his research revealed the following:

Gender: Females had greater dendritic values and variability than males.
Hemisphere: The left hemisphere had greater overall dendritic measurements than the right, but the results were not consistent with each individual.
Education: Level of education had a "consistent and substantial effect" on dendritic branching: The higher the level, the greater the measurements.

Can enrichment actually make you smarter? The answer to this question is still unclear. William Calvin, PhD. a University of Washington neurobiologist (Calvin and Ojemann 1994), however, says that cortical area growth does have something to do with "being smart," even though the internal efficiency of our "wiring" and connections are *more* significant. A student's early sensory deprivation can play a role: "If there is a bad experience, the wrong synapses are shed and the system malfunctions," says Greenough (Fuchs, ct. al 1990). Retaining excess synapses can be harmful, as in the case of Fragile X mental retardation.

Figure 11.2
Impoverished vs. Enriched Neurons

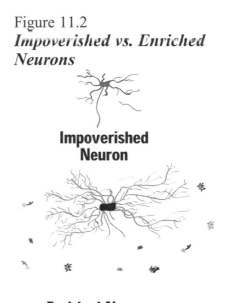

Impoverished Neuron

Enriched Neuron

Summary of Enrichment Findings

Age: The effects of enrichment have been robust at all ages (in both rat and human studies).

Hope: Recent studies have shown that the human brain can and does grow new cells. So far, neurogenesis has been confirmed only in the hippocampus, an area essential for learning and memory.

Speed: Specific changes in neurons were found in as few as 48 hours after exposure. In just one week, newborn rats in an enriched environment developed a 7 to 11 percent larger cortex than those in deprived conditions. In two weeks, the sensory integration area of the brain developed 16 percent more.

Strategies: Complex learning tasks are better than simple ones; more exercise is better than inactivity. Challenging tasks are better than easy ones. Interaction is better than isolation.

Boredom: A boring environment had a greater thinning effect on the cortex than an enriched environment had on the thickening of the cortex. Thus, it may be more critical to enrich the impoverished over the gifted; or ideally provide enrichment for all The brain of adolescent rats were especially devastated by boredom.

Source: Marion Diamond, PhD. *Magic Trees of the Mind.* 1998. Dutton: New York

In working with children, Craig Ramey, PhD. at the University of Alabama found (1992) that he could increase intelligence with mental stimulation. Ramey's intervention program studied children of low IQ parents. Divided into two groups (one control group), the children who were exposed to the enriched environment scored significantly higher (20 points) on post-treatment IQ tests. And the results lasted: When the children were retested after ten years, the effects of early intervention had endured. This provides quite an endorsement for challenging learning environments.

Human Neurogenesis is Possible!

The early studies demonstrated that enrichment of the brain leads to greater spine growth on the dendrites (connection points for cell-to-cell interaction), heavier cell bodies, longer dendrites, and more glial (support) cell growth. As early as 1985, Joseph Altman, PhD. of Purdue University (1993) claimed that the human brain can not only grow better dendrites, but can also grow new cells (neurogenesis). The scientific establishment, however, was not ready for this radical claim. The mainstream thinking was that yes, the human brain can be enriched, but growing new cells was impossible.

Then in 1997, a research effort led by scientists at San Diego's Salk Institute of Neuroscience discovered that (O'Leary 1997; Van Pragg, et. al 1999) neurogenesis is, in fact, a reality in rat brains (at least in the hippocampus area of the brain). A year later, the study was extended to humans; and the findings were reconfirmed (Eriksson, et. al 1998). The human brain also has the capability of growing new neurons!

Even though we inevitably lose brain cells each day, new ones can be germinated in a fertile environment. The impact of this finding on the general public has yet to be fully realized, but the scientific community is buoyed by the medical potential of these recent findings. Injuries once viewed as permanent, may soon be repairable with accelerated cell growth prompting. A cure for the dreaded disease Alzheimer's may soon exist. Although we are still a long way from the reality of these prospects, scientists are hopeful.

The Five Keys to Enrichment

In examining the many "enrichment" studies that have been conducted over the past few decades, the following common factors have emerged:

First, to get the enrichment effect, the stimulus must be new. An old stimulus just won't do: It must be novel. Second, the stimulus must be challenging. Routine efforts do little for the brain's growth. Third, the stimulus must be coherent and meaningful. Random input will not enrich the brain. Fourth, the learning has to take place over time. How much time depends on the extent of the neural changes, but the only changes that happen instantly are stimulus response learning. And finally, there must be a way for the brain to learn from the challenging, novel stimuli: This means feedback. For example, if you're learning to walk a tightrope and you make a mistake, you fall: That's feedback. If you press a lever and you get food or you don't: That's feedback. The more consistent, specific, timely, and learner controlled the feedback is, the better. There you have it! In a nutshell, the critical ingredients for enriching the brain are novelty, challenge, coherence, time, and feedback.

Figure 11.3
Enrichment Keys

☑ **Challenge**
time • standards
resources • circumstances

☑ **Novelty**
contrasting • new

☑ **Feedback**
timely • specific • in control often

☑ **Coherence**
meaningful • choice

☑ **Time**
greater changes need more

What This Means to You

Create a more multi-sensory environment. Add posters, aromas, music, and relevant activities. Increase social interaction and group work. Move to novel locations frequently (i.e., take fieldtrips, go outdoors, exchange rooms with another teacher for the day, etc.) On a daily basis, modify the environment in some minor way (i.e., seating, displays, bulletin boards, etc.). Encourage students to explore new ideas and express themselves creatively. Provide quality, not just quantity, time. Teach and practice critical skills like logic, categorizing, counting, labeling, language, cause and effect, debate, and critical thinking. Provide positive feedback; and celebrate accomplishments with fun celebrations. Use words from several languages in a variety of contexts. Reduce all forms of severe negative experience, punishment, or disapproval. And most of all, offer students choices so that their learning is meaningful.

The work of Greenough and colleagues (1992) and J. E. Black (1989) confirmed that for the enrichment effect to occur, the challenges presented must engender learning, as opposed to mere activity or exercise. When Black isolated other factors, such as aging and stress, from complex environments, he affirmed that it was the *learning*, not simply the motor activity, that caused the optimal brain growth. Based on this, we know that *how* you enrich an environment is critical.

What's So Novel About Novelty?

Arnold Scheibel, PhD. director of The Brain Research Institute at University of California, Los Angeles (1994) says, "Unfamiliar activities are the brain's best friend." The fact that the brain is so stimulated by novelty may be a survival response: Anything new may be threatening to the status quo; and thus, represents a potential danger. Once we have grown accustomed to an environment or situation, however, it becomes routine and the reticular formation in our brain begins to operate at a lower level. Once a new or novel stimuli is reintroduced, the reticular formation gets alerted once again and the brain is stimulated to grow.

The enrichment effect does not take months or years necessarily to show up. Significant "structural modifications" in the dendritic fields of cortical neurons have been reported evident in just four days. Greenough and Anderson (1991) suggest that brain enrichment happens in stages—from surface level to depth growth. They draw four important conclusions:

1. Rats in enriched environments actually grow heavier brains with more dendritic connections that communicate better. They also exhibit increased synapses, greater thickness in sensory areas, increased enzymes, and more glial cells (the ones that assist in growth and signal transmission).

2. Enriched environments need to be varied and changed often (every 2 to 4 weeks) to maintain the positive differences in rat intelligence. In studies, this meant frequently introducing other rats, more toys, and additional challenges; and this holds true for humans.

3. Rats of any age can experience increased intelligence if they are provided challenging and frequent new learning experiences.

4. The real world—outside of the cages (even the enriched ones)—provided one of the best environments for brain growth.

Environmental Effects on Rats' Cortical Structure

Commonly Studied Conditions Rated from Most to Least Effective

1. **Complex Environment:** Exploration, toys, object-filled spaces produced robust dendritic growth.
2. **Social Environment:** Interaction with families and peers produced moderate dendritic growth.
3. **Isolated Environment:** Rats kept in isolation produced no dendritic changes.

In Other Experiments

1. **Acrobatic Learning:** Providing challenges produced the greatest dendritic growth.
2. **Treadmill Exercise:** This exercise provided no choice, required limited learning, but increased blood flow and improved dendritic growth.
3. **Voluntary Exercise:** This exercise provided choice and free access. Exercisers had some increased blood flow and slightly better learning.
2. **Inactivity Condition:** Rats kept in isolation produced no dendritic changes.

Schools today are developing greater interest in creating the right kind of enriched environments for students. One of the most convincing arguments comes from the former director of the Institute of Mental Health, Frederick Goodwin, PhD. He says "...there is now an increasing understanding that the environment can affect you...you can't make a 70 IQ person into a 150 IQ person, but you can change their IQ measure in different ways, perhaps as much as 20 points up or down, based on the environment."

Have you ever noticed how much more passion and motivation learners exhibit when they are talking about real-world experiences versus "book learning"? Real-life learning provides a valuable springboard for delving deeper into the meaning or analysis of things. Some learning opportunities that inspire this include field trips, travel or study abroad, library study, the home environment, the park, on-the-job training, a convention, rally, special meeting, or vacation—*anything rich and varied that naturally occurs in life.*

Feedback Spurs Learning

While enriched environments (both mental and physical) are important, something else is equally critical. Research by noted brain expert Santiago Ramon y Cajal (1988) has emphasized that the brain needs feedback from its own activities for optimal learning.

> ## The best feedback is immediate, positive, and dramatic.

Feedback is critical, but that feedback does not necessarily have to be teacher generated. One of the best ways to encourage self feedback and boost thinking is to have learners reflect and record their own perceptions on audio tape. This examination into one's own thinking, sensing, and organizing process provides a powerful vehicle for the brain's development as a problem-solver and thinker.

A teacher's greatest feedback resource may be other learners. And, yet many learning environments are not organized to take advantage of this asset. Group work or teams are ideal for learning—especially when they are multi-age and multi-status groupings. Group work can help learners feel valued and cared for, in which case our brain releases the neurotransmitters of pleasure—endorphins and dopamine. This helps us enjoy our work more. Secondly, groups provide a superb vehicle for social and academic reinforcement. When students talk to other students they get direct feedback on their ideas as well as their behaviors.

Figure 11.4
Learning Requires the Formation of New Networks

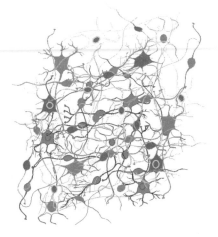

The most effective feedback is specific and immediate. For example, video games and computers both provide very specific and immediate feedback, as does peer editing of a student's story. Also, interaction among learners and with outside sources can provide valuable feedback. A great deal of feedback is obtained non-verbally. Facial expressions and body language tell us a lot about our performance on a nonconscious, if not conscious, level. Building a classroom model, playing a learning game, creating a class video, or planning a community project, are all activities that provide indirect feedback from the interaction process.

Ideally, feedback will involve some learner choice: That is, it can be generated and modified at will. If it's not relevant or if it cannot be immediately applied, however, performance won't be altered. Recall a college class where your only feedback may have come from a mid-term or final: That's an example of poor, other-controlled feedback! Fortunately, immediate and self-generated feedback can be achieved in many simple ways. Have learners review their own work against a performance criteria. Provide self-assessment guidelines; post grading criteria; have students review their personal goals; and use computer learning programs if appropriate.

To summarize what we've learned about enrichment, consider the following general truths:

▼ **Learners do best when they are presented with novel stimulation— something out of the ordinary.**

▼ **Beware of learner overload. Don't provide too much new material at a time. A presentation of thirty to ninety minutes with intense (preferably non-stop) sensory stimulation is good, with a rest period to follow.**

▼ **Provide proper down time after new learning. Repeat new learning twenty- four to forty-eight hours following the initial encounter, then daily, and every other day subsequently.**

▼ **Interacting with peers, teachers, or other adults regarding the subject mat- ter allows learners to create a conceptual framework for the learning and gather critical feedback.**

▼ **Consistent feedback helps learners improve the quality of their understand- ing and observe their own progress.**

▼ **When learners are provided with a roadmap or framework for the new learning—an overall picture of where they are and where they are going— understanding is enhanced.**

Activating More of the Brain

Intelligence is largely the ability to bring together random bits of information to inform thinking, problem solving, and analysis. The brain relies on a multitude of cir- cuits to do this effectively. These connections are called "phase relationships" because they tie together simultaneous stimuli. When learners are provided with more consistent feedback and better quality feedback, they are better able to tie pieces of the learning puzzle together and integrate the information into higher quality rela- tionships and patterns.

A strategy known as "pole-bridging," coined by Researcher Win Wenger, PhD. (1992), highlights the way the brain connects information and processes it both from front to back and side to side. To "pole-bridge," simply talk about what you're doing, while you're doing it. Talk deliberately, perceptively, and purposely about the process; then have learners record their perceptions of the learning on paper. This strategy can dramatically increase learning. Some studies have documented gains from one to three IQ points *per hour* of "pole-bridging" practice.

Many of the "great thinkers" in history, for example Leonardo da Vinci, have kept elaborate journals of their work. Perhaps these recordings represent a sort of self-feedback mechanism. As a child, you had plenty of environmental stimulation, but you also got the all-important feedback. When you first learned to ride a bike, you experienced immediate and conclusive feedback: Either you stayed up or fell down. Imagine trying to learn to ride a bike *without knowing how you were doing until a month later*. You would go nuts!

We may be accidentally retarding thinking, intelligence, and brain growth, and ultimately creating "slow learners," by the lack of feedback and by the wide lag time or feedback loop we have built into the typical learning environment.

If after reading this chapter, you want to start increasing the enrichment opportunities in your teaching/learning environment, begin first by simply increasing the frequency and quality of learner feedback. With this intervention alone, you will notice immediate improvement in learners' motivation and achievement. Some simple and practical suggestions follow:

Enrichment Tips for Teachers

▼ Greet learners at the door.
▼ Frequently comment on previous learning.
▼ Encourage peer teaching and interaction.
▼ Provide daily or weekly reviews (self, teacher, or peer generated).
▼ Have learners talk themselves through their thinking process (out loud).
▼ Have teams keep progress charts for their group and post results.
▼ Encourage students to keep a learning journal.
▼ Provide "mock tests" that won't be applied to the grading scale.
▼ Have students pair up for test preparation study.
▼ Have students correct their own homework, quizzes, tests, etc.
▼ Have learners do a group presentation, whereby they receive subsequent group feedback (take the time to teach learners how to provide effective critical feedback versus criticism; otherwise the strategy will backfire).

Reflection Questions

1. What from this chapter was novel, fresh, or new to you? What was familiar or "old hat"?

2. In what ways, do you already apply the information in this chapter?

3. What three questions might you now generate about this material?

4. How did you react emotionally to the information in this chapter?

5. How did you react cognitively to the information? Do you agree or disagree with the author's point of view? Why?

6. In what ways might you translate the principles presented in this chapter into practical everyday useful ideas?

7. If these things are, in fact, true about the brain, what should we do differently? What resources of time, people, and money could be redirected? In what ways might you suggest we start doing this?

8. What were the most interesting insights you gained from this material?

9. If you were to plan your next step for making your curriculum more brain-based, what would that be?

10. What obstacles might you encounter? How might you realistically deal with them?

The Role of Movement and Exercise

12

The Role of Movement and Exercise

Despite research findings to the contrary, the erroneous separation of mind and body in the traditional education system stubbornly persists. Indeed, many special education teachers, sensory integration teachers, occupational therapists, and physical education teachers have long recognized the connection between physical and mental learning, but overall, schools have not kept up with the research that links physical movement with thinking processes.

Henrietta Leiner, PhD. and Alan Leiner, PhD. two Stanford University neuroscientists, were at the forefront of this research (1993), which ultimately refined "the cognitive map." Their research centered on the cerebellum (Latin for "little brain") located at the base of the brain. Although this cauliflower-shaped tissue clump takes up just *one-tenth* of our brain by volume, it contains *more than half* of all our neurons and some forty million nerve fibers—forty times more than even the highly complex optical tract.

The nerve fibers not only feed information from the cortex to the cerebellum, but the researchers found, it works in reverse as well. In other words, the communication between these two critical brain areas is a like two-way highway system. Previously, the cerebellum was thought to merely process signals from the cerebrum and send them to the motor cortex. But, the Leiners explain this is only part of the big picture. "The mistake was in assuming the signals went only to the motor cortex. They don't." The last place information is processed in the cerebellum, before it is sent to the cortex, is the dentate nucleus.

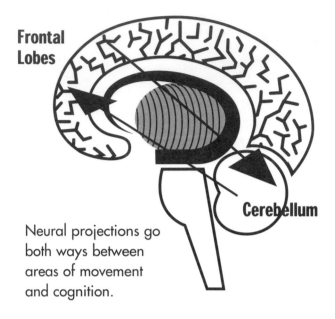

Figure 12.1
The Relationship Between Movement and Learning

Frontal Lobes

Cerebellum

Neural projections go both ways between areas of movement and cognition.

Although most mammals don't possess a dentate nucleus, primates (with high learning capabilities) do. A smaller area, the neodentate nucleus is present only in humans and may play a significant role in thinking. When neurologist Robert Dow, PhD. noted that one of his patients with cerebellar damage, also exhibited impaired cognitive function, the link between movement and thinking (and the cerebellum and cerebrum) was gaining stature. Today, we recognize that this sub-section of the brain (the cerebellum), long known for its role in posture, coordination, balance and movement, may be our brain's sleeping giant.

Motor Development and Learning

Neurophysiologist Carla Hannaford, PhD. (1995) says that the vestibular (inner ear) and cerebellar system (motor activity) is the first sensory system to mature. The semi-circular canals of our inner ear and the vestibular nuclei are information gathering and feedback mechanisms that inform our movements. As impulses travel through nerve tracts back and forth from the cerebellum to the rest of the brain, including the visual system and the sensory cortex, the vestibular nuclei help fine tune our movements and also activate the reticular activating system (RAS) near the top of the brain stem.

The reticular activating system, which receives incoming sensory data, constitutes our attentional system. The interaction between the two systems helps us keep our balance, translate thinking into action, and coordinate body movements. Typical playground games and motions like swinging, rolling, and jumping stimulate this system. "When we don't move and activate the vestibular system, we are not taking in information from the environment," Hannaford warns.

One of the simplest, but possibly most critical "exercises" for optimal learning is one that is sorely missing from children's lives today—games and movements that stimulate the vestibular system. All infants, children and teens can benefit from movement games that require learners to spin and turn. At the higher grades, participation in sports and pursuits that require energetic physical action (i.e., swimming, diving, dancing, tumbling) can serve learning; while at the lower levels, simple games, like Triangle Tag, for example, can encourage the beneficial movements. In Triangle Tag three players form a triangle by holding hands, while a fourth player stands outside the group and tries to tag whoever is "it" on the inside. The triangle team must spin to protect the "it" from the tagger! This is just one idea; there are hundreds of simple games that can facilitate the desired movements.

Peter Strick, PhD. (1995) at the Veteran Affairs Medical Center of Syracuse, New York established another important link. His staff traced a pathway from the cerebellum (see figure 12.3) back to parts of the brain involved in memory, attention, and spatial perception. Amazingly, the part of the brain that processes movement is the same part of the brain that processes learning.

In Philadelphia, Glen Doman, PhD. (1994) has had spectacular success with autistic and brain damaged children by using intense sensory integration therapy. And, many teachers who have integrated productive "play" into their curriculums have enjoyed positive results. Figure 12.2 illustrates how basic motor movements are related to required academic skill sets.

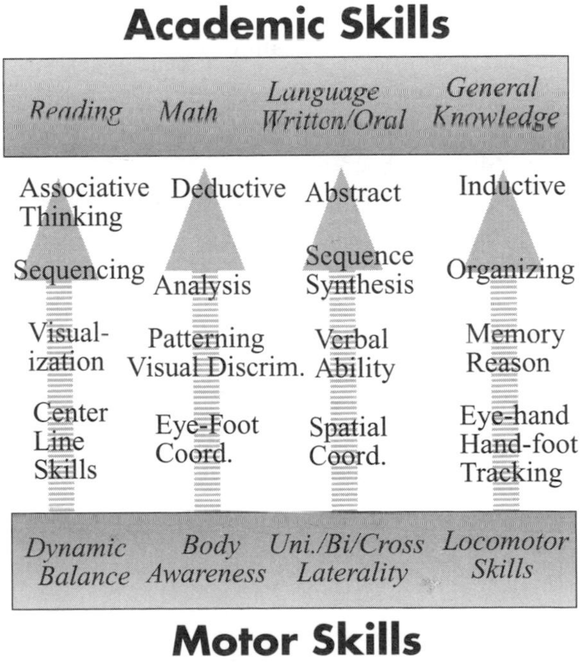

At a recent Society for Neuroscience Conference in San Diego W. T. Thatch, Jr., PhD. chair of the symposium entitled "The Role of the Cerebellum in Cognition," cited eighty studies that suggest strong links between

Figure 12.2
Academic and Motor Skills

Academic Skills

| Reading | Math | Language Written/Oral | General Knowledge |

Associative Thinking · Deductive · Abstract · Inductive

Sequencing · Analysis · Sequence Synthesis · Organizing

Visual-ization · Patterning Visual Discrim. · Verbal Ability · Memory Reason

Center Line Skills · Eye-Foot Coord. · Spatial Coord. · Eye-hand Hand-foot Tracking

| Dynamic Balance | Body Awareness | Uni./Bi/Cross Laterality | Locomotor Skills |

Motor Skills

the cerebellum and memory, spatial perception, language, attention, emotion, non-verbal cues, and even decision-making.

The Cerebral Code Revealed

Our brain creates movements by sending a deluge of nerve impulses to either the muscles or the larynx. Since each muscle gets the message at a slightly different time, it's a bit like a well-timed explosion on a special effects team. This amazing brain-body sequence has been referred to as a spatiotemporal (space-time) pattern. Researcher William Calvin (Calvin and Ojemann 1994) calls it a cerebral code. While simple movements like gum-chewing are controlled by basic brain circuits nearest the spinal cord, more complex movements require wider areas of the brain that include the prefrontal cortex and the rear two-thirds of the frontal lobes (see figure 12.3), particularly the dorsolateral frontal lobes. This is the an area of the brain often used for problem-solving, planning, and sequencing.

The area known as the anterior cingulate (see figure 12.3) is particularly active when novel movements or new combinations are initiated. This particular area seems to tie some movements to learning. Some early studies indicated that if our movements are impaired, the cerebellum and its connections to other areas of the brain are compromised. These findings, strongly implicate the value of physical education, movement, and games in boosting cognition.

Figure 12.3
Key Brain Areas Involved in Movement

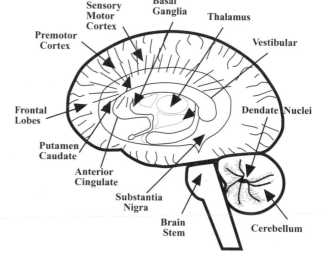

Growing Up Active

Many researchers believe that sensory-motor integration is fundamental to school readiness. In one study in Seattle, Washington third grade students studied language arts concepts through dance activities which included regular spinning, crawling, rolling, rocking, tumbling, pointing, and matching. Although the district-wide reading scores showed an annual average decrease of 2 percent, the students involved in the dance activities exhibited an increase in reading scores (MAT) of 13 percent in six months.

Lyelle Palmer, PhD. of Winona State University (Palmer and McDonald 1990) has also documented significant gains in attention and reading from similar stimulation activities. While many educators recognize this connection, nearly as many dismiss it once children pass the early elementary grades. The relationship between movement and learning, however, continues throughout life.

Some believe that sensory stimulation is so important, that deprived of it, infants may not develop the movement-pleasure link in the brain. Although fewer connections are made in the research between the cerebellum and the brain's pleasure centers, there is a growing concern that some infants deprived of touch, movement, and/or interaction, may grow up to have a violent disposition. Unable to experience pleasure through usual channels of pleasurable activity, their need for intense states, one of which is violence, may propel them towards anti-social responses. With sufficient supply of the needed "drug" (movement), the child is fine; deprive him/her of it, however, and problems arise.

Physical Education and Learning

The President's Council on Fitness and Sports states that all K-12 kids need at least thirty minutes a day of physical movement to stimulate the brain; and the research supports this claim. In fact, Larry Abraham, PhD. in the Department of Kinesiology at University of Texas at Austin says, "Classroom teachers should have kids move for the same reason that physical education teachers have kids count." Physical education, movement, drama, and the arts all add, rather than detract, from the "core curriculum."

In William Greenough's experiments at the University of Illinois (1991, 1992), rats that exercised in an enriched environment had a greater number of connections among neurons than those that didn't. They also had more capillaries around the brain's neurons than the sedentary rats. In the same way that exercise shapes up our muscles, heart, lungs, and bones, it also strengthens our basal ganglia, cerebellum, and corpus callosum—key areas of the brain. And, yet only an astonishingly low 36 percent of K-12 American students participate in a daily physical education program. We know exercise fuels the brain with oxygen, but it also triggers the release of neurotrophins, which enhance growth, impact mood, cement memory, and enhance connections between neurons.

Mark Hallet, PhD. at the National Institute of Neuroanatomy, says that excellence in physical performance probably uses 100 percent of the brain. There is no known cognitive activity that can claim this. Fred Gage, a neurobiologist and geneticist at the world-renowned Salk Institute in La Jolla, California (1999), says that regular exercise may stimulate the growth of new brain cells and prolong the survival of existing cells. In describing the results of studies in this area, Gage calls the differences between the exercisers and non exercisers, "striking."

Researchers James Pollatschek, PhD. and Frank Hagen, PhD. say, "Children engaged in daily physical education show superior motor fitness, academic performance, and attitude toward school as compared to their non-exercising counterparts." University of Nebraska researcher Richard Dienstbier, PhD. (1989) says that aerobic and other forms of "toughening exercises" can have lasting mental benefits. The secret, he says, is that physical exercise alone seems to "train a quick adrenaline-noradrenaline response and rapid recovery." In other words, by working out your body, your brain will also become more adept at responding to mental challenges. Moderate amounts of exercise, "three times a week, twenty minutes a day, can have very beneficial effects," he adds.

Neuroscientists at University of California, Irvine discovered that exercise triggers the release of BDNF, a brain-derived neurotrophic factor. This natural substance enhances cognition by boosting the ability of neurons to communicate with each other. When the Irvine researchers examined aging rats that had exercised daily on a running wheel, they found elevated BDNF levels in various areas of the brain, including the hippocampus which is critical for memory processing. BDNF has been shown to accelerate the development of long-term potentiation (LTP) or memory formation in young rats. When researchers bred mice that lacked the BDNF gene, they found that the animals had markedly reduced LTP in the hippocampus. They were then able to correct the defect by reintroducing the BDNF gene into hippocampal neurons in these mice. "Our findings have potential implications for improving learning and memory in young animals and children," said researcher Bai Lu from the National Institute of Child Health and Human Development. Ira Black, a researcher at the Robert Wood Johnson Medical School, and colleagues who discovered the potential effects of BDNF on LTP, believe that the findings also offer new possibilities for studying and treating memory deficits in disorders such as Alzheimer's disease.

In another study, a Utah psychologist Robert Dustman, PhD. (1990), divided subjects into three categories: vigorous aerobic exercisers, moderate non-aerobic exercisers, and total non exercisers. The results supported findings from similar studies. The aerobic exercisers showed an improvement in short-term memory, faster reaction times, and were more creative than the non aerobic exercisers. Perhaps the most dramatic results were experienced in the Vanves and Blanshard projects in Canada, which revealed that when physical education was increased to one-third of the school day, academic scores increased.

Beyond this, since exercise can reduce stress, an ultimate fringe benefit exists, as well. Thus, physical exercise is still one of the best ways to stimulate the brain and boost learning.

Be purposeful about integrating movement activities into everyday learning. Provide much more than mere hands-on activities. Facilitate daily stretching exercises, walk and talks, dancing, role playing, seat-changing, quick energizers, and movement games. The whole notion of using only logical thinking in a mathematics class flies in the face of current brain research. Brain-compatible learning means weaving math, movement, geography, social skills, role-playing, science, and physical education together.

How Physical Activity Boosts Learning

Exercise does several things for the brain. First, it enhances circulation so that individual neurons can get more oxygen and nutrients. Second, it may spur the production of a hormone NGF (nerve growth factor) that enhances brain function. Third, gross motor repetitive movements can stimulate the production of dopamine, a mood-enhancing neurotransmitter.

"Aerobic exercise can definitely improve thinking and learning," says Dienstbier (1989) because, he adds, "it alone seems to train a quick adrenaline-noradrenaline response and rapid recovery." This adrenal response is critical to facing and coping with challenges. Ned Herrmann, PhD. (1988) suggests that even a brisk twenty-minute walk can be enough to serve both the body and the mind. "The main thing is to get out and move your body around," he states.

Why Play Belongs in Learning

While it's counterproductive to make play *more* important than academic subject matter, movement must become *as honorable and important* as the so-called "book work." Hopefully, we can better allocate our resources in ways that harness the hidden power of movement, activities, and sports. One of the most powerful reasons to engage learners in purposeful play is biological: All mammals engage in play. The play is a way to learn behaviors in a non-threatening way. Lion cubs will wrestle with each other in playful fighting; and as they grow the moves they learned with their cute playmates translate to survival skills. Similarly, when humans engage in play, it allows us to learn motor, emotional, social, and cognitive skills in an environment that can sustain a less-than-perfect learning performance.

What This Means to You

There are plenty of ways for learners to learn skills in playful formats. The games that others think are too loose, nonacademic, or unstructured may be the very games that learners need most. Integrate fact learning with games such as tag, ball toss, dodgeball, cooperative games, "New Games" and drama activities. In addition, there is intrinsic value in sports, puppets, dancing, role-plays, acting, impromptus, and simulations. Never assume that your learners will get sufficient exercise elsewhere. At the very least, encourage physical activity for your learners away from the classroom; and if possible, offer a few moments of stretching or deep breathing in class to increase all-around productivity.

Stimulation of Body and Mind

Apparently, if you don't want to lose your marbles, you'd better use them throughout your life. French researcher and neuroepidemiologist Jean-Francois Dartigues (1994) says that non-intellectuals are more likely to face senility later in life. Dartigues did a study of 3,700 people over the age of 65 in which he correlated their intellectual functioning with their former occupations. Then he adjusted for variables such as age, sex, and even environmental and toxic risks. He found that the subjects who performed best on the tests were not those with the greatest formal education, but those who had the most intellectually demanding careers.

In Dartigues's study, after retiring, former farm workers were *over six times more likely to become mentally impaired* than those who were in more intellectual occupations, such as teachers, trainers, executives, managers, and other white collar professionals (see figure 12.4). But for farm managers, whose job forced more challenging thinking, the rate was only 2.9 times that of intellectual occupations.

Figure 12.4
Affects of Challenging vs. Non-Challenging Occupations on Mental Impairment

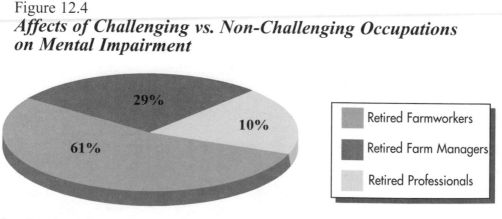

Nobel laureate Eric Kandel and neuroscientist Michael Merzenich studied the effects of digital manipulation on the brain of an owl monkey with interesting results. The monkey was provided with manipulatives for an hour a day for three months, while the scientists carefully measured and recorded the areas of the brain that related to the particular digits the monkey was restricted to using. When the contrasting effects of the digits *not* used for manipulation were compared to those that were, the scientists discovered a substantial increase in size and neural connections within the brain areas related to the digits used in the daily manipulations, demonstrating that physical activity can physically alter brain tissue.

For a human example, consider how a high proportion of concert pianists stay mentally sharp and verbally articulate well into old age. Some speculate that the long-term stimulation of the fingers seems to stimulate the mind. Elderly individuals who play cards, chess, or shuffleboard regularly also have a greater chance of staying sharp longer than those who engage only in gross motor activities, such as walking or jogging.

 ## What This Means to You

- Use more slow stretching and breathing exercises to increase circulation and oxygen flow to the brain.
- Incorporate energizers every twenty minutes or so.
- Make sure that some of your planned activities have a built-in component of physical movement (going outside to do a project, working on jigsaw puzzles, etc.).
- Provide manipulatives: Have students hold, mold, and manipulate clay or other objects.
- Give learners permission to get up without permission, to move around, stretch, or change postures, so that they can monitor and manage their own energy levels.
- Facilitate hand movements each day with clapping games, dancing, puzzles, and manipulatives. Invent new ways to shake hands or greet each other.
- Engage learners in cooperative activities and group work.
- Provide activities that offer varying levels of physical and mental challenge with plenty of feedback mechanisms for support.
- Offer novel activities, learning locations, and choices that require moving.
- Encourage student-generated learning goals, ideas, and experiences.

Physiology and Learner Posture Affect Thinking

Teachers have long intuited that a slumped over student is probably learning less than an alert one in an upright posture. But how direct is the link between learning and a student's physiology? "The human body, as represented in the brain is the indispensable frame of reference for the neural processes we call thinking," says Antonio Damasio (1994). "It is, in fact, the one grounding reference point of reality for our ability to make sense of the world."

The research of Max Vercruyssen, PhD. of the University of Southern California suggests that blood flow and oxygen to the brain are partly responsible for the posture effect on learning. He found that when subjects were asked to stand, their heartrate increased by ten beats per minute on average. As a result more blood goes to the brain, thereby activating the central nervous system to increase neural firing. Standing up, he concludes, creates more attentional arousal, speeds up information processing by 5 to 20 percent, and increases blood flow and oxygen to the brain by 10 to 15 percent.

> *Standing students are likely to be more alert and ready to learn, as their quickened heartrate supports greater blood flow and oxygen to the brain.*

The human brain, which thrives on oxygen, may in many instances be starved for it in the classroom! Researchers at a Florida University found that dolphins (oxygen breathing mammals) exchange nearly 90 percent of their lung's capacity each time they surface for a breath. Thus, most of their "stale" air is exchanged with fresh oxygen. When you compare this to human studies that suggest learners generally only exchange 10 to 25 percent of their lung's capacity with each breath in an enclosed classroom, one can begin to conjecture the consequences. Oxygen-starved students are likely to feel sleepy, as evidenced by their posture.

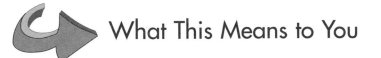

What This Means to You

We are *not* wasting precious learning time by including physical education and movement activities in our lesson plans. Rather, we *are* wasting time by having students sit too much. When energy lags, have learners stand up while you continue to talk for a few minutes. Then facilitate a diffusion activity or energizer, or ask them to start a relevant discussion with a partner. Once their attentional systems have been reactivated, allow them the choice of sitting or standing.

How Relaxation and Stress Affect Learning

In a study of thirty-nine older adults conducted at Stanford University, School of Medicine, researchers determined that a memory training course was more effective when students were relaxed. The study compared two groups. The first was taught to relax every muscle in their body, from head to toe, prior to the memory training. The other group was simply given a lecture on positive attitudes. Both groups then attended a three-hour memory training course and were ultimately tested on what they learned. The overall score of the group that received the relaxation instruction was 25 percent higher than the control group.

Although moderate (and learner-controlled) stress is known to be conducive to new learning, at the other end of the relaxation continuum, trauma or long-term high stress, is known to be detrimental. Threats, even in the form of a simple negative remark, can affect our physiology and impact attitude, motivation, and learning. The reptilian portion of our brain is designed to respond quickly to threats, and in so doing, everything else becomes secondary. Teacher threats are not uncommon in the school environment. They can be so subtle, in fact, that only the non-conscious mind reacts.

> *"I'll just stand here and wait until YOU decide you're ready to learn!"*

The above thinly disguised threat implies disapproval, and smacks of control. "I'll withhold my wisdom, class progress, and test information *until* you behave the way I want you to behave." Threats like these negatively impact learning over time, and reduce the teacher-student relationship to one that resembles a master-servant arrangement.

What This Means to You

Reduce or eliminate threats. Physical relaxation may be more important to learning than previously realized. Teach your students about the benefits of relaxation. Better yet, make it part of the daily routine.

The Contributions of James Asher

To millions of teachers around the world who are pleading with students to *please sit down and be quiet*, James Asher is a rebel. A pioneer in second-language learning and the developer of the Total Physical Response (TPR) approach, Asher maintains that learning on an immediate, physical, and gut level speeds acquisition dramatically (1986). Asher's hypothesis is "teach the body; it learns as well as the mind." To use his approach successfully, the following conditions are recommended:

▼ **The teacher creates a strong positive rapport and relationship with students.**

▼ **The learning climate is cooperative, playful, active, and fun.**

▼ **The teacher establishes an environment of mutual respect.**

▼ **Imperative instructions are given to students in a commanding, but gentle manner.**

▼ **The students respond rapidly without analyzing the input.**

Asher's TPR approach associates a body movement with new learning. In teaching Spanish, for example, Asher might simply stand up, and verbalize the Spanish word for "stand." Then he might touch his knee and say the word in Spanish; or tell his students to follow him while he walks around the room and repeats the Spanish word for walk. The approach is very natural, much like how a parent teaches an infant. Although, Asher created the approach for teaching languages, it is transferable to other subjects, as well. For example, it can help learners remember vocabulary words, spelling, geography, science concepts, social studies, collaboration skills, and math formulas.

What This Means to You

Associate new learning with various physical movements. Draw from the dramatic arts, the fine arts, music/band, and sports. Engage your class in regular role playing, charades, games, and movement activities. Students can organize extemporaneous pantomimes to dramatize a key point. Incorporate overviews of future learning or reviews of past learning in one-minute commercials adapted from popular television advertisements.

Energizer Ideas

▼ Use the body to measure things around the room and report the results: "This cabinet is 99 knuckles long".

▼ Play a Simon Says game with content built into the game: "Simon says point to the South; or Simon says point to five different sources of information in this room."

▼ Do a giant class mind-map or break into teams and do group mind-maps.

▼ Have students move around the room, like a scavenger hunt. "Get up and touch seven objects around the room that represent the visible spectrum or colors of the rainbow."

▼ Relate locations to new learning. For example, ask students to "move to the side of the room where you first learned about the food chain related to our pet snake."

▼ Conduct thinking games and values exercises that require learners to move. For example, ask learners to "move to the left side of the room if they feel more like an ant or to the right side of the room if they feel more like an elephant."

▼ Even simple games we learned as children are great. Have learners jump rope and sing rhymes that reflect new learning.

▼ Spell difficult words to the old tune of B-I-N-G-O while clapping out each letter until the whole word is spelled.

▼ Wake the class up with a silly stint of Hokie Pokie, Ring Around the Rosie, or London Bridges. Even adults can benefit from these childhood favorites.

Energizer Ideas Continued

▼ Conduct a ball toss game and incorporate content from prior learning. Great for reviews, vocabulary-reinforcement, storytelling, or self-disclosure.

▼ Have students rewrite lyrics to familiar songs substituting new words.

▼ Play verbal Tug of War, where dyads choose a topic from a list and each must devise an argument. After the verbal competition, the whole class engages in a traditional game of tug of war with dyad partners on opposite sides.

▼ Use Cross-laterals, such as arm and leg cross-overs. Cross-lateral movements activate both brain hemispheres for greater integration of learning. "Pat your head and rub your belly; or touch your left shoulder with your right hand" are examples of cross-laterals. Others include marching in place while patting opposite knees, touching opposite eyes, knees, elbows, heels, etc.

▼ Facilitate stretching and breathing exercises. Rotate leaders.

▼ Provide frequent breaks for water or walking around; or open up this option for learners anytime they need it.

▼ Ask the students to plan and lead a class session or break into teams and have each present an activity to the rest of the class.

Reflection Questions

1. What from this chapter was novel, fresh, or new to you? What was familiar or "old hat"?

2. In what ways, do you already apply the information in this chapter?

3. What three questions might you now generate about this material?

4. How did you react emotionally to the information in this chapter?

5. How did you react cognitively to the information? Do you agree or disagree with the author's point of view? Why?

6. In what ways might you translate the principles presented in this chapter into practical everyday useful ideas?

7. If these things are, in fact, true about the brain, what should we do differently? What resources of time, people, and money could be redirected? In what ways might you suggest we start doing this?

8. What were the most interesting insights you gained from this material?

9. If you were to plan your next step for making your curriculum more brain-based, what would that be?

10. What obstacles might you encounter? How might you realistically deal with them?

Enhancing Cognition

Environment

Will and Volition

Life Experience

Genes

Lifestyle Choices

Teaching Thinking

Chaos and Confusion Valuable to Learner

What Exactly Is Thinking Anyway?

Eye Movements and Thinking

Questions Promote Better Learning

Answer Patterns Provide Thinking Clues

The Value of Discussions

Brain Activated By Problem Solving

Competitive or Cooperative Learning

The Role of Intuition

13

Enhancing Cognition

Problem solving is a survival imperative. In history, those most skilled in problem solving flourished, while the less skilled perished. The motivation to learn
that which is necessary for survival is intrinsic. Teachers can capitalize on this
natural aptitude by explicitly focusing on the related attributes of good problem
solvers, primarily critical thinking skills. Fortunately, nature does some of the work
for us, but there's still a great deal we can do in the classroom to ensure learners
develop high-level thinking skills. Let's start with a review of some of the primary
factors that influence thinking or cognition.

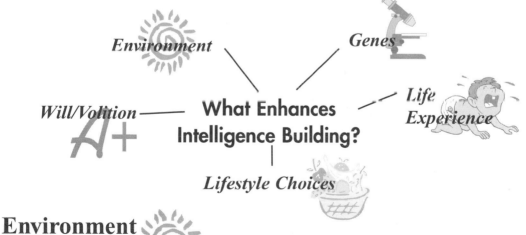

Environment

A challenging environment forces the brain to flex its thinking "muscles." Intrinsic
motivation kicks in as we effort towards reversing the uncomfortable biochemical
state called stress. On the other hand, when the body reaches the biochemical state of
balance called homeostasis, motivation to achieve classically drops. When an environment provides an equal amount of challenge and stress with empowerment and
support, you get an ideal learning situation whereby progress proceeds most rapidly.

We've seen this principle in operation many times over as communities join together to rebuild after a major catastrophe. Or consider how quickly New York City grew around the turn of the century when inundated with new immigrants. Faced with overcrowded conditions, a massive effort was mobilized to expand the city's infrastructure and relieve some stress. While workers gained new skills at an unprecedented rate, the stress/success/empowerment loop propelled further development; and one of the world's greatest cities was born.

We know that the under-challenged learner may relieve boredom with disruptive behavior, while the overly-challenged learner is likely to feel defeated and withdraw unless some resolution or success is achieved. Resting precariously between these two critical points is the magic learning moment. As presented in Chapter 5: Optimal Environments and Chapter 9: Attentional States, we also know that teachers who provide a safe and challenging environment, while staying attuned to learner states and responding appropriately to them, facilitate a great number of teachable moments.

Will and Volition

Riding closely on the heels of the environment factor is the motivation factor, also known as will or volition. Really the two are inseparable. When an environment is conducive to learning, positive motivation naturally follows. However, when daily life is unchallenging (or dysfunctional in some other way), even the brightest learner can end up squandering their intellectual potential. Until a person gets motivated to use and enhance their cognitive skills, they are likely to remain ensconced and stagnant in their relative comfort. The best way to strengthen learner motivation is to provide meaningfulness, learner choices, and emotional support while affirming the individual.

Life Experience

The emerging brain research has provided good evidence that our brain is biologically molded by life experiences—most especially in infancy. At birth we immediately begin experiencing basic needs (or problems), which are either met or not. The baby who wails with hunger, for example, and is promptly satisfied with a feeding, experiences a deep sense of success. The ignored baby, on the other hand, experiences a poignant sense of failure. Multiplied a thousand times in a few years, we soon begin to behave in ways that reflect this fundamental "programming." Influenced strongly by our sense of personal power or (all too often) sense of powerlessness, our life experiences build upon one another, usually reinforcing our early programming.

Genes

Although the nature versus nurture debate has reigned for years, the current cognitive science and neuroscience research suggests that both positions are correct. As previously pointed out, life experiences most certainly impact cognitive responses. Our genes, however, influence such things as alertness, memory, and sensory acuity, as well—all significant intelligence factors. Consider, for example, how rare it is for parents with very low IQs to produce offspring with very high IQs. Nevertheless, genes alone do not account for genius-level IQs. Thus, we begin to see the interrelated nature of these influences.

Lifestyle Choices

Cognitive enrichment possibilities are ever inherent in our daily decisions—from the foods we eat and people we socialize with to the amount of physical and mental exercise and sleep we get. Our brain, like our body, is either nurtured or neglected by our actions. Poor nutrition, lack of mental or physical challenge, abuse of drugs and alcohol, repeated blows to the head, and extreme stress are cognitive killers. Although we lose brain cells every day, emerging brain research suggests that we may also generate new cells. Neuroscientist Fred Gage and colleagues at the Salk Institute in San Diego report (Van Pragg, et al. 1999), that new brain cells generated in exercising mice are in fact functional neurons that boost the rodents' cognitive skills. "What I find most exciting, Gage concludes "is that taken together, the studies suggest that throughout one's life, one's behavior can change the structure of the brain, and that these changes can in turn affect how we behave in our environment."

Figure 13.1
Cognitive Development Timeline

Abstractions
Skills develop from 10-20 years

Representations
Skills develop from 2-7 years

Actions
Skills develop from 3-13 months

Reflexes
Skills develop from 3-11 weeks

Although the developmental stages highlighted in figure 13.1 vary from individual to individual depending on the related factors previously mentioned, in general our cognitive development proceeds along a predictable timeline. At birth, we possess only reflexes, but babies are quick learners. The development of basic skills generally takes place within three to eleven weeks; and in three to thirteen months, the infant becomes capable of basic actions, such as putting food in their mouth or taking a blanket off of themselves. Until this time, however, babies have only the basic cognitive capabilities exhibited by non-human primates.

The toddler soon develops, however, the basic representational framework that accompanies language development and sets humans apart in the primate world. Skills accompanying this stage include identifying objects and locations, consciously using body language to make a point, drawing cause and effect conclusions, imagining scenarios, and verbalizing their needs and feelings with words.

The peak of the cognitive path—abstract thinking—however, is not reached until the later elementary to high-school grade levels. Abstract thinking is reflected in such tasks as identifying universal truths, beauty, ethical dilemmas, and cultural frameworks. By adulthood most of us possess fully matured frontal lobes, the area of the brain thought largely responsible for this highest form of cognition.

> *Being especially good at problem solving does not guarantee success in life; but being especially poor at it practically guarantees failure.*

Teaching Thinking

Can intelligent thinking be taught? Absolutely yes. It not only can be taught, it is a fundamental part of the essential skills package necessary for success in today's world. A primary focus on creativity, life skills, and problem solving makes the teaching of thinking meaningful and productive for learners. These aspects of intelligence, though long undervalued in the traditional school setting, play an important role in intelligence. The following list offers a breakdown of some of the skills that ought to be emphasized at the abstractions level of development in the teaching of problem solving and critical thinking:

▼ **Gathering information and utilizing resources**

▼ **Developing flexibility in form and style**

▼ **Asking high-quality questions**

▼ **Weighing evidence before drawing conclusions**

▼ **Using metaphors and models**

▼ **Conceptualizing strategies (mind-mapping, pros and cons lists, outlines, etc.)**

▼ **Dealing productively with ambiguity, differences, and novelty**

▼ **Generating possibilities and probabilities (brainstorming, formulas, surveys, cause and effect)**

▼ Debate and discussion skills

▼ Identifying mistakes, discrepancies, and illogic

▼ Examining alternative approaches (shifting frame of reference, thinking out of the box, etc.)

▼ Hypotheses-testing strategies

▼ Developing objectivity

▼ Generalization and pattern detection (identifying and organizing information, translating information, cross-over applications)

▼ Sequencing events

> *While the intellect asks, "Is it possible?" Only intelligence asks the question, "Is it appropriate?"*

What This Means to You

From a brain-based perspective, the most effective way to teach thinking skills is to incorporate real-world problems under authentic (or simulated) conditions. With young children simple games can produce a suitable environment for teaching thinking. With adolescents, sharing our own thinking processes, working through personal challenges with them, assigning complex, group-oriented projects, and analyzing case studies, are all excellent ways to instill thinking skills. Most importantly, at any level, model high-level thinking. That is, verbalize your own thinking process as you weigh evidence, consider ramifications, and make decisions.

The specific strategies listed on the following page are flexible enough to be modified for various age groups and learning environments.

Problem-Solving Strategies

▼ "Reframe" a problem so that it is not a problem.

▼ Discover the course of the problem so as to prevent reoccurrence.

▼ Adjust your attitude to deal with life's difficulties.

▼ Consider how process impacts results.

▼ Analyze and discuss thinking (metacognition).

▼ Use various styles and models of thinking.

▼ Exhibit how your thinking skills add value and joy to your life.

▼ Apply your thinking skills so as to enhance the lives of others.

▼ Assign or read stories imbued with personal meaning—literally the oldest strategy "in the book."

▼ Assign team projects; and incorporate a metacognition component (i.e., have team members keep a journal of the issues, challenges, and decisions faced and how they're resolved.

▼ Facilitate a group discussion where you role model (and/or comment on) higher-order thinking skills.

▼ Think out loud.

▼ Solve a problem or case study together using brainstorming, discussion, deduction, and decision-making skills.

▼ Set up debates between students or teams of students; and have them comment on the process.

▼ Put each learner in the role of teacher. Provide plenty of support and personal choice in the process.

▼ In groups of three, learners are given the opportunity to play the role of listener, talker, and reviewer respectively while discussing a problem. The reviewer provides feedback to talker and listener before exchanging roles.

▼ Assign projects that require reflection and personal expression.

▼ Take on class projects that benefit the school or community and require students to use a wide range of real-life skills.

▼ Require learners to make mind-maps or graphic organizers that reflect models or ways of thinking, patterns, sequences, and levels of detail.

▼ Honor the individual's feelings. Feelings are neither intangible or elusive, but rather a very real and legitimate part of the thinking process.

The following excerpt, also from *Turning Learning Inside Out* (Leff and Levin 1994), reflects a brain-based learning environment where encouraging the use of thinking skills is one of the teacher's primary objectives:

Fletch Coolidge asks his high school science class to brainstorm a list of world problems. Working in small study groups, they narrow the list to ten. Then they brainstorm how the science topic of the week (weather) could impact, illuminate, or solve the problems. Overpopulation would be impacted by a natural weather disaster or flooding could slow down tanks in a war. The class discusses these impacts. Then other academic areas are discussed and their relationship to the topic of the week. Does physical education relate to an army at war? How about home economics or math? Finally, students are asked to take these concepts home for discussion with their family and the assess the personal impact.

Chaos and Confusion Valuable to Learner

The behaviorist model of teaching (reward-punishment) with an emphasis on an orderly sequential delivery system has been the norm of classroom teaching for decades. The brain-based model of teaching, however, subscribes to a more real-life approach that is less rule based and more discovery based. A little suspense, surprise, disequilibrium, uncertainty, and some disorder (also known as challenge), can go a long way in producing a higher level of intrinsic motivation in students, report Howard Gardner, PhD. (1993) and Robert Sternberg, PhD. (1994).

Most of the time our brain simply runs stored "programs." This, however, is not learning, but replication. Only when we are stopped in our tracks by a problem or situation that forces us to think or rethink is there the possibility of new learning. This impasse is the opportunity to make progress; and our brain approaches it one of three ways: It either retreats to a tried and true method, which probably doesn't facilitate new learning; or it nibbles into new territory; or it radically reorganizes itself for the task, says Thomas Kuhn, author of *The Structure of Scientific Revolutions* (1996).

If some instability creates purposeful activity and direction, perhaps our orderly time-sequenced lesson plans need a makeover. Does this mean we should throw away our lesson planning altogether then? Hardly! Paradoxically, routine and ritual are necessary for optimal learning, as they balance out the chaos and uncertainty. Again, it is the precarious balance between the two points that support the teachable moment. Teachers who create sloppy lessons with scattered thinking and poor preparation will get rebellion. The brain-based model does not encourage lack of organization. Rather, the model suggests less teacher control and rigidity; and an orchestrated learning environment reinforced by solid organization, positive rituals, and infused with choice, novelty, and challenge.

Figure 13.2
Ritual vs. Novelty Comparisons

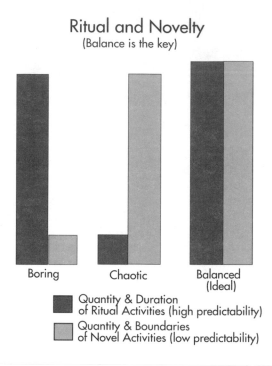

Some educators have dubbed this approach "positive dissatisfaction" or "controlled frustration" (Pogrow 1994). And besides getting engaged learners with significant gains in traditional academic subjects, the technique seems to encourage quality thinking, patience, and mental toughness. To exemplify the concept, let's pretend you have a few learners working together on team project when an interpersonal conflict erupts. Rather than intervening to solve the immediate quarrel, you challenge and support the learners to work through their conflict. You can suggest some strategies for doing this, but you allow the momentum of the controlled frustration to propel the learners towards resolution and the satisfaction of using their own problem-solving abilities.

What This Means to You

We need to allow for more variety and real-life problem-solving in our learning contexts. This does not mean that we should embrace thoughtless chaos, but rather that we should encourage a sort of "orchestrated disequilibrium" more frequently. Utilize learner-generated role-playing, meaningful group projects, simulation games and activities, experiments, field trips, and guest participants for deeper learning. Allow learners the space to work through their problems in a safe and supportive environment. Minimize unnecessary interventions and time constraints that take away from authentic problem solving.

What Exactly is Thinking Anyway?

When we say, "I am thinking," what we are really saying is, I'm trying to manipulate internal symbols in a meaningful way. Thinking is a process whereby the brain accesses prior representations for understanding or creates a new model if one does not exist. The following categories represent some of these modes of representational thinking.

1. *Symbolic Language*
Includes pictures, symbols, sounds, words, or "internal movies." This also includes verbal expression, music, or technological communications, such as computer programming languages.

2. *Indirect Knowledge*
Includes mental models, procedural thinking, physical patterns, and other implicit knowledge, such as feelings. How you feel about something or having a sense about something plays a large role in the decision-making process.

3. *Direct Sensations*
Includes touch, natural sounds, scenes, and the experience of nature.

When we break thinking down into the above three categories, we see how difficult it is to measure it. Our mind, body, and feelings are all involved. There is no separation. Knowing this, it will be no surprise to you to hear that *how* we are thinking can be discerned by observing the body. When we are tense or happy, nothing necessarily has to be said for another to interpret our thinking. Our eyes, also, offer valuable clues as to our thinking.

Eye Movements and Thinking

As illustrated in figure 13.3, there are seven basic eye movements that relate to thinking. The best way to determine the particular eye (and thinking) pattern for a learner is to observe that person in a real-life no stress situation. Controlled, laboratory testing has yielded inconsistent results, but the real-world relationship between eye movements and cognitive functioning has been well documented. Cognitive activity occurring in one hemisphere *triggers* eye movements in the opposite hemisphere.

1. *Visual thinking of stored picture memories:* Looking up and to the left allows one to access stored pictures (visual recall). Questions to ask yourself for verification: What car was parked next to yours in the parking lot? Describe your bedroom. Walk me through the clothes in your closet.

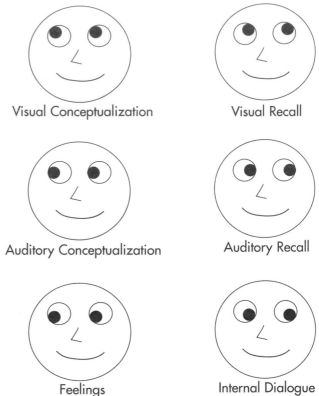

Figure 13.3
Eye Movements and Thinking

Visual Conceptualization

Visual Recall

Auditory Conceptualization

Auditory Recall

Feelings

Internal Dialogue

2. *Visual thinking of created new pictures:* Looking up and to the right is where your eyes usually go to create new images. Questions to ask yourself for verification: How would you look with a radically different haircut? What can you do to rearrange your living room? What would a dog look like with cat's legs?

3. *Auditory thinking and recalling sounds:* Eyes go to the left to access stored sounds (what was said or heard). Questions you can ask yourself for verification: What did the other person say as you concluded your last phone conversation? What's the ninth word of the Happy Birthday song? As a child, how did your mother call your name when she was mad at you?

4. *Auditory thinking and creating new sounds:* Eyes go off to the right to create new sounds. Questions you can ask yourself for verification: How would a dog sound if it had a voice like a pig? What sound would you get if you heard a siren and a rooster at the same time?"

5. *Internal dialogue (talking to yourself):* Eyes most commonly move downward and to the left. Notice others' eyes as they walk down the street alone.

6. *Experiencing feelings:* Eyes go down and to the right. Try it. Ask someone about something which you know they have strong feelings about.

7. *Automatic responses:* Eyes look straight ahead when no thinking is necessary, as when verbalizing an automatic response. For example, when asked "How are you?" Your polite answer, "fine, thank you" does not require a search through your brain for the answer.

> *Eye movements facilitate the processing*
> *and retrieval of information to and from the brain.*

With learners who are having trouble spelling, for example, the following strategies can better hook the brain:

1. *Access feelings with regard to the word:* Start with eyes looking down.
2. *Visualize the image of the word:* Move eyes up and to the right.
3. *Cement a word in auditory memory:* Say the letters while looking to the right.
4. *Cement a word kinesthetically:* Trace the letters of it with your finger.
5. *Recall a stored image of the word:* Close eyes and look to the left.
6. *Write out the correct spelling on paper:* Review it and look up to the left.
7. *To cement the success:* Look down to the right and celebrate the feeling of empowerment.

 ## What This Means to You

When you post students' work up on bulletin boards, put it low if you want to access feelings; head high if you want to facilitate discussion; or overhead if you want them to store the visual images in memory. When you present new material, stand to the right of learners (on the right side of the classroom from *their* point of view). When you review, stand to the left of learners (from their point of view). This simple strategy enables learners to process and access the new information more efficiently. At test time, if you tell students to keep their eyes on their own paper, their ability to access information in their brain may be thwarted. As an alternative, have students spread out. This lowers everyone's stress levels.

Questions Promote Better Learning

Since moving our eyes around helps us access information from our memory, we can learn about students' cognition process by asking questions and observing their eyes. Asking questions also elicits deeper thinking than providing mere answers. When we are asked a question that requires a yes or no answer, our brain surprisingly continues, nonconsciously, to process alternatives to the answer. Thus, questions generate sustained enriching brain activity.

Naturally, the better the quality of the question, the more the brain is challenged to think. This strategy, long ago dubbed The Socratic Method, may have more than history going for it; it may actually be best for the brain. In-depth questions activate more of the brain. And the more of the brain that's activated, the more likely retrieval will be. Instead of asking, for example, "What is it called when things keep falling back towards the earth?" Ask a more meaningful question, such as "What would life be like on earth without gravity; and could we survive?"

When we reframe and restate concepts into questions, we encourage a free flow of creativity and critical thinking. Let's say, for example, you've asked your class to design a clock with no moving parts and no face. Although they discuss the matter briefly, they are stumped and inform you it can't be done. Rather than simply imparting the information that they've neglected, ask them some important questions. For example, "There are many ways we communicate in the world, what are they? And how do you suspect the ancients told time?" Now with some more food for thought, the class is able to solve the problem, and confidence soars.

Answer Patterns Provide Thinking Clues

Another benefit of question asking is that we can analyze wrong answers and discover meaningful information. Often wrong answers fit a pattern and reveal something important about the process. If you only listen, however, for the expected answer, you are likely to miss out on the more interpretive and qualitative possibilities.

> *"Profoundly informed people often read more ambiguity into a question than is intended."*
>
> —J. W. Powell

This student, for example, may score lower on a multiple-choice exam than accurately reflects his/her knowledge. On such a test, there is no room for further elucidation or explanation. Their answers reflect, perhaps, a more profound understanding of the topic than the single answer possibility allows.

Here is another example that illustrates how prescribed answers can be mismeasured or underestimated by the unthinking teacher: A physics teacher includes a test question that reads, "Using a barometer, how can you tell the height of a building?" The answer the teacher is looking for is, "measure and compare the air pressure at the bottom of the building and at the top; then use a prescribed formula to compute the difference." The student, however, who provides a different (although perfectly legitimate) answer is not given credit for his/her problem-solving abilities. This error in our own thinking teaches learners to regurgitate the prescribed answers, rather than to rely and build on their own unlimited thinking powers. Give it a try. Can you think of an alternative answer for the problem?

Did you consider any of the following possibilities? Or did you come up with a completely different solution? 1) Tie a string onto the barometer and throw it out the top of the building. Then when it lands, measure the length of the string needed; 2) On a sunny day, use the shadow cast by the barometer and the building as a comparison and compute the ratio; 3) Go to the stairwell of the building and using the barometer as a ruler, count how many times you need to flip it end-over-end to get to the top. Then multiply that number by the length of the barometer; 4) Take the barometer to the building inspector, engineer or architect and offer to trade the barometer for the exact height of the building... etc. You get the idea!

 ## What This Means to You

We have been missing out on a huge opportunity for learning about our learners by asking too few questions and giving too many answers. So-called wrong answers can supply us with valuable information about the teaching and learning experience of an individual or group. Provide self-assessment opportunities to engage thinking skills. Allow learners the opportunity to share and shape their discoveries rather than always being evaluated and told what is right and wrong. Predetermined questions and answers can limit risk taking, critical thinking, and higher-level problem-solving.

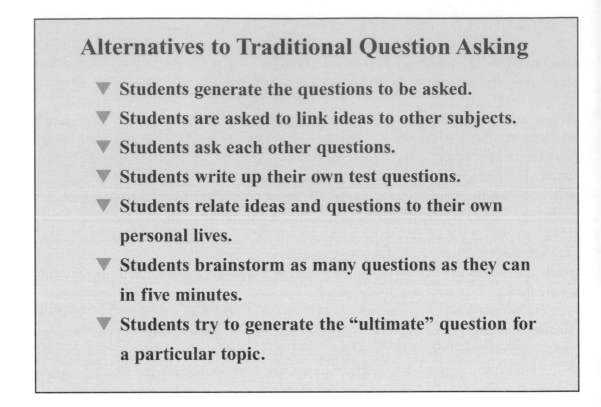

Alternatives to Traditional Question Asking

▼ Students generate the questions to be asked.

▼ Students are asked to link ideas to other subjects.

▼ Students ask each other questions.

▼ Students write up their own test questions.

▼ Students relate ideas and questions to their own personal lives.

▼ Students brainstorm as many questions as they can in five minutes.

▼ Students try to generate the "ultimate" question for a particular topic.

The more we discover about learning and the brain, the more it becomes evident that our old "factory-model" of teaching has done a great disservice to the magnificent minds with which learners come to us. We are given as educators, budding Einsteins, Mozarts, Robert Frosts, and Helen Kellers, but traditional teaching methods often turn them into bored, frustrated, and disillusioned dropouts who never get a chance to experience their own greatness.

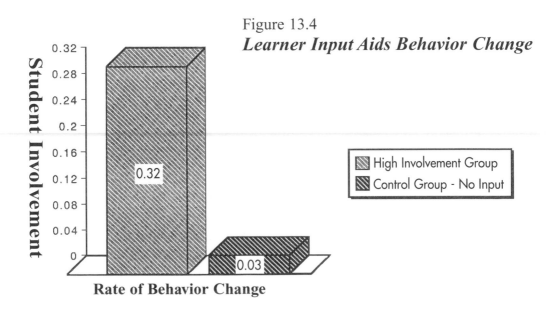

Figure 13.4
Learner Input Aids Behavior Change

High Involvement Group
Control Group - No Input

Student Involvement

Rate of Behavior Change

The Value of Discussions

Dr. Lewin, while conducting USDA experiments, discovered that learners are more likely to integrate new learning and implement changes when lecture is followed by discussion. One study compared the results of a group of students who were given a lecture and then allowed to leave (the control group) with a group of learners who were given a lecture and then asked to discuss it (the treatment group). The results revealed a three percent change in behavior in the control group compared to a 32 percent rate of change in the treatment group's behavior. While this study speaks to the importance of discussion in the learning environment, it also underscores the importance of participants making the learning *their own*.

Traditionally class time (at least at the upper levels) has consisted of a teacher lecturing for forty-five minutes until the bell rings, at which time students jump up and make their way to their next class. Brain-based learning advocates a brief lecture or presentation, a chunk of time for discussion, a reflection exercise, and a confirmation of the learning. The rhythm is more like this: Share information, problem solve, discover, discuss, then confirm.

 ## What This Means to You

Teaching more or faster is not the solution. The problem is that the learners have not *made the information their own*. Group discussions provide time to integrate, trouble-shoot, and "buy-in" to the new learning. Provide consistent opportunities for learners to stop and discuss what they have learned. Let them talk about how it might affect them personally and what they can do about it. Brief discussions can be just as powerful as long ones.

Brain Activated By Problem Solving

University of Wisconsin psychology professor Dr. Denney says that "problem-solving is to the brain what aerobic exercise is to the body. It creates a virtual explosion of activity, causing synapses to form, neurotransmitters to activate, and blood flow to increase." Her studies suggest that the brain that is worked out with mental weights, remains younger, smarter, and more creative longer in life. Especially good for the brain are challenging, novel, and complex tasks that require intense thinking and multi-tasking (doing more than one type of thinking at a time).

At Harvard University, a researcher conducted a study of the elderly. First he divided them into two groups. One group was asked to sit and reminisce about the old days, when they were younger. The other group was asked to play act, pretending to be in the year 1959. They listened to old radio programs, watched old speeches, watched old TV shows, and did activities they used to do. They acted, thought, talked, and role-played as if they were years younger. The results were spectacular. After just one week, the role-playing group showed a dramatic increase in their scores on intelligence and reaction times. The other group showed no improvement.

Marian Diamond, PhD. (1988) reminds us that boredom is a serious problem. She cites rat studies that show boredom does more harm to the brain than enrichment does good! Withdrawal from the world and reduction of stimulation most certainly contribute to senility and depression, while activity and challenge promotes health and well being.

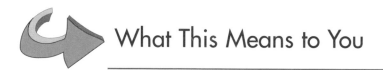 ## What This Means to You

Our traditional system does not teach learners to think. Learners who spend all of their free time "doing nothing" can get out of shape—not just physically, but mentally. Television is not exercise; active thinking and problem-solving is. We, as instructional leaders, have to set the example and provide the climate that reinforces critical thinking and problem-solving. There are a host of resources on the market now that provide "mental workouts" of many types—from brain teasers to crossword puzzles. Make sure that you are not just teaching or training, but that you are "growing better brains." Use visualization, problem solving, debates, projects, and drama. Reduce lecture time, seat-work, and other rote activities. Challenge your students' brains; and be sure to give them the resources to meet the challenge.

Competitive or Cooperative Learning

Which is better? The answer to this question is that both have their place. The world is highly competitive and it's important to be able to compete when necessary. At the same time, the brain learns poorly under the negative stress conditions caused by excess anxiety or fear. But what's anxiety causing for one individual can be enjoyable and challenging to another. We are all stressed by different things, so we must be careful about drawing broad conclusions. In general, however, both approaches in a supportive and organized environment can probably benefit learners.

Nevertheless, others believe competition of all sorts should be done away with in the classroom. Alfie Kohn argues strongly in his book, *No Contest: The Case Against Competition* (1987), that competition has vastly undermined educational and business systems. In summary, he states:

> *There is little, if any, viable evidence that a constant competitive structure in the classroom is associated with outcomes that are indicative of positive self-worth, continuing motivation, or quality of task engagement.*

Certainly, the competitive learning model has seen its share of time on the playing field. The "curve" system of grading is based on a competitive or win-lose model. In order for one student to win, another must lose, when in reality, what does one student's evaluation and assessment have to do with anothers? Either you have a certain level of understanding and mastery in a subject area or you need more time. Artificial competition, such as that set up by grading on a curve, is more harmful overall than beneficial.

Many educators today want to see the cooperative learning model get equal playing time. Among the pioneers of cooperative learning, Robert Slavin (1990) and David Johnson and R. T. Johnson (1994) found that when positive cooperative structures were in place, *some inter-group competition could exist without reducing motivation.* In fact, the more you use cooperative groups, the more competition can be incorporated without upsetting the balance.

The Role of Intuition in the Thinking Process

When we simply *feel* that something's true, that doesn't make it true. Nevertheless, what we call intuition is often triggered by nonconscious learning picked up along life's winding pathway. So, how do we know when we really know something or just think we know something? The fact is, the majority of our knowledge is implicit—that is, there is no symbolic language attached to it. For example, we certainly know how to get up from a chair, but could you accurately write out the steps for doing so?

Figure 13.5
Orbitofrontal Area and Basil Ganglia

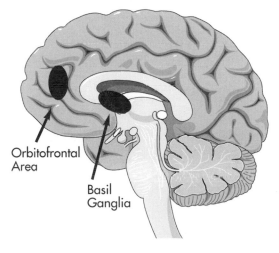

Orbitofrontal Area

Basil Ganglia

Two areas of the brain, the basal ganglia and the orbitofrontal cortex, (see figure 13.5) seem to be primarily responsible for intuition. The basal ganglia helps us regulate, manage, and translate our emotions into thinking. Situated near the eye sockets and at the bottom (ventral) of the frontal lobes is the orbitofrontal area. This area helps integrate our emotions and thinking. This is where values are weighed, emotions are mediated, and thinking is modulated. When this area is healthy, violent, immature, or inappropriate behaviors are inhibited: We exhibit normal inhibition. If either of these two brain areas is malfunctioning, however, our intuition will be affected.

However, a third structure—the amygdala—also contributes to intuition. This almond-shaped brain area processes and stores intense emotions, such as trauma, celebrations, violence, weddings, phobias and more. Since there is no connection directly from the amygdala to the language areas of the brain, we store these experiences, but usually have inadequate language to verbalize them. For example, a child abandoned by a parent may exhibit a pattern later in life where he/she leaves relationships before the partner can leave them. In spite of the repeated pattern, the adult child does not make the connection: He/she has no language for it. Normally we have no memory of early traumas (the amygdala is mature at birth, but the frontal lobes are not developed enough to make logical sense of the incident). Later on, our well-meaning "intuition" guides us in ways that may no longer be relevant: The emotion is deeply embedded in the amygdala.

 ## What This Means to You

We can help learners understand the role of intuition and emotions in learning and thinking by validating them. Ask students how an element of a lesson makes them feel? Encourage learners to venture a guess when they are unsure of an answer. Realize that when learners act out illogically, a biological response may have been triggered that they don't have the awareness to stop. Learners who have had damage to key areas of the brain also may exhibit inappropriate behaviors which they cannot be expected to control. The most effective response is to affect a change in the student's state. Redirect them. Put on some relaxing music or take a stretching and deep breathing break. Model solid problem-solving skills and your learners will follow.

Reflection Questions

1. What from this chapter was novel, fresh, or new to you? What was familiar or "old hat"?

2. In what ways, do you already apply the information in this chapter?

3. What three questions might you now generate about this material?

4. How did you react emotionally to the information in this chapter?

5. How did you react cognitively to the information? Do you agree or disagree with the author's point of view? Why?

6. In what ways might you translate the principles presented in this chapter into practical everyday useful ideas?

7. If these things are, in fact, true about the brain, what should we do differently? What resources of time, people, and money could be redirected? In what ways might you suggest we start doing this?

8. What were the most interesting insights you gained from this material?

9. If you were to plan your next step for making your curriculum more brain-based, what would that be?

10. What obstacles might you encounter? How might you realistically deal with them?

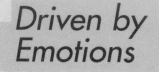

Driven by Emotions

14

Driven by Emotions

We've come full circle, from an ancient culture that focused primarily on emotions (to the point of practically disregarding logic) to a modern culture that's rediscovering the value of emotions; and, indeed, realizing that our emotions inform our logic. Only a few decades ago, showing your emotions was considered a sign of weakness. Strong men showed none and weak women showed too many, was the thinking. But what does the current brain research tell us that has caused us to change our minds?

"Emotions drive attention, create meaning, and have their own memory pathways," says Joseph LeDoux, PhD. (1996). These attributes unequivocally epitomize the learning process. Harvard professor Jerome Kagan (1990) says, "The rationalists who are convinced that feelings interfere with the most adaptive choices have the matter completely backwards. A reliance on logic alone without the capacity to feel would lead most people to do many more foolish things." The popularity of the best-selling book *Emotional Intelligence* (Goleman 1995), underscores our increased acceptance of the important role emotions play in learning and decision-making; but where's the science?

Figure 14.1
Outdated Western Model of Learning

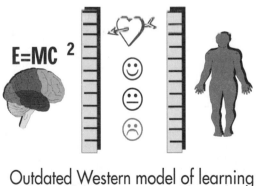

Outdated Western model of learning hints clear separation of mind, emotions, and body.

This model is not supported by recent brain research.

What We've Discovered About Emotions Lately

Discoveries that have shed light on the brain and learning over the past twenty-five years have also been instrumental in reshaping our thinking about emotions. With the advent of sophisticated neuro-imaging devices, we've been able to observe the internal (in addition to external) responses of both brain-damaged and non-brain damaged individuals; and the actual biochemical process and pathways established in response to various emotions. We've identified a host of neurotransmitters and peptides that influence our emotions; and we've just begun to understand how these chemical messengers impact learning and memory.

During the 1990s—the official "Decade of the Brain"—four highly respected neuroscientists, Antonio and Hanna Damasio of the University of Iowa, Joseph LeDoux of New York University, and Candace Pert of Georgetown University Medical Center emerged with important implications about the role of emotions.

The Role of Emotions in Learning

In *Descartes' Error: Emotion, Reason, and the Human Brain* (1994), Damasio argues that the brain, mind, body, and emotions form a linked system. He criticizes the typical neurologist's narrow-minded view of emotions: "...uncontrolled or misdirected emotion can be a major source of irrational behavior...[but] a reduction in emotion may constitute an equally important source of irrational behavior. Certain aspects of the process of emotion and feeling are indispensable for rationality," he adds. "Emotions are not separate, but rather enmeshed in the neural networks of reason." Damasio's work, based mostly on animal and human studies of subjects with brain damage, established that damage to particular areas of the brain—especially to the prefrontal lobe (bilaterally) and the amygdala—eliminated the ability to feel emotion, and as a result, faulty cognition occurred.

In *The Emotional Brain* (1996) LeDoux analyzes the anatomy of an emotion. Basing his work on a meta-analysis of previous research (including his own), LeDoux argues that emotions or "arousal" is important in all mental functions and "contributes significantly to attention, perception, memory, and problem solving." In fact, "without arousal," he continues, "we fail to notice what is going on—we don't attend to the details. But too much arousal is not good either." If we are overaroused, we become tense and anxious and unproductive. LeDoux subscribes to the theory that various systems contribute to arousal, with four of them located in the brain stem. Each area contains different neurotransmitters that are released by their axon terminals when the cells are activated by the presence of novel or otherwise significant stimuli.

According to Jeff Tooby, PhD. of University of California, Santa Barbara, the circuitry of emotion is widely distributed in our brain. While the old model linked only the mid-brain ("the limbic system") to emotions, other areas are now implicated, as well, including the orbitofrontal cortex and the ventral frontal lobes, to start. But there's more.

Although some researchers cite the orbitofrontal cortex as the central-processing area that orchestrates our emotions and cognition, emotions are not the exclusive domain of the brain, claims Candace Pert, PhD. author of *Molecules of Emotion* (1997). She says, emotions aren't just in the brain, they operate throughout the body. Pert's work over the past thirty years, including the discovery of the opiate receptor in 1972, helped establish a biomolecular basis for our emotions. "Emotional states or moods," she explains, "are produced by the various neuropeptides (and neurotransmitters) that attach to our cells." What we experience as an emotion or feeling is also a mechanism for activating a particular neuronal circuit—simultaneously throughout the brain and body—which generates a physiologically-based behavior, she says.

Many others, including McGaugh (1989,1990), MacLean (1978, 1990), and Goleman (1995) have written about the critical role of emotions in learning, as well. Paul MacLean, PhD. an early pioneer in brain research, says that the most disturbing thing about the way the brain is "wired up" is the mid-area system which insists that ultimately the learner must feel that something is true before it is *believed* (1978). MacLean says with puzzlement:

> *"The mid-area system, this primitive brain that can neither read nor write, provides us with the feeling of what is real, true, and important"*

The New Paradigm: "Emotional Logic"

The old way of thinking about the brain is that mind, body, and feelings are separate entities, but there's really no division between these functions. Our emotions help us to focus our reason and logic. Our logical side may help us, for example, set a goal, but it is our emotional side that provides the passion to persevere through trying times. Certainly excessive or undisciplined emotions can harm our rational thinking, but a lack of emotion can also make for equally flawed thinking, Damasio (1994) reminds us.

Holistic learning means that we acknowledge learners' emotions, feelings, beliefs, cravings, problems, attitudes, and skills; and include them in the learning process. While the outdated academic model addressed primarily the explicit aspects of the learner and learning (i.e., facts and figures, things we can touch and see, etc.), the prevailing model contends we learn best with our minds, hearts, *and* bodies engaged. The more aspects of self we can tap into for learners, the more effective we'll be as educators.

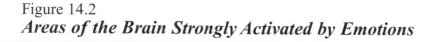

> *All learning involves our body, emotions, attitudes, and physical well being. Brain-based learning advocates that we address these multiple variables more often and more comprehensively.*

The influence of emotions on our behavior is immense. Because they give us a "live" report at all times on the body's response, they receive priority status. Scientists believe the critical networks that process emotions link the limbic system, the prefrontal cortices, and perhaps most importantly, the brain areas that map and integrate signals from the body (see figure 14.2). We know that damage to the limbic system (primarily the amygdala and anterior cingulate) impairs primary emotions (innate fear, surprise, etc.). But, damage to the prefrontal cortices compromises the processing of secondary emotion—that is, our feelings about our thoughts, says Damasio (1994). Emotions let us mind our body's physical reaction to the world.

Figure 14.2
Areas of the Brain Strongly Activated by Emotions

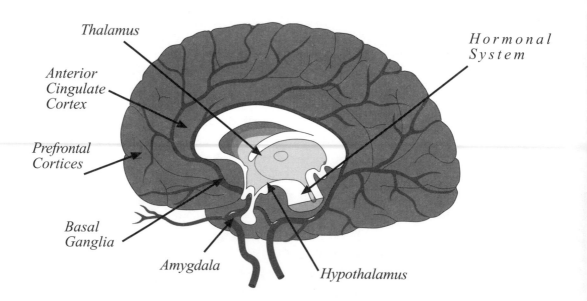

When our body experiences primary emotions, our brain "reads" them as part of the critical information that ensures our survival. Our body serves as a critical frame of reference for the internal creation of our reality. In other words, the body generates the sensory data, feeds it to the brain, and then integrates it with emotions and intellect to form a "thinking triumvirate" for optimal performance and decision making. An over-reliance or under-reliance on any one of the elements can impair our quality of thinking.

Our thinking is not "contaminated" by emotions: Rather, our emotions are an integral aspect of our neural operating system. Emotions speed our thinking by providing an immediate physical response to circumstances. When a result makes us feel good, naturally we're going to select it over a result that makes us feel badly. And when we value something strongly, whether it be a principle or a person, or a thing, that relationship becomes "emotionally charged." If our emotions have been badly neglected by others (especially early in life), "emotional problems," fortified by an overproduction of some neurotransmitters, can result. Such intense reactions to our emotions, however, are a survival benefit and allow us to preserve that which is important, including our lives.

 ## What This Means to You

Develop a greater awareness of all the factors influencing your learners; and take the time to influence as many of these variables as you can. Although we clearly cannot control all of them, we can surely influence many more of them than traditionally expected. The emotional state of your learners is at least as important as the intellectual-cognitive content of your presentation. Never avoid emotions; deal with them gently and personally. Allow negatives ones to be processed and positive ones to be celebrated. Elicit positive emotional states from learners with enjoyable activities, games, humor, personal attention, and acts of caring. Modeling these states will teach learners indirectly how to better manage their own optimal states for learning. Allow your learners time to de-stress before presenting new information. Reflect on your priorities, as a teacher. Do you put your learners' emotions and feelings on par with the mastery of content and skill learning? Remember, the two are directly biologically linked.

The Chemistry of Emotion

Brain chemicals (neurotransmitters and neuropeptides) are released from neurons and transmitted to wide areas of the brain and body. From excitement to calm, from depression to euphoria, these chemicals influence our thinking and behaviors. They are responsible for the lift we get from a cup or two of coffee; the thrill of a roller-coaster ride; and the common experience of having a "gut feeling"—as when neuropeptides released in your brain land at receptor sites in the gastrointestinal tract. Some of the most influential chemical inputs on feelings and behavior include serotonin, acetylcholine, dopamine, and norepinephrine, which are released from areas such as the brain stem. These chemicals linger in our system; and once an emotion occurs, it is hard for the cortex to simply shut it off. From our desire to learn to our etiquette in the cafeteria, how we act usually reflects how we feel.

Are Feelings and Emotions the Same?

Neuroscientists usually separate emotions and feelings. Emotions are generated from biologically-automated pathways and have been found in cross-cultural studies to be experienced by people universally. These six universal emotions are joy, fear, surprise, disgust, anger, and sadness. Feelings, on the other hand, are our culturally and environmentally developed *responses* to circumstances. Examples include worry, anticipation, frustration, cynicism, and optimism.

Although analyzing feelings is problematic, we have a vast array of highly specific and scientific ways to measure emotions. These measurements include electrodermal (skin) responses, heart rate, blood pressure, EEG activity, and brain-imaging techniques. With these common medical procedures, it's fairly easy to get readings on a student's response to fear; however, we have yet to find a way to measure the more illusive experience of feelings—for example, a student's level of sympathy for a fellow classmate.

Feelings and emotions travel along separate biological pathways in the brain. While feelings may take a slower, more circuitous route, emotions always access the brain's "superhighways." These pathways are reserved for information that takes emotional priority over our measured thinking—a survival mechanism that ensures intense emotionally-laden events get attended to immediately.

In an emergency situation, stopping to weigh and judge our feelings could cost us our life. When a lion is chasing you, this is not the time for reflection and contemplation. As the author of *Emotional Intelligence* Daniel Goleman points out, this priority status (although it has a critical purpose) also allows us to become "emotionally hijacked" by our responses. Our emotional system is acting simultaneously independently as well as cooperatively with our cortex. A student who is getting threatening looks from another student, for example, may strike out at him before he even "thinks" about it. The teacher's "behavior-improvement lecture" in response to the event will likely do little to change "automated" responses such as this. Rather, students need to learn emotional intelligence skills in a way that acknowledges what's happening in their own body, and then reinforces more positive responses over time.

The Amazing Amygdala

While other areas of the brain help process emotions, the amygdala—an almond shaped structure within the limbic system (see figures 14.2 and 14.3)—is highly involved. Buried deep in the front half of the temporal lobes, it is mature at birth and stores intense emotions, both negative and positive.

The amygdala exerts a tremendous influence over our cortex. The cortex, for example, has more inputs *from* the amygdala than the reverse; yet the information flows both ways. It's reactive, while the frontal lobes are reflective. Although the amygdala seems to have twelve to fifteen distinct emotive regions within it, so far only two (those linked to fear) have been specifically identified. Other emotions, such as intense pleasure may be linked to other areas.

Figure 14.3
Amygdala Location

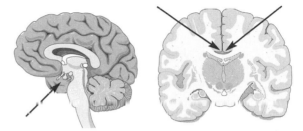

The amygdala is activated by intense emotions.

We have two amygdalas, left and right. They are buried in the medial frontal temporal lobes and are well connected to the rest of the brain.

The amygdala's primary task may be its responsibility for bringing emotional content to memory. Because the amygdala connects to the hippocampus, it has long been believed to play a role in memory. While most now believe the amygdala does not itself process memory, it is believed to be a source of emotions that imbue memory with meaning (Turkington 1996). It is most concerned with our survival and the emotional flavoring or interpretation of feelings in a situation.

Hot Buttons and the Amygdala

Have you ever had a "hot button" triggered by a student, family member, or colleague? Most of us have. This automatic response (usually considered negative) to a perceived threat of some kind, is probably the reactivation of an old pattern triggered by your amygdala. The perceived threat might only be a put-down, withdrawal of attention, or a sarcastic comment, but it feels on a very deep level like a threat to our emotional or physical safety. Whether we're six or sixty, when our amygdala says, "Hey! Survival is at stake—strike back!" we usually do. Fortunately, unproductive patterns of behavior resulting from early neglect or trauma can be altered with awareness and practice.

We rarely ever get angry for the reasons we think. Rather, each time we react, it's the re-triggering of an earlier, stored reaction. The trigger may be nearly insignificant; nevertheless, your brain says, "React! This is horrible!" Over time, the body can become a storehouse of defensive postures. When a "hot button" is pushed, we (or our students) may not be able to stop our immediate reaction. But we can pause for a moment (if the threat is, in fact, insignificant) and then take a slow, deep breath to relax. After we've allowed ourselves to get "past" the reactive behavior, we can then choose to act more appropriately.

> *Since survival is the most important function of the brain, the physiology involved most heavily in this role (our emotional processing center) dominates our everyday lives in more ways than we can imagine.*

 ## What This Means to You

Integrate emotions into the learning process. One simple way to do this is by encouraging learners to reflect on their feelings. In response to a reading assignment, for example, you might ask a question like, "When you read what happened to Johnny after he told the truth, how did you feel?" Asking students how they feel about a topic will help cement the learning in their memory. Remember, the best thinking is integrated with emotions. Some behaviors are going to occur regardless of what you do; and many of them can feel destructive. Accept the need for them; and help learners move through the experience towards a more positive outcome.

Here are three immediate strategies for providing alternative productive outlets for what are basically powerful, biological expressions:

- Establish new, positive, and productive rituals such as arrival handshakes, music fanfare, positive greetings, hugs, high-fives, etc.

- Set a tone of teamwork with class rituals such as team names, cheers, gestures, games, and friendly competition.

- Encourage participation rituals such as a class applause when learners contribute or present; closing rituals with songs, affirmations, discussion, journal writing, cheers, self-assessment, gestures, etc.; and your own personal form of ritual to celebrate a learner's achievement such as a special student award, note of praise sent home, extra privileges, etc.

These positive feedback circuits capitalize on the value of emotions for cementing learning. It is in fact, the emotional response that animates us, not the logical one. We are emotional beings. Even when we evaluate student performance, it's all about how we feel about what we've seen and heard. The feelings strongly flavor our evaluation. We call it a professional opinion, but to say there's no emotion involved would be a case of serious denial.

Our emotions are our personalities. When researchers examined subjects with most of their frontal lobe (the area of so-called highest intelligence) damaged or removed, a significant score reduction on standard intelligence tests was evident. When researchers examined subjects with damage or removal of their amygdala, there was even more profound personality change. Deficits to the amygdala result in a greatly reduced (if not extinct) capacity for creative play, imagination, and emotional nuances that drive the arts, humor, imagination, love, music, and altruism. These are the very cornerstones of personality—the qualities of those who have made great contributions to our world, such as the genius of Quincy Jones, Martha Graham, Steven Hawking, Eddie Murphy, and Mother Teresa. Our emotions, in fact, drive our creativity.

Emotions as Mind-Body States

Emotions impact student behavior by creating distinct mind-body states. A state is an exact frozen moment composed of a specific posture, breathing rate, and chemical balance in the body. The presence or absence of norepinephrine, vasopressin, testosterone, serotonin, progesterone, dopamine, and dozens of other chemicals dramatically alter a person's frame of mind and body. How important are states to us? They are all that we have: They are our feelings, desires, memories, and motivations. We are driven by our emotions. Everything we do is motivated by them. When your students buy a new pair of Nikes, they are not likely in *need* of new shoes, but are rather seeking more confidence or popularity. A state change is what their after! Even buying drugs is evidence of the desire for a state change—perhaps to feel better, or to simply feel *something*, or nothing, as the case may be. We need to pay attention to this. Those who help their students feel good about themselves through learning success, quality friendships, and celebrations are doing the very things the learning brain craves.

Neurosurgeon Richard Bergland (1986) says, "Thought is not caged in the brain but is scattered all over the body." He adds that there is

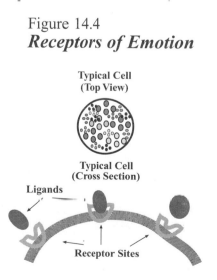

Figure 14.4
Receptors of Emotion

**Typical Cell
(Top View)**

**Typical Cell
(Cross Section)**

Ligands

Receptor Sites

little doubt in his mind that the brain operates more like a gland than a computer. It produces hormones, is bathed in them, and is run by them. Emotions are the catalyst that impact the conversion of mind into physical matter in the body. They are distributed as white blood cells and peptide molecules throughout the body. Emotions trigger the chemical changes that change our moods, behaviors, and eventually, our lives. If people and activities are the content in our lives, emotions are both the contexts and the values we hold.

Outlets For Expression

Many behaviors, like flocking, dominating, and preening, are simply a carry-over from our ancient survival patterns. However, some of these common ritualistic behaviors can be counter-productive to learning unless positive outlets for them are provided.

Some examples of these rituals are put downs or taunting, compulsions rigid routines, fads, cliques, peer pressure, arguing over meaningless subjects, competing for approval, "trying on roles," "nesting" or personalizing a space, "top dog" type behaviors, flocking in teams, flirting with each other, and adhering to group mentality. Traditionally, teachers invest a great deal of energy combating these ever-evolving rituals mostly to no avail. But there are alternatives.

Rituals can fulfill learners needs without being counterproductive to learning. Brain-based learning environments acknowledge the anthropology of such behaviors and recognize their value to the organism. They focus on understanding the brain and working with its natural tendencies instead of fighting them in an attempt to suppress them.

A brain-based environment supports the expression of emotions by:

▼ **Creating a brain-affirming learning climate.**

▼ **Acknowledging the role of chemicals in behavior.**

▼ **Not denying the importance and recognition of feelings and emotions.**

▼ **Providing more personally meaningful projects and more individual choice.**

▼ **Using productive rituals to adjust mind-body states.**

▼ **Maintaining an absence of threat, high stress, and artificial deadlines.**

▼ **Ensuring that the resources necessary for success are available to every learner.**

▼ Creating multi-status groups of learners supported by peer review and feedback.

▼ Using self-assessment tools for non-threatening feedback.

▼ Assigning large group-oriented projects that require learners to learn to work with others and problem solve for the greater good.

The Thinking Tool of Emotions

For years we believed that thinking was the main domain of our frontal lobes. That is, we credited this area with our brilliant, "best of humanity" thoughts. We know now that the frontal lobes may allow us to elaborate on the details of our goals and plans, but it's our emotions that drive their execution in our lives. That's why when we ask students to set their goals, it's just as important to ask them *why* they want to reach them, as it is to ask *what* their goals are. You might say, "Write down three good reasons why reaching your goals is important to you." Then, have the students share their answers with others.

> *Remember, it is the emotions behind the goals that provide the energy to accomplish them.*

Some suggest that emotions are a form of intelligence—a distillation of learned wisdom that may even be hard-wired into our DNA. In other words, we have been biologically shaped to be fearful, worried, surprised, suspicious, joyful, and relieved, almost on cue. Emotions are a critical source of information for learning and ought to be used to inform us, rather than considered something to subdue and ignore. Students who feel tentative or afraid to speak in front of a group of their peers, for instance, may have a very legitimate and even logical reason for the fear: Failing might cost them significant loss of social status.

Emotions help us make better and faster decisions. In fact, we make thousands of micro-decisions daily that illuminate, for example, our character as either good or bad, dependable or not, honest or sleazy, gossipy or noble, creative or straight-laced, generous or stingy. Each of those decisions is made with a guiding hand—our values. All values are simply emotional states. If my value is honesty, then I feel badly when I'm dishonest. Conversely, I feel good when I do honest things. In a sense, our character is shaped by the conscience of our emotions. While too much or too little emotion is usually counterproductive, our everyday emotions play an important role in our lives; and make us who we are.

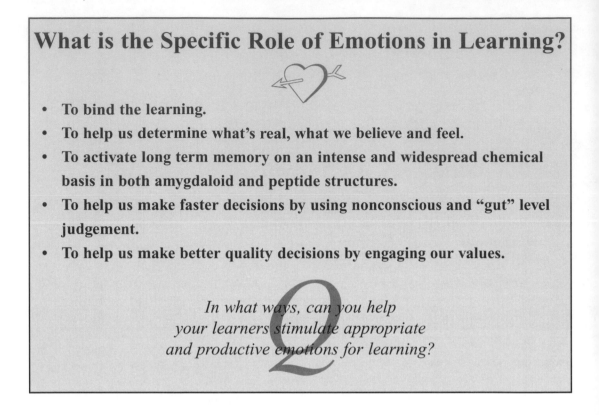

What is the Specific Role of Emotions in Learning?

- **To bind the learning.**
- **To help us determine what's real, what we believe and feel.**
- **To activate long term memory on an intense and widespread chemical basis in both amygdaloid and peptide structures.**
- **To help us make faster decisions by using nonconscious and "gut" level judgement.**
- **To help us make better quality decisions by engaging our values.**

In what ways, can you help your learners stimulate appropriate and productive emotions for learning?

We remember that which is most emotionally-laden because:

▼ **Emotional events receive preferential processing.**
▼ **The brain is over-stimulated when strong emotions are present.**
▼ **Emotions give us a more activated and chemically stimulated brain, which helps us recall things better.**
▼ **The more intense the amygdala arousal, the stronger the imprint.**

In fact, University of California, San Diego neurobiologist and memory expert Larry Squire (1987, 1992), says emotions are so important, they have their own memory pathways. Hence, it's common for students to remember most events like the death of a friend, a field trip, or a hands-on science experiment far longer than a mere lecture. As teachers, we can purposely engage productive emotions.

We've come a long way! The old thinking was, "First, get control of the students, then do the teaching." Today, neuroscientists would say, "First engage the emotions appropriately, then continue to engage them." Engaging emotions must be intrinsic to the curriculum, rather than something attached to it as an afterthought.

We simply cannot run a good school without acknowledging emotions and integrating them into our daily operations. Many schools do this already: They have pep rallies, athletic competitions, guest speakers, poetry presentations, community projects, storytelling, debates, clubs, sports, drama performances, and comedy routines. Which forms of emotional expression are you orchestrating?

The following are strategies you can incorporate to help your learners understand the importance of their own emotions in the learning process:

• **Role Model:** Exhibit a love of learning. Bring something to class that you're in the process of learning about—something that really excites you. Build suspense, smile, tell a true emotional story, show off a new CD, bring a favorite book in, or discuss a recently read one, bring a pet to school, get involved in community work, but most importantly, show enthusiasm.

• **Celebrate:** Throw parties; provide acknowledgments; and incorporate high-fives, team cheers, food, music, decorations, and costumes! Show off student work. For example, when students are done doing a group mind-map, have them share it with others. Tell the groups to find at least two things they like about each others mind-maps. Do this in an atmosphere of celebration: Have background music on, encourage applause, and provide some words of praise for a job well done.

• **Controversy:** Set up a debate, dialogue, academic decathlon, game show, or panel discussion. Any time you vest two groups in competing interests, you'll get action! Theater and drama can create strong emotions, as well: The bigger the production, and the higher the stakes, the more emotions will be engaged. Event planning on this scale evokes stress, fun, anxiety, anticipation, suspense, excitement, and relief: What better way to engage a wide range of emotions?

• **Physical Rituals:** There are innumerable examples of classroom rituals that can inspire and engage emotions. A few examples include, clapping patterns, cheers, chants, movements, or theme songs. Incorporate arrival and departure rituals that are fun, quick, and frequent to prevent boredom. Obviously, rituals need to be age-appropriate.

• **Introspection:** Incorporate assignments that require journaling, small-group discussions, story swapping, surveys, interviews, and other reflection tasks. Use people and issues to engage students personally. Ask students to write or talk about a current event that has drawn attention. Help learners make personal connections between current events, the current curriculum, and their own everyday lives.

Learning Has to "Feel Right"

The work of Richard Bandler (1988) reveals that our brain has three criteria which must be fulfilled in order for it to "know that it knows something"—also called the self-convincer state. Although the criteria vary from person to person, in general, the brain needs the following three forms of verification for learning in order to truly believe it:

1) **Modality:** The learning must be reinforced in the learner's dependent modality (i.e., either visual, auditory, or kinesthetic). We must see it, hear it, or feel it. Examples include a written test score, a compliment, holding a trophy, a smile on a another person's face, a positive peer assessment, or an audience's applause.

2) **Frequency:** The new learning must get reinforced with repetition. The necessary repetition varies from one to twenty times depending on the individual. For example, some learners reinforce their own learning by looking over prior tests and rereading the questions and answers numerous times. Some may want to watch a video about a subject they're studying, as well as read a couple of books about it, and experience a related field trip. Others might only feel they really know something after teaching it to others.

3) **Duration:** The learning must be validated for a length of time—anywhere from two seconds to several days depending again upon the individual. Thus, the learner may learn something in their dependent modality, and even get it reinforced for a few hours, but they still don't feel like they know it. An unspecified duration of time, however, may alter this feeling. This is another reason why review is such an important learning step.

Once a learner has experienced learning in their preferred modality, the right number of times, and for the right length of time, they will feel that it is now true. When this happens, we believe it in our gut. Until then, it's only data, with little meaning.

Think about how often you've questioned your own sense of knowing something. Have you ever left the house and then suddenly wonder, "Did I lock the door? Did I unplug the iron? Did I turn on my answering machine?" Or perhaps you look at a word you've just spelled out and wonder, "Is this right"? This is not a memory problem. It is a case of not believing yourself. If you do believe yourself, you've achieved the self-convincer state.

We've all heard someone say, "I'll believe it when I see it." This is clearly a case of the visual learner who *has* to *see* something to believe it. Another might say, "I saw it, but I just don't believe it." And yet another may need to call their neighbor and get their opinion before they feel they know. Someone else may say, "If I can touch it, hold it, or be there first hand, I'll believe it." These three responses represent the major modality variables—visual, auditory, and kinesthetic.

Self-convincers are especially critical when it comes to changing beliefs. If a student already believes that he or she is going to succeed, only "maintenance reinforcement" is required to preserve that belief. But if a student believes that he/she is a failure and you want them to get convinced otherwise, all three of the criteria must be met. Otherwise, the student's internal belief will remain the same.

In general, "at-risk," slow, discouraged, or low-level learners don't usually possess strong self-convincing strategies. They may either self-convince too easily, meaning they think they know something before they really do; or, they don't self-convince easily enough, meaning their learning self-confidence is very low. "Gifted" learners, on the other hand, may merely possess more accurate self-convincing skills, and as a result, exhibit more self confidence.

 ## What This Means to You

Many learners access the self-convincer state on their own. They simply know how to convince themselves of what they know or want to know. They tend to have more self-confidence, perhaps even arrogance. But others aren't so easily convinced. We've all heard a child remark to their parents that they learned nothing at school. Although they may have actually learned a lot, brain-based learning says we must elicit the self-convincer state to ensure the learner feels they know it.

To ensure that all learners leave your class in a state of "knowing what they know," provide activities that give them a chance to validate their learning. The activities should cross all three modalities, be repeated numerous times, and last for several hours or days. Some examples of approaches that meet this criteria include setting up peer assessment opportunities, conducting role plays, assigning journal writing, creating self-assessment instruments, assigning tasks that require team work, and peer teaching. When enough of these activities are conducted, students will leave your class feeling like they've really learned something.

For those who "self-convince" too easily, and think they "know it all" long before they really do, there's another solution. These are usually the more contextual-global learners. Give them a checklist of criteria for the learning; and ask them to assess themselves based on the specific measures. This will help acquire a more realistic view of their mastery level.

> *Learners not only need to learn,*
> *but they need to know that they*
> *learned what was taught.*

At the end of an activity, listen for expressions that confirm learners are processing the veracity of an experience, such as "It just doesn't *feel* right" or, "I'll believe it when I *see* it" or Wait until my friend *hears* about this." These phrases indicate an attempt to feel convinced about something. Only then will there be actual belief.

Once students are sucked into the self-confidence/intrinsic motivation loop, future learning is easy. Rituals that celebrate learning go a long way towards moving learners into that success loop. Even beyond making the learning more fun, they seal the new learning as real and worth remembering.

Reflection Questions

1. What from this chapter was novel, fresh, or new to you? What was familiar or "old hat"?

2. In what ways, do you already apply the information in this chapter?

3. What three questions might you now generate about this material?

4. How did you react emotionally to the information in this chapter?

5. How did you react cognitively to the information? Do you agree or disagree with the author's point of view? Why?

6. In what ways might you translate the principles presented in this chapter into practical everyday useful ideas?

7. If these things are, in fact, true about the brain, what should we do differently? What resources of time, people, and money could be redirected? In what ways might you suggest we start doing this?

8. What were the most interesting insights you gained from this material?

9. If you were to plan your next step for making your curriculum more brain-based, what would that be?

10. What obstacles might you encounter? How might you realistically deal with them?

Memory and Recall

15

Memory and Recall

How do your students store and recall what they've learned? Surprisingly, there's no single master filing cabinet residing in our brain; nor does our brain archive our memories by number or some other linear system. It seems that the process is much more complex and holistic than this.

How Our Memory Works

It is important to think *process*, rather than *location* when discussing our memory system. Neuroscientist Daniel Schacter, PhD. (1996) suggests that *multiple memory locations and systems* are, in fact, responsible for our learning and recall. His research suggests that different learning tasks may require different ways to store and recall information.

Researchers emphasize that it's the *retrieval process* which activates dormant neurons to trigger our memories. They argue that you cannot

Figure 15.1
How Memories Are Formed

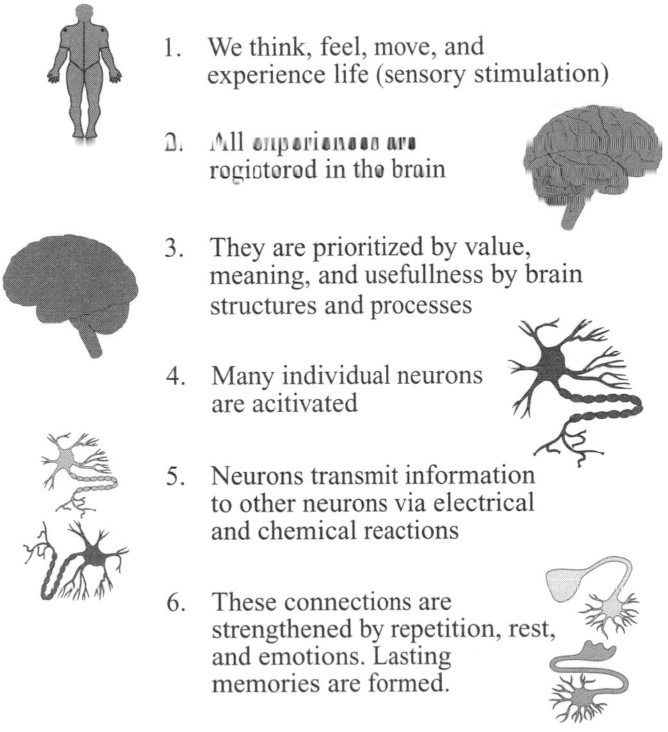

1. We think, feel, move, and experience life (sensory stimulation)

2. All experiences are registered in the brain

3. They are prioritized by value, meaning, and usefullness by brain structures and processes

4. Many individual neurons are acitivated

5. Neurons transmit information to other neurons via electrical and chemical reactions

6. These connections are strengthened by repetition, rest, and emotions. Lasting memories are formed.

separate memory and retrieval—that memory is determined by what kind of retrieval process is activated. Each type of learning requires its own type of triggering. When enough of the right type of neurons, firing in the right way, are stimulated, you get successful retrieval. In larger patterns, whole neuronal fields can be activated. For example, at hearing the word "school," hundreds of neuronal circuits may be activated triggering a "cerebral thunderstorm." This is due to the many associations and experiences most of us have with the subject.

One theory is that memories are frozen patterns waiting for a resonating signal to awaken them, like a bumpy road that makes no sound until a car drives over it. Neurobiologist William Calvin (1996) says that the content may be embedded in "spatiotemporal themes" which potentially create a critical mass needed for retrieval. In other words, when enough of a thought's identical copies have been made for the cerebral code to trip an "action switch," the memory is recalled. This computational theory provides one explanation as to why a student might remember an answer to a question after a test is over that he/she couldn't quite retrieve in the moment. It can take some time for a critical mass of thought patterns to be activated—especially if a lot of competing processing is happening.

Where Our Memories Live

There is no one area of the brain that is solely responsible for memory. Most of our memories are well-distributed throughout the cortex. This "spread the risk" strategy explains why a person can lose 20 percent of their cortex and still "have a good memory." It also helps explain why a student can have a great recall for one subject, like sports statistics, and a poor recall for another, like names and faces.

Memories of sound are stored in the auditory cortex. Memories of names, nouns, and pronouns are traced to the temporal lobe. The amygdala is quite active for implicit, usually negative, emotional events. Learned skills involve the basal ganglia structures. The cerebellum is also very critical for associative memory formation, particularly when precise timing is involved as in the learning of motor skills. Researchers have found that an area of the inner brain, the hippocampus, becomes quite active for the formation of spatial and other explicit memories, such as memory for speaking, reading, and even our recall *about* an emotional event.

When you think of an idea, hear your internal voice, get an image, recall music, or see a color in your mind's eye, you are reconstructing the original memory. Your brain creates a composite of the various elements of the experience "on the spot." This means you only remember something once: After that, you're remembering the memory! And as time goes by, our versions change. And our memories get more and more "recreated" and less and less true to the event. Your instant recreation of the original takes a split second (usually) and operates a bit like a volunteer fire department:

There's no building, office, or central system, but when a fire breaks out, the volunteers quickly unite from various locals to (hopefully) extinguish the blaze. Your memory is "on-call" at all times of the day and night.

There are two theories on how this miraculous process happens. One is that we have "indexes" which contain the instructions (not the content) for the brain on how to rekindle the content. These "convergence zones," as they've been called (Damasio 1994), unite the pieces of a memory during the retrieval process. For the sake of analogy, consider that your semantic memory works like "just in time" manufacturing: It creates a "car on the spot" in it's own auto parts store upon demand—an ingenious process considering the "parts" are reusable on

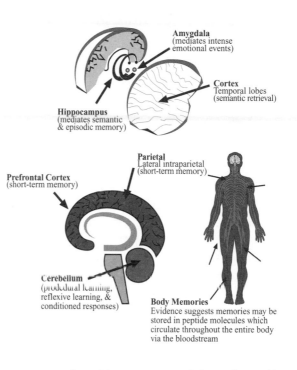

Figure 15.2
Locations of Memory Activations

the next "car" or any other item you want to remember. For most word-based recall, we use mental "indexes" to help us find the word we want. A word like classroom is very likely linked to several related subjects like school, learning, kids, teacher, and principal. Our language is a classic example of having to pull hundreds of words "off the shelf" within seconds, to assemble even the most common sentence. This theory explains why when we are trying to say something, often a similar word (close, but still wrong) comes out of our mouth.

Long-Term Potentiation: What Is It?

The expression scientists have used to identify the actual molecular process involved in the formation of explicit memories is long-term potentiation or LTP. This process is defined as a rapid alteration in the strength of the synaptic connections as a result of stimulation. Susumu Tonegawa, PhD. a Nobel laureate at MIT (1995) discovered that LTP is actually mediated by genes, which trigger a series of complex cascading steps.

At the same time, neurobiologist Eric Kandel's team from Columbia University (1992, 1994) identified a critical protein molecule known as CREB that serves as a logic switch, signaling to nerve cells whether to store the information in short- or long-term memory. Jerry Yin, PhD. at Cold Spring Harbor Laboratory and colleagues demonstrated (1995) that CREB-activation gives fruit flies a photographic memory, the ability to remember after just one trial what ordinarily requires many trials. Researchers believe the physical substrate of memory is stored as changes in neurons along specific pathways. This means that, in a sense, memory is a probability that neurons will fire in a particular way.

Chemicals Impact Memory

Many modulatory compounds can enhance or depress recall if given at the time of learning. Researchers suspect that calcium deficiencies may be one explanation for the memory loss often experienced by the elderly. Norepinephrine is a neurotransmitter that is linked to memories associated with stress. Recently, vitamin A has been found to assist in memory formation. Phenylalanine, found in dairy products, helps manufacture norepinephrine, also involved in alertness and attention. Adrenaline acts as a memory fixative, locking up memories of exciting or traumatic events. The brain uses the neurotransmitter acetylcholine in long-term memory formation. Increased levels of this neurotransmitter are linked to subjects with better recall. Lecithin, found in eggs, salmon, and lean beef, is a dietary source which raises the choline levels and has been shown to boost recall in repeated trials. Studies show that even the presence of household sugar in the bloodstream can enhance memory.

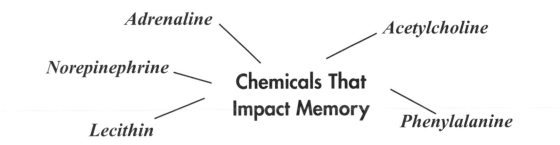

Scientists postulate that the chemistry of our body (which regulates our physiological states), is a critical element in the subsequent triggering of our recall. Learning acquired under a particular state (happy sad, stressed, relaxed, etc.) is most easily recalled in that same state. This phenomenon of getting better recall by matching the state of learning with the state of testing/evaluating even works with chocolate. Eat chocolate during the learning and you'll recall more at test time if you, once again, eat chocolate. Realistically, however, this is only a small piece of the whole puzzle.

Memory Is State Dependent

Stanford University psychologist Gordon Bower and associates (1990, 1992) confirm that each mental, physical, and emotional state "binds up" information within that particular state. In other words, states like anxiety, curiosity, depression, joy, and confidence also trigger information learned while in that state.

"It is as though the two states constitute different libraries. A given memory record can be retrieved only by returning to that library, or physiological state, in which the event was first stored," says Bower. In other words, learners who hear a lecture while a certain baroque music composition is playing will test better if that same music is replayed at exam time.

Practical Applications:

▼ **Facilitate reviews that engage all five senses.**

▼ **Encourage discussions about learners' feelings and emotions regarding new learning.**

▼ **Get learners to incorporate the new learning in some way to their own personal life.**

▼ **Use storyboards (like oversized comic strip panels) to present key ideas.**

▼ **Make a video or audio tape: The more complex the better.**

▼ **Use pegwords to link numbers or pictures to an idea for ease in recall.**

▼ **Create or re-do a song with lyrics that represent the new learning.**

How and *where* we learn may be as important to the brain as *what* we learn. Why is this? Because the success of memory retrieval is very state, time, and context dependent. In experiments with color, location, and movement, findings suggest the recency effects are enhanced by identifying the stimulus at the time of the state change. In other words, if you pause and take notice of the circumstances of your learning, it will subsequently be easier to trigger its recall.

Research suggests that context is even critical to the memory of infants (Amabile and Rovee-Collier 1991; Boller and Rovee-Collier 1992; Hayne, Rovee-Collier, and Borza 1991). In these studies, it was demonstrated that babies better remembered faces and sounds when the same contextual (location) cues initially used were repeated. Each physiological state is a moment in time that locks together two elements—the mind/body circumstances (feelings, emotions, arousal) and the contextual circumstances (sights, sounds, location, etc.). Thus, studying and cramming for a final exam may present a problem. If your students study in a hyped-up state with coffee or other stimulants to keep them awake, unless they can match this state during test time, they may perform below their abilities.

Have you ever had the experience of hearing a favorite song or melody and suddenly you are transported back in time and place? Or have you ever decided you want something from another room, but once you're there, you can't remember what it was you came for? So, then you go back to the original place, and remember your intention. These are examples of context-bound memory cues.

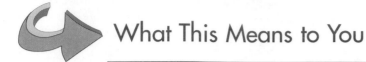

What This Means to You

Many learners may actually know the material they are being tested on, but may not demonstrate it well during exam time. If they study under low stress, but take the exam under high stress, for example, their brain may recall less efficiently than if the physiological states were matched. With so much subjectivity involved in the evaluation of learning, brain-based learning advocates that learners be evaluated with a wide range of methods and instruments, including portfolios, quizzes, projects, presentations, and tests that consider multiple learning objectives, while emphasizing multiple intelligences.

Students who might be thought of as "lazy learners" may, in fact, be simply recalling only what they can. Just because a particular student may be good at recalling names and dates, this doesn't necessarily mean they'll be good at recalling a poem, for instance. Learning is stored in distinctive pathways. If you can't retrieve it through one pathway, it may be accessible via another.

Figure 15.3
What Is Memory?

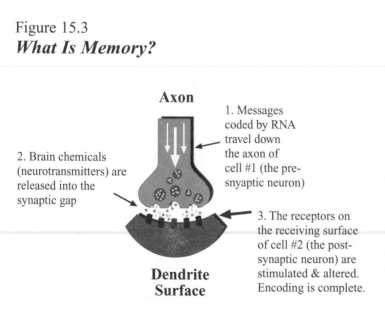

Axon

1. Messages coded by RNA travel down the axon of cell #1 (the pre-snyaptic neuron)

2. Brain chemicals (neurotransmitters) are released into the synaptic gap

3. The receptors on the receiving surface of cell #2 (the post-synaptic neuron) are stimulated & altered. Encoding is complete.

Dendrite Surface

The fact that information is "state-bound" also lends credibility to the role of simulations, case-studies, role plays, and drama performances in the learning process. This may explain why the physical concrete learning that happens when students act out new material better prepares them for real life. Pilots use simulators for training; the military creates mock war situations; and theater groups do rehearsals. In formalized learning situations, increased real-life simulation can also increase the applications of the learning. And, of course, this strategy is most productive when physiological, emotional, and mental states are matched as closely as possible between practice and reality. This is why the popular self-defense courses that rely on mock attackers are so effective. And for this same reason, fire, safety, and health emergency drills are important and should be rehearsed periodically with some sense of urgency and an appropriate level of intensity.

Practical Applications for Better Recall

▼ **Have learners build a working model that embodies the key elements of an idea or lesson.**

▼ **Encourage student study groups.**

▼ **Encourage good nutrition.**

▼ **Create a positive association with the material; engage emotions.**

▼ **Assign partner reviews, but provide for choice in the process.**

▼ **Use dramatic concert readings; read key points with a musical backdrop.**

▼ **Have learners mind-map a subject and share their work within small groups; review them or do second ones a week later.**

▼ **Set up peer-teaching situations or class presentations by the students.**

▼ **Do a one-month follow-up activity to reinforce "new" learning.**

▼ **Learn in different places so that each location provides a context cue.**

Why is it that learners tend to remember much more when learning is associated with a field trip, performance, disaster, guest speaker, complex project, or novel study location? Quite simply, when all of our senses are stimulated and our emotions aroused, multiple memory pathways are engaged.

What Do We Mean by Memory Pathways?

There are many ways to classify memory, for example, short-term, long-term, declarative, nondeclarative, reflexive, procedural, etc.; and the brain deals with each of them in distinctive ways. The two major memory pathways we'll focus on for our purposes here are 1) implicit,

Figure 15.4

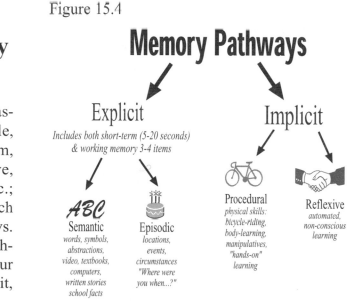

Memory Pathways

Explicit

Includes both short-term (5-20 seconds) & working memory 3-4 items

ABC
Semantic
words, symbols, abstractions, video, textbooks, computers, written stories school facts

Episodic
locations, events, circumstances "Where were you when...?"

Implicit

Procedural
physical skills: bicycle-riding, body-learning, manipulatives, "hands-on" learning

Reflexive
automated, non-conscious learning

and 2) explicit, meaning basically automatically learned or learned by effort. These two memory types can be further divided into subgroups, as figure 15.4 illustrates.

> *Our brain sorts and stores information based on whether it is heavily embedded in context or in content*

The difference between the two primary ways our brain deals with new information can be described quite simply: Information embedded in *context* is "episodic" memory, which means it is stored in relationship to a particular location, circumstance, or episode; and information embedded in *content* is "semantic" memory (facts), which is usually derived from reading and studying (O'Keefe and Nadel 1978).

Episodic memory has unlimited capacity, forms quickly, is easily updated, requires no practice, is effortless, and is used naturally by everyone. *What did you have for dinner last night?* This question, for example, triggers your episodic memory. Not only will context cues help you remember the answer, your memory can be triggered by a body movement or posture, particular music, smell, sound, sight, taste, etc. You will likely think, *what was I doing last night?* in order to trigger some context cues.

The formation of this contextual memory pathway is motivated by curiosity, novelty, life experience, and expectations. It's enhanced by intensified sensory input (sights, sounds, smells, taste, touch). The information can also be stored in a fabric or weave of "mental space," which is a thematic map of the intellectual landscape, where learning occurs as a result of changes in location or circumstances.

Information embedded in *content*, on the other hand, is usually learned (or attempted to be learned) through rote practice or memorization. It requires rehearsal, is resistant to change, is isolated from context, has strict limits, inherently lacks meaning, and is linked to extrinsic motivation. If I ask you, for example, "Who was the author of that book we read last week in class?" your semantic memory is being tapped. This memory pathway is more difficult to establish; it is unnatural and requires practice and consistent rehearsal to encode. This is why we forget so much of the curriculum we are taught in school. In spite of this, our episodic memory is absorbing knowledge all the time, which is what our brain attends to first.

> *Semantic memory (facts and figures) may be a relatively new requirement in the history of humankind. When did we start needing to know addresses, presidents, city capitals, and math formulas?*

Engaging Multiple Memory Pathways

For the brain to remember *content* when it is removed from *context* is a difficult task; yet, this is the type of learning typified by traditional school-work and homework. How often have you heard or said, "Study for Friday's test by reviewing Chapter Six"? Although this is the least efficient way to learn, it is the way most teachers teach. With some imagination, however, we can create a more context-driven environment that makes learning more memorable. This can be done by using real-life simulations, story-telling, ethnic celebrations, virtual learning, field trips, etc. Also when various cultural viewpoints are presented, the learning becomes more relevant to a greater number of students. For example, incorporate diverse languages, foods, environments, holidays, guest speakers, and classroom visitors.

For most teachers, planning time is short, so a simple alternatives have to suffice. Although it would be ideal to enmesh your students in the places they're learning about, this is unrealistic in many cases. So although a trip to China to learn about the country's political system is out of the question, asking your students to plan out such a trip is not. Of course, to accomplish the task, they will have to learn something about the political climate, geography, money, language, passports, weather, foods, people, and customs. Students would have to problem solve, organize, do research, discuss viewpoints, and discover what resources might help them in attending to the task.

Should we throw out "book learning?" No. Just because the brain is generally very poor at learning this way, the solution is not to discard the source. Semantic learning does have its place. When you ask for directions, for example, you want the shortest route from A to B. You don't want to drive all over the city to figure it out (although that would create a stronger "contextual map"). On the other hand, if you ask others what of significance have they learned in the last year, 90 percent of what they'll tell you will probably be contextually-embedded information as opposed to rote or semantic learning.

What This Means to You

Learners may seem to forget a great deal of what is taught, but the problem may stem from an over-reliance on a singular memory system. We may have accidentally created generations of "slow" learners who easily forget; and at no fault of their own. There are better ways to reach learners so that recall improves and self-confidence soars. First, do what you can to avoid excessive use of semantic memory strategies.

Through the use of real-life simulations, thematic instruction, interactive contextual learning, and a focus on multiple intelligences, we can activate multiple memory systems so that learning sticks. When you present a new topic, have learners read about it, listen to a relevant lecture about it, have a discussion regarding it, and watch a related video. Then follow up with complex projects, role-playing, at-home assignments, and related music, discussion, field trips, games, and simulations.

Instead of putting most of the emphasis on memorization and recall, it may be smarter and more efficient to place more emphasis on the context in which something is learned. Contextual learning simply provides more spatial and locational "hooks" and allows learners more time to make personal connections. Reading, hearing, or experiencing the background on a topic aids understanding and recall. The placement of information being learned into a conceptual context, such as historical or comparative, boosts recall, as well.

Other Influences on Recall

Research has verified that an easy way to remember something is to make it new, different, novel. This is because our brain has a high attentional bias towards something which does not fit a normal or expected pattern. When the brain perceives something as different, our stress hormones are released and the result is better attention. If it's perceived as a negative threat, the body may release cortisol; but if it's perceived as a positive stress (challenge), the body releases adrenaline. McGaugh and associates (1989, 1990) and other researchers suggest these chemicals act as memory fixatives.

The BEM Principle

The acronym B.E.M. stands for beginning, end, and middle. When information is presented, it is most likely remembered in this sequence. In other words, what is presented at the beginning is the most memorable, followed by that which is presented at the end, and lastly by that which is presented in the middle. Why does this happen? Researchers speculate that an attentional bias exists at the beginning and end. The *novelty factor* inherent in beginnings and the *emotional release* of endings foster chemical changes in the brain. These changes in our chemistry "tag" the learning and make it more memorable. Figure 15.5 illustrates this memory phenomenon.

There is a distinctly different mental set at the beginning and end of an experience (anticipation, suspense, novelty, and challenge) than there is at the middle of it when the status quo, nothing new, boredom mental state, sets in. Thus, when reviewing a list of items, notes, or facts, or presenting a lengthy lesson, remember to break up the middle part of the session with some surprise elements, a brain break, and/or some conscious strategies for remembering the material presented during this time.

Figure 15.5
Learner Recall of Class Material

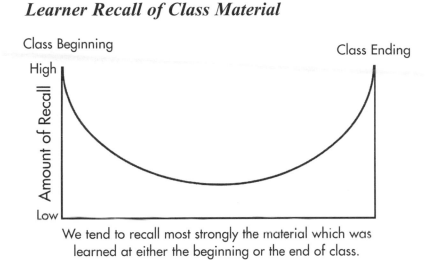

We tend to recall most strongly the material which was learned at either the beginning or the end of class.

What This Means to You

Your students may be able to remember much more if you provide more novelty in the lesson plans and more beginnings and ends (with shortened middles). Introduce short modules of learning instead of long ones. Break up long sessions into several shorter ones.

All learning requires consistent review and updating. Even medical doctors are required by law to "continue" their education. Make time for reviews in class and consistently draw from prior learning to reinforce connections. There are many ways to keep the memory of learned information alive in your learners. Have students participate in weekly peer-review sessions; or have them create a mind-map representing their current understanding of a topic. Assign class murals, mindscapes, and student projects. Continual revision, week after week, encodes the learning in more complex neural networks.

More Memory, Storage, and Retrieval Ideas

▼ Increase the use of storytelling, visualization, and metaphors in your presentations.

▼ Attach a strong emotion to new learning with a purposely designed intense activity.

▼ Review or repeat new learning within ten minutes; then after forty-eight hours; and again after a week.

▼ Attach concrete reminders to new learning, like a token or artifact.

▼ Act out new learning in a skit or role play.

▼ Attach an acrostic to new learning (first letter of each key word forms new word) and other mnemonic techniques.

▼ Depict new learning on a large, colorful poster and put it up in the room.

▼ Ask students to identify patterns and to look for connections with prior learning.

▼ Personalize the lesson by incorporating students' names, ethnic customs, and real-life issues.

▼ Ask learners to summarize new learning with a mind-map.

▼ Give new learning strong context with field trips, guest speakers, and concrete objects to touch and feel.

▼ Have students identify "What's in it for me?" to increase meaningfulness and motivation.

▼ Start a new learning session with something exotic, then familiar, then unusual again.

▼ Increase accountability with frequent reviews and "check-ups."

▼ Incorporate real-life problems and situations to teach about content, as well as process.

▼ Facilitate frequent group discussions on new material.

▼ Incorporate journal writing and other forms of personal reflection.

▼ Provide down time and frequent short breaks to consolidate learning.

Reflection Questions

1. What from this chapter was novel, fresh, or new to you? What was familiar or "old hat"?

2. In what ways, do you already apply the information in this chapter?

3. What three questions might you now generate about this material?

4. How did you react emotionally to the information in this chapter?

5. How did you react cognitively to the information? Do you agree or disagree with the author's point of view? Why?

6. In what ways might you translate the principles presented in this chapter into practical everyday useful ideas?

7. If these things are, in fact, true about the brain, what should we do differently? What resources of time, people, and money could be redirected? In what ways might you suggest we start doing this?

8. What were the most interesting insights you gained from this material?

9. If you were to plan your next step for making your curriculum more brain-based, what would that be?

10. What obstacles might you encounter? How might you realistically deal with them?

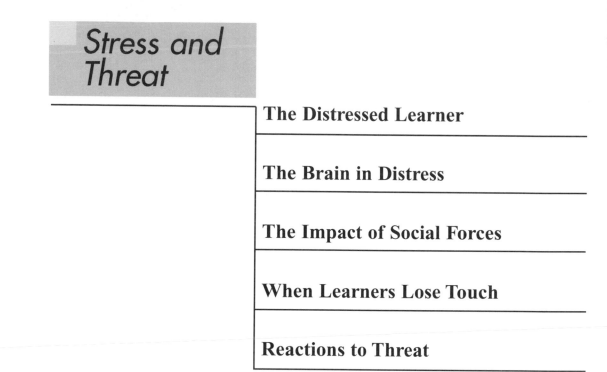

Stress and
Threat

16

Stress and Threat

All of us experience "good stress" and "bad stress." The positive forms of stress occur when we feel moderately challenged and believe we can "rise to the occasion." In these cases, the body releases chemicals like adrenaline and norepinephrine, which actually heighten our perceptions, increase motivation, and strengthen our bodies—all conditions which enhance learning.
Positive stress (eustress) occurs when we have:

▼ **The desire to solve a particular problem**
▼ **The ability to resolve the problem**
▼ **Some sense of control over circumstances**
▼ **Sufficient rest between challenges**
▼ **A perceived potential solution to the problem**

The negative form of stress (distress) occurs when we feel threatened by some physical or emotional danger, intimidation, embarrassment, loss of prestige, fear of rejection or failure, unrealistic time constraints, or a perceived lack of choice.
Distress occurs when we:

▼ **Are confronted with a problem we don't want to solve**
▼ **Don't perceive a solution to the problem**
▼ **Lack the resources to solve the problem**
▼ **Feel the risk levels involved are unacceptable**
▼ **Have little or no control over circumstances**
▼ **Experience repeated situations of intense prolonged stress**

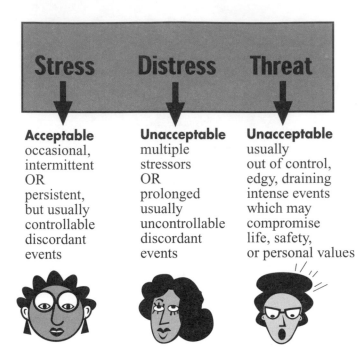

Figure 16.1
Stress vs. Distress and Threat

Stress	**Distress**	**Threat**
Acceptable	**Unacceptable**	**Unacceptable**
occasional, intermittent OR persistent, but usually controllable discordant events	multiple stressors OR prolonged usually uncontrollable discordant events	usually out of control, edgy, draining intense events which may compromise life, safety, or personal values

The Distressed Learner

The difference between positive or moderate stress and distress or threat is distinct: Moderate stress is good for learning, while distress and threat are not! The body responds to high or chronic stress by releasing the hormone cortisol from the adrenal glands. While small amounts can feel good and be a motivating force, too much depresses the immune system, tenses muscles, and impairs learning. Ultimately, high cortisol levels can result in feelings of despair or overwhelm. Worse yet, prolonged release of cortisol can destroy hippocampal neurons associated with learning (Sapolsky 1996, 1999; Sylwester 1995). Even short-term elevation of cortisol can create confusion and poor distinctions between what's important and what's not (Vincent 1990).

Whether the perceived stress or threat is physical, environmental, academic, or emotional, the result on our body over time is the same—a depressed immune system, tensing of the large muscles, blood-clotting, and high blood pressure. This physical state is the perfect response for facing a saber-toothed tiger in the jungle; but in school, the triggering of this survival mechanism usually leads to behavior and learning problems.

The issue gets more complicated when you consider that what might be perceived as high stress and threat to one person may not be to another. The subjective nature of stress makes it a complex dynamic that can be difficult to manage. A critical point, however, is that the brain's reality is born from our perception; and perception is mutable. This is why it is so important to give learners choice in the learning process: The more control they feel they have, the more they will exercise it; and the better they will become at managing their own stress states.

Many learners who are under-performing may be simply over-stressed. At the elementary level, the student may not even be cognizant of the problem. To some learners achieving at a higher level may simply feel like an impossibility. If all you've ever known is poverty, for example, it's difficult to realize an alternative—a necessary step in the resolution process. Identifying the core stress; then creating an awareness of alternatives; and ultimately working towards a desirable change,

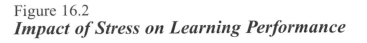

Figure 16.2
Impact of Stress on Learning Performance

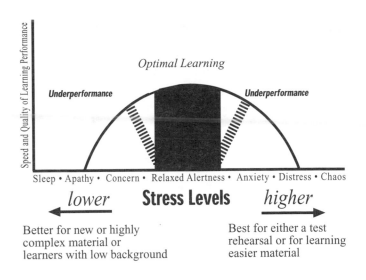

are the cornerstones of empowerment. And it is this foundation that is critical to optimal learning. Remember, if the brain is in survival mode, it won't effectively process and recall even simple semantic facts like "nine times three equals twenty-seven." You can bet, however, that it will remember information such as, "Today is Daddy's payday, which means he'll come home drunk: I better stay away from him tonight." A child in this state won't likely complete their homework assignment, as their emotions are (therefore attention) drawn away to more immediate matters.

 What This Means to You

Ensure that learners have the necessary resources and support to complete the assignments you give them; and ultimately, to resolve high-stress issues that may be harming them outside of class. Keep in mind that learners will experience undue stress if they do not: 1) Perceive a solution is possible; 2) Have the necessary resources to solve a problem; 3) Have a sense of control over a bad situation; 4) Have sufficient time to learn; or 5) Have the ability or awareness to manage their stress. Seek help if you suspect a learner is facing threat and high stress outside the classroom. Routinely incorporate brief stretching, breathing exercises, and "purposeful play" in the classroom. Model respectful interactions and non-threatening communication. Introduce activities and games that add an element of moderate challenge, fun, and stress-free learning to your classroom environment.

The Brain in Distress

The area of the brain most affected by high stress or threat is the hippocampus, which is very sensitive to cortisol. Over time, cortisol may weaken the brain's locale memory and indexing systems, and may narrow perceptual "mapping." The hippocampus is also the center of the body's immune system, so the chronic release of cortisol weakens the body's ability to fight disease.

> *Learners in a state of fear or threat not only experience reduced cognitive abilities, but their immune system suffers, as well.*

A chronically high cortisol level leads to physical changes in the brain that are significant. Stanford scientist Robert Sapolsky (1992, 1996, 1999) found atrophy levels of 8 to 24 percent in the hippocampus of Vietnam veterans with post-traumatic stress disorder. "We have known for many years that stress can interfere with neuron production in the *fetal* brain and that it can damage and even kill pre-existing neurons," said Sapolsky. "Now we have evidence, as well, that when there is neuron production in the *adult* brain, stress can also disrupt it." High levels of distress can cause the death of brain cells in the hippocampus—an area critical to explicit memory formation. Chronic stress also impairs student's ability to sort out what's important and what's not.

There are other problems. Chronic stress makes students more susceptible to illness. In one study (Johnston-Brooks, et al. 1998), learners examined just prior to test time revealed depressed immune systems and lower levels of an important antibody for

Figure 16.3
Stress and Distress Pathways

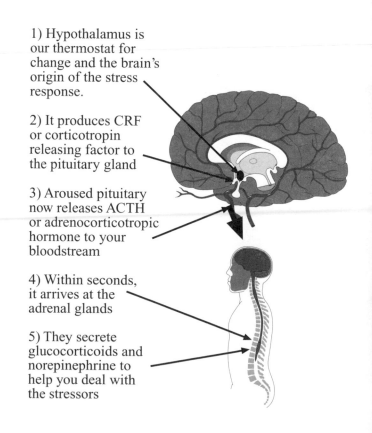

1) Hypothalamus is our thermostat for change and the brain's origin of the stress response.

2) It produces CRF or corticotropin releasing factor to the pituitary gland

3) Aroused pituitary now releases ACTH or adrenocorticotropic hormone to your bloodstream

4) Within seconds, it arrives at the adrenal glands

5) They secrete glucocorticoids and norepinephrine to help you deal with the stressors

fighting infection. Such findings may help explain the viscous academic performance cycle most of us have become all too familiar with: More test stress means more illness and missed classes which eventually means lower test scores; and the cycle of failure continues. In addition to increased cortisol levels, recent studies (Casolini, et al. 1993) also link chronic stress to low serotonin levels, which are suspect risk factors for violent and aggressive behavior patterns.

A stressful physical environment adds to the problem. Crowded conditions, fear of violence or peer retaliation, even fluorescent lighting, can impact learner stress. All of these stress factors can contribute to the low achievement/low self-esteem cycle of failure that can occur in spite of a child's high IQ or natural intelligence. Stressed children typically experience constricted breathing which can alter how they focus and blink as they adapt to the stress. Distress can impact the learner in other ways, too. In figure 16.4 you see how various levels of distress, including a traumatic event, can impact our memory.

Figure 16.4
Stress, Trauma, and Memory

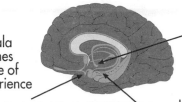

Amygdala establishes the value of an experience

HPA stands for Hypothalamus Pituitary and Adrenals, the brain's stress response curcuit

Hippocampus is the brain's index for our semantic & episodic types of retrieval

Stress Levels

High levels (distress), sustained levels, or trauma means:
Strongly impaired or highly selective memory. Excess activiation of the amygdula through trauma may inhibit hippocampal functioning. Excess and chronic stress commonly leads to neuronal death in hippocampus.

Moderate stress means:
General facilitatation of memory storage

Very low stress means:
Neutral or minimal impact on memory; no excessive hormonal activation

The good news, however, is that moderate levels of stress actually seem to facilitate storage and retrieval of memories. Moderate stress, such as that caused by an emergent deadline, may also provide the impetus or motivation necessary to accomplish a challenging task. If the learner feels capable of the challenge before them and has the support to persevere through the difficult times, the stress state can help establish an optimal learning environment. Some studies suggest, on the other hand, that low-stress environments increase student receptivity to complex and novel learning.

The Impact of Social Forces

Our emotional environment is influenced by many stressors—many of which cannot be avoided. For an adult, it's the noise, erratic drivers, mean-spirited customers, hard-headed colleagues, selfish bosses, broken down copy machines, insensitive family members, financial worries, and screaming children that provide the emotional stress. For youth, it's no different: A typical school day is full of broken promises, hurt feelings, and fear of the unknown. The project that flopped, the low math score, the bully's unkind remarks, the insensitive teacher, the pressure to conform, the pressure to perform, the popularity contest, decisions about values and choices, and concerns about money—all of these "glitches" can be a source of stress which the brain often responds to as threats. Accepting our different roles in various social situations can be difficult for adults, let alone youngsters still grappling with self-identity issues. However, if we have a lot of support we can manage the stress more effectively than if we don't have a good support system. Support can come from many places; and does not necessarily have to originate at home to positively influence learners.

According to a recent study by Sally Reis and Eva Diaz (1999), despite lack of parental involvement in the academic pursuits of nine ethnically diverse and economically disadvantaged high-school females, the students continued to perform well on achievement tests and in other academic endeavors. The students attributed their success to interaction with other high-achieving students, teachers, and mentors—all which helped deepen a strong belief in self, the study reports. Thus, student achievement may be less related to the parental support factor than to the enrichment factor of the educational setting.

 ## What This Means to You

Social status or popularity, especially among teens, represents a key source of stress for learners. A student, for example, who may be "top dog" at home, but just "one of many" in a classroom of thirty, may feel "stressed out" at school. However, such a student may shine if given a leadership role. Since the brain's chemistry can actually change in response to one's perception of social status, it makes good sense to shift leadership roles often and ensure all students have a chance to lead *and* follow. Providing an enriched learning environment at school can contribute a great deal to a student's support system. The less support a child may be receiving at home, the more they need to be enriched and supported at school. A simple step you can take to offset the many stressors learners face is provide more predictability through school and classroom rituals. Predictable events, like a graded paper returned when promised or a peer cheer for completing a project on time, helps put the unsettled brain at ease.

When Learners Lose Touch

The funny thing about distress is that our body adapts *too* well to it. In figure 16.5 there are three lines, representing three different levels of stress. The lowest one is acceptable stress. It increases in the morning, levels off mid-day, then drops in the evening. The very top line represents stress that has become "out of control." This is the level of stress none of us like—the irritable, short-fused, aching shoulders, migraine headache level. Adults who have learned to manage their stress may respond to this over-stressed state by taking time off work to relax. The problem, however, is that the temporary reduction of stress takes us back temporarily to the middle stress level in the illustration; but once we become complacent again, we find ourselves back in the high-stress state. Our mid-line becomes our new baseline; and before we know it, it's increasing again.

Many educators and trainers are in a perpetual state of the mid-line "crisis." They no longer feel the distress as their body has adapted. However this is a dangerous state to be in: Having lost touch with their bodies, they only feel distressed when they've capped out at the highest level. As many as 30 to 50 percent of all educators may find themselves in this situation. The bad news is that, in this state, effective staff development is virtually impossible. When the mind body system is "under siege," the body will accept only the "tried and true," because the additional

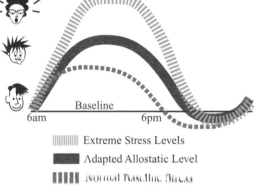

Figure 16.5
Adaptation to High Stress Creates an Allostatic State

||||||||| Extreme Stress Levels

▬▬▬ Adapted Allostatic Level

▮▮▮▮ Normal Baseline Stress

stress of any change may "break the bank." The good news is, however, that through a thoughtful program of personal change, we can all lower our distress levels—an important first step in returning ourselves to an optimal learning state.

 What This Means to You

Incorporate stretching and breathing sessions, quiet walks, support groups, music, and art therapy in your own life. Give your students and yourself down time or reflection time to get in touch with your stress levels. Reducing sugar and caffeine intake can help moderate the effects of stress. Only when you are effectively managing your own stress levels, can you be at your best for others.

Reactions to Threat

High stress or threat has no place in schools. This is a given. Our military, which purposely creates a stressful environment for accelerated learning, is a well-known departure from the rule. The very essence of "boot camp" is to create a stressful environment that resembles a war environment. Thus, threats and punishment are commonplace. However, even the military's teaching approach changes when a soldier is being trained for a technical job or a leadership position that requires critical recall and strategic thinking, rather than purely obedience. Teaching soldiers to obey commands at all costs is, in fact, a very different learning task than teaching them to show good judgment and be critical thinkers.

For the most part, the brain responds to threat exposure in predictable ways. The moment a threat is detected, the brain jumps into high gear. The amygdala is at the center of all our fear and threat responses. It focuses our attention and receives immediate direct inputs from the thalamus, sensory cortex, the hippocampus, and the frontal lobes. Neural projections (bundles of fibers) from the amygdala then activate the entire sympathetic system. Normally, it triggers the release of adrenaline, vasopressin, and cortisol. These chemicals immediately change the way we think, feel, and act.

Figure 16.6
Simplified Biological Reaction to Threat

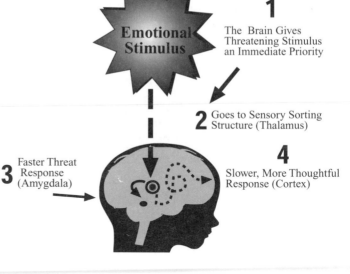

1 The Brain Gives Threatening Stimulus an Immediate Priority

2 Goes to Sensory Sorting Structure (Thalamus)

3 Faster Threat Response (Amygdala)

4 Slower, More Thoughtful Response (Cortex)

New research reveals that threatening environments can trigger chemical imbalances; and especially worrisome, is the reduced level of serotonin. Serotonin is a strong modulator of our emotions and subsequent behaviors; and when serotonin levels fall, violence often rises. Threats also elevate levels of vasopressin, which has been linked to aggression. These imbalances can trigger impulsive and aggressive behavior that, some believe, can lead to a lifetime of violence.

Students who have experienced early chronic exposure to threat and high stress, particularly those who have come from violent backgrounds, usually have attention difficulties. Survival behaviors, such as consistent and constant shifting of eyes, voice, and attention are the norm, as they unconsciously scan the room for "potential predators" or "prey." For survivals sake, the brain's receptor sites have adapted to the dangers in their normal environment. These learners often swing or swat at other students to establish "rank" and control. Such "territorialism" can be heard in comments such as, "Don't look at me that way!" Misreading danger cues is common for the "stressed out" learner. What may be perceived as a friendly gesture by someone who is emotionally well adjusted, may be experienced as a threat by one who has lived with chronic threat. While this behavior makes for frustrated teachers, it makes perfect sense to the student whose life seems to depend on it.

The list of potential threats to learners is endless; and they can exist anywhere, from one's own home to a neighbor's home, from the hallway outside your classroom to the gang that rules the hood. It could be an over-stressed parent, a boyfriend, a rude classmate, an unknowing teacher who threatens a student with humiliation, detention, or embarrassment, or a combination of these stressors. When the brain is put on alert, defense mechanisms and behaviors are activated, which is great for survival, but not good for learning.

Figure 16.7
Common Sources of Threat to Learning

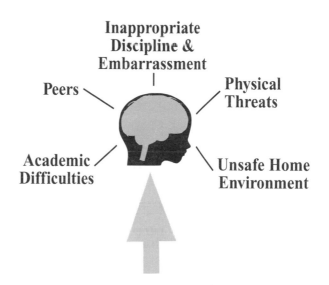

There are other costs to threats, such as induced or learned helplessness. Since survival always overrides pattern-detection and complex problem solving, stressed students are less able to understand subtle connections, patterns, and implications. Under threat, the brain uses less of the reflective, "higher-order" thinking skills of the frontal lobes and resorts to using more of the reflexive nature of the amygdala. In addition, only immediate consequences are likely considered in the decision-making process. These results have tremendous implications for learning. Non-stressed learners will exhibit better thinking, understanding, attention, concentration, and recall. For a simple example, consider how when you are taking a test, an answer can be on the tip of your tongue, but not quite accessible. But the moment you turn in the test, the answer pops into your head.

Blood flow changes to the brain also negatively impact the threatened learner. Wayne Drevets, PhD. of the University of Pittsburgh (Drevets and Raichle 1998) says that when faced with threat, we experience an increased blood flow to the lower (ventral) frontal lobes and a decreased flow to the upper (dorsal) areas of the frontal lobes. This means the area of the brain that processes emotions is getting the lion's share of the blood creating a sense of overwhelm, while the brain area used for critical thinking, judgment, and creativity is shorted.

Threats are defined as any stimulus that causes the brain to trigger a sense of fear, mistrust, anxiety, or general helplessness. This state can be a result of physical harm or perceived danger (usually from teachers, parents or peers); intellectual harm (unrealistic performance expectations or time constraints, or lack of resources, support, positive role models); or emotional harm (embarrassment, humiliation, or isolation) Under any type of perceived threat, the brain:

Figure 16.8
Impact of Threat on Cerebral Blood Flow

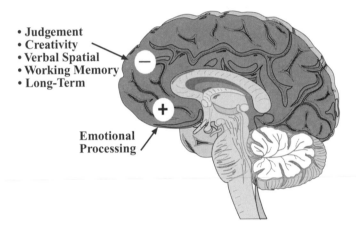

• Judgement
• Creativity
• Verbal Spatial
• Working Memory
• Long-Term

Emotional Processing

▼ **Loses its ability to correctly interpret subtle clues from the environment**

▼ **Reverts to familiar "tried and true" behaviors**

▼ **Loses some of it's ability to index, store, and access information**

▼ **Becomes more automatic and limited in its responses**

▼ **Loses some of its ability to perceive relationships and patterns**

▼ **Is less able to use "higher-order" thinking skills**

▼ **Loses some long-term memory capacity**

▼ **Tends to overreact to stimuli in a phobic-like way**

Avoid calling on learners unless they volunteer. Eliminate discipline policies that are fear or threat-based. Avoid score keeping, overt comparisons, or situations that cause embarrassment to students. Never threaten a student by saying you'll send them to a higher authority, kick them out, or call their parents. Provide an enriched environment with lots of opportunities for interactions with caring adults and other learners. Reduce testing and grade stress by providing more frequent reviews, feedback, and remedial support. Make assessments more genuine and meaningful by recognizing the personal challenges of individual students and acknowledging even slight progress.

Figure 16.9
Create Conditions for Learning

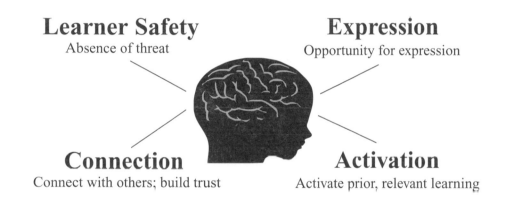

Learner Safety
Absence of threat

Expression
Opportunity for expression

Connection
Connect with others; build trust

Activation
Activate prior, relevant learning

Common Teacher Threats

▼ **Every minute you're late is going to cost you.**

▼ **You know what's going to happen if you don't do what you're told, don't you?**

▼ **If you do that one more time, you're staying after school.**

▼ **You're not going to recess until you clean up your desks.**

▼ **If I have to tell you again, you'll be sorry.**

▼ **Wait until I tell your mother/father about this; they will not be happy.**

▼ **The more time you waste talking, the less computer time you'll have.**

What This Means to You

Here are four ways you can reduce the impact of threat on your learners:

1) Increase their sense of safety at school. Encourage discussions about their fears, worries, and causes of stress. Sometimes just the opportunity to talk about the issues helps reduce the burden. Incorporate small group activities; and model effective communication and problem solving. Increase teams and other strategies for developing group identity and support. When necessary, seek outside help and support.

2) Encourage positive relationships among learners. Give them time to relate to each other in ways that go beyond superficial. Allow for personal choice in the process of creating teams. Once teams are formed, allow learners to remain with the group long enough to develop strong interpersonal relations. Help learners resolve conflicts by being there for support, but not enforcing your influence too strongly. Help them with their decision-making and problem-solving skills, but don't solve the problem or make decisions for them. Initiate team cheers, applause, and other affirming rituals that make students feel good.

3) Provide numerous opportunities for learners to express themselves. This can be initiated through the use of art, dance, poetry, singing, sharing, journal reflection, sports, debate, and small group activities. Give students the opportunity to set their own ground-rules and classroom standards. What they help create, they will buy into, and adhere to with less resistance.

4) Activate prior learning by reviewing the previous lesson(s). Offer generous feedback; and set up mechanisms for self-evaluation and peer review. This simple strategy, if nothing else, will reduce learner stress and increase confidence immensely.

When you create a safe and relaxed learning environment with an absence of threat and high stress, many learners will surprise you. They'll very quickly exhibit improved thinking and problem-solving skills and fewer disruptions and behavioral problems. Although no one can be expected to provide the perfect environment (there is no such thing), providing an emotionally and physically safe environment with plenty of opportunity for enrichment will go a long way towards offsetting life's little (and sometimes big) imperfections.

Reflection Questions

1. What from this chapter was novel, fresh, or new to you? What was familiar or "old hat"?

2. In what ways, do you already apply the information in this chapter?

3. What three questions might you now generate about this material?

4. How did you react emotionally to the information in this chapter?

5. How did you react cognitively to the information? Do you agree or disagree with the author's point of view? Why?

6. In what ways might you translate the principles presented in this chapter into practical everyday useful ideas?

7. If these things are, in fact, true about the brain, what should we do differently? What resources of time, people, and money could be redirected? In what ways might you suggest we start doing this?

8. What were the most interesting insights you gained from this material?

9. If you were to plan your next step for making your curriculum more brain-based, what would that be?

10. What obstacles might you encounter? How might you realistically deal with them?

Music with a Purpose

Mind-Body Effects

The Musical Brain

Music and Learning

Impact on Moods and Stress

Most Beneficial Music Selections

Music as a Carrier to the Nonconscious

Engage the Brain with Concert Readings

Music with a Purpose

We've known for eons that music can have a mind-altering effect on humans. And, you've probably heard recently that listening to Mozart can be beneficial to learning. But are there ways to maximize the value of music in the academic environment? And, are some kinds of music better for learning than others? Is there research to support these claims; and how substantial are they? All of these questions are important. Clearly everyone loves music. And if we can benefit cognitively from listening to it, certainly we are interested. Let's start by reviewing some of the findings about music's effect on the brain-body system and the implications for educators.

Mind-Body Effects

Music is an essential aspect of human life; and our responses to it may even be hard-wired into our brain. The authors of *The Biological Origins of Music* (Wallen, Merker, and Brown 1999) say that music may be a universal form of communication that has influenced species preservation and played a role in mate attraction, bonding, and harmony. Norman Weinberger, a neuroscientist at the University of California at Irvine, says (1995), "An increasing number of findings support the theory that the brain is specialized for the building blocks of music." His research suggests that the auditory cortex responds to pitch and tones rather than simply raw sound frequencies; and that individual brain cells process melodic contour. Other specific correlates in the brain (areas that respond specifically to music) are illustrated in figure 17.1 on the following page.

Figure 17.1
Neural Correlates for Music Processing

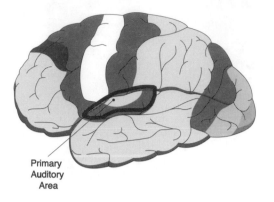

Primary
Auditory
Area

In the auditory cortex, specific groups of neurons have been identified which do the following:
- process pitch
- process timbre
- process melodic contour
- process beat (meter) in right hemisphere
- process rhythm in left hemisphere

Summary: Music sensitivity may be built into our brains. If so, most likely, there is strong adaptive value.

Manfred Clynes, PhD., author of *Music, Mind, and Brain* (1982), explains how music engages the whole brain. Music's harmonic structure, interval quality, timbre, and the spatial, temporal, long-term patterns are recognized by our *non-dominant* hemisphere (in most of us, the right hemisphere). On the other hand, the short-term signatures in music, like rapidly varying volume, rapid and accurate pitch trajectory, pacing, and lyrics are recognized by the *dominant* hemisphere (in most of us, the left). Over the last hundred years, music has shifted towards types that stimulate our dominant hemisphere more (as our tastes have moved towards more avant-garde styles) and less towards the non-dominant hemisphere (as would be expected of baroque or classical). In other words, today's music engages more of the brain.

Music's impact can also be felt on our heart rate, as measured by our pulse, which tends to synchronize with the beat of the music we're hearing. The faster the music, the faster our pulse. Jean Houston, PhD. has often said in her workshops that music "raises the molecular structure of the body...." The body resonates at a stable molecular wavelength. Music has its own frequencies, which either resonate or conflict with our body's own rhythms. When both are resonating on the same frequency, we feel "in sync," we learn better, and we're more aware and alert.

As summarized in the book *Accelerated Learning with Music* (Webb and Webb 1990), music's potential effects on the mind and body include the following:

▼ **Increases muscular energy**

▼ **Increases molecular energy**

▼ **Influences heartbeat**

▼ **Alters metabolism**

▼ **Reduces pain and stress**

▼ **Speeds healing and recovery in surgery patients**

▼ **Relieves fatigue**

▼ **Aids in the release of emotions**

▼ **Stimulates creativity, sensitivity, and thinking**

The Musical Brain

Music elicits emotional responses, receptive or aggressive states, and stimulates the limbic system. The limbic system and subcortical region of the brain are involved in engaging musical and emotional responses, as well as mediating long-term memory. This means that when information is imbued with music, there's a greater likelihood that the brain will encode it in long-term memory.

Interestingly enough, researchers (Bever and Chiarello 1974) found that the brain responds differently to music depending on the listener's depth of analysis. In neuro-imaging studies blood flow and brain activity in the brains of professional musicians and non-musicians were compared, as they listened to music. When the musical novice listened, the right hemisphere "lit up", while the left hemisphere and amygdala were more activated when the professional musician listened.

Activations occur in various parts of the brain depending on the specific learning task involved. The brain responds differently depending on if you are learning music by hearing it, playing it, reading it, being told about it, visualizing a score, recalling a concert, or experiencing strong emotions involving music. Each of these events is registered and processed differently in the brain. For example, melody activates the right brain, while harmony and rhythm activate more of the left brain; and measuring beats activates the cerebellum.

It is deplorable that in some public schools music is considered a "right-brain frill." Robert Zatorre, a neuropsychologist at the Montreal

Figure 17.2
How Areas of the Brain Are Differently Activated by Music

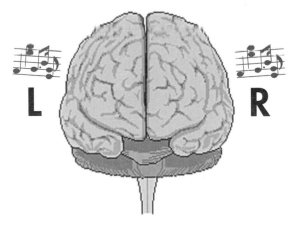

- Musician: L Brain vs. Non-Musician: R Brain (Analyze vs. entertain)
- Harmony and Rhythm: L Brain
- Melody: R Brain
- Beat/Spatial: Cerebellum

Neurological Institute says (1997), "I have very little doubt that when you're listening to a real piece of music, it is engaging your entire brain." And reading or composing music particularly engages both sides of the brain. Music in the curriculum, both as a subject of study and as accompaniment to the learning process, may be a valuable tool for the integration of thinking across both brain hemispheres.

Music and Learning

In studies with pre-schoolers, secondary students, and college students, computer-generated images of brain activity revealed striking similarities to the written score of Mozart-composed music. Coincidence, or not? Could it be that Mozart activates the brain in a way that we are biologically receptive to or programmed for? Further study is necessary, but the promise of music's potential for engaging learning is enticing. Consider that each of the countries with the highest science and math results in the world have a strong music and arts programs.

Consider a 1987 National Music Educators Conference report that cites students taking music courses scored 20 to 40 points higher on standardized college entrance exams. And, a college entrance examination board study (Educational Testing Services 1999) suggests that students who took four or more years of music classes scored higher on both verbal and math tests. Another study examined the effect of two years of keyboarding lessons on preschoolers (Rauscher, et al. 1997). The results are illustrated in figure 17.3.

Figure 17.3

Preschool Keyboarding Practice Enhances Long-Term Spatial/Temporal Reasoning

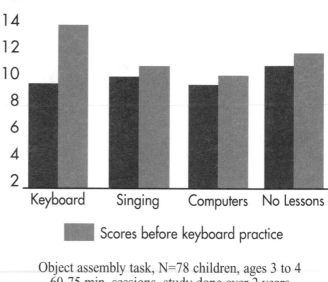

Object assembly task, N=78 children, ages 3 to 4
60-75 min. sessions, study done over 2 years
Mean score for age groupings (Wechsler)

Source: Rauscher et al. (1997) Neurological Research, Vol. 19, Feb.

Music can actually prime the brain's neural pathways. Researcher Frances Rauscher, PhD. contends (1997) that neural firing patterns are basically the same for music appreciation and abstract reasoning. Rausher's early studies (Rauscher, et al. 1993) at the Center for the Neurobiology of Learning and Memory at University of California, Irvine campus measured the impact of listening to Mozart before taking a test. The students who listened to classical music for ten minutes (Mozart's Sonata for Two Pianos in D Major) raised their test scores in spatial and abstract reasoning. And, on an intelligence test, the gain was 9 points after just ten minutes. Those who listened only to a relaxation tape or had silence, on the other hand, showed only slight improvement at best. Rauscher notes that this suggests a causal relationship, not a correlation. Although the effect in the brain is only temporary (5 to 15 minutes), the results can be duplicated with additional reactivation at any time.

Discretion is important when interpreting and applying these results. For example, although the Irvine studies may suggest that listening to Mozart before testing is valuable; listening *during* a test would likely cause neural competition by interfering with the brain's neural firing patterns (Felix 1993). Thus, there are appropriate times for music in the learning process, just as there are appropriate times for quiet. When studies compare the gains after listening to Mozart compared to relaxation music, or white noise, or simple subsets of music (tones, beats, and rhythms) results differ.

Neuroscientist Larry Parsons, at the University of Texas's Imaging Center in San Antonio discovered that while Mozart beat the control group in spatial reasoning enhancement, other simple subsets of music actually helped the experimental subjects do far better than did listening to Mozart. What this suggests is that it may be rhythms, tones, or patterns of music that enhance learning.

And there are other issues. Rats that listened to Mozart and improved their maze-running, did so very specifically: They improved in the spatial task of object rotation, but not the more demanding reasoning and problem-solving skills. So, for the moment, the so-called "Mozart Effect" is still unclear; and its applications to the classroom are only speculative. The degree to which learning may be enhanced and the specific learning tasks impacted remain the focus of current research.

Robert Monroe, PhD., engineer and founder of the Monroe Institute, has produced audiotapes which use specific beat frequencies to create synchronized rhythmic patterns of concentration. He calls them "Hemi-Sync" and they are designed to help the left and right hemisphere of the brain work together for increased concentration, learning, and memory. He reports a multitude of success stories with a wide range of learners from first graders to seniors.

Professional musician and educator Steven Halpern (1985, 1999) claims that not only is the study of music beneficial in itself, but the introduction of it into the school curriculum aids math, reading, and science learning. The absence of art and music, on the other hand, can retard brain development in children," he adds. Halpern produces recordings that are predictable, therefore not distracting, to the ear.

The learning benefits attributed to music are:

▼ Relaxation and stress reduction (stress inhibits learning)

▼ The fostering of creativity through brain-wave activation

▼ The stimulation of imagination and thinking

▼ The stimulation of motor skills, speaking, and vocabulary

▼ A reduction in discipline problems

▼ The focusing and alignment of group energy

▼ Vehicle for conscious and subconscious information transmission

> *"Significant positive effects of music during learning have been reported, especially with music from the baroque and classical periods; however, positive effects of music played during testing are not consistently supported."*
> —Uschi Felix

 ## What This Means to You

We may be under-utilizing music in the context of learning. We rely so much on our own voices to deliver meaning, yet music is a terrific carrier of information to the brain. The new research describing "The Mozart Effect" (Campbell 1997) tells us that music may be a powerful tool in building reasoning power, memory, and intelligence. If you're not using music in your teaching, this may be a good time to start. If you are already, this may be a good time to expand or enhance your repertoire.

Music should be used purposefully and judiciously for best results. Too much can saturate the listener, reducing its effectiveness. As a general rule, music should be used no more than 30 percent of total class time (unless, of course, it's a music class). And, *how* the music is used is as important as the *type* of music used. Many educators have claimed success using reggae, Latin, pop, jazz, new age, big band, waltz, hip hop, rock, and soul. Don't get caught up in using only Mozart, just because that's what we've heard the most about. Mozart is great; but it is just one piece of the larger puzzle. Other types of sound are beneficial, as well. Even clapping games, singing, nature sounds, and simple rhythms alter physiological states and create more receptivity for learning.

Impact on Moods and Stress

Don Campbell, author of *The Mozart Effect* (1997), summarizes how music lowers stress: It impacts our heart rate, influences the brain's chemicals, and creates a receptive state of mind. Consider, for example, how you might be driving along in your car listening to the radio and maybe feeling a bit blah or stressed when one of your all-time favorite songs comes on. Maybe it's one you recall from a special time as a teenager or college student. Or maybe it's a song that brings back memories of a first love. Whatever the associations, you immediately feel better. Once again, music has worked its charms.

> *Some sounds and music produce optimal learning states, as well as energizing the body for maximum wellness and optimism.*

Music affects all of us: Its reputation as a universal language is well deserved. Manfred Clynes, PhD. research (1982) involving forty Central Australian Aborigines of the Warlbiri Tribe suggests that sounds of joy, love, reverence, grief, anger, sex and hate are recognized across cultures. The Aborigines' recognition scores, in fact, equaled those of university students at the University of New South Wales, MIT, and the University of California at Berkeley.

In Japan, one group of anesthetized surgery patients listened to music with headphones while another group did not. The "music" group exhibited lower stress. In your classroom, you may have found that when you play relaxing music, or Baroque in the major key, your students tend to settle down and focus. From bedtime lullabies to sacred drumming rituals, music has always been used to induce a focused, calm, trance-like state that hypnotists call a "suggestive state." Whatever name you give it, learning in this state is more efficient than when the learner is stressed out, tense, distracted, or hyper.

Music and acoustic pioneer Alfred Tomatis, PhD (1983) says that sound provides an electrical charge to energize the brain. His research suggests that cells in the cortex of the brain act like small batteries, which generate the electricity you see in an EEG printout. Amazingly enough, the brain's own batteries are not charged by metabolism, they are charged externally, through sound. Dr. Tomatis discovered that specific high frequencies sped up the brain's recharging process. This recharge affect impacted posture, energy flow, attitude, and muscle tone. The frequencies with the greatest impact were in the 8000 hertz range. Other research (Clynes 1982; Zatorre 1997) suggests that low-frequency tones discharge mental and physical energy, while specific higher tones power up the brain.

Music is an effective instrument for enhancing mood and eliciting a state of learning receptivity. Ideal for this purpose is music that is played in a major key and provides positive upbeat messages. Broadway musicals and theme songs from epic motion pictures work well in many instances. Ask your students what music they like to listen to at home. Incorporate some of their collective taste, even if only in limited doses. Provide a wide variety of types and choices; and incorporate music from diverse cultures. Experiment with many types and learning purposes to find what works best for your particular students and subject matter. Use music to mark a special occasion or announcement, to change the energy level in the room, to celebrate a success, or to accompany a closing or transition time. Some learners like background music played in the classroom, while others don't. One way to satisfy everyone is to provide an area of the room where learners can use headphones to listen without disturbing others.

What Music Selections Are Most Beneficial?

The answer to this question depends on the individual and what the intended state is. We know that the brain's attention is drawn by variations rather than predictable patterns; thus, if you want to increase writing focus, for example, Baroque on low in the background is great. Since Baroque, unlike most other types of music, is highly predictable, it poses less of a distraction problem. If you want to increase your group's energy level, however, selections like the theme song from "Rocky", "Jump," by Van Halen or "Let's Get Excited," by The Pointer Sister's are great. Then again, if you want learners to relax, nature sounds or soft piano music is ideal.

Accelerated Learning Pioneer Georgi Lozanov (1979, 1991) says that classical (circa 1750-1825) and romantic (circa 1820-1900) are better for introducing new information. He suggests Baroque (circa 1600-1750) as background accompaniment or for reviews at the end of a session.

Dr. Clynes (1982) says that, there is a greater consistency in the body's pulse response to classical music than to rock music. In other words, you will get more predictable responses with classical music. This doesn't mean that contemporary music cannot work; just that much of it elicits less predictable responses.

Researcher Jeff King, PhD. has studied the neurophysiological response of particular music selections on the brain. His results suggest that there is no statistically significant difference between using Baroque or New Age music in the effectiveness of inducing alpha states for learning. Dr. King used music from the recording "Duotones" by the artist Kenny G, but speculated that other similar music types may work as well. Multiple independent tests were performed for all samples, and King concluded that either New Age or Baroque music could be used to enhance learning.

 ## What This Means to You

Think about the specific physiological and emotional state that you would like to evoke; and choose music that elicits that state. Since different types of music elicit different psycho-physiological states, incorporate a variety of music types. For example, as learners are arriving, play music that creates a state of anticipation or excitement (epic movie themes, Olympic fanfare, the andante movements in major keys of Vivaldi's "Four Seasons," or Bach's "Brandenburg Concertos" in major keys). For storytelling, use music that has built-in peaks and valleys and that engages fantasy and emotion (classical or romantic). To deliver content with a musical accompaniment, use classical or romantic music. For closed-eye review or background accompaniment, low-volume Baroque is optimal. Many other forms of expression also work from world beat, folk, jazz, or country to gospel, marches, pop, positive rap, or new age. Experiment and use what works for your particular circumstances. Have learners rewrite well-known songs with words that reflect what they're currently learning. Give learners the opportunity to experiment (in a structured way) with music in the classroom.

Music as a Carrier to the Nonconscious

Music carries with it more than just feelings: The melody can act as a vehicle for the words, as well. This powerful communication transfer can happen on either a conscious or nonconscious level. As described by the Webbs (1990), "Music acts as a premium signal carrier, whose rhythms, patterns, contrasts, and varying tonalities encode any new information." You may have noticed how easily children pick up the words to new songs. It's the melody that helps them learn the words. For example, consider how you learned the alphabet. If you're like most of us, you absorbed this fundamental information to the tune of "Twinkle, Twinkle Little Star." As infants, we hear the melody over and over; and when it's time to learn the alphabet, we simply "glue" the letters to the tune. This is done so unconsciously that most of us don't even realize, the Alphabet Song and "Twinkle, Twinkle Little Star" are sung to the same tune.

Some educators are capitalizing on the use of melody as a carrier of information by creating musical "sound tracks" for their presentations. This purposeful combination of music with planned content was first described by the renowned educational innovator and founder of accelerated learning Georgi Lozanov in the 1970s. In a nutshell, the approach incorporates a movie-like sound track effect, whereby, the material you present is accompanied with a musical "concert" interplay. The teacher becomes the "orchestra conductor." "Sound surfing," as it's been called by some, works by combining the educator's voice, as one instrument in the learning process, with an appropriate musical selection based on the intent of the lesson.

What This Means to You

There are many ways we can use music to carry messages into the minds of receptive learners. One is to use learner-generated songs. Have your students select five songs that they already know well (like Jingle Bells, Happy Birthday, simple and traditional folk songs, etc.). Then re-write the song's lyrics with new words from the lesson. Sing the song several times. The new lyrics will bind easily to the minds of learners.

Engaging the Brain with Concert Readings

While it's true that music can engage the brain, a combination of words and music can dramatically increase the results. A "concert reading" is the purposeful use of music as a partner for delivering a large volume of content to the brain. According to Dr. Lozanov (1979, 1991), a "well-executed concert can do 60 percent of your teaching work in about 5 percent of the time."

Lozanov discovered that well-delivered concerts can open gateways to learning, reach the subconscious, create better understanding of subject matter, activate long-term memory, and reduce overall learning time. There are three types or phases of a concert reading in the accelerated learning approach.

1. Preview

This is the initial globalization period, whereby the "big picture" is the primary focus. Incorporate intriguing, attention-getting music with a short, light, and fun content overview. This can be accomplished with content in chorus, parable, chant, or poem form. This phase builds confidence and anticipation; and should be conducted at the beginning of a new session when a fresh topic is introduced. In general, keep previews down to a length of three to seven minutes—short enough to be dramatic, inspiring, or shocking.

2. Active Concerts

This is the period in which you present the heart of the content in a dramatic way using an interplay of classical or romantic selections. With their eyes open, students simply listen to the "concert" without effort to remember it. The material is presented in context incorporating metaphors, dramatic readings, a script, or text. This phase is most effective at the middle or near the end of a learning session. The active concert period will be most effective if five to fifteen minutes in duration, and when conducted no more than every five to ten hours of class time. The first thirty seconds of the active concert should be music only. As the music pauses or gets quieter, deliver your material; then as it picks up again, return to music listening only. This technique has been called "sound surfing."

3. Passive Review

This is the period in which you let the music and message carry a low-key review of the new material to the learner's unconscious while they passively relax with their eyes closed. The same material as used in the active concert phase can be repeated, but use a baroque accompaniment rather than a romantic selection. This phase generally lasts from five to eight minutes and is conducted at the end of a learning session.

When performing a concert reading with music, you can use just one phase or all three. The following tips may also be useful:

▼ Make sure that you know your own content well and are comfortable with the meaning of it. Tell students what you'll be covering in the concert reading; and provide them with a short verbal preview. Do this even if you are providing handouts covering the new material.

▼ Make sure that you have listened to your music many times so that you know it well. How long does the introductory movement last? When does the volume increase and decrease? How about the pacing and tempo? How long is the piece?

▼ Create a relaxing environment: Tone down bright lighting; get learners up and moving a bit first; do some deep breathing; provide some positive suggestions of expectancy; and encourage learners to get comfortable.

▼ Create Some Credibility: Announce the name of the musical selection, the composer, the time period, and what it's known for. This will prevent listeners from wondering about the music and feeling distracted.

▼ The volume ought to be loud enough to be dramatic during the non-speaking parts and soft enough so that you can talk during the quieter times of the selection.

▼ Create anticipation from the start: Pause and get the audience's attention. Wait until the introductory movement of the selection is over, then begin with gusto.

▼ Give your reading a dramatic edge. Make large movements and gestures to emphasize key points. Think of yourself as a Shakespearean performer and enjoy putting on a show. Finish with a dramatic statement or memorable closing remark.

▼ Experiment! Doing concert readings is a great way to have fun, be creative, and embed some powerful learning. Repetition is the secret to comfort. And with comfort, you will perform confidently and competently.

The Best Uses of Recorded Music

Entrainment
We often synchronize our body's pacing with common rhythms and beats

Memories Triggered
Elicit prior events, places, and people to trigger strong states

Socialization
Music can bring people together

Calming
To slow and calm the mind and body

Better Cognitive States Elicited
Manage learner states since specific music can enhance precise states for learning

Priming
Activate precise, specific neural pathways for learning content, performing a task, or creativity

Emotions
Music, sung, heard, or performed, can trigger the release of the brain's natural opiates and hormones

Binding Learning and Meaning
This process creates a memory link between concept and state, making recall more likely

Delivery System for Content
Words can be embedded with music

Movement
Get people up and moving: Dance, work, transit, talk, or take action

---

Reflection Questions

1. What from this chapter was novel, fresh, or new to you? What was familiar or "old hat"?

2. In what ways, do you already apply the information in this chapter?

3. What three questions might you now generate about this material?

4. How did you react emotionally to the information in this chapter?

5. How did you react cognitively to the information? Do you agree or disagree with the author's point of view? Why?

6. In what ways might you translate the principles presented in this chapter into practical everyday useful ideas?

7. If these things are, in fact, true about the brain, what should we do differently? What resources of time, people, and money could be redirected? In what ways might you suggest we start doing this?

8. What were the most interesting insights you gained from this material?

9. If you were to plan your next step for making your curriculum more brain-based, what would that be?

10. What obstacles might you encounter? How might you realistically deal with them?

Rewards, Motivation, and Creativity

18

Rewards, Motivation and Creativity

An all too common question asked by teachers is "How do I motivate my students?" The answer is both simple and complex. First of all, *the human brain loves to learn:* Our very survival, in fact, is dependent upon learning. We are all biologically driven to seek out novelty, social contact, food sources, shelter, and enjoyment. Each of these experiences is incorporated into the species through learning. In other words, learners have a built-in motivation mechanism that *does not require* a teacher's input or manipulation to work. Our brains have hungrily absorbed information, integrated it, made meaning out of it, remembered it, and used it at the appropriate times for eons.

The question itself may imply a deeper issue which is in opposition to the motivation scheme—teacher control. When teachers are operating under the assumption that more teacher control is better, learner motivation is going to be a problem. The more fundamental question is "What is my responsibility as a teacher?" If you believe your job is to be a learning catalyst (one who lights a fire for learning), rather than someone who stands and delivers information once you have your students' attention, then motivating your learners will likely be a non-issue. After all, in a brain-based learning environment, the learners are already motivated (just the way they were when they walked in your door). Remember, all human beings are born with intrinsic motivation: We don't need someone to monitor it, unless that is, a brain-antagonistic environment has been set up.

The Folly of Labeling Learners

The unmotivated learner is a myth. The root of the problem is not so much the learner, but rather the conditions for learning that are less than ideal in most school contexts. A great number of kids have been labeled "underachievers," yet when we stop to consider the amount of motivation it takes just for some under-supported children to get to school, we tend to rethink our labels. Once a learner is in their seat, the teacher's role is to elicit the learners' natural motivation. If a learner is severely stressed, they may not be able to process information as efficiently as other learners, but their motivation to solve their problems, you can bet, is strong. Negative behaviors are commonly reinforced in the artificial and unresponsive school environment. And, identifying, classifying, grouping, labeling, evaluating, comparing, and assessing learners perpetuates the problem.

> *There is no such thing as an unmotivated learner.*
> *There are, however, temporary unmotivated states*
> *in which learners are either reinforced and supported*
> *or neglected and labeled.*

All of us have two different sources of motivation acting upon us—that which arises from within (intrinsic) and that which is externally reinforced from the outside (extrinsic). The ideal source for learning motivation is intrinsic for many reasons, the most obvious of which is that even without the artificial controls of a classroom environment, the student will continue to achieve.

The following techniques de-motivate learners and drive away intrinsic motivation:

▼ Coercion, control, and manipulation
▼ Weak, critical, or negatively competitive relationships
▼ Infrequent or vague feedback
▼ Racism or sexism, or prejudice of any kind
▼ Outcome-based education (unless learners help generate the outcomes)
▼ Inconsistent policies and rules
▼ Top-down management and policy-making
▼ Repetitive, rote learning
▼ Inappropriate or limited learning styles

▼ Sarcasm, put-downs, and criticism

▼ The perception of irrelevant content

▼ Boring, single-media presentation

▼ Reward systems of any kind

▼ Teaching in just one or two of the multiple intelligences

▼ Systems that limit personal goal achievement

▼ Responsibility without authority

Under ordinary circumstances, most good learning environments will encourage active student learning; and healthy brains usually make good choices. However, unhealthy brains often make poor choices. Learners who have acquired a condition called "learned helplessness" generally fall into the second category. The good news is, however, you can do something about it. But you have to be informed so that you can recognize and act on your awareness.

Learned Helplessness

Helplessness can devastate even the brightest learners. Since being active is our natural state, what causes a student to feel helpless? What causes learners to sit in class like a lump on a log and not participate? Temporary helplessness is one thing: What we're talking about here is a chronic condition or disorder that develops over time. The following symptoms often accompany the condition of learned helplessness:

Symptoms of Learned Helplessness

▼ Not caring what happens

▼ Giving up before starting; or sabotaging positive outcomes

▼ Motivational and emotional deficits; depression, anxiety

▼ Not acting upon a request; or not following directions

▼ Increased attraction to hostile humor

▼ Cognitive impairment

▼ A belief that the outcome of an event is independent of input

▼ Passivity instead of activity

▼ Self-imposed limitations that exacerbate passivity

Students who are suffering from learned helplessness are not necessarily hostile or argumentative. They simply don't want to take action because they truly believe there is no dependable cause-and-effect relationship between their efforts and the outcome. When you truly believe you don't have any control over your environment, why try?

Following are some of the probable causes of learned helplessness:

▼ Learned helplessness can be developed over time from repeated exposure to trauma and high stress. It's most likely to occur when one feels *both* out of control *and* lacking influence.

▼ Helplessness can be influenced by society. In many cultures, the prevailing attitude is that whatever happens, good or bad, "it is God's will." This is a different point of view than, "God gave us the power to choose our destiny."

▼ Helplessness can be learned in a specific context through repeated uncontrollable experiences. For example, one might be otherwise capable, but feel helpless in math class due to multiple prior failures.

▼ People can learn to become helpless through observation of others encountering uncontrollable events. Viewing global disasters on television day after day, for example, may be a contributing factor; or growing up in a welfare-supported family where a vicious cycle of poverty prevails over a long period of time.

▼ Well intended, but overly controlling relationships can strengthen helplessness. A parent who does a child's work for them, or a teacher who takes over when a student seeks help, can both be culprits.

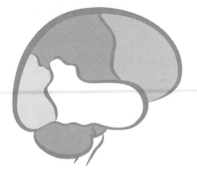

Changes in the Brain

There can be no change in student behavior without a corresponding change in the brain. Body-mind, mind-body: There is no separation. Here are some of the changes we see in the brain when a robust condition of learned helplessness is evident:

Brain Changes Relative to Learned Helplessness

▼ Decreased amounts of norepinephrine—an important compound that contributes to our arousal system

▼ Lowered amounts of GABA (a common neurotransmitter), with links to anxiety

▼ Decreased amounts of available serotonin and dopamine—the "feel good" neurotransmitter

▼ Increased activation in the amygdala—the almond-shaped structure that is involved in intense emotions

▼ Increases in both the autonomic nervous system and the sympathetic nervous system—both of which are involved in the stimulation of the stress-related hormone cortisol

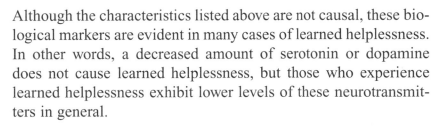

Conditions and Constraints

Although the characteristics listed above are not causal, these biological markers are evident in many cases of learned helplessness. In other words, a decreased amount of serotonin or dopamine does not cause learned helplessness, but those who experience learned helplessness exhibit lower levels of these neurotransmitters in general.

There are varying levels of susceptibility to learned helplessness. It turns out that only about two thirds of students are likely candidates. This is because many individuals are "immunized" against it by many previous successful experiences where they have experienced control in their environment; and there is a greater susceptibility among those who are aggressive or dominant in a group. This is counterintuitive: Those who *seem* to be the most social, outgoing, assertive, strong, and in control are, in fact, the most likely to be a victim of learned helplessness.

Some links with depression have been identified. One of the few distinctions between learned helplessness and depression, in fact, is that depression triggers a generalized belief that responding will be ineffective; whereas those with learned helplessness believe that responding is independent of the outcome. This is a subtle, but important, difference.

The criteria for the official learned helplessness status is an inappropriate passivity via mental or behavioral actions to meet the demands of the situation. Can it be contextual? Yes, an example would be a student who is active in all classes but math.

Perhaps this student "learned" through prior failures that there is no casual relationship between his behaviors and the outcome of his math studies. Learned helplessness can be evoked or triggered by a location, person, or event. This transient quality makes it even more difficult to diagnose and treat.

Unlearning Learned Helplessness

It should be noted that most of time, when we see an unmotivated student, it is *not* a case of learned helplessness. It is more likely a *temporary motivation deficit* due to lack of clear goals, under-arousal, malnutrition, value conflicts, inactivity, conflicting learning styles, prejudice, or lack of resources.

Learned helplessness, the genuine stuff, *is a serious and chronic condition*. It is not treated by a few compliments and a smile. Teachers who have students who fit the description should know that they are in for a challenging test of their patience and skill. The good news is there are some steps you can take to facilitate hope and contribute to the healing. All of them have one important thing in common: They increase the student's perception of their *ability to control* the outcome of an event.

Encourage engagement in the following types of experiences:

▼ **Community service (scouts, Red Cross, cross-age tutoring)**

▼ **Activist roles (changing school or community policies)**

▼ **Classroom activities with some choice involved (field trips, teamwork, ball toss)**

▼ **Personal skills (CPR, martial arts, academic competitions)**

▼ **Physical immersion events (Outward Bound, camping, SuperCamp, boot camp)**

▼ **Active hobbies (taking care of animals, skating, sports)**

▼ **Family contributions (making meals, clean-up, yardwork, car work)**

▼ **Sports, theater, music programs**

Giving the learner more control over their environment is the first step towards boosting confidence. In his book, *Choice Theory*, (1999) William Glasser says, this effect happens whether the control is real or illusory. In an experiment on noise and control, two groups were put into a noisy room. One group had no control over the noise and the other had a placebo control knob that they thought gave them control over the loud noise. The subjects reported their moods before and after each equally-administered 100 decibel session. Neither group actually did have control over their environment, but one of them had the perception that it did. After the group who perceived no control ended their sessions, subjects reported increases in depression, anxiety, helplessness, stress, and tension, while the other group reported being affected very little.

The state of helplessness is a common one for students who do poorly in school. It's common for students in schools where the administration or teaching staff is controlling, manipulative, and coercive. Since the natural state of the brain is curiosity and motivation, schools and staff have to ask themselves hard questions such as, "What are we doing that makes learners feel powerless? In what ways might out behavior create helplessness; and how can we change this?"

 ## What This Means to You

Participation and motivation are boosted by inclusion, ownership, and choice. They are impaired by autocratic insistence and tight control. Make a list of choices you provide to learners. Do they have control of their environment? For example, who maintains the temperature, volume, lights, and other physical elements in your room? Do students feel free to get up and walk around when they need to move; can they get water when their thirsty? Can they take a break from one type of learning if they feel a need to so? As you provide more learner control, you will find that participation and motivation increase quite naturally.

Excessive Praise Detrimental

Researcher Alfie Kohn (1993) says that children can become negatively dependent on praise, just as they can on any other external reward. This dependency can lead to lower self-confidence, loss of intrinsic joy in the learning process, and decreased self-esteem. When the reward is withdrawn, the learner feels let down. Praise is also interpreted by some as manipulative; and relying on it can easily backfire. The learner may feel controlled and resent the scrutiny; or they may feel self-conscious and inadequate if they sense any insincerity on the part of the praiser.

Researcher Roy Baumeister's experiments (1984) verified that heavy praise given to a learner can be detrimental to learning. While intermittent praise can be positive, praise from authority figures can increase "pressure to perform" and result in performance anxiety. Subjects who were given praise right before a skills test consistently performed worse than those who did not receive praise. Students heavily praised became more tentative in their answers and gave up on their own ideas more quickly than those who were not.

If a teacher continually praises students for doing their homework or for sitting quietly in class, for example, soon the learner discovers that it is the praise that he/she seeks, not the behavior that the teacher is attempting to reinforce.

 ## What This Means to You

The most striking and permanent interpretation of a positive judgment is that it's still a judgment. Reduce your praise and increase peer feedback and support which is more motivating to the learner. Encourage rather than praise. Say, "You're on the right track," or "Give it your best effort." Give praise that is not contingent on performance. Encourage the learner to take risks. Provide affirmation, not back-slapping. When the task is completed, ask the learner what his or her assessment is. In this way, the learner begins to develop a sense of quality about the learning, instead of feeling pressure to perform the right way. Teach learners how to provide supportive feedback to each other.

Motivation and Rewards

In a never-ending effort to control, manipulate, manage, and influence learners, some educators have become accustomed to using rewards; but considering the brain's natural operational principles, the technique is not productive. To understand this irony, first let's define "reward."

> *A reward is a compensation or consequence which 1) is predictable; and 2) has market value.*

If it is only predictable, but has no market value (i.e., a smile, a hug, a compliment, a random gift or token, an awards assembly, public approval, etc.), then it is simply an acknowledgment, not a reward. If it has market value, but absolutely no predictability (a spontaneous party, pizza, cookies, gift certificates, small gifts, trips, tickets, etc.), then it is a celebration, not a reward. However, if students know that by behaving a certain way, there's a chance that they might get a prize, that's enough predictability to be called a "reward." The determining criteria is simple:

If you offer learners something that meets both criteria, you are, in fact, bribing the learner. A reward system, regardless of what you try to call it, carries an implicit and covert threat: If you don't meet the criteria, you will not receive the reward or some opportunities will be withdrawn. As you can tell, the issue has a great deal to do with intent. And that's sometimes tough to read.

Rewards and the Human Brain

What do rewards do to the brain? The brain, which has its own built-in reward system (see figure 18.1), is highly customized to the individual. This system can be tracked and observed with tracers injected into the blood which measure the release of the chemical dopamine—the "feel good" neurotransmitter.

This customized reward system develops over time based on the person's unique experiences and perceptions. And each person's system responds to rewards differently. This means what is a reward to one person may not be much of a reward to another. Events and thoughts can change the system by altering the receptivity of the receptor sites to the brain's endogenous opiates.

The reward system habituates easily, which means that although a reward may be motivational at first, soon thereafter, the ante must be increased for the pleasure to remain stable,

Figure 18.1
The Brain's Internal Reward System

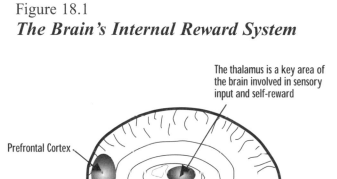

The thalamus is a key area of the brain involved in sensory input and self-reward

Prefrontal Cortex

Receptor sites for the molecules which trigger pleasure are distributed throughout the body but are concentrated here in this "reward circuit"

Dopamine is produced at the top of the brain stem and pushed outward

not unlike an addict who needs ever greater amounts of a drug to get the same high. The first time a person uses cocaine, the rush of pleasure may be 500 times that of their normal experience; but by the second time, it may drop to 200 times; and by the third, the brain may release only 100 times the amount of dopamine in response. You can imagine what a predicament this puts the brain in. The promise of pleasure entices, but each time the drug is used, the pleasure is less. The brain has habituated.

In school, this means that what worked the first time might be insufficient the next time; and the need for an ever increasing value of reward is sought. The gold stars that worked for first graders become cookies for third graders and pizza for fifth graders. Before you know it, you can't provide what the student desires. It's a vicious cycle! Thus, rewards in the learning process must be used judiciously, if at all, to accomplish increased learning.

The Detrimental Effects of Rewards

Brandeis University researcher Teresa Amabile, PhD. (1989) suggests extrinsic motivation inhibits intrinsic motivation. "The ability to be creative is strongly linked to intrinsic motivation, since it gives the brain 'freedom of intellectual expression,' which fuels even more thinking and motivation," she says.

A reward system prevents the establishment of intrinsic motivation because there's rarely an incentive to be creative—only to exhibit the requested behavior. "Creativity" is rarely measured in relation to a reward system—in fact, the two are usually at far ends of the scale. You either get intrinsically motivated creative thinking or extrinsically motivated repetitive, rote, predictable behaviors.

Dr. Amabile, in fact, found that reward systems lower the quality of the work produced. She conducted more than two dozen studies over nearly twenty years with the same results: In the long run, rewards didn't work. Among artists, creativity (as judged by their peers) dropped subsequent to signing a contract to sell their work upon completion. The fact that financial rewards were pending lessened their fullest expression.

> *"A system of rewards and punishments can be selectively demotivating in the long term, especially when others have control over the system."*
>
> —Geoffrey and Renate Caine

Geoffrey Caine, PhD. and Renate Caine, PhD., contend (1990) that the existence of any behavior-oriented threats and anxiety, coupled with a lack of learner input and control, will "downshift" learner thinking and cause them to prefer repeated, predictable responses to lower their anxiety. This may make teachers think the reward system is working, but to initiate changes within this system becomes more difficult, since any change increases "threat and anxiety" to both students and teachers.

Learners who have been bribed for either good work or good behavior find that soon the last reward wasn't good enough. A bigger and better one is wanted. Soon, all intrinsic motivation has been killed off and the learner is labeled as "unmotivated." Like a rat in a cage pushing a food bar, the learner behavior becomes just good enough to get the reward.

Some, like Dr. Kohn (1993), contend that *all* rewards are bad; but Martin Ford (1992) argues that it depends on whether the reward creates a conflict with the learner's existing goals. There are three times when this is most likely to occur.

Rewards Conflict with Learner Goals When:

1. *The learner feels manipulated by the reward*
   "You just want me to dress your way."

2. *The reward interferes with the real reason for the learning*
   "Now that I'm getting rewarded for getting good grades, I care only about what's on the test."

3. *The reward devalues the task and the learner feels bribed*
   "This class must be pretty bad if they're giving us a bribe just to attend."

Consider, for example, a school that is having problems with truancy and low attendance. The administrative staff decides, as an incentive, to reward those who come every day. Now, each student gets a reward for having a 100 percent attendance during the month. The school has worked out an arrangement with local businesses, where the reward is a free meal at McDonalds or Pizza Hut. Students immediately feel bribed for coming to school. They think, "The situation must be really bad for them to bribe us." But learners still respond to the rewarded behavior. "It's stupid, but we'll play the game," they say. Now school is about "working the system," instead of learning.

Strategies for Eliciting Intrinsic Motivation

1. Meet learner's needs and goals.

The brain is designed biologically to survive. It will learn what it *needs* to learn to survive. Make it a top priority to discover what needs your learners have and engage those needs. If students need what you have, they're interested. If the content relates to the student's own personal life, they're interested. For example, six-year-old students have higher needs for security, predictability, and teacher acceptance than fourteen-year-olds; whereas, the teens' needs are more likely to be about peer acceptance, a sense of importance, and hope for the future. And, an eighteen-year-old learner is likely more interested in autonomy and independence. Use what's appropriate for the age level of your students.

2. Provide a sense of control and choice.

Creativity and choice allow the learner to express him or herself and feel valued. The opposite of this is manipulation, coercion, and control.

3. Encourage and provide for positive social bonding.

This can come in many forms—a likable teacher, classmate, situation, or group. Encourage teamwork, collaboration, and group activities.

4. Support a sense of curiosity.

Inquiring minds want to know: This is the nature of the human brain. Keep engaging curiosity—it works! Newspaper tabloids and electronic tabloids have played off our curiosity for years: Just witness all the stories about Elvis, aliens, Princess Diana, Hollywood celebrities, and UFOs.

5. Engage strong emotions.

Engage emotions productively with compelling stories, games, personal examples, celebration, role-plays, debates, rituals, and music. We are driven to act upon our emotions because they are compelling decision makers.

6. Encourage adequate nutrition.

Better nutrition means more mental alertness. Learn about how diet influences the thinking and learning process. Write up a list of suggestions to give to your students and their parents. Suggest specific brain foods (eggs, fish, nuts, leafy dark green vegetables, apples, bananas, and others known to increase mental alertness).

7. Incorporate multiple intelligences.

Hook learners in through their strengths which may range from spatial, bodily-kinesthetic, interpersonal, and verbal-linguistic to intrapersonal, musical-rhythmic, and mathematical-logical. We are particularly motivated when we can demonstrate our strengths and proclivities.

8. Share success stories.
Tell inspiring stories about other learners who have surmounted obstacles to succeed. Develop a mythology and culture of success. Consider how just walking onto an ivy-league campus, like Oxford, Harvard, Stanford, Wharton, or Notre Dame, can elicit feelings of motivation.

9. Provide acknowledgments.
These include assemblies, certificates, group notices, team reports, compliments, and appropriate praise. Positive associations fuel further action.

10. Increase frequency of feedback.
Make it your part-time job to see that learners get a lot of feedback during each class. Use charts, discussion, peer teaching, projects, and role-plays. Feedback needs to be nonjudgemental and immediate.

11. Manage physiological states.
Learn to read and manage states. There is no such thing as an unmotivated learner, only unmotivated states. Elicit anticipation and challenge states in your learners and in yourself.

12. Provide hope of success.
Learners need to know that it's possible for them to succeed. Regardless of the obstacles or how far behind they may be, hope is essential. Jerome Frank, PhD. of Johns Hopkins (1985) strongly believes that hope works like a powerful drug and is essential to restoring demoralization. Every learning context must provide some kind of hope.

13. Role-model the joy of learning.
Since over 99 percent of all learning is nonconscious, the more excited you are about learning, the more motivated your learners will likely be.

14. Mark successes and achievements with celebrations.
These include peer acknowledgment, parties, food, high-fives, cheers, etc. These create the atmosphere of success and can trigger the release of endorphins that further boost learning and motivation.

15. Maintain a physically- and emotionally-safe learning environment.
An environment where it is safe to make mistakes, ask questions, and offer contributions is essential. Meet learners' physical needs for adequate lighting, water, food, movement, and comfortable seating. Also, ensure learners are physically safe from building hazards. Make sure students know you are always available to discuss any concerns about their safety including concerns about other students.

16. Incorporate learners' individual learning styles.

Provide both choice in how learners learn, and diversity in what they learn so that students can use their preferred learning styles.

17. Instill positive beliefs about capability and context.

Reinforce learners as they meet difficult challenges. Tell them that you know they can succeed and accomplish their goals. Discover what beliefs an individual may be maintaining about him or herself that might be holding them back; and work to affect them positively.

All of the strategies mentioned above cost nothing (no rewards or bribes are necessary); and they work. It is certainly more preparation and work, initially, to create a climate of intrinsic motivation, but it pays off in the long run. Teachers who rely on extrinsic motivation may be vastly underestimating three things: 1) The power and limitations of their influence; 2) The desire of the learner to be intrinsically motivated; and 3) the long-term ease of reinforcing intrinsic rewards.

Rewards...

▼ **Reduce the learner's ability to solve complex problems without extrinsic motivators.**

▼ **Reduce learner responsiveness to the environment.**

▼ **Result in increased stereotypical, low-risk, low-creativity behavior.**

▼ **Increase learner attentiveness to, and reliance upon, external systems of rewards and punishments.**

Researcher Edward Deci (1987) says there is evidence linking *extrinsic* motivation to positive outcomes in work involving non-creative tasks, memorized skills, and repetitive tasks. In order to get learners to be creative, however, and have greater subject interest, higher self-esteem, and the ability to be reflective, there must be *intrinsic* motivation. Reward systems prevent this, but make no mistake about it, some learners will respond to rewards in the short term.

> *Learners who are experiencing stress and anxiety in their environment will prefer external motivation, meaning a system of reliable rewards.*

Paradoxically, *the more unmotivating the environment is, the more the learner seeks rewards*. The rewards are initially welcomed by the learner, who needs predictability and certainty. Stressed and anxious learners are more likely to look to others for safe, predictable role modeling, to listen to others for goals, and to increase their own stereotyped, lower-order thinking. But, this creates a "Catch-22." Rewards, at a low level, work. The teacher continues their usage. The learner now is a victim of the "glass ceiling" principle: They learn to perform to the lowest level needed to get the reward. Geoffrey Caine (1990) says, "In effect, they prefer external forms of motivation and lose sight of internal motivation."

For example, I often have teachers say to me, "My students seem to like the reward system. They complain when it is dropped and their performance goes down." The teacher uses this as evidence to say, "I know I shouldn't bribe them, but the system works!"

> *In the long run, rewards do more damage than good towards motivating the so-called underachiever.*

The problem is that the system does work—too well. But then again, holding a gun to someone's head works, too! It will get them to do all kinds of things, but it's just not good for the learner's brain (among other things). Rewards lead to learners who become preoccupied with "playing the game" and not really doing quality learning. Why? Quite simply, the ability to alter perceptual maps, to do higher-order thinking, and to create complex thematic relationships with the subject is not available to the brain when it experiences the anxiety of a reward system.

The more you use a reward system, the more you evoke the "two-headed dichotomous dragon." This means 1) the psychological anxiety of performance increases; and 2) every reward carries with it an implied certainty of success or failure. But which one? The learner then wants to reduce the uncertainty, so they pick tasks that have a high degree of predictability (often boring, repetitive skills). The learner also is more likely to pick goals set by others, instead of oneself (even the goals he/she does pick are often the basic, overworked, media-reinforced, cliché types).

What This Means to You

Replace rewards with positive alternatives. These include meeting learner goals, peer support, positive rituals, self-assessment, acknowledgments, the love of learning, enthusiasm, increased feedback, more options for creativity, and more student control. Rewards are doing more harm than good: They encourage results other than those originally intended. Phase out reward systems. It makes more sense to make school or work a worthwhile place to be, rather than trying to bribe people to attend or perform. When you incorporate the brain-based strategies in this book, rewards will become totally unnecessary.

Rewarded Actions Lose Appeal

In research by Alan Kazdin, PhD. (1997) following a decade of post-reward analysis, he concludes that when the goodies stop, the behavior stops, too. Dr. Kazdin, *who once was a proponent of rewards*, set up a token economy system in a health care institution. At first, he was excited about the behavior changes. In his first publication, *The Rich Reward of Rewards*, he talked about how much patient behavior had changed. And that's what people remembered the most. But ten years later, in *The Token Economy: Review and Evaluation*, the author has determined that although the rewards worked temporarily, they did not maintain the desirable outcomes.

> *"Removal of token reinforcement results in decrements in desirable responses and a return to baseline or near-baseline levels of performance."*
> —Alan Kazdin

Every learner has his or her own bias which they bring to a particular context. The biases constitute personal beliefs, hopes, expectations, fears, values, and emotions. These are what hold a behavior in place. In fact, Leslie Hart (1983) says, "To change the behavior, the biases must be changed, not the behavior directly." The rewards are designed to change the behavior, not the biases. Hence, any reward-driven activity is likely to fail in the long run.

We all know teachers often offer rewards for attendance, homework, or good behavior. Pizza Hut had a program designed to reward students for reading by offering pizzas. The follow-up, however, would likely confirm that those who read the most were those who were reading already: They just decided to play the game. And, learners who were not ordinarily reading before the promotion, likely returned to their prior habits.

What This Means to You

Many learners would become more intrinsically motivated if given a chance; but as long as a reward system is in place, they'll play the game and undermine their own progress in the long term. Reduce or eliminate all rewards. Phase out slowly any rewards you are now using. Incorporate positive alternatives: Celebrations, Variety, Novelty, and Feedback.

Should You *Ever* Use Rewards?

If rewards are really counterproductive, is there ever a time and place for them? Yes, says Dr. Kohn (1993). "If your objective is to get people to temporarily obey an order, show up on time, and do what they're told, rewards can work." But, he adds emphatically, "rewards are simply changing the specific, in-the-moment behavior and not the person." If your objective, however, is to help your learners authentically achieve, rewards simply don't work.

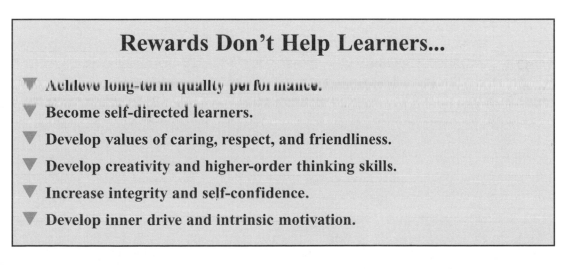

Rewards Don't Help Learners...

▼ Achieve long-term quality performance.

▼ Become self-directed learners.

▼ Develop values of caring, respect, and friendliness.

▼ Develop creativity and higher-order thinking skills.

▼ Increase integrity and self-confidence.

▼ Develop inner drive and intrinsic motivation.

A group of fourth graders were asked what kind of reward they'd like for doing a simple classroom task. They were given that reward for doing it, as promised. Later, when it was time to do the task again, they performed more poorly than the group which was never offered a reward.

Here's an example of when, however, a reward might be used. You have a bunch of chairs to move to another room. It's the end of the day; you're tired and hungry. You ask a couple of students if they'd be willing to help you move them after class. They say, "No, not really." But you're desperate, so you say, "How about if I get you both a Coke?" They change their minds and decide it's worth it. The chairs get moved. Everybody's happy. The reward was appropriate.

Alternatives for Bribery and Rewards

There are many positive alternatives to bribing students for better behaviors. The first and most powerful one is to make school more meaningful, relevant, and fun: Then, you won't have to bribe students.

If you are using any kind of reward system, let it run its course and end it as soon as you reasonably can. If you stop it abruptly, you may get a rebellion. The learners will need to "de-tox" from the "reward drug." Remember, the research says:

> *Learners who have been on a reward system will become conditioned to prefer it over free choice.*

But replacing rewards with alternatives gets a bit tricky in two cases. First, in schools, *the entire system of marking and grading is a reward and punishment system*. The rewards are good grades which lead to teacher approval, scholarships, and university entry. How can an instructional leader work properly (without bribes and rewards) within a system that is so thoroughly entrenched? What if other teachers use rewards, but you don't? You will have your work cut out for you, but if you provide learners with reasoning behind your approach, learners will eventually prefer your methods. Be patient.

Secondly, there are many "gray areas." Receiving a certificate may be just an acknowledgment when you give it, but what if the parent rewards the learner with money when it is taken home? Then it becomes a reward in spite of your best intentions. The solution is to try to make parents aware of the destructive effects of rewards at an open house night or by letter. You don't have to bribe learners to learn. The human brain loves to learn! Simply follow the "rules" for brain-compatible learning and learners' thirst and hunger to learn will return.

What the Reward Proponents Say

Behaviorists treat learners as empty vessels that need to be filled. In this paradigm, the way you get learners to learn is to first gain control, then control *what* and *how* they learn it; and if they aren't interested, you simply bribe them. Those who are steadfast in their insistence on rewards usually defend themselves on the following grounds:

Proponents of Reward Systems Often Claim...

1. Rewards are necessary. "After all, what's the intrinsic reward for computing the problem 4 + 4?"
2. The studies on intrinsic rewards are theoretical only.
3. Rewards are harmless.
4. The real world uses rewards.
5. Rewards are effective.

Those who have discovered the power of alternatives know the answers already. But for the others, here are some comments about the five points raised above:

1. "Rewards are necessary." This is false. In the "control paradigm," students have been so conditioned, that even simple learning begs for a motivating cue. This is because their natural love of learning has been manipulated out of them. But there are millions of students who learn based on curiosity, joy, and their natural love of learning. Learners who say they want rewards have simply been conditioned to want them.

2. "The studies on intrinsic rewards are theoretical only." This is false. Hundreds of studies on the follies of rewards have been done with real people in everyday situations. Out of the top twenty-five high schools in 1993 in America, only two of them used a reward system (aside from grades). Twenty three of them relied on quality, real-life learning. One of the most innovative programs for almost twenty years, SuperCamp, *uses no rewards* and its results have been reported in doctoral dissertations, in *Quantum Teaching* (DePorter, et al. 1999), *The Learning Revolution* (Dryden and Vos 1994), and on over two hundred radio and television stations and in hundreds of newspapers worldwide. It has over 25,000 graduates and one, five, and ten year studies demonstrate that its methods worked.

3. "Rewards are harmless." False. Consistent studies have documented that, under the context of a reward, the brain operates differently. Behaviors become more predictable, stereotyped, rigid, and narrow. In other words, you can get a desired behavior with rewards, but you won't get intrinsically motivated students with a passion for learning.

4. "The real world uses rewards." In some cases, yes; in many other cases, no. Critics say that everyone gets rewards for their work, but that's not true. Many people work because they love what they do. The majority of teachers went into their profession because they liked the satisfaction of helping others grow and succeed, even though other jobs pay better.

5. "Rewards are effective." For rote, repetitive tasks, yes, rewards will enhance performance for a while; but then the novelty of the reward wears off and the performance drops. Remember, someone can hold a loaded gun to your head and get you to do almost anything. It's effective, isn't it? But this doesn't make it right. Rewarded behaviors rarely continue after the rewards are removed, unless the learner did not depend on the reward to begin with.

Replacing Rewards in Learning

When you begin to remove rewards from your learning environment, don't expect a standing ovation. Research has shown that many learners prefer rewards even though it is counter-productive to their learning. Why? It's predictable. Take your time phasing out rewards. Allow existing programs to expire on their own. Then ask students for their partnership in replacing extrinsic rewards with intrinsic rewards. Teachers who make unilateral decisions about classroom operations, while ignoring student input, reinforce a sense of powerlessness. Rather, engage students in an active, discussion about the real cost of rewards and the real rewards of learning.

If you replace rewards with more student choice, feedback, and empowerment, learners will begin to choose to learn for their own reasons. This transition to learning for learning's sake will not happen over night. Students will need time and support in directing their focus inward—on their own needs, values, goals, belief systems, and emotions. Thus, the removal of external rewards is only the first step. Now, students need to be supported while their locus of control shifts from external to internal. When you stop hearing, "Is this going to be on the test?" you'll know you have achieved the goal. What this question tells you about learners is that they've had the love of learning bribed out of them by unknowing teachers. Since they don't think learning is any fun, they need a bribe for their effort. The goal of brain-based teaching, is to let the brain reward itself for its own growth, just as it is naturally equipped to do.

Reflection Questions

1. What from this chapter was novel, fresh, or new to you? What was familiar or "old hat"?

2. In what ways, do you already apply the information in this chapter?

3. What three questions might you now generate about this material?

4. How did you react emotionally to the information in this chapter?

5. How did you react cognitively to the information? Do you agree or disagree with the author's point of view? Why?

6. In what ways might you translate the principles presented in this chapter into practical everyday useful ideas?

7. If these things are, in fact, true about the brain, what should we do differently? What resources of time, people, and money could be redirected? In what ways might you suggest we start doing this?

8. What were the most interesting insights you gained from this material?

9. If you were to plan your next step for making your curriculum more brain-based, what would that be?

10. What obstacles might you encounter? How might you realistically deal with them?

Meaning-Making

Meaning-Making

The brain is designed to seek meaning. Until we provide learners with the resources (time, context, other learners, materials, opportunities) to discover meaning in what we ask them to learn, we will continue to produce robots and underachievers. Correspondingly, until we provide more meaningful forms of assessment, educators will have little incentive to pursue teaching for deep meaning. Students will simply skim a few facts off the top, pass the test, and call it an education. If *this* constitutes an education, then we're in trouble. Fortunately, however, some educators are providing a meaningful learning curriculum, in spite of the continued thrust towards standardized testing and standards-based outcomes.

There's an enormous difference between memorizing a few key facts and having an authentic grasp of a subject: It's the difference between doing well on a multiple choice test and being able to hold a substantial discussion about a topic. It's the difference between reading about hospitals and being hospitalized for a week. It's the difference between eating out at a Mexican food restaurant and living in Mexico for a year. It's the difference between memorizing a few "math facts" and being able to tutor another student in mathematics.

Requiring students to learn lists of information has little to do with true learning. It's a "throw-back" and "hang-over" from mid-twentieth century schoolrooms. It's not that kids can't do it; it's simply a poor use of time. The brain is not very good at learning isolated information and especially when it is devoid of any joy or meaning. In fact, rote learning is the best way to turn kids off to nearly any topic.

Authentic, meaningful learning requires the student to process information in his/her own way, along his/her own timeline, and in relation to his/her own perceptual maps. Sorting, analyzing, and drawing conclusions in the context of one's own life is the only learning that sticks.

In fact, the research (Russell 1984; Shaffer and Resnick 1999) suggests that teachers who try to give learners as many facts as possible are doing both their students and themselves a disservice (see figure 19.1)

Figure 19.1
High or Low Density Content

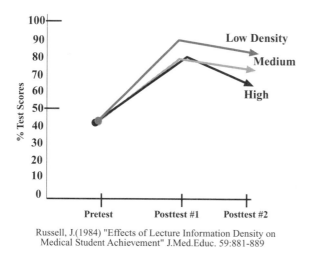

Russell, J.(1984) "Effects of Lecture Information Density on Medical Student Achievement" J.Med.Educ. 59:881-889

Two Types of Meaning

Researchers tell us there are two types of meaning: "reference" and "sense" meaning. Others refer to meaning as "surface" or "deeply-felt." The first is a sort of pointer, a dictionary definition, that refers to the lexical territory of the word. For example, raincoat is an "over-sized waterproof cloth or plastic garment." But the "sense" meaning of the word is different. While I know what a raincoat is, it means little to me personally, as I live in a climate where it rarely rains. The raincoat I own is used only rarely (when I travel) and seems like a waste of closet space most of the time.

Contrast this to a very different "sense" or a "deeply felt" meaning one might have about the word raincoat if one lives in a rainy climate. Perhaps, then your raincoat not only protects you from severe weather, but it is a well-worn friend that preserves your health, protects your nice clothes underneath, and elicits many compliments. Your raincoat, thus, has "meaning-sense" to you developed over time and made meaningful through personal experience.

In the classroom, the concept of the Vietnam War can either be explored at the surface level or on the deeply-felt meaning level. The latter might happen if the teacher is a Vietnam veteran who shares remembered experiences with his or her students. As we explore meaningful learning in this chapter, it is the "sense" meaning that we're after, rather than the dictionary-type "pointer" meaning which leaves emotions untouched.

The Biology of Meaning

Many of our deeply-felt meanings in life are "built-in," sort of "hard-wired" into our brains. An example would be the human response of sadness to sickness and death. Humans have simply learned over the centuries that life is valuable and to be protected. The meaning which is not "hard-wired" is a bit trickier. The importance one gives to attending college, for example, is derived from "constructed" meaning, which is influenced by those around us, the culture, and our personal experiences over time.

There is no single place in the brain where meaning occurs. Brain scans reveal that different areas are activated depending on the nature of the event and the type of meaning derived from it. Events that trigger our so-called "hot buttons" are stored in the amygdala. When something is meaningful during reading, there's usually more activity (as measured by glucose consumption) in the left frontal, temporal, or parietal lobe, says University of Oregon's Michael Posner and associates (1997). If it's a more spiritual meaning, it's probably a parietal lobe activity, says University of California, San Diego's V. S. Ramachandran (1998). If it's an emotionally felt meaning, it may have activity in the frontal, occipital, and mid-brain areas, says University of Iowa's Antonio Damasio (1994). If it's an "Ah-ha!" type of meaning, it is more likely a left-frontal lobe activity. These diverse areas of activation suggest that the concept of meaning may also be diverse.

What Triggers a Sense of Meaning?

Factors for meaning-making are 1) relevance; 2) emotions; and 3) context. *Relevance* is a function of the brain making a connection from existing neural sites. *Emotions* are triggered by the brain's chemistry and tag the learning as important; and context triggers pattern-making which relates to the activation of larger neural fields. In other words, if the information is personal to us, if we feel deeply about it, and if it makes sense, chances are pretty good we'll find it meaningful.

Anything meaningful has at least one of these three ingredients, but the reverse is not true. Something could be relevant and still be meaningless. For example, eating a nutritionally sound diet is very relevant, even though it may hold little meaning to a teenager. Of the three items, the one most commonly associated with meaning-making is relevance.

Relevance

Relevance actually happens on a cellular level. An already-existing neuron simply "connects" with a nearby neuron to make a connection. If the content is irrelevant (lacks understanding or emotional valence), it's unlikely a connection will be made.

While neurons are constantly firing, much of the time it's an inaudible chatter. The meaning we experience happens when a multitude of connections or the activation of a neural field takes place. In the brain, a "nearby" connection is often less than a centimeter away. The brain's nerve cells rarely move, they simply extend their axons to connect with other dendrites. If they can't make the connection, it's going to be harder to establish relevance. These connections are what form the basis of our personality, thinking, and consciousness.

Some thoughts activate entire neural fields that may cross cell and axonal boundaries. The greater the number of links and associations that your brain creates, the more firmly the information is "woven in" neurologically. Unfortunately, many students find that classroom information lacks the personal relevance necessary for authentic learning.

 ## What This Means to You

Never assume that because something is relevant to you, it's relevant to your students. Help them discover their own connections rather than imposing your own. Give students time to link prior learning with current learning through explorations encouraged by special events, discussions, and introspection. Use the power of family history, stories, myth, legends, and metaphors to help make learning relevant for students. Throughout human history, stories have been fundamental to understanding and valuing the people and lessons of the past. Encourage learners to use their own words with regard to new learning. You might also tie in local or national celebrations. Encourage students to share their own experience. Set up pair shares, small group discussions, and team projects. Use "free association" techniques to help learners explore the personal relevance of subjects. You might ask questions like "Have you ever had this happen? If, so how did it feel?" Or, "Could you compare and contrast this to an experience you've had in your own life?"

Emotions

Intense emotions trigger the release of the neurotransmitters adrenaline, norepinephrine, and vasopressin. These chemicals act as signals to the brain, saying, "This is important—remember this." There's little doubt about it, emotions and meaning are linked. You may ask, "Which comes first, the emotion or the meaning?" This is a bit like the proverbial "chicken and egg" question. The systems are so interconnected that chemicals of emotion are released virtually simultaneously with cognition.

Why
Goals
Volition
The "Drive"

EMOTIONS

Links with Emotions

Researchers have found critical links between emotions and the cognitive patterning needed for learning. Many have documented how emotions directly influence learning. First, the "flavor" or "color" of our experiences are likely to make us either want more of it (it was pleasurable) or less of it (it was boring or painful). Second, positive emotions allow the brain to make better perceptual maps, meaning when we are feeling positive, we are able to better sort out our experiences and recall with more clarity. In fact, Candace Pert (1997) at Georgetown University, says: "The brain is just a little box with emotions packed into it."

> *The old model of learning separated mind, body, and emotions. We now know differently. Emotions are a critical part of a learner's ability to think rationally and experience meaning.*

For the moment, let's assume a learner arrives distraught over a dispute at home. He is irritable, inattentive, and learns very little. He thinks of class as a waste of time and does not want to be told what to do. Contrast this with a very different experience: A learner has just had a recent success or positive relationship encounter. The day is rosy, the birds are singing, and he's happy. As a result, he learns better and has positive memories of the class. Here are some specific strategies you can use to reinforce the positive and manage the negative:

 What This Means to You

Provide learners with positive and emotionally-safe ways to express their emotions—negative or positive. Suggestions include:
- A mind-calming visualization or relaxation exercise
- Physical activity—a walk, cross-crawl, stretching, or games
- Dialogue time with partners, a small group, or sharing time
- Internal reflection—journal-writing, self-assessment, and goal-setting
- Metaphorical rituals like a "dumping box" near the door so learners can "toss away" bad feelings or memories
- Role-play, theater, drama, mime, and simulations
- Music—playing instruments, singing, chanting, cheers, and shouts
- Debate a controversial issue; hold a tug-of-war; or stage an improvisation
- Movement—dance, games, exercises, stretching, and play
- Excursions, guest speakers, trips, novel or challenging activities

When we pay more attention to the emotional states of learners, dramatic shifts happen. Unless the learner is in a relaxed state of positive expectancy, very little learning can take place. As instructional leaders, we have the power to influence the emotional state of learners in three profound ways:

Enhance the Emotional State of Learners...

1. **With activities that release stress.**
2. **With activities that increase bonding.**
3. **By providing a forum for emotions to be acknowledged and expressed.**

Richard Lazarus (1984) says, "The dramatic plot or personal meaning that defines each emotion is universal in the human species regardless of culture; no competent person fails to understand strong emotional events..." Emotions engage meaning and predict future learning because they involve our goals, beliefs, biases, and expectancies. You can tap into this process. When your students do goal-setting, it is their emotions that create the goal, as well as the "vesting" in the achievement of the goal.

 ## What This Means to You

Add higher stakes through goal-setting or by conducting public performances to evoke emotional investment. Create immersion environments where your entire room reflects the subject at hand (i.e., decorated as a particular city, place, or foreign country). Involve the students in the design. Perhaps it's a rain forest, an airplane, a business, or a particular period of time. Encourage students to share their inner worlds with each other. Have them discuss their goals, thoughts, and ideals. Develop greater peer collaboration. Assign cooperative projects. Use partners, long-standing teams, or temporary groups that are activated with specialized activities. Encourage the use of more relationship-driven learning by facilitating apprenticeships with experts. Multi-age classrooms, big-brother programs, and community-active adults are perfect examples of support systems that engage deep meaning for learners. Do fewer, but more complex projects, especially lengthy multi-level projects with sufficient time and resources provided. Students in a science class might plan, for example, a five-year trip to Mars. Such a project would involve skills in math, science, problem solving, research, economics, and social studies.

In a classroom, emotional states are an important condition around which educators must orchestrate learning. Students may be bored with the lesson, afraid of an upcoming test, or despondent about a drive-by shooting. They may be hyper-energized by an upcoming sports competition, an emotional crisis, or looming deadline. Instead of trying to eliminate learners' emotions by ignoring them (which doesn't work), it makes more sense for us to integrate them into our curriculum. When we ignore the emotional components of any subject we teach, we deprive students of meaningfulness. Emotions drive attention, meaning, and memory. To take advantage of this principle, acknowledge emotions in the learning process.

Context and Patterns

Perception is the act of the brain constructing a map. This process involves brain structures that are responsible for categorization, discrimination, and regrouping. Stanford neuroscientist Karl Pribram (1971) states that the brain's way of understanding is more through pattern discrimination than singular facts or lists. "The initial stages of processing are largely parallel rather than serial, and feature analysis results from patterns matching rather than feature detection."

Leslie Hart, author of *Human Brain, Human Learning* (1983), says, "It can be stated flatly, the human brain is not organized or designed for linear, one-path thought. Rather, it operates by simultaneously going down many paths. We identify an object, for example, by gathering information—often in less than a second—on size, color, shape, surface texture, weight, smell, and movement...." Dr. Hart emphasizes the importance of presenting material in larger patterns first: "Once we begin to look critically at this notion of teaching in a logical sequence, we can see that usually a giant, and utterly wrong, assumption has been made. That assumption is that "a subject can be fragmented into little bits, and the student when presented with the bits, will be quite able to assemble the parts and emerge with the whole—even though they've never been provided with an inkling of the whole!"

The cortex is both a pattern-maker and pattern-detector. The ability to make meaningful sense out of countless bits of data is critical to understanding and motivation. Since the brain's craving for meaning is automatic, patterning occurs all the time. Each pattern that is discovered can then be added to the learner's "perceptual maps" relieving the brain of the confusion, anxiety, or stress. It "maximizes" again and is then ready for more challenge.

Every pattern that the brain is able to create means that it can then relegate that new "blueprint" to the nonconscious. From a survival point of view, it is critical to create patterns as quickly as possible. The process of creating a pattern or perceptual map utilizes both the conscious and nonconscious brain.

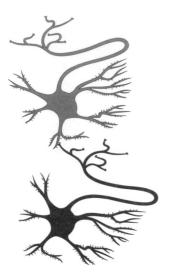

Neurons don't contain information, they simply translate, conduct, and connect to others which resonate with their own frequency. All cells are simultaneously sending and receiving information. New information, which has no established pattern or frequency must find uncommitted fields that resonate. Mapping can help trigger these fields. Fields can shift, rearrange, and form new fields (neural mapping). In fact, the more fields tapped, the greater your depth of meaning, feedback, and understanding.

But, in this process of establishing a neural, then mental map, the brain is less able to generate other parallel maps as it is "thematically distracted." The brain forms quick hierarchies to extract or create patterns. To the brain, there is a certain survival risk and vulnerability while a pattern is being created. But the payoff is big. The patterns give context to information that would be otherwise dismissed as meaningless. This desire to form some kind of meaningful pattern out of our learning seems innate. Children create games that organize behaviors; and they arrange objects into patterns rather than leave them random. Adults organize dishes, cars, tools, sewing articles, businesses, file cabinets, and book chapters. Researchers believe this patterning may begin on a micro level.

Individual neurons do not seem to exhibit learning, only groups of neurons. These networks or "clouds" of neurons seem to be able to recognize and respond to meaningful learning. In fact, scientists are currently testing models of perception and learning that may mimic the brain's visual system. These "connectionist" models mirror neuronal groups and synapses. Although we are cautioned in calling it a biological match, early findings are encouraging.

Other areas of neurobiology suggest pattern-making may be innate. In a classic experiment (Easterbrook, et al. 1999), infants were shown a series of drawings. Each illustration had exactly the same elements as a human face. But only one had them in a coherent, human face shape and form. The others had the eyes, nose, hair and mouth scrambled. To determine the interest and value to an infant, careful recordings were made of which figures were preferred by "gaze time." The pattern of a human face in its correct form, was preferred by infants, even those only a few days old. Infants as young as ten months

or less are drawn to, and can recognize, patterns quicker than non-patterns. On video-tape, infants show puzzled looks when presented with scattered "unpatterned" material. These studies suggest we are wired to pay attention to certain patterns.

In tests of visual perception, researchers have shown not only that we are "naturals" at learning pattern discrimination, but at applying it to other models. It's the making of familiar connections (relevance) and locating conforming neural networks (pattern-making), in fact, that is critical to the formation of meaning. How important is the process of pattern-making to the brain? Author of *Endangered Minds* (1990) Jane Healy says, "I am increasingly convinced that patterns are the key to intelligence. Patterning information means really organizing and associating new information with previously developed mental hooks."

Using the pattern-detecting and pattern-making areas of the brain is critical to proper development. Dr. Healy adds, "Children who don't learn to search for meaning are often good 'technicians' in the first and second grade because they can deal with isolated data, but when the demands for comprehension increase, they hit the wall. They simply can't assemble it and make sense out of it; while those who can are considered more intelligent."

Exposing learners to interdisciplinary and cross-disciplinary models helps expose students to more patterns, which in turn translates to more relevance, context, and connections. It's the ability to see ideas in relation to others, as well as how individual facts become meaningful in a larger "field" of information, that ought to be considered important. How does economics relate to geography; mathematics to art and music; and ecology to politics?

 ## What This Means to You

Context can be either explicit or implicit. Implicit learning forms a powerful pattern called a mental model. Teachers who reveal their own mental models and elicit student models may be surprised at the value. When you open your own "windows of the mind," you make the implicit explicit. Ask students *how* they know *what* they know through the use of "how" questions. "How does democracy work? How does the weather change? How does our body digest food? How do you go about solving problems?" These will draw out the patterns of thinking that can expose the boundaries, limitations, and genius in your students.

Pattern Detection

Pattern-detection has been taught exquisitely well by countless teachers: One in particular is former Soviet Union high-school teacher Victor Shatalov. The math and science achievement scores of Dr. Shatalov's students rank among the highest in the world. His success is attributed to the high standards for success he maintains and his "nobody will fail" attitude. He makes a practice of describing the mental model he is using as he incorporates such techniques as color-coded graphic organizers, frequent shifts from global to detail learning, and active interaction with materials. He emphasizes relevance, context, and common patterns. The following teaching strategies can be used to help learners develop good pattern-detection skills:

 What This Means to You

- Ask students questions that force them to consider a larger context. For example, "Are high-school shootings random or part of a larger pattern?"
- Point out patterns in nature. "Can you see all the leaf shapes in the trees?"
- Introduce the skill of grouping objects, ideas, names, facts, and other key ideas.
- Simply read to kids; then guide them in establishing some basic patterns depicted in the reading. These might be cycles of cause-and-effect, problems and resolutions, or intense drama and down time.
- Ask questions that compare and contrast things in the natural environment.
- Give children the opportunity to play cards, build with blocks, and solve puzzles.
- Incorporate stitchery or sewing with patterns. Sort items related to sewing, building, or other hobbies.
- Assign class projects that require pattern conceptualization (i.e., a classroom library/book loan system, a school store, yearbook, newspaper, etc.)
- Pay attention to patterns: Discuss the patterns exhibited by wildlife, such as bird calls and migration patterns.
- At the start of each new topic, provide global visual overviews (i.e., overheads, videos, and posters).
- Incorporate motor skills: Walk learners through a process that ensures new learning corresponds to a physical place, location, or movement.
- Pre-expose learners with oral previews, applicable games in texts or handouts, metaphorical descriptions, and posted mind-maps of the topic.
- Encourage learners to evaluate the pros and cons of a topic, discuss its relevance, and demonstrate their conceptual patterning with models, plays, and projects.

Many students who have done poorly in the past may simply need a larger "map" of the material. In one study, two groups of college students were given an essay-format post-exam in a geology class. Those who had received instruction in conceptual mapping outperformed those who didn't.

Role-Plays and Games Enhance Meaning

Making learning physical is "old hat" to most primary teachers. And the whole idea of taking academic learning and embedding it within creative expression or entertainment is also centuries old. But does the method of re-contextualizing the learning really work? Does brain-based learning research support this type of learning? Yes, it does. It allows the brain to make complex perceptual maps. It has a high likelihood of engaging emotions. Being physical is much more naturally engaging, motivating, and likely to extend learning. When the focus is on performing, rather than learning, stress can be reduced, while creativity increases. Since knowledge is "state bound," what is learned during a role-play may be accessible during that same situation later on. This is the basic premise of self-defense courses that rely on "model muggers;" as well as, other simulation trainings, such as those used with pilots.

Most importantly, in these simulation contexts learning becomes more meaningful and enjoyable. More choice and creativity are exercised; and there is minimal negative evaluative pressure. It is easier to push through negative inner thoughts when everyone is caught up in the excitement of producing, planning, researching, and marketing a grand performance. When the stakes are higher, learning may take on more relevance. Reaching multiple goals (social, artistic, emotional, academic, etc.) is easier when the learner's heart and mind is engaged. The student actor will learn in spite of him/herself by virtue of memorizing lines and creating scenes, if nothing else.

What This Means to You

Students learn much more than they can consciously know when they work together to put on a school play. Many teachers and professors think that active, physical response learning and role-plays are, well, elementary. Brain research says otherwise. Activate the brain through presentations, skits, mock debates, "Jeopardy" shows, and humorous treatments of commercials, songs, etc. Include creative and/or entertaining activities as a regular part of the learning process.

Multiple Roles Enhance Learning

Research conducted at Stanford University (Levin 1996), suggests that taking on many roles enhances learning. The optimal environment is one in which learners are at different times partners, teammates, individuals, and teachers. This diversity of roles provides for greater contextual immersion learning that better replicates real life. By providing for many roles and status levels, instructors can ensure that all learners will be able to find at least one contextually suitable activity that they can strongly invest in.

You may have many very smart learners, but in the absence of favorable circumstances, their intelligence goes unnoticed. All of us are gifted; the context provides the evidence. There are many ways to utilize multiple status roles. Change the learner's status through the use of teams, alter-egos, peer tutoring, study buddies, multi-age projects, and multi-grade projects. Involvement in the community or with other classes provides more opportunity for real-life involvement, novelty, surprise, and meaningfulness.

Textbooks themselves do not provide meaning. Meaning is constructed. Encourage the use of integrated learning. Tap into learner's prior knowledge. And operate out of the context that learners *have to learn to create meaning for themselves* in what they learn. The conditions for meaning-making can be encouraged and orchestrated, but it is the learner who must construct the meaning. The genius of this process is that when the teacher gets out of the way of the learner, the learner can create, from scratch, real meaning in the learning.

Reflection Questions

1. What from this chapter was novel, fresh, or new to you? What was familiar or "old hat"?

2. In what ways, do you already apply the information in this chapter?

3. What three questions might you now generate about this material?

4. How did you react emotionally to the information in this chapter?

5. How did you react cognitively to the information? Do you agree or disagree with the author's point of view? Why?

6. In what ways might you translate the principles presented in this chapter into practical everyday useful ideas?

7. If these things are, in fact, true about the brain, what should we do differently? What resources of time, people, and money could be redirected? In what ways might you suggest we start doing this?

8. What were the most interesting insights you gained from this material?

9. If you were to plan your next step for making your curriculum more brain-based, what would that be?

10. What obstacles might you encounter? How might you realistically deal with them?

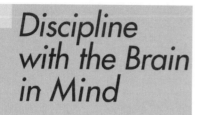

Discipline
with the Brain
in Mind

A Realistic Discipline Approach

Preventing Discipline Problems

High Control Can Backfire

Impact of Constant Subtle Threats

Levels of Discipline

Discipline with the Brain in Mind

Brain-based discipline takes into consideration what we now know about the brain and learning. It accepts our natural tendencies and responds more sensibly to problems. The primary source of discipline problems is a poor learning environment filled with threat, stress, lack of choice, inappropriate learning activities, and limited learning modalities.

A Realistic Discipline Approach

Discipline problems are *always* multi-causal—that is, related to various environmental and physiological factors. A primary biological correlation to discipline problems is dysfunction of the orbitofrontal cortex (see figure 20.1). This is the area right behind the eye sockets in the ventral (lower) frontal lobes. Other brain functions that impact behavior and discipline include the mid-brain area, particularly the amygdala (the area that deals with intense emotions); the thalamus, which deals with attentional priorities; and the balance or imbalance of neurotransmitters.

Environmentally, discipline problems can stem from irrelevant learning experiences and insufficient activation of the orbitofrontal area; or a combination of low serotonin and high noradrenaline levels plus a threatening emotional climate. It should be emphasized that behavior problems almost always relate to a combination of these factors. The better you are at recognizing the potential problems, the more preventative work can be done; and prevention always beats a remedial approach.

Figure 20.1
Orbitofrontal Cortex

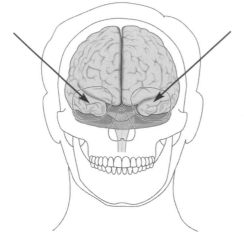

The orbitofrontal cortex is where thinking and emotions are integrated with sensations

When it comes to discipline, all of us have "mental models" that influence our approach. We formed them many years ago. They may, or may not, be very functional. Regardless, these models are the primary decision-makers for us. These frameworks or cause-and-effect propositions are either useful or not. Here's an example of a *non-brain-based* mental discipline model.

Non-Brain-Based Model of Discipline

Teacher gets control ➾ *by suppressing emotions* ➾ *so teacher can teach* ➾ *so supposedly students can learn* ➾ *suppressed emotions hurt learning* ➾ *students learn less* ➾ *teachers coerce more* ➾ *students act out emotions* ➾ *state of learning suffers.*

Some teachers would argue that the above scenario is absolutely necessary for running "a tight ship." The problem is, you may get a tight ship, but you'll also get impaired learning and cautious low-risk learners. In the worst-case scenario, you may also get students with so much pent-up aggression that they lash out at others with unspeakable acts of violence, as we've seen recently. What does a framework or mental model look like that is more brain-based? Here's an example:

Brain-Based Model of Discipline

Appropriate outlets are provided for expression of emotions ➾ *learners feel good* ➾ *boundaries and structure are respected* ➾ *learners learn more* ➾ *discipline problems diminish* ➾ *more choice is offered* ➾ *more learning is fostered* ➾ *less direct disciplining is needed* ➾ *everyone wins.*

The following six premises reflect the fundamentals for establishing a brain-based discipline approach that truly supports learners:

1. Disruptions are a normal part of living.

Disruptions happen! Some can be prevented, but some are inevitable. Life is chaotic and uncertain: If we are to make schools more relevant, we must learn to treat most non-emergencies as enjoyable challenges and sources of curiosity. It is easier to adapt than to try to change the world to meet your point of view. Ask yourself, "What are the two or three most common disruptions and how can I deal with them positively and proactively?"

Message to students: "School is real life."

2. The classroom is a "learning environment."

Within this learning environment, occasional discipline issues arise. The classroom is *not* the military where learning better occur, or else...! Student teachers are often taught that *first*, you get control, *then* you teach, and supposedly then *they* learn. But this is backwards thinking. The worst environment for authentic learning is one where fear, control, and high stress prevail. The optimal learning environment is supported by moderate stress for motivation; enough novelty to inspire curiosity; and enough challenge to move students towards higher levels of achievement. When learners are engaged, discipline problems disappear.

Message to students: "What we are about is learning."

3. Students are all basically good.

Students are just trying to manage their everyday lives. In spite of how you may feel some days, students don't wake up in the morning plotting strategies to make your day terrible. They do have normal needs, however, for expression, control, attention, and love. Some of the ways they express their needs are inappropriate for the classroom; and part of your job is showing them appropriate alternatives. Provide productive outlets for their frustrations and need for attention.

Message to students: "You are a human being, I respect you."

4. The best discipline is the kind nobody notices.

The single best discipline system is engaged learning. When kids are engaged, they act out less. It's crazy to formally discipline every student "mistake." The less students *know* they are being disciplined, the better. Keep the focus on "learning" by reading learner states and creating consistent engagement, novelty, challenge, and diversity. The more outraged you become about discipline problems, the more they occur. (If *you're* upset, who's in control?) Remember this: "Where the attention goes, the energy flows!" Keep your attention focused on the joy and excitement of learning.

Message to students: "Teacher has things handled; learning is fun."

5. Discipline problems are simply feedback to you.

Most problems are "in the moment" reactions. The first line of defense is a non-verbal response. Rather than words or lectures, use actions: Initiate a transition that alters the energy or mind state of learners. After all, most problem-behaviors originate from the area of the brain unable to will away an inappropriate behavior. Redirect learning with a change of pace. Save the left-brain discussion of rules for the last line of defense.

Message to students: "I'm aware of your mind state; let's alter the circumstances."

6. Prevention solves 95 percent of the problems

When students are engaged and allowed to express themselves, aggressive behaviors are reduced. When you maintain this awareness, inappropriate states for learning can be managed before they become a major problem. Plan transitions so that empty time is minimized. Work with students who require more of your attention "behind the scenes." The best teachers don't struggle with discipline problems—*not* because they have students who are always well-behaved, but because they create the conditions for optimal learning.

Message to students: "Let's focus on the important thing—learning."

Preventing Discipline Problems

The above six premises reflect a major paradigm shift. When teachers approach discipline from a brain-based perspective, the very nature of the problem changes. Students are not being bad to make your life miserable; they are simply expressing their state of mind. You are the orchestra conductor, pay attention to your musicians, and move them ever closer towards a harmonious whole, not by force, but by subtle tactics that reach for the best in them. The following strategies all reflect a brain-based perspective:

▼ Limit the amount of focused learning time: Switch back and forth from focused to diffused to down time activities.

▼ Use baroque, jazz, and environmental music (with sounds of waterfalls, rain, oceans, the rain forest, etc.) in the background at low levels to soothe and inspire.

▼ Create more "W-I-I-F-M" for students (What's in it for me?). *Ask them* to elicit good reasons for doing something or learning about a particular topic. Start with their needs. The more learning is aligned with students' goals, instead of someone's else's, the more engagement you'll get.

▼ Make rules fair, clear, and enforceable; and the fewer, the better. Make sure that students know the reasons behind every rule. Post them up in the room.

▼ Create a sense of family. Have students learn in teams; help each other; and work cooperatively towards achieving group goals. Teams can provide a source of fun, socialization, and positive peer pressure.

▼ Make positive eye contact with each of your students within the first few minutes of class. Also connect with parents as early in the year as you can at open houses, by phone, or with *positive* notes home.

▼ Boost ownership: Increase ways for students to have more input in their classroom. Install a suggestion box and respond to comments in a timely manner.

▼ Provide ample auditory outlets for expression. Learn to encourage, not suppress, student emotions. Incorporate partner affirmations, group time, discussions, movement activities, team events, sharing, etc. Give learners time to de-stress and interact with other students.

▼ As a group, brainstorm solutions to problems. Create mind-maps and explore topics with free-word association activities.

▼ Make the classroom visually interesting. Allow students to provide input; and seek their help in achieving a stimulating environment. Make it busy, colorful, fresh, challenging, wild, and relevant.

▼ Anticipate and respond swiftly to student states. As soon as you see something building, be proactive. Incorporate a stretch break, game, or partner shift. Frustration usually leads to apathy, anger, or revenge; Don't ignore the signs of frustration, boredom, or helplessness.

▼ Make rapport-building a part-time job. Start with the kids you relate to least and reach out to them both verbally and non-verbally. Know the tendencies of auditory learners who tend to talk a lot; as well as the rebellious learners who accidentally disrupt class in an attempt to learn. They're often pointing out what does not make sense to them, what's wrong, different, missing, or confusing.

▼ To keep the brain switched on, keep the body moving many times per hour. Incorporate active games, stretching, outdoor activities, and experiments.

▼ Make sure you've incorporated strategies into your own life to de-stress and download your body each day. What helps you relax?

▼ Set goals for yourself. Improve areas of concern you may have, like parent communications, administrative policies, or communications with other teachers/staff.

▼ Give clear, mobilizing directions: Make sure you provide the where, when, who, what; then re-check for understanding, and finally provide a congruent call to action. Be consistent, so students become conditioned to listen carefully. "We've been sitting for awhile (why), so in a few seconds when I say go (when), we'll all (who) stand up and stretch, circle the room (where), find a partner, give them a high-five, then have a seat (what) again. Got it? Ready, set, go!"(call to action).

▼ Give learners more choices. Provide more suggestions and fewer directives. Allow them to pick from a list of ten problems, issues, or topics: Choose either this or that topic, or this or that time priority. Choices work!

▼ From the very start, get parents involved in your discipline approach. Send home a brief note about your philosophy. Share more with them at appropriate times; seek agreement.

▼ Build personal relationships with students by getting to know them and their families. Have lunch with a student; or take a special interest in an activity or hobby they may be pursuing. What are their personal interests? Who helps them with their homework? What are their favorite stories?

▼ Engage multiple intelligences. Make sure that when you plan out your week, you have exposed students to all of them.

▼ Provide outlets for students to talk about the things that are important to them—discussion time, sharing circles, partner activities, etc.

▼ Encourage students to develop pen-pal relationships, either with other students at the school, or online, or with mentors/volunteers.

▼ Give students an opportunity to evaluate your teaching. Provide an evaluation form or have learners brainstorm ways they think their learning environment might be improved.

▼ Eliminate threats, rewards, and unfair demands.

High Control Can Backfire

Although the tendency of teachers in dealing with a large group is to establish conformity, this approach almost always backfires.

> *Highly controlling motivational strategies such as real or implied threats, strong punishments, compelling rewards, and forced competition are sometimes effective; however, they are likely to produce negative developmental consequences if they are repeated across many different behavioral episodes.*

In other words, by consistently using controlling means on your learners, you'll undermine their overall success. People lose interest in activities when they feel coerced or manipulated to engage in those activities, even when the motivational strategies used are intended to be positive and motivating.

In most cases, school starts off being fun and motivating with high initial interest. That enthusiasm, however, is typically replaced with resentment, complacency, and avoidance as controlling strategies are used, creativity discouraged, choice reduced, and parental pressure intensified. Sadly, intrinsic motivation is sidelined for another year.

 What This Means to You

We may have much more to do with the behaviors of our learners than we previously thought. Hold a staff meeting. Get everyone aligned on this issue. Develop a policy that everyone can buy into. Eliminate rewards; replace them with the alternatives of choice, creativity, enthusiasm, multi-context learning, and celebration.

The Impact of Constant Subtle Threats

Teachers who pause and say to the class with a stern voice, "I'll just wait until you're ready to learn" may be doing more harm than good. This subtle control tactic ("I'll withhold my teaching as long as you are withholding your good behavior") is a simple example of the continual threats that pervade a typical classroom, in spite of the

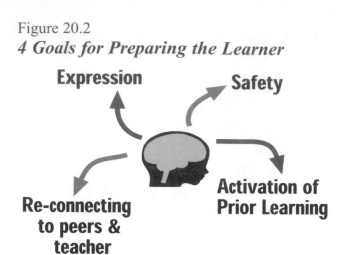

Figure 20.2
4 Goals for Preparing the Learner

Expression

Safety

Re-connecting to peers & teacher

Activation of Prior Learning

fact that threatening learners fosters more of the same behavior we wish to discourage.

A threat is any stimulus that causes the brain to trigger defensiveness or a sense of helplessness in the learner. For example, assigning a project without providing the resources and support to carry it out successfully is a subtle threat. Announcing a pop quiz is another example. The brain sits in a state of stress; and the learner's self-esteem, confidence, and peer acceptance is at stake.

Threats adversely affect one's ability to plan for the long term and to stay engaged at a task long enough to achieve success. Although the ability to postpone immediate gratification is important in the learning process, the child who is forced to sit at the piano for two hours a day to practice may, indeed, learn to play the instrument, but the price may be too high. Resentment can squelch whatever intrinsic joy they experienced in playing the piano to begin with. When this happens, we have contributed to the most devastating of all consequences—the distaste of learning.

Many teachers have difficulties with learners diagnosed as ADHD (attention deficit hyperactivity disorder). These individuals can be a tremendous challenge with restless, unfocused, and impulsive behaviors. Many researchers say ADHD is partially caused by specific neurotransmitter deficiencies in the brainstem (both serotonin and dopamine) and inhibition problems in the orbitofrontal cortex. In some cases, properly prescribed drugs such as Ritalin™ and Cylert™ can make dramatic improvements in behavior. However, other alternatives ought to be explored first, leaving medication as a last resort.

What This Means to You

We ought to reconsider what constitutes a threat in the learning environment. Any system of learning which uses heavy authority, position, laws, threats, rules, punishments, and rewards will, over the long run, perpetuate the very behaviors it is trying to eliminate. The techniques may work initially, but soon learning will suffer.

Learners who feel picked on and threatened by adults are least likely to change behavior because the part of their brain that deals with "perceptual mapping" and complex behavior change is unable to be engaged. Both adults and teenagers stay in peer groups for identity and safety. So-called "low achievers" who are constantly threatened, disciplined, and bribed with rewards may be unable to work for delayed gratification. The part of their brain they need to use, the frontal lobes, are less likely to be engaged under a system where others have control and they feel pressured to perform like a rat in a cage.

This may explain many of the common behaviors of gangs, so-called "low-achievers," and unmotivated learners. The more they are threatened, the more defensive behaviors they develop. Remember, when the brain senses danger, higher-order thinking skills take a back seat to survival concerns.

 ## What This Means to You

Identify areas of threat, both implicit and explicit, in your learning environment and introduce alternative forms of motivation, such as novelty, curiosity, positive social bonding, and relevant content to replace them. Avoid reliance on extrinsic rewards.

Levels of Discipline

When a student is misbehaving, remember, he is *not* a problem. He usually has no problem; *you are the one* who is upset. He/she is simply acting inappropriately, just like you have at some time in your life. Short term, you simply want to change the learner's state into a better one. Long term, you want the learner to learn to better manage his or her own behaviors.

> *Most discipline problems are inappropriately*
> *expressed emotions: Find more productive outlets*
> *for them and you'll dramatically reduce discipline problems.*

Based on what we know about the brain, the mid-brain area is most responsible for discipline problems. Since it regulates arousal thresholds, attention cycles, and learning biases, some steps are obvious. First, we ought to accept that the brain has an attentional bias for contrast, novelty, and emotion. When we ignore this, many learners get bored and restless. Timing is important, as well: Due to our brain's focus-diffusion cycles, more complex, detailed learning should be conducted in the morning, and more global, physical learning should take place in the afternoon.

As a general rule, we can expect to keep learner interest for about the amount of minutes represented by the learner's age. For example, the attention span of an average ten-year-old is ten minutes. Rarely, will a student ever be able to concentrate on a lecture for more than twenty-five minutes at one time. The internal-external shifts in our attention are natural and reflect our need for time to internally process the external stimuli that's accumulated in our brain. Thus the concept of "on task" is totally irrelevant; the brain is "on task" even when you don't have a learner's attention. The brain does not work like a machine. It cannot be forced to focus.

There are many "levels" of discipline. Someone who is doing bodily harm or property damage needs immediate and different strategies than someone who's talking too much. In general, the first tact should be simply to stop disruptive behavior with as little notice and fanfare as possible. In other words, keep the solution "invisible" while you continue to teach. Following are some strategies for dealing appropriately with various levels of discipline issues, starting with the least serious (Level 1) to the most serious (Level 4).

Level 1
Invisible: *Nobody knows but the teacher*

Focus on changing the state of the learner, not the behavior. When the state changes, the behaviors automatically change. Keep the focus on learning and be indirect. Many things can change the physiological state of the student such as: 1) a change in activities, regrouping, stretch break, or seat change; 2) a deep breathing exercise; 3) a change in the tonality of your voice; 4) a shift of your position in the room; 5) drawing attention away from the disruptive person; 6) putting on some background music; 7) altering the lighting in the room; 8) facilitating a movement game, like Simon Says or game show simulation; 9) sending the problem student on an errand for you; 10) assigning the problem student a special class job; 11) increasing your excitement or energy level; 12) name dropping—use the names of three or more students in a sentence; "How many of you, Jason, Tim, Tracy, and Becky, need more paper?" 13) using "shhh" more creatively like "You sssssshhhould find this interesting"; 14) using gestures or a gentle touch; 15) changing your facial expression;

16) having a team cheer contest; 17) having group leaders facilitate an activity; and 18) admonishing the object of the noise making instead of the student; i.e., Bad pencil! If it doesn't quiet down, I'll have to put it in the bad pencil box."

Level 2
Minor Attention: *No big deal attitude towards matter*

Be direct and light; and use no or low-threat consequences such as providing direct eye contact and asking the student to stop the behavior. For example, "Brian, can you keep it down? I'd really appreciate that." Or, "Cindy, by keeping your hands to yourself, we can finish without any more interruptions and get out on time." Tonality, intent, congruency, and consistency can positively influence the disruptive student most of the time.

Use no threats, follow through on all consequences, and avoid keeping a student after school. For most kids, staying after simply reinforces their dislike of school even more. Try *not* to punish students: sitting and brooding about their mistakes or misconduct will only form more bad associations about school. Help learners to feel good about themselves instead.

Level 3
Substantial Attention: *A serious infraction to be addressed*

If one, or just a few, students are causing trouble, don't disrupt everyone with your discipline approach. Continue talking to the whole class, but interject a story quickly about a dog or a kid that you once yelled at loudly. In the story, turn to the noisy kids and say you got so mad, you had to tell the dog to "Quiet down!" Continue with your story. The behavior will stop. There are many other statements you can make in the context of a story that will get the attention of your intended students.

If you feel you must discipline the entire class, never get "heavy" from the front of the room where you teach. This "contaminates" your ritual teaching space. Rather go to a place in the room that is your consistent "hot spot" where you can let off some steam. This does not mean *screaming* at the class; but if that we don't occasionally vent, our own pent-up emotions can be miscommunicated. When you feel that all of your other efforts have failed, stand in your designated spot and use your "heavy" voice, strong disciplining eye contact, and state something brief, but loud, like "courtesy please!" or "boys and girls!" or "ladies and gentlemen!" Once you've "had it out," return to your normal voice, tonality, facial expression, and position in the room. Don't lecture or recite the rules. Return your focus to learning.

Level 4
Serious Talk Time: *What's really up?*

Before you get to this stage, ask yourself if you've really done everything you can to make class interesting, relevant, and empowering. Are you incorporating multiple learning styles and intelligences? Are you providing various choices for learners? If you've done your part, and the student is still acting out, the next step is to get the student to take responsibility for his/her behavior.

Call a meeting with the student preferably outside of class time. Meet with them alone first to see if the problem can be resolved between the two of you. Ask questions and listen to the student's story without blaming. Follow these guidelines: 1) Allow for emotions to be expressed and gain rapport; 2) Communicate and discover each other's concerns; 3) Create new agreements each is willing to keep; and 4) Agree on a way to monitor or manage the plan. If the student does not maintain his/her agreements, you may have to repeat the process with higher stakes, such as administrative or parented or therapeutic involvement.

Reflection Questions

1. What from this chapter was novel, fresh, or new to you? What was familiar or "old hat"?

2. In what ways, do you already apply the information in this chapter?

3. What three questions might you now generate about this material?

4. How did you react emotionally to the information in this chapter?

5. How did you react cognitively to the information? Do you agree or disagree with the author's point of view? Why?

6. In what ways might you translate the principles presented in this chapter into practical everyday useful ideas?

7. If these things are, in fact, true about the brain, what should we do differently? What resources of time, people, and money could be redirected? In what ways might you suggest we start doing this?

8. What were the most interesting insights you gained from this material?

9. If you were to plan your next step for making your curriculum more brain-based, what would that be?

10. What obstacles might you encounter? How might you realistically deal with them?

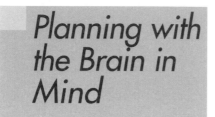

Planning with the Brain in Mind

Planning with the Brain in Mind

Many different planning approaches have been suggested to teachers over the years as the "right" way to teach; but the difference between those and planning with the brain in mind is the underlying assumption involved. Where traditional lesson planning is based on the thinking, "Plan what there is to *teach*, then teach it"; the brain-based practitioner asks, "What is there to *learn*, and how can it *best* be learned?"

Putting Learners First

What at first may be perceived of as a backwards approach to planning is really not: Brain-based learning starts with the learner, not the content. The lesson is based on creating optimal conditions for natural learning. Contrary to traditional belief, the brain rarely learns in a sequential format: i.e., "Introduce Unit A; learn it, test students on it; then go to Unit B..." We learn best by immersion; by jumping into the fray, then thinking our way out of it. In brain-based learning, we get our feet wet in Unit K; then find solutions in Units A, D, and G. This is real life. Rather than proceeding in a straight line manner, we move ahead, back, and around like a spiral. This is the brain's natural tendency. This is not to say that planning or structure is not necessary. In fact, planning is more important today than ever as there's more to learn. The issue is rather a reprioritizing our values, as we learn to plan in a way that is natural to the brain.

Old Style Lesson Planning

The old way of teaching was to take a subject like math, science, or history and divide it into smaller chunks called units; then sub-divide the units into weekly and daily lesson plans; then present micro chunks of the whole in a linear fashion. It sounds logical. But it is not the way our brain is best designed to learn.

Imagine yourself as a three or four-year-old child; and you've just received your first bicycle for your birthday. You're all excited and want nothing more than to jump on it and go! But wait...you can't. Your parents have decided that you should learn to ride your bicycle in the "proper" way first. Replicating the traditional approach used in schools, they insist on teaching you how to ride your bike with the following progression:

Unit A: Safety
Personal safety
Hand signals
Defensive attitude
Neighborhood safety
Possible hazards
Crosswalks
Laws, customs and rules

Unit B: Bicycle Logistics
History of the bicycle
Types of bikes
Product specifications
Parts of the bike
Tire repair
Costs

Unit C: The Skills of Riding
Proper mount and dismount
Proper use of trainer wheels
Body positioning
Advanced riding skills

Unit D: Everyday Use
Bicycle storage
Permission
Maintenance

Naturally, before your parents have even completed Unit A, you've lost interest and gone on to do something else. The brain is far more capable than we usually give it credit for. A child's natural urge to jump on the bike and try to ride it is really more compatible with the brain. They've already watched others learn to ride; they ask a few questions, garner support, and get on. Low and behold, after a few faults and fumbles, they learn to ride their bike quite naturally.

> *The brain learns best in real-life, immersion-style multi-path learning: Fragmented, piecemeal teaching can forever kill the joy and love of learning.*

If you think about it, the way a child generally learns to ride a bike is how you learned some of the most complex things in your life—your native language, for example. Did you study the rules of grammar before you began speaking? Did you take classes in speaking? Were you tested on it? Of course not! Although you received plenty of informal feedback, you weren't "taught" your native language: You rather "picked it up."

Uncovering the Learning

Is it possible that our brain can "pick up" other subjects, as well? Is it possible to learn science, history, accounting, geography, math, life skills, literature, and the arts by default? Of course it is! This, in fact, is how our brain is designed to learn—multi-path, in and out of order, on many levels, from a variety of feedback sources, and in various contexts. We learn best with complex learning: moving from chaos to clarity, following our natural passions and interests, exploring issues, focusing on key points, and with a trial and error approach. As teachers, we need to plan learning with this in mind. Within the structure of your curriculum, provide flexibility.

> *Complex learning is a process that better reflects the way the human brain is naturally designed to learn.*

The underlying premise is that our world is an integrated whole; and that one of the greatest gifts we can offer our students is a bridge from classroom education to the real world. A brain-based approach to planning urges you to follow the threads woven through the fabric of your students' world. Use textbooks only as supplemental materials. In this fast-moving information age, students need to learn how to rely on multiple sources of information. Include magazines, computers, videos, television, journals, and fieldtrips in your lesson planning.

Brain-Based Planning Strategies

Brain-based lesson planning does not follow a template—mainly because the basic premise of brain-based learning is that every brain is unique, so a "one size fits all" approach does not work. Learning different things requires different approaches for different people depending on variables such as prior learning, experience, preferred modalities, and the type of skill being taught. Thus, a toolbox rather than a template is the basis for brain-based lesson planning.

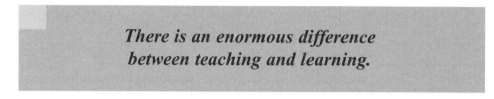

> ***There is an enormous difference between teaching and learning.***

There are a wide range of tools that help encourage the brain to absorb, process, and store experiences and information meaningfully. The following general strategies reflect a brain-based approach to lesson planning. They are followed by a more detailed sequence of guidelines that reflect the seven stages of learning.

 ## What This Means to You

- Pre-expose learners to new material in advance: The more background they have, the greater number of connections they'll make.
- Discover what your students background is in the subject; and customize your planning to their experience level and preferred learning style.
- Create a supportive, challenging, complex, no threat classroom environment where questions and exploration are encouraged.
- Ensure that your materials and presentation strategies are age-appropriate.
- Acquisition happens both formally and informally; provide learning experiences that reflect real life.
- Always plan for elaboration; presenting is not learning. The student must process the learning before they own it.
- Help learners encode learning in their memory with appropriate usage of down time, emotions, real-life associations, and mnemonic techniques.
- Functional integration only happens over time and with repeated reviews.

The 7-Stage Brain-Based Planning Outline

The following strategies are organized below in a sequence that makes sense to the brain. The list is by no means exhaustive: You'll be able to add many more to it based on the demographics of your particular learners. After you've prepared your lesson plans, use the outline as a checklist to ensure you've planned activities that satisfy the goals of each learning stage:

Stage 1: Pre-exposure

This phase provides the brain with an overview of the new learning before really digging in: Pre-exposure helps the brain develop better conceptual maps.

▼ Post an overview of the new topic up on the bulletin board: Mind-maps work great for this.

▼ Teach learn-to-learn skills and memory strategies.

▼ Encourage good brain nutrition, including drinking plenty of water.

▼ Role model and practice coping, self-esteem, and life skills.

▼ Create a strong immersion learning environment; make it interesting!

▼ Consider time-of-day brain cycles and rhythms when planning morning and afternoon activities.

▼ Discover students' interests and background; start where they are in their knowledge base, not where you think they are.

▼ Have learners set their own goals; and discuss class goals for each unit.

▼ Post many colorful peripherals, including positive affirmations.

▼ Plan brain "wake-ups" (i.e., cross-laterals or relax-stretching) every hour.

▼ Plan activities where students can move around and choose from a menu of offerings.

▼ State strong positive expectations; and allow learners to voice theirs, too.

▼ Build strong positive rapport with learners.

▼ Read learning states and make any adjustments as you proceed through the lessons.

Stage 2: Preparation

This is the phase where you create the curiosity or excitement. It's similar to the "anticipatory set" but goes farther in preparing the learner.

▼ Create a "you are there" experience; give learners a real-world grounding.

▼ Provide the context for learning the topic (Can be a repeat of the overview; the classic "big picture").

▼ Elicit from learners what possible value and relevance the topic has to them personally. They must feel connected to the learning before they'll internalize it. Encourage their expression of how they feel it is, or is not, relevant.

▼ The brain learns particularly well from concrete experiences first! Provide something real, physical, or concrete. Conduct an experiment; go on a fieldtrip; or obtain a guest speaker who is professionally involved with the topic.

▼ Create complex interdisciplinary tie-ins to the session.

▼ Provide a "hook", surprise, or bit of novelty to engage learner emotions.

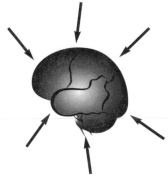

Stage 3: Initiation and Acquisition

This stage provides the immersion: Flood with content! Instead of the singular, lock-step, sequential, one-bite-at-a-time presentation, provide an initial virtual overload of ideas, details, complexity, and meanings. Allow a sense of temporary overwhelm to occur in learners: This will be followed by anticipation, curiosity, and a determination to discover meaning for oneself. Over time it all gets sorted out, by the learner, brilliantly. If that sounds like the real world of learning, outside the classroom, you're right; it is.

▼ Provide concrete learning experiences (i.e., a case study or experiment, a field trip, interviews, hands-on learning).

▼ Provide activities that employ a majority (if not all) of the multiple intelligences.

▼ Offer a group or team project that encompasses building, finding, exploring, or designing.

▼ Attend the theater; put on a skit; produce a commercial; or create a class/school newspaper.

▼ Provide enough choice that learners have the opportunity to explore the subject using their preferred learning modality: visual, auditory, kinesthetic, etc.

▼ A well-designed computer program can be helpful at this stage.

Stage 4: Elaboration

This is the processing stage. It requires genuine thinking on the part of the learner. This is the time to make intellectual sense of the learning.

▼ Provide an open-ended debriefing of the previous activity.
▼ Tie things together so that learning across disciplines occurs (i.e., read a sci-fi story about outer-space while studying the solar system; discuss how literature relates to science).
▼ Have learners design an evaluation procedure or rubric for their own learning (i.e., write test questions, facilitate peer reviews, design mind-maps, etc.)
▼ Have learners explore the topic online or at the library.
▼ Watch a video, view slides, or see a theatrical production on the topic.
▼ Stimulate small group discussions; have groups report back to entire class.
▼ Create individual and/or group mind-maps reflecting the new material.
▼ Hold a school forum, debate, essay contest, or panel discussion.
▼ Hold a question and answer period.
▼ Have students do the teaching (i.e., in small groups, as class presenters, in pairs).

Stage 5: Incubation and Memory Encoding

This phases emphasizes the importance of down time and review time. The brain learns most effectively over time, not all at once.

▼ Provide time for unguided reflection—down time.
▼ Have learners keep a journal of their learning.
▼ Have learners take a walk in pairs and discuss the topic.
▼ Provide stretching and relaxation exercises.
▼ Provide a music-listening area.
▼ Ask learners to discuss new learning with their family and friends.

Stage 6: Verification and Confidence Check

This phase is not just for the benefit of the teacher; learners need to confirm their learning for themselves, as well. Learning is best remembered when the student possesses a model or metaphor regarding the new concepts or materials.

▼ Have learners present their learning to others.
▼ Students interview and evaluate each other.
▼ Students write about what they've learned (i.e., journal, essay, news article, report).

▼ Students demonstrate learning with a project (i.e., working model, mind-map, video, newsletter).
▼ Students present a role-play, skit, or theatrical performance.
▼ Quiz (verbal and/or written)

Stage 7: Celebration and Integration

In the celebration phase it is critical to engage emotions. Make it fun, light, and joyful. This step instills the all-important love of learning. Never miss it!

▼ Have a class toast (with juice)!
▼ Provide sharing time (i.e., peer sharing, demonstration, acknowledgments).
▼ Play music, hang streamers, and blow horns.
▼ Invite another class, parents, the principal, or community guests in to view projects.

▼ Facilitate a class-designed and produced celebration party.
▼ Incorporate the new learning in future lessons! Never introduce something, then drop it. If it's not important enough to refer to in the future, don't waste time on it to begin with.

What This Means to You

It is critical as we plan learning with the brain in mind to ask a different set of questions: Rather than, *what* should I teach, ask *how* will students *best* learn? As you plan the learning, keep the focus on the basic principles that support the brain's natural learning tendencies. Follow through from pre-exposure to celebration, making sure that none of the phases in-between are skipped. Learning happens over time. Create a complex, integrated, interdisciplinary curriculum that provides for plenty of learner choice. Provide structure, but in an environment that respects the unique nature of each learner and their individual needs and experiences.

Reflection Questions

1. What from this chapter was novel, fresh, or new to you? What was familiar or "old hat"?

2. In what ways, do you already apply the information in this chapter?

3. What three questions might you now generate about this material?

4. How did you react emotionally to the information in this chapter?

5. How did you react cognitively to the information? Do you agree or disagree with the author's point of view? Why?

6. In what ways might you translate the principles presented in this chapter into practical everyday useful ideas?

7. If these things are, in fact, true about the brain, what should we do differently? What resources of time, people, and money could be redirected? In what ways might you suggest we start doing this?

8. What were the most interesting insights you gained from this material?

9. If you were to plan your next step for making your curriculum more brain-based, what would that be?

10. What obstacles might you encounter? How might you realistically deal with them?

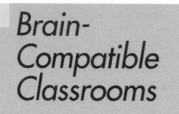

Brain-
Compatible
Classrooms

The School as a Learning Community

The Essentials of Brain-Based Learning

22

Brain-Compatible Classrooms

The way to maximize learning results is to fit all of the pieces of the puzzle together. This means planning the curriculum with the brain in mind; presenting it with the brain in mind; creating the environment with the brain in mind; and assessing it with the brain in mind. Ideally, your school will buy into becoming a total learning community where teaching with the brain in mind is the norm. A chain is only as strong as its weakest link: The link you must start with is yourself. From there, the next step becomes addressing the bigger picture. As you know, problems will occur in the weakest area, so this is where your attention will naturally flow. Don't get discouraged. We've come a long way in our knowledge, but now we have a long way to go in applying it. As others view the changes in your teaching approach, awareness of brain based learning will grow exponentially.

We have to nibble away at our goals, making progress in small chunks, rather than expecting the whole world to change overnight. As an administrator, teacher, or trainer, however, you will experience some immediate success by integrating some of the practical, simple brain-based strategies presented in this book. A little success encourages more success. So just jump on the bike and start pedaling. Before you know it, you'll be riding like an expert without ever looking back.

This chapter is a summary of the puzzle pieces presented thus far. If it seems like a review, that's okay: Remember, frequent review is good for the brain.

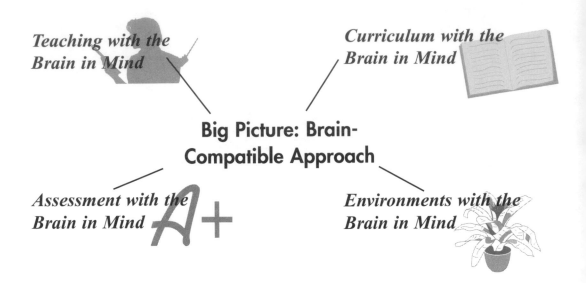

Teaching with the Brain in Mind

Curriculum with the Brain in Mind

Big Picture: Brain-Compatible Approach

Assessment with the Brain in Mind

Environments with the Brain in Mind

The School as a Learning Community

None of us work in a vacuum; and the more we address the whole, the easier the parts will fall into place. Once you've created a brain-based environment for *your* learners, it's time to seek support from the larger community, the school. A class-room that is the only learning oasis on campus will soon find it is in jeopardy of being sabotaged. Support on the macro level forms the foundation for long-term success on the micro level; thus, seek assistance from the larger learning communi-ty in achieving the following goals:

▼ Acknowledgment of Value

Ensure that everyone feels like they are a contributing member of the community. If they don't, they will be prone to disrupt the system, and/or experience feelings of inadequacy and depression. Daily affirmations, notes of appreciation, and occasion-al celebrations go a long way towards acknowledging the efforts of everyone in the learning community.

▼ Everyone Feels Cared For

Make sure that no one falls through the cracks. *Everyone* should be in a peer group, on a committee, or involved in some way with a supportive crew.

▼ Freedom of Expression

Make sure everyone has a creative voice in the community. It may be volunteering for a local non-profit or impacting change as a community activist or playing in the marching band or being on the chess team. For some, it's simply being able to raise their hand in class, get called on, and share their feelings without the fear of humil-iation.

▼ Encourage Affiliation

Encourage healthy levels of affiliation among students, parents, teachers, and committee members. Provide many group learning experiences, team efforts, and a variety of bonding activities.

▼ Accountability

We feel accountable when the rules, policies, and norms of the groups at large are consistently enforced by common regulation. As soon as this consistency is broken, we feel we can act with impunity and the system begins to break down.

▼ Hope of Success

Everyone absolutely must feel as if there's hope in their efforts. Hope is defined differently by each of us, but the bottom line is that hope is about bettering one's situation. Hope may come in the form of potential scholarships or an opportunity to make a up a test due to illness, or progress towards higher test scores. Hope is best achieved by individuals progression toward their goals.

▼ Orchestrated Common Experiences

Look for ways to develop common ground on a schoolwide and community-wide basis. Some ideas include assemblies, sporting events, celebrations, etc.

▼ Physically Safe Environment

Make physical safety a top priority. Do not tolerate bullying, threats, or fighting. Encourage learners to "use their words" and communicate verbally rather than physically. Also eliminate social and emotional distress by making it a safe environment to make mistakes without embarrassment.

▼ Trust of Others

Trust comes from both the frequency of contact and the predictability of another's behavior. We all want to know that we are safe to express ourselves; and that we will be treated fairly and with respect. Practice providing this in all relationships—with students, parents, other teachers, administration, and the larger world.

▼ Consistency of Structure

A community has to have more than a set of rules, guidelines, and values; it must also have predictable rituals and traditions that everyone participates in. For example, birthdays, holidays, openings, closings, and openhouses are all opportunities to strengthen community support.

The Essentials of Brain-Based Learning

A good way to work with these guidelines is to write each concept on an index card and then list some of the specific, practical strategies you can do to make that guideline happen. Consider introducing one new concept a week; then be rigorous in your implementation. Remember, you'll still be integrating the concepts from the previous weeks, too; but after a while, your new approach will be automatic.

★ Pre-Exposure and Priming

Make sure that learners are pre-exposed to the content and context of the new topic at least one week in advance of starting it. This helps establish some background and relevance in the subject and expedites future learning. Post a summary or mind-map of the proceeding unit on the bulletin board a couple of weeks prior to starting it. Let students notice and ask you about it, rather than calling it to their attention.

★ Sufficient Time for Learning

Time is an essential ingredient and always a factor in the learning equation. The urge to cover more and more content often results in incomplete learning. Provide sufficient time for learning to begin with. Make sure you plan time for review and reflection, as well. These are requirements for authentic learning.

★ Low or No Threat

Interact daily with each learner. Provide frequent, non-judgmental feedback. Be sure to activate prior learning so that learners draw connections between new subjects and past learning. Manage states without making threats; redirect learners as the need arises. Remember, it's not *what* you teach, but *how* they *best* learn. Keep the focus on learning.

★ Prep for Final Performance

If you expect learners to take a test to demonstrate their learning, it is your responsibility to prepare them for success on it. We are doing a disservice to learners if they are set up to fail. Every time a student fails or experiences a "poor performance," we are reinforcing that self-image. Ensure that learners rehearse for their "final performance," and that their preparation includes a similar stress condition as they'll likely experience at test time. Do not give pop (or surprise) quizzes. Rather, provide ungraded pre-tests so that learners can decipher their strengths and weaknesses before their test scores are "final."

★ High Engagement

Make this statement your mantra: "*Involve*, don't tell." Get students "on the bicycle," rather than *telling* them how to ride it. The bulk of your lesson planning activities ought to engage learners physically and socially, so that they are continuously interacting and taking action.

★ Positive Emotional Engagement

Teach learners to manage their own learning states. How students feel is critical to the decision to learn, the quality of learning, and the ability to recall the learning. Reduce negative states by changing activities frequently, providing choice, attending to physical needs (i.e., moving, stretching, providing drinking water, downtime, etc.); and by keeping the stakes and challenge level high. Be supportive and provide frequent opportunities for feedback.

★ Learner Choice

There is a fine line between too little and too much choice; and the balance is related to other factors as well, such as, trust, rapport, and past experiences. When you provide a brain-friendly learning environment, learners feel empowered. When they feel empowered, it isn't necessary for them to have a choice in everything because they will trust you have their best interest at heart. The key element here is perception: If learners perceive they have power in the relationship, they will demand less of it. Everyone needs to feel like they have some control over their destiny, whether they're five or fifty years old.

★ Moderate to High Challenge

Create enough challenge that what you are asking students to do is worth doing. Any activity can be made more challenging by adjusting any of the following factors: 1) time (increase or decrease the amount of time you give for an activity); 2) standards (raise or lower the final product standards); 3) resources (increase or decrease the availability of resources for doing the task); 4) altering the circumstances (learners have to do the task silently, or by themselves, or in the dark, or with three partners, or for public performance, etc.).

★ Strong Peer Support

Students will be willing to take on more challenge if they know they can count on peer support. Encouraging positive peer affiliation is an ongoing process that is supported by frequent group assignments and team efforts. Use formal and informal groupings; use frequent pairs activities; encourage socializing at appropriate times; and emphasize cooperative learning. Assist learners in setting up outside study groups and/or paired homework assignments. The old model of learners competing against each other for the best grades ought to be replaced with learners helping each other to achieve the best learning results for the greatest number of people.

★ Mastery Goals

Students, for the most part, do what is expected of them. Set high standards; provide benchmarks; and acknowledge learners for reaching them. Share and post your goals for the class, as well as learner goals.

★ Sufficient Non-Learning Time

The brain is not good at non-stop learning. In fact, *not* learning is necessary for the brain to process and transfer learning from short- to long-term memory. So make sure your students have sufficient reflection time. Down time can be in the form of journal time, recess, break time, listening to music, lunch time, or activities such as a walk with a partner.

★ Balancing Novelty and Predictability

The optimal learning environment provides a balance of novelty or surprise and predictability and ritual. Constant novelty is too stressful for students; while constant predictability is too boring. Too much of one or the other usually results in behavior problems. The best balance is high amounts of both novelty and predictability.

★ Safe for Taking Risks

Ensure that the culture in your classroom is one that supports emotional safety. This can be done by adopting a zero tolerance policy for teasing, humiliation, put downs, or name calling. Get learner buy-in by discussing the need for a safe learning environment. Ask learners how it feels to be humiliated or laughed at. Conduct role plays emphasizing appropriate responses when someone does put another person down. And ask the class to determine what the consequences ought to be for breaking a groundrule. Post a sign to remind learners of their agreements. Always model appropriate responses for such things as incorrect answers: "Good try, Michael; you're using your brain. Do you want to give it another shot? Would someone else like to give it a shot?"

★ Moderate Stress

A little stress is good; but too much is bad. Again, it is the balance that is important here. Stress levels influence learner states. Monitor the tension in your class and manage it accordingly. If it's too high, it's time for humor, movement, games, or quiet time; if it's too low, it's time to raise the stakes or challenge level.

★ Alternating Low to High Energy

A biological mechanism in human beings, called circadian rhythms, moves our energy from low to high and back again along a regular timeline. This roller coaster of energy levels is easier to deal with when you recognize it as a natural aspect of our lives. We are influenced by hourly, daily, weekly, monthly, and seasonal cycles. Acknowledge this influence on learners; and work to accommodate their natural ups and downs. This is another reason why providing choice is so important.

★ Multi-Modal Input

Engage as many modalities as possible by providing learners with options and choices. Ensure learning activities offer auditory, visual, and kinesthetic components. Provide visual aids, guest speakers, partner learning, cross-age tutoring, independent time, computer assistance, audiobooks, and fieldtrips. Remember the importance of the three Vs and the three Cs: Variety, variety, variety; and choice, choice, choice!

★ Frequent Feedback

All of the previous goals are supported by frequent feedback. Ensure that every student gets some kind of feedback every thirty minutes or so each school day. This does not mean you personally have to provide that feedback. Rather, set up mechanisms whereby learners receive feedback from their peers, teaching assistants, and self-reviews, as well as feedback based on grades and your own verbal feedback.

★ Celebrate the Learning

It's easy after all these demands on your time to forget to celebrate the learning, but this is a critical step
for optimal learning. Like the athletic team that cele-
brates their hard work after each win, learners need to
feel acknowledged for their efforts. It also adds an
element of fun to the process and engages learners
emotions. From something as casual as a simple
high-five to a more elaborate student-planned party, be sure to close each learning
session with some kind of a celebration or acknowledgment.

Remember no class is 100 percent brain-based or 100 percent brain-antagonistic. We
are all "in process"—moving towards ever greater insights and better implementation.

Reflection Questions

1. What from this chapter was novel, fresh, or new to you? What was familiar or "old hat"?

2. In what ways, do you already apply the information in this chapter?

3. What three questions might you now generate about this material?

4. How did you react emotionally to the information in this chapter?

5. How did you react cognitively to the information? Do you agree or disagree with the author's point of view? Why?

6. In what ways might you translate the principles presented in this chapter into practical everyday useful ideas?

7. If these things are, in fact, true about the brain, what should we do differently? What resources of time, people, and money could be redirected? In what ways might you suggest we start doing this?

8. What were the most interesting insights you gained from this material?

9. If you were to plan your next step for making your curriculum more brain-based, what would that be?

10. What obstacles might you encounter? How might you realistically deal with them?

Curriculum with the Brain in Mind

Brain-Compatible Curriculum

Social Fluency

Personal Development

Artistic Expression

Information Literacy

Scientific Inquiry

Suggestions for Grades K to 5

Suggestions for Grades 6 to 12+

Curriculum with the Brain in Mind

Many ideas have been established thus far about the function, needs, priorities, and purpose of the brain; but how do we make the leap from brain-based teaching strategies to brain-based content? This chapter explores how *what* you teach is relevant to *how* the brain learns best.

No doubt, many of the things you already do are good for the brain. This is no coincidence. Remember, the brain's primary mission is to ensure our survival. Therefore, it is very good at seeking pleasure (food, social bonding, and mating); avoiding pain (physical harm, embarrassment, negative judgments, etc.); and novelty-seeking (finding interesting diversions). These natural tendencies provide the basis for a brain-based curriculum. Our job is to *maintain* a focus that is meaningful and relevant to the brain.

Brain-Compatible Curriculum

Given what we know about the brain—and its quest for curiosity, affiliation, challenge, and creature comforts—the following curriculum elements all make a great deal of sense and embody the principles we have been exploring in this book.

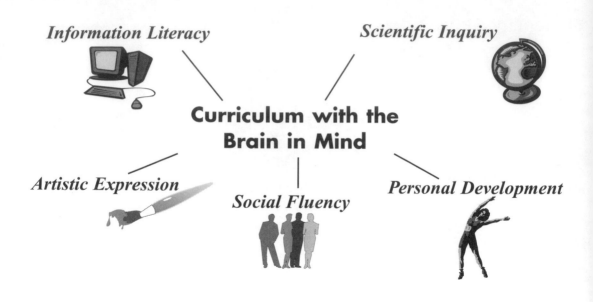

Information Literacy

Scientific Inquiry

Curriculum with the Brain in Mind

Artistic Expression

Social Fluency

Personal Development

Social Fluency

As human beings, we rely on one another and learn from each other. In fact, our very survival depends upon our relationships with others. Therefore, ensuring every learner develops the requisite set of social skills to interact productively in the world is essential. Humans cannot grow up isolated and expect to succeed in society: The very word "society" implies a complex web of social interactions and rules that provide the basis for a community. What could be more important in the big picture than learning how to get along with others? This aspect of the curriculum ought to include the following subject areas:

Emotional Intelligence

Identifying and labeling feelings
Reading others moods and feelings
Managing your own moods and feelings
Controlling impulses; delaying gratification
Expressing feelings appropriately and productively
Compassion and empathy for others

Appreciating Diversity

Accepting the differences of culture, race, religion, ethnicity, and life style
Exploring the injustice of intolerance
Types of differences
The politics of differences and diversity

Language Skills

Learning how to use the native language accurately and artfully
The ability to express oneself in a complex social world
Learning a non-native language; awareness of other languages

Workplace Literacy

The importance of livelihood
Careers and jobs
Bosses, colleagues, and subordinates: The workplace hierarchy
Getting along in the work setting; problem-solving and conflict resolution

Religious/Spiritual Identities

The role of religion and/or spirituality
Similarities and differences among religions
Religious freedom versus persecution

Appropriate Family Behaviors

The purpose of family (as a unit of safety)
Differences in family structures (biological, adoptive, divorced, and non-traditional)
Functional versus dysfunctional
A child's rights
Affecting change in the family unit

Teamwork/Cooperation

The importance of teamwork
Group roles
Competition versus cooperation; and the need for both

Conflict Resolution

The nature of conflict
Approaches to resolving conflict
Understanding frames of reference

Democracy/Political Action

The history/role of government
Types of government
Approaches to impacting change in a democracy
Voting

These skills ought to be addressed both explicitly and implicitly in an age-appropriate manner; and purposefully integrated across the curriculum.

Personal Development

In Maslow's hierarchy of needs, self-actualization (or the ability to achieve ones goals) lies at the peak of the pyramid with survival needs (food and shelter) at the base of the pyramid. Nevertheless, developing the personal power or skills to maximize one's potential is a critical goal in a society that values innovation and achievement. In the past, an emphasis on personal-development skills was reserved for the elite, whose birthright ensured their basic needs were met. Today, teaching the skills for personal success across the economic divide promises improved access and opportunity for all regardless of social class. This aspect of the curriculum ought to address the following areas:

Stress Management

The role of exercise, relaxation, imagery, sleep, and lifestyle choices

Physical Fitness

Healthy body, healthy mind
Kinds of fitness: stretching, strength training, aerobics
Sports and activities
Body image

Metacognition and Reflection

Developing self-reflection skills and insight
Positive inner dialogue
Learning from mistakes
Recognizing strengths and weaknesses
Analytical skills; compare and contrast, pros and cons, etc.

Sense of Meaning and Purpose

Self-acceptance, self-esteem, and self-confidence
Loves, passions, and hobbies
Goals and goal setting

Nutrition/Health/Eating Habits

The role of water; hydration awareness
The value of vitamins, minerals, and a good diet
The dangers of additives, growth hormones, herbicides, pesticides, excess
    fats, sugars, carbohydrates, dieting, and drugs
Feeding your brain and body

Goal-setting and Achievement

Setting measurable goals and objectives
Decision-making and follow through
Vigilance and persistence

Learning-to-Learn Skills

Memory strategies
Note-taking strategies
Study skills, test-preparation skills
Utilizing resources, incorporating feedback, and time management

Personal/Ethical Responsibility

What are ethics?
What is integrity?
Agreements, contracts, and dilemmas
Consequences, cause-and-effect, and analyzing risk
Problem solving and whistle blowing

Artistic Expression

All human beings have a basic need to express their thoughts and feelings. And, many individuals actually subsist on the fruits of their artistic/expressive talents (i.e., graphic artists, painters, sculptors, writers, architects, jewelers, product/fashion designers, interior decorators, musicians, performers, actors, conductors, florists, etc.). Learners need to be, at the very least, exposed to the various means of artistic expression; and ideally, provided with formal instruction in some of them. This aspect of the curriculum ought to include the following mediums:

Music

The history and role of music in society
Types of music
Active versus passive engagement
The parts of music
Singing, reading music, and choral arrangements
Types of instruments
Playing an instrument
Famous musicians

Writing/Storytelling

The role of writing in history
Journal reflection
Poetry
Fiction, non-fiction, and the different genres
Scriptwriting, songwriting, and speechwriting
Famous writers and poets

Dance

Forms of dance
Choreography
The integration of mind, body, and emotions
Famous dancers

Sculpture

Types of mediums
Role in history
Building, shaping, arranging, and model making
Famous sculptors

Theater

History of the theater
Types of plays and roles
Organizing a production
Famous playwrights, stage performers, and directors

Sports, Hobbies, and Crafts

Quality of life
The role of recreation
Types of activities and inherent risks
The role of physical challenge
Mastery as a means of expression
Hand-eye coordination, motor skills, and balance

Design

Types of designers
The role of aesthetics
The elements of design; form versus function
Computer-aided design; technological factors
Famous designers

Imaging

Types of images (i.e., painting, drawing, montage, photography, graphics, etc.)
The role of imagination
Famous artists

Information Literacy

Humans rely on accurate, accessible, and comprehensive information to survive. From newspapers, magazines, meeting minutes, and annual reports to radio, telephone, television, and computer communications, our lives revolve around giving and getting information. How do we access information? How do we process and manage it? This aspect of the curriculum ought to address the following skill areas:

Reading and Writing

The foundations of a modern education
The role of literature
Rules of grammar, syntax, and style
Types of communication
Writing formats
Steps in the writing process
Vocabulary and spelling
Following a set of directions

Hunting and Gathering Skills

Research methods
The library, cataloging, and organizational systems
The Internet

Cognitive Manipulation

Extracting, analyzing, critiquing, sorting, grouping, generalizing, evaluating, synthesizing, presenting, and orchestrating information
Famous inventors, philosophers, thinkers, and strategists

Speaking/Presentation Skills

Reasoning, arguing, debating, persuading, marketing, and sharing information.
Famous presenters, teachers, motivational speakers, and politicians

Digital/Technology Skills

Computer skills
Printing, reproduction, and transmission
The impact of innovation; rapid rate of change

Scientific Inquiry

The ability to rationalize and think makes humans unique in the animal kingdom. Asking questions, analyzing situations, setting up experiments, strategizing solutions, formulating plans of action, and interpreting results are basic steps in the scientific process. Whether it's figuring out how to fix a broken water faucet or planning a career, we all need to be good thinkers. The best thinkers understand the natural world and the elements, formulas, rules, and factors that influence it. This aspect of the curriculum ought to address the following areas:

Environmental Studies

Protecting our natural resources
The ecosystem (here and abroad)
Evaluating, problem-solving, and political action
Responsible industry; responsible consumerism

Future/Global Studies

Global change, conflict, and relationships
Potential scenarios, problems, and solutions
Planning for the future; the costs of progress
The impact of new scientific discoveries
Astronomy, our solar system, and outer space

Physics/Biology/Chemistry

The nature of reality
The underpinnings of the universe
The elements of science
Famous scientists

Mathematics

Numbers as a universal language
Types of mathematics
A vehicle for problem solving
Business and practical math applications
Rules and formulas
Famous mathematicians

Suggestions for Grades K through 5

▼ Reduce computer use to a minimum (too early; too much opportunity cost).

▼ Increase language exposure (a great time for learning a second language!).

▼ Mandatory music and arts training (3 times a week, 50-60 minutes per session to build strong neural networks for later math and science skills).

▼ Mandatory physical education (30+ minutes per day).

▼ Emphasis on emotional intelligence skills (begin it early, and keep it going).

▼ Increase health education (nutrition, drug/substance awareness, anti-violence training).

▼ Emphasis on learning-to-learn skills; how to utilize information resources versus traditional content and rote memorization.

Suggestions for Grades 6 through 12+

▼ Strong emphasis on learning-to-learn skills and lifelong learning.

▼ Emphasize social skills, cooperative learning, teamwork, and interpersonal relations.

▼ Provide exposure to computers; multiple functions and research potential.

▼ Delve deeply into a few subjects, rather than surveying a great number.

▼ Emphasize life skills (financial planning, bookkeeping, career planning, mental health, physical health, recreation, conflict resolution, interpersonal relationships, and decision making).

▼ Reduce emphasis on rote learning, semantic learning, and superfluous content.

What This Means to You

While it's true that teachers aren't at liberty to teach only what they want to teach; it's also true that we have an ethical, moral, and professional responsibility to ensure every student receives the benefit of our life experience and professional judgment about what learners need to know to flourish in the twenty-first century. We are important in the process: If we weren't, we could just teach via television—a proposition that would surely be brain antagonistic. As conductors of the orchestra, we must be fully present and accountable for our learner's performance. Be prepared to meet some resistance as you introduce your modifications to the curriculum. Part of being a brain-based practitioner is acting as an advocate for change. As with anything that requires people to re-examine themselves, pushing for a more brain-friendly curriculum will cause some people to get defensive, territorial, and even aggressive. As you would encourage your students—do the best you can and *that* is progress enough. Before you know it, you'll be the expert everyone wants to emulate.

Reflection Questions

1. What from this chapter was novel, fresh, or new to you? What was familiar or "old hat"?

2. In what ways, do you already apply the information in this chapter?

3. What three questions might you now generate about this material?

4. How did you react emotionally to the information in this chapter?

5. How did you react cognitively to the information? Do you agree or disagree with the author's point of view? Why?

6. In what ways might you translate the principles presented in this chapter into practical everyday useful ideas?

7. If these things are, in fact, true about the brain, what should we do differently? What resources of time, people, and money could be redirected? In what ways might you suggest we start doing this?

8. What were the most interesting insights you gained from this material?

9. If you were to plan your next step for making your curriculum more brain-based, what would that be?

10. What obstacles might you encounter? How might you realistically deal with them?

Rethinking Assessment

What's Not Working

Mistakes to Avoid

Brain-Based Assessment Overview

Content

Emotions

Context

Processing

Embodiment

Assessing Authentic Learning

Focusing on Feedback

Improving Test Scores

Rethinking Assessment

Even though the dictionary definition of learning is quite simple—to gain knowledge, understanding, or skill by study or experience—when we attempt to measure learning, the complexity of the definition emerges. Even neuroscientists have a tough time agreeing on what constitutes learning. Why? Because much of what is important in learning, is difficult to measure. For example, Sally may provide the correct answer to a mathematics equation, but does she understand the underlying rules and formulas; does she recognize the broader context and meaning of the problem; and does she have the ability to apply what she's learned for real-life problem solving? The traditional evaluation of a student's learning disregards these questions altogether. It merely asks, Did the student get the right answer?

What's Not Working

Most of the time when we think we are assessing learning, we are merely getting feedback on how well a student plays the game of school. Perhaps more disturbing is the fact that *what* we normally assess is superficial and irrelevant to the brain. Not only do we need to reevaluate our fundamental premises about assessment, we need to broaden our evaluation techniques so that learners receive the benefit of a fair and authentic assessment process.

"Authentic assessment" reflects a commitment of moving beyond *quantity* of learning to *quality* of learning; that is, asking the tougher questions and broadening our definition of learning. Accurately assessing learners is part science, part art. Most teacher-education programs fall short in this department. We are taught that the way to evaluate learning is to test students with "quantifiable" instruments that can be scored and defended expediently. Authentic assessment requires more from the teacher than this; and it rejects the notion that quality of learning can be accurately assessed simply by observation and testing means. Authentic assessment asks the question *why* when a learner performs short of our expectations.

Just because Sammy doesn't demonstrate good reading skills in class doesn't necessarily mean he's a poor reader. When we delve deeper into Sammy's learning process, we may discover that in spite of his weak "public" performance he, in fact, reads faster and with better retention than 90 percent of his peers. There could be a number of explanations for this. It is quite possible, for example, that Sammy's verbal skills are just on the slower end of the normal development continuum: Boys generally develop their verbal skills later than girls. Other factors may be at play here, as well. Sammy may be under-challenged; or perhaps the material he's been given lacks meaning for him; or maybe he's afraid of being ridiculed, judged harshly, or punished for making a mistake. Has anyone bothered to make these determinations?

Unfortunately, we misdiagnose learners often. Sammy's now grouped with the "slower readers." It won't be long before he perceives himself as a poor reader and associates the task with negative emotions. The worst thing is that the consequences of our superficial assessment are likely long term, if not permanent—all because we missed what was really going on in Sammy's normal development. "Normal development" is a key concept here because most teachers have accepted the artificial standards erroneously identified as appropriate for each grade level, when in fact, normal development in children fluctuates by three years. This means that as second graders, Sally may be three years ahead of Sammy in verbal proficiency; and this is perfectly normal. Following are some of the most common mistakes we make in the evaluation process:

Mistakes to Avoid

Mistake #1:
Pushing for Higher Standards Without the Necessary Resources

The new trend towards setting school standards higher is a misguided ploy that will backfire at the expense of children's lives. Why? Because when you raise the bar and tighten the consequences without providing the resources to accomplish the task, we *all* fail. The more we experience failure, the more vicious the cycle becomes. The result may be short-term improvements in test scores, but what suffers is authentic learning and assessment. Everyone rebels against high-stakes pressure that smacks of control. This is like saying to teachers, you'll teach them or else...; while saying to learners, you'll learn or else...! This is the opposite of a threat-free, brain-based learning environment.

There's no doubt that accountability is important; and there are ways to achieve greater accountability without employing draconian measures that reduce teachers to technicians. Already more than half of all new teachers leave the profession within seven years of entering it. Everyone who goes into teaching knows it's not a high-paying job, so the money isn't the issue. What is the issue is the frustrations involved and the lack of rewards and support. When any of us are pressured to perform, we experience stress; and the greater the stress, the more learning suffers. Rather than holding the front lines more responsible for fighting the escalating battle, the "generals" need to take more responsibility and use more strategic means for winning the war. This means investing for the long term, rather than gambling with students' (and teachers') lives and self-esteem for short-term results.

With more and more inclusion classes, teachers are seeing greater numbers of kids with special needs; and most teachers lack the training to deal with them. For starters, consider how many of the following common problems *you* have been trained to identify and act upon. Do you know what the symptoms of these conditions are? Do you know what to do once you identify a potential problem? Do you know which cases should be referred out? Don't feel bad if the answer is no. The fact is, most teachers don't; yet, between 25 and 40 percent of all students in our classes today are facing challenges related to one or more of the following special needs:

▼ **Abuse and/or neglect (physical/sexual/emotional, sleep deprivation, learned helplessness, fear, and high stress)**

▼ **Mental disorders (antisocial disorder, anxiety disorder, attachment disorder, depression, post-traumatic stress disorder, obsessive compulsive disorder, bipolar, borderline personality disorder, eating disorders, schizophrenia, oppositional defiant disorder)**

▼ **Learning disorders (attention deficit hyperactivity disorder, auditory processing deficits, reading deficits, dyslexia)**

▼ **Physical disabilities (mild autism, brain injury, epilepsy, diabetes, fetal alcohol syndrome, motor skill deficits, seizures, Tourette's syndrome)**

▼ **Substance dependency (drugs and/or alcohol, food, cigarettes, caffeine)**

▼ **Cultural Issues (refugees, language deficits, values differences, high stress)**

▼ **Poverty Issues (nutritional deficits, learned helplessness, high stress, peer/social ridicule)**

So teachers are being expected to ensure that all learners meet the new standards, but where are the increased training programs to support their efforts? Ideally, districts will provide more comprehensive in-service programs to help meet the increased demand on teachers, but even this will not provide an overnight solution. The overall impact of raising standards without increasing the stability of the infrastructure is higher stress, lower morale, and greater teacher turnover. Is this what our teachers, kids, and schools need?

Mistake #2:
Lock-Step Testing Ignores Brain Development

Cognitive psychologists have established a pretty good idea of how and when the brain develops in childhood; but the fact is, determining what is critical for children to learn at each specific grade level is not a precise science. Although certain learning tasks, like reading in first grade, make good general sense; It is quite another thing to mandate that *all* first graders exhibit a particular reading level or face remedial measures. This pressure-cooker formula reflects the old "demand model" of learning: It implies that if your learners don't demonstrate the prescribed benchmarks by the assigned time, you are not doing your job right. However, brains develop differently and some are not ready for reading in first grade.

What one student is doing academically does not necessarily relate to another student. Their backgrounds may be a world apart. The bell-shaped curve may have served learners at one time, but in the diverse culture we live today, the bell curve does not reflect reality! The only thing that really matters is how a student is doing compared to their previous performance!

> ***Comparing one student to another is one of the most irrelevant and damaging assessment strategies ever devised.***

When we recognize the wide variation in human development, we begin to see how the faulty assumptions of the old assessment model hinder learning.

Mistake #3:
Short-Term Testing Ignores How the Brain Learns

The first problem is that *authentic learning takes time.* The second problem is that *most of what's important is* not *being measured.*

> *Biologically, the best, most valuable, and deepest learning does not produce any tangible results for a considerable time.*

We've all witnessed students who vehemently resist new ideas or face learning challenges only to see them emerge years later more well rounded and successful in life than the straight-A students. And we've all witnessed the straight-A students—those who met grade expectations, filled in all the boxes correctly, and got good marks—not succeed in the real world. To use a metaphor, consider this: If you keep pulling up your newly planted fruit tree to see how it is doing, you will damage its root system; and you won't learn anything about its long-term health. Testing students before they are ready creates frustration, disillusionment, and a distrust of the system. Learning takes time to germinate: Provide fertilizer and water, tend to the earth around it; but keep in mind that rushing its maturity won't make it grow any faster.

Mistake #4:
Most Testing Ignores Building-Block Learning

Some subjects prepare learners for later learning: These so-called "prep" subjects may be important, but difficult to measure. For example, research has suggested that early music exposure helps learners develop subsequent math and science skills. Does this mean that we should grade learners on their level of mastery with a musical instrument; or does it mean we ought to expose learners to classical music? How should we assess the learning of music; or should we?

When we compare music with physical education, we see a similar dilemma. How should we grade a learner who may not exhibit great athletic prowess, but runs around and participates as best he/she can? Is this student not building spatial, counting, and problem-solving skills; enhancing their cardiovascular system; lowering their stress level; building social skills; receiving settling benefits; and experiencing a low-threat learning environment for trial and error learning in spite of his/her lack of athletic talent? So here we have two examples of curriculum activities that are important to subsequent learning; and yet problematic to assess.

Mistake #5: Most Testing Ignores Real-World Applications

Certainly it is possible to measure whether a student has memorized something or is able to summarize a topic, but does this reflect what we want to teach? In a competitive global society, will the learner best be served by this ability; or will there be a greater advantage in having high-level thinking and conceptual analysis skills; knowing how to work in a team environment; possessing a high level of motivation to achieve; and/or solving problems through model-building, research, systems analysis, and good communication skills?

We waste huge amounts of student and teacher time by filling up brains with trivia that will not be remembered one year later. The national and state assessment designers were sold a bill of goods. They bought into the "cultural literacy" ideology that insists a graduate should have memorized a heap of facts. But content-based knowledge is always accessible to anyone who has a computer, television, phone, or fax. Asking learners to memorize an increasingly larger body of facts to be replayed at test time is ludicrous and irrelevant; and ultimately, a poor use of valuable class time.

Rather we need to do fewer things, but do them better: We ought to be focusing on developing positive learners who exhibit critical thinking ability, basic skills proficiency, a love of learning, and the capability to work with others in a cooperative manner. To achieve these goals, we need to reduce (not increase) the content we test on and update our evaluation criteria. Even with today's so called high standards, high-school graduates still can't name the last five presidents, what countries make up NATO, who authored the Declaration of Independence, or who was in the War of 1812. Why do we continue to waste valuable school time teaching things learners have already demonstrated they don't learn?

Brain-Based Assessment Overview

Now that we've reviewed *what's wrong* with the traditional assessment approach, let's explore *what's right*. The following five areas provide a basis for authentic assessment:

1. **Content** (what learners know)

2. **Emotions** (how learners feel about it)

3. **Context** (how learners relate it to the world)

4. **Processing** (how learners manipulate data)

5. **Embodiment** (how deep the learning goes; how they apply it).

These areas of assessment are inclusive of mind, body, and heart; as well as past, present, and future. Learners may express what they know using multiple mediums like drawings, charts, lists, dialogues, actions, demonstrations, debates, or maps.

> *Let's make what's important more measurable,
> rather than making what's measurable more important.*

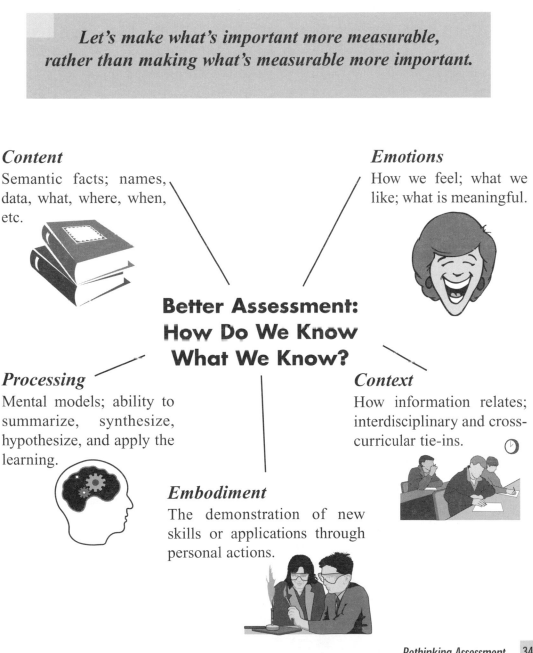

Content
Semantic facts; names, data, what, where, when, etc.

Emotions
How we feel; what we like; what is meaningful.

**Better Assessment:
How Do We Know
What We Know?**

Processing
Mental models; ability to summarize, synthesize, hypothesize, and apply the learning.

Context
How information relates; interdisciplinary and cross-curricular tie-ins.

Embodiment
The demonstration of new skills or applications through personal actions.

1. Content

The prevailing wisdom is that the old-style true-false and/or multiple choice/matching tests are out of step with authentic assessment. And this is true to a certain extent; however, there is still a place for traditional testing, so long as its limitations are recognized. For example, a learner who has not mastered the language (perhaps they're a foreigner, or have a learning disability, or are disabled) may, or may not (depending on the individual circumstance), be better assessed by answering questions in a traditional test format. And traditional testing can help us assess all learners to some degree, albeit narrowly.

The critical question though is, *how much weight* should old-style content tests be assigned the overall assessment package? And I'll give you a direct answer: Less than half. Much of our knowledge is only demonstrated with prompting; that is, our memory is triggered by cues. This is why answering essay questions is usually more difficult than answering a multiple-choice question. So, multiple-choice and true-false questions aren't necessarily bad, it's just that we shouldn't rely on them as much as we traditionally have for assessing learners.

 What This Means to You

Don't throw out the true-false, matching, or multiple-choice tests completely; just don't make them the mainstay of your assessment program. They do, however, trigger and measure some types of learning. In addition to tests or quizzes, give learners an opportunity to demonstrate their knowledge in their preferred learning modality. See that you assess more than content knowledge. Evaluate a learners progress over time. And make sure that students are well aware of the various ways they can demonstrate learning. Ask yourself the tough questions when a student isn't seemingly working up to his/her potential. Try to get a picture of the learner's unique experience. Show an interest in their feelings. Ask questions. What might be interfering with his/her concentration? If your district is enforcing standard-based outcomes and you don't feel supported, do what you would expect your own learners to do: Ask for help and be specific about what you need.

2. Emotions

Events that tap into our emotions are remembered: Likewise, learning that taps into our emotions will be remembered. In other words, how you feel about a topic or subject is critical.

Either you like it or you don't; and if you don't, you won't likely want to explore the subject again. When we tap into a learner's positive emotions, the learning becomes more meaningful.

As we increase students' awareness about the different types of learning and how we learn (metacognition), we help them understand why some subjects are easier for them than others. Draw a distinction for them between knowledge (usually surface knowledge) and meaning (something that clarifies what's happening in our world or extends our existing natural knowledge). Surface knowledge will be forgotten shortly after a test is given, while what's intrinsically meaningful to the individual learner will be lasting. This is why comparing students to one another is erroneous. The faulty premise that students should all be learning the same thing at the same time is based on a model that disregards the importance of personal relevance and normal differences in the developmental process.

Give learners the opportunity to discuss what is personally meaningful to them and how the subjects they're studying connect to their own lives. If we want to evaluate authentic learning, we need to start here. Rather than "testing" students, why not "interview" them. Let's acknowledge the importance of emotions in the educational setting by addressing rather than ignoring them. This consequently is the learning that makes education rewarding, rich, and timeless. It's also the kind of learning that spurs intrinsic motivation, while superficial knowledge requires constant external reinforcers and ultimatums. As we focus on authentic learning and engaging emotions, classroom management flows more effortlessly and naturally.

3. Context

In assessing students more accurately, we definitely need to consider their ability to generalize or contextualize what they've learned. In other words, we need to ask, "Now that you have learned ABC, how does this apply to DEF? Many believe that applying knowledge is strongly related to real-life, survival skills; and what could be more important than this? In fact, intelligence is *very* related to the ability to generalize learning from one platform to another, which requires planning, metacognition, and both inductive and deductive reasoning skills. While teaching students about thinking and learning, we are also providing them with the framework to be productive and to succeed in the world.

It's important for learners to be able to ask questions and formulate thinking in a safe environment where exploration of concepts, feelings, and emotions is encouraged. Ask learners how they know something and where it fits into their life. Demonstrate how learning can be deep, shallow, impertinent, or profound. Asking more or fewer questions is irrelevant; it's the quality of the question that counts. Keep in mind that the answer to one well-formed open-ended question can provide a more authentic and comprehensive basis for assessment of a learner than how they did on a twenty-question surface level test.

Expect learners to demonstrate the depth and quality of learning with mind-maps, cross-subject debates, integrated subject demonstrations, and panel discussions. These projects provide a strong basis for assessing learners ability to generalize their learning.

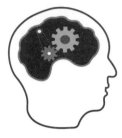

4. Processing

Some areas of processing are easier to assess than others. For example, it's pretty simple to determine whether students can summarize and draw conclusions. But what about the more important and complex processing skills? How do you measure a learner's ability to hypothesize, form mental models and comparisons, sort and manipulate data, present and defend their position, and ultimately apply the principles. Although these are tough criteria to measure, they are strong indicators of the depth of a student's learning. In the big picture analysis, it is the cognitive skills, not the content, that will be the primary measure of a student's long-term success in today's world.

5. Embodiment

When a learner "embodies" learning, they have incorporated it into their life in a meaningful way. The student who takes the initiative to solve a problem or influence others with their knowledge is demonstrating that they have internalized the learning and are able to act on it in a real-life context. Schools that encourage this depth of learning are on the cutting edge. Examples of projects that encourage this level of integration are year-book publications, school papers, school stores, internships and work-study, travel abroad programs, theater productions, competitive athletics, and other "extracurricular" activities. It is very difficult to measure a learner's degree of embodiment on a multiple-choice, true-false, or matching test. Even an essay test does not really demonstrate how well a learner has embodied the learning; rather it suggests how well a learner can talk (or more specifically, write) about the learning. This does not necessarily reflect actions or integration of the learning.

27 Ideas for Assessing Authentic Learning

Outlined below are some ideas for evaluating a student's content understanding in ways that reinforce their learning without inducing the anxiety state usually associated with testing. These strategies also give emotions a seat at the assessment table. Remember (and remind students) that much of the value in the assignments is in the emotional responses they elicit; and in the planning and production process. The finished product is important, but focusing on issues such as problem solving, interpersonal relations, conflict resolution, accountability, group dynamics, follow-through, and self-assessment throughout the life of the project are also critical learning functions.

1. News Brief or Newspaper

Have students mock-up the front page of a newspaper that covers relevant learning topics. Emphasize multiple points of view, personal experiences, and the process necessary for creating an accurate finished product (i.e., drafts, checking facts, dividing responsibilities, editing, proofreading, presentation).

2. Class Yearbook

Create a class yearbook: Brainstorm the possibilities. What should be included? What events of the year will go down in history? What music was popular? What was learned? Include students' artwork, poems, photographs, and other contributions.

3. Wall-Sized Mural

Have the class choose a theme related to what you're learning. Then map out an image depicting the subject matter on a large piece of butcher paper. Once the sketch is completed everyone can participate in the painting of it. When it's done hang it in a conspicuous location for all to enjoy. If the mural is really good, you might want to see if there's interest from the community in having the mural painted in a public area. Civic projects are great for meaning-making and building relevance.

4. Storyboards

Disney cartoonists pioneered the concept of storyboarding: Start with a sequence of roughly drawn pictures that capture the action or key events of a story or topic. Put them up on a wall as a timeline illustration or visual history of the subject.

5. Student-Generated Tests or Quizzes

Establish some basic criteria; then have students decide what's important to be tested on and what's not. Have them write the questions.

6. Multi-Media Creation

Have students make a video, cassette tape, or CD that will help others learn the subject they are studying. Insist on good quality; and ensure learners have access to the necessary resources and equipment.

7. Pre/Post-Test Comparisons

Design pre- and post-surveys that examine learners' feelings about a subject. Not all of the questions have to deal overtly with the subject of emotions. You might ask on a science survey, for example, 1) Do you watch the Discovery Channel on TV or read science magazines and books? 2) Have you ever done a science experiment? If so, how did you feel about it? 3) On a scale of 1 to 10 (with 1 low and 10 high), what's the likelihood that when you grow up your career will involve an aspect of science? You get the point. What you're trying to do is get a reading on the learner's emotional reaction to the subject. At the end of the term or unit, have students complete the same survey again; and then compare the differences between the two surveys.

8. Storytelling

Have student write or tell a story about the subject. This gives them an opportunity to relate feelings and emotions through the eyes and voice of a fictional character. This strategy also reinforces personal meaning.

9. Learning Logs

Sometimes referred to as Learning Logs, have students keep a freeform or structured diary about their learning. Journal-writing is both a strong and reflective medium for expressing emotions. Encourage learners to relate subject matter to their own lives, while describing real-life applications for the content.

10. Demonstrations/Student Teachers

Have learners demonstrate an application for the learning or facilitate a group experience. Teach students how to act as peer or student teachers. As you know, teaching others is a great way to reinforce your own learning. It is also a non-threatening way to evaluate depth of learning and applications to real-life situations.

11. Community Projects

Students can actively demonstrate their learning with community projects, such as volunteering for a special event or becoming an activist for an important cause. It may be a social, ecological, or business concern. One high school junior in Portland, frustrated by her school's closure of the arts and music program, began a letter-writing campaign that resulted eventually (through her persistence) in a benefit performance by Jackson Browne. The concert raised enough money to save the arts/music program; and the student definitely got a real-life boost in her self-confidence and social-skills.

12. Theatrical Performance

Produce a play or skit that relates to the current unit of study. Allow students the opportunity to plan the process, as well as the content and final production. Keep the emphasis on "having fun," while also reinforcing learning.

13. Model-Making

This is a particularly good way to measure a learner's depth of understanding with regard to physical laws and scientific principles, while keeping the focus on experimentation and exploration. Again, the emphasis ought to be on the process, as well as the final product.

14. Artwork/Drawing

Not only is art a good medium for exploring emotions, it is a safe way for students to express themselves. It is also a great way to channel concentration and energy and manage states. When approached as a "down time" activity, it can also help learners subconsciously process content and integrate learning.

15. Sculpture

Many students optimally demonstrate their learning (and learn best) with "hands on" activities that allow them to manipulate concepts and physical objects. Creativity and risk-taking are also encouraged as learners design works of art that draw out their emotions and challenge them.

16. Music

Have learners use music to represent and extend their learning. They can set key words and concepts to music and then perform it; or have them come up with their own idea.

17. Commercials/Short Films

Give learners the opportunity to translate their learning into a short film or commercial. Emphasize the process more than the final product: Assist them in each stage, from brainstorming the topic as a group, writing the script, and auditioning for the key roles to rehearsing, filming, and editing. This project requires a vast array of skills that will be invaluable in the student's future work and personal life.

18. Case Study Problem

Give students an opportunity to design, build, and demonstrate their learning with a physical representation of the topic or unit. Observe what parts of the task they like and excel at; and what parts are problematic to them. To get the process started, you might want to throw out a problem related to the content they're learning—preferably one that can be solved in a variety of ways.

19. Group Discussions

Give groups of learners a task or problem and some ground rules. Then observe how individuals participate in the process. Provide some discussion and reflection questions after they solve the problem that help them focus on the process they used. Have a spokesperson for each group report on the groups process to the rest of the class.

20. Informal Interviews

Much can be assessed about a student's learning simply by talking to them in a casual, relaxed manner. Informally interview students; and have learners interview each other. The ability to formulate questions, extrapolate answers, and synthesize the information in writing will be extremely valuable to students' future learning and work life.

21. Game Design

Have students incorporate current learning into a game, such as Simon Says, Monopoly, Jeopardy, Wheel of Fortune, Concentration, card games, ball toss, etc.

22. Personal Goals

Have students create a set of personal learning goals. Teach them how to make them measurable. Emphasize the importance of short-term and long-term objectives. Teach them how to integrate their goals into their own ongoing self-assessment program. Encourage them to re-evaluate their goals on a regular basis and to track their progress.

23. Mind-Mapping

As a group or alone (or both), have students create a mind-map of their current learning. A mind-map is a webbed, thematic graphic organizer that illustrates information and connections between topics with colorful doodles and lines connecting topics. These open-ended depictions of a student's thinking process can provide an excellent vehicle for evaluating learning. The process also reinforces learner's understanding of relationships, themes, and associations between ideas.

24. Debates

Debates provide a forum for learners to defend their learning and verbalize their knowledge. Half of the value is in preparing for the debates. Expect an array of emotions to surface as learners struggle with presenting a point of view that may not necessarily reflect their own. Be very specific about your criteria for assessment, so that learners understand they are not being graded by *what* they say, but how they say it and how well prepared they are.

25. Mini-Conference

Have students plan (and carry out if you're really brave) a mini-conference around a topic related to the current unit of study. This is an opportunity for students to gather information from the community at large, invite speakers, organize logistics, and pull off a special event with higher than usual stakes involved.

26. Timelines

Have learners create a chronological graphic timeline that reflects the historical development of the topic they're studying. This project can help you evaluate research skills, as well as the learner's integration of the subject with related learning.

27. Montage or Collage

Using any combination of mediums, have students create an original work of art that reflects their learning. Emphasize freedom of expression and originality. There is no right or wrong way to approach the task. One popular technique, however, is to cut out and arrange print images that resonate with the learner and draw connections between concepts. Looking through magazines for photographs is also a great way to get students sparked for goal-setting. Have them make a collage that incorporates their short and long-term goals.

All of the above evaluation strategies respect differences in developmental stages and reflect the type of learning that is difficult to measure in the short run. Rather than presenting learners with a barrage of standardized tests (or pulling up the fruit tree to see if it's growing properly), we water, fertilize, and appreciate the organism knowing fully that by nurturing it, growth happens.

Focusing on Feedback

Grades are too often relied on as the primary means of student feedback. This strategy reflects a "too little, too late, too general" approach which is doomed to fail. By contrast, when we concentrate on ensuring learner feedback from multiple sources (including self-assessment) every thirty minutes, learners begin to view feedback as healthy guidance rather than critical judgment.

> *The brain hunts for feedback to ensure its survival, growth, and progress.*

Not only is feedback important to the brain, it is important to all stakeholders in the education system—parents, teachers, administrators, and the community at large.

Feedback Tips

▼ The more often, the better.
▼ The more immediate, the better.
▼ The greater the specificity, the better.
▼ The more appropriately dramatic, the better.
▼ The more delayed, the less productive.

What This Means to You

To optimize learning, make it a rule that learners get feedback every thirty minutes. This does not mean you personally have to talk to each student every half hour. Although this would be ideal, it is highly unlikely that you would realistically be able to keep this up over the long haul. Rather, incorporate various forms of feedback that don't all rely on you. Teach learners how to assess themselves: Provide self-quiz materials, rubrics, and guided reflection activities. Also use group and partner assessment techniques, such as holding discussions where learners get ideas validated or reshaped; set up peer teaching opportunities, debates, partner mind-mapping activities, group observation/feedback exercises, team discussions; or simply ask for a show of hands in response to reflection questions you throw out. The most effective feedback is non-judgmental: It simply takes note, observes, and gently guides the learner towards the agreed upon goal.

We know reporting is essential; yet many teachers agree that grading students in the traditional manner has strong disadvantages. But what are the alternatives in a brain-based school? It is fully possible to approach grading in a more holistic manner; that is, utilizing all of the following strategies to guide learners on a daily basis and eventually report their progress for the term.

Brain-Friendly Assessment in a Nutshell

▼ Increase feedback from yourself and other sources (including other students).
▼ Encourage group work; include discussion groups, long-term team projects, theatrical productions, brainstorming, debates, and games.
▼ Encourage learners to use self-assessment techniques; introduce rubrics, study groups, and self quizzes.
▼ Replace external rewards of any kind with acknowledgment of the intrinsic rewards of success.

continued...

continued...

▼ **Focus on substantial long-term group assignments that impact the larger community, as well as learners.**

▼ **Keep all student work in a portfolio file and refer to their progress often.**

▼ **Compare learners only to themselves, not other learners.**

▼ **Emphasize mastery, rather than a bell-shaped (or any shaped) curve.**

▼ **Discuss your assessment philosophy and approach with all stakeholders (how and why it works and your expectations).**

▼ **Post your grading policy/approach in a highly visible location in the room; make it colorful and attractive so that students won't perceive it as a threat, but rather as a friendly reminder.**

Many schools are currently moving towards this model. They are doubling and tripling the quantity of feedback students get. And they are getting the learners involved in setting criteria for assessment. Even many major universities are recognizing the weaknesses of traditional standardized achievement tests and rigid once-a-term testing. They also are beginning to emphasize consistent feedback and a more holistic approach to grading.

> *Multiple-choice, true-and-false, and fill-in tests are not brain-antagonistic; they're simply part of the overall assessment process. Each can help reveal some of what students know; but alone they present an incomplete picture of authentic learning.*

Outcome-based learning, where students have little say in the process, is outdated and obsolete; however, we still see a reliance on this demand model at the highest levels of education. We can do all the insisting we want to, but students (and teachers) don't perform better with more stress and threat. Punishing with disapproval when demands aren't met is not a long-term solution. A long-term solution recognizes the importance of happier, threat-free students and teachers who feel supported by a compassionate, caring, and fair system that recognizes everyone's natural desire to succeed in life.

Improving Test Scores

While the thrust of this chapter was to explore more authentic ways to assess learners, keep in mind that testing is still a reality in our school systems and will likely be for a long time. Therefore, we also need to prepare learners for this aspect of education. There are very few "points of power" when it comes to improving test scores; however, the following tips can positively impact student performance and test-taking skills:

Tips for Boosting Test Scores

▼ **Improve the original learning:** Use the strategies in this book to see that students integrate the learning in meaningful ways.

▼ Teach study skills and memory-enhancing techniques, such as mnemonics.

▼ **Review learning at frequent intervals:** after one day, one week, and one month.

▼ **Rehearse the test.** The questions don't have to be exactly alike: There is value in the process itself. Do try to duplicate the stressful conditions, however; and recognize that the more similar the practice session is to the final session, the more helpful it will be.

▼ Teach students how to approach the various types of tests and test questions. For example, discuss time restraints, quick scanning techniques, prioritizing, self-imposed time limits, test-taking objectives, types of questions, and educated guessing.

▼ **Prepare learners to manage their own states.** We can all get discouraged or frustrated, but during a test, these can be devastating. Teach students how to do deep breathing for relaxation; emphasize the value of positive self-talk; discuss issues of posture, hydration, lighting, and resting the eyes; and address the impact of high-energy foods eaten prior to testing.

▼ Make students aware of what they can and can't do during testing. Can they stand, walk around, or take a stretch break? Will they have access to water or can they bring their own? Can they suck on hard candies or chew gum as a stress reducer? Can they use any learning aids?

▼ After the test, provide a debriefing session where students can discuss their experiences and feel supported. Testing is a stress-inducing experience and one that should not be left unaddressed. Lead learners in a discussion about how they might better prepare for the next test if they feel they did poorly; or what study techniques they want to repeat for the next test if they feel they did well.

Reflection Questions

1. What from this chapter was novel, fresh, or new to you? What was familiar or "old hat"?

2. In what ways, do you already apply the information in this chapter?

3. What three questions might you now generate about this material?

4. How did you react emotionally to the information in this chapter?

5. How did you react cognitively to the information? Do you agree or disagree with the author's point of view? Why?

6. In what ways might you translate the principles presented in this chapter into practical everyday useful ideas?

7. If these things are, in fact, true about the brain, what should we do differently? What resources of time, people, and money could be redirected? In what ways might you suggest we start doing this?

8. What were the most interesting insights you gained from this material?

9. If you were to plan your next step for making your curriculum more brain-based, what would that be?

10. What obstacles might you encounter? How might you realistically deal with them?

Brain-Based Reform

The Bigger Picture

Fatal Paths to Avoid

Involving Learners in the Reform

Transforming Your School

Brain-Friendly Schools

Assessing the Learning Community

Becoming a Local Expert

25

Brain-Based Reform

Based on everything you now know about the brain and learning, what do you think are the hallmarks of brain-based reform? Do you think the traditional restructuring approach, such as enforcing outcomes-based standards, will result in the kind of change that our schools desperately need? If not, why? Asking ourselves these questions will help us embody the learning we've done so far. Do you think there's a way to reform the reforms so that they are student-centered and teacher-supported? The key issues that need to be addressed if we hope to improve student achievement across the board (and which are often neglected) include the following:

▼ Most school staff (including teachers, assistants, and administrators) are overwhelmed by the enormous responsibility they have to turn out learners who test well. The more we emphasize outcomes-based standards based on grade level, the more distress and feelings of resignation teachers experience. Positive change is unlikely to happen in this physiological and emotional state.

▼ Many educational systems are increasing the accountability load on teachers without enhancing their training, resources, and support. Most communities are unwilling to fund the requisite staff-development time necessary to make substantial changes. This is partly a problem of ignorance; and partly a problem of trading in long-term reform for short-term results that provide "immediate gratification" for special interest entities, such as politicians.

▼ Classrooms today are dramatically less homogenous than they were just a couple of decades ago. Teachers are expected to prepare learners for the next grade who don't speak (never mind understand) the language. Along with language barriers, learners from a multitude of cultural, ethnic, and religious backgrounds pose issues around norms and values. Some students have never been in one classroom for a complete year; others have known only violence; some are undernourished; and others have been taught that the way to survive is to dominate others. In addition to this, students with special needs are being mainstreamed into a class of thirty students with one teacher. These special needs can range from physical to emotional or mental. What teacher wouldn't be overly challenged in such an environment?

▼ All of the prior concerns are exacerbated when the teacher has only a few weeks or years of classroom teaching experience under their belt. This is like throwing a rookie lion trainer into a pit of lions and saying, "We're leaving now, but we expect you to train these dangerous animals to perform the following stunts; and unfortunately, we can't provide you with much assistance, but we'll be sure to return at the end of the term to determine if you were capable of meeting our expectations."

▼ Most of the restructuring changes are token substitutes for real reform. Substantial change requires a long-term commitment that addresses mental models, paradigm shifts, present weaknesses, training shortcomings, and infrastructure decisions that support real learning. Most administrators are in denial about how significant the changes must be; and how challenging it really is to affect change on this level.

The Bigger Picture

To achieve better results in learner achievement, we need to focus on the factors we have the most control over: environment, environment, environment! When students are supported by a more responsive environment, their behaviors change quickly. In spite of all the educational reforms that are in the works, there is a critical element that will do more to motivate learners than any other.

> *Make schools more like real life:*
> *Integrate the curriculum, incorporate real problems,*
> *organize simulation activities, supply plenty of novelty*
> *and feedback, and seek student cooperation by earning*
> *their interest and respect.*

Schools, businesses, and organizations of all kinds can implement top-down restructuring measures all they want to, but until they make the true distinction between what motivates learners in "real life" and what is going on in their respective environments, the result will always be the same: Naturally good, curious, and motivated individuals will become demotivated, unempowered, and branded "lazy." Rather than expending more energy on judging learners, we need to spend more time determining how we can best serve and nurture them.

> *Authentic school reform must be committed to long-term, personal, systemic, and organizational change—anything less is doomed to fail.*

Educational leaders who are committed to true and substantial reform will learn from past mistakes. We've gone down these fatal paths before. It's time to try something new based on what we now know about the biology of learning.

Fatal Paths to Avoid

▼ **Incorporating 100 percent curriculum mandates (removes student choice and buy in).**

▼ **Conducting high-stakes testing (creates teaching to the test and causes student's brains to "minimize"). Instead create more frequent assessment and use multiple assessment strategies.**

▼ **Increasing staff pressure to achieve outcomes-based standards (more stress without support disempowers teachers and learners alike).**

▼ **Focusing primarily on short-term assessment (measuring semantic learning is superfluous, as it will be forgotten shortly after test time). Instead provide a rich and constant stream of feedback to learners.**

▼ **Using assessment practices that focus only on immediate and/or easily measured results (many aspects of authentic learning cannot be measured). Instead focus on the joy of learning and how we learn best.**

▼ **Expecting teachers to increase student achievement results without providing the additional training and support necessary to meet the needs of diverse student populations (inclusion will backfire unless teachers are intensively trained to deal with physical, mental, and emotional disorders, as well as cultural differences and non-English speaking learners).**

▼ **Responding to bureaucratic demands at the cost of ensuring a responsive organizational climate for teachers and students.**

▼ **Implementing rigid performance evaluations of teachers (causes teachers to perform according to the assessments; discourages creativity).**

▼ Incorporating testing standards that don't account for the one-to-three year range of cognitive and developmental differences that are perfectly normal in children and teens.

▼ Reinforcing high teacher control in classrooms (creates resentment and learner apathy).

▼ Encouraging "stand and deliver" teaching practices that rely on lecture, lecture, and more lecture.

▼ Providing special programs for so-called "gifted" and talented learners: All learners deserve the enrichment afforded the "gifted" (and gifted learners enhance the regular classroom).

▼ Encouraging punitive discipline measures, rewards, bribery, and control tactics. School is not prison; treat students with respect and dignity and expect them to want to learn for the sake of learning; make learning fun.

Involving Learners in the Reform

The following school reform approaches work because they put students and teachers at the center of the change movement:

✔ Ask for student input; then incorporate it.

✔ Reorganize classroom routines incorporating more partner work.

✔ Elicit learner goals and align curriculum accordingly.

✔ Keep focus on learner goals; review and revise frequently.

✔ Provide an environment which is responsive to student needs.

✔ Infuse learning with emotion, novelty, and enthusiasm.

✔ Incorporate student values, such as autonomy, peer approval, and personal responsibility.

✔ Create teacher-to-teacher support networks that encourage sharing, rapport, and problem solving.

✔ Establish a "bottom-up" administrative approach whereby students feel their beliefs, goals, and values matter and are consistently integrated into the overall school design.

Schools that incorporate the brain-based learning methods outlined in this book are consistently more successful than those that don't. But then how do we define success? Quite simply, systematic success means fewer dropouts, deeper authentic learning, and increased enjoyment, critical thinking, risk taking, and creativity. Success is teaching learners about learning—how to do it and the intrinsic benefits derived from it. But this requires more than just applying a few brain-based techniques. A brain-based school must concentrate on becoming a learning organization. Pulling from the works of *Ten Steps to a Learning Organization* (1993) and *The Fifth Discipline Fieldbook* (1992), the following sequence of steps is recommended for transforming a school into a learning organization:

7 Steps to Transforming Your School into a Learning Organization

1. Assess the Existing Culture

This requires observation over time and a safe environment for others to tell the truth about their perceptions regarding the organization. Use both formal and informal means to determine what works and what doesn't. What is the predominant thinking? What overt and covert assumptions are influencing the environment? How are decisions made and supported (or not supported)? The findings (if they're honest) may result in some despair, but only after the truth is acknowledged can the real work begin.

2. Build a Collective Vision

This step involves identifying a mutually agreed upon mission statement and collective vision for a successful learning organization. Based on discussions, reflection, and consensus, map out the steps in a visually stimulating manner. Avoid identifying specific strategies at this time. Post the "mission map" or "vision statement" in a highly visible location.

3. Establish a Learning Climate

Identify and promote positive teaching practices that will aid the organization in reaching its vision. Share what's working on a consistent basis. Reward appropriate risk-taking behaviors with acknowledgments and celebrations. Allow for mistakes; celebrate lessons learned; and supply lots of feedback. This goes for both students and teachers. Remember your aim is to produce good learners, not robots.

4. Encourage Personal Mastery

Support each member of the learning team to create a personal vision, guiding life statement, and both long- and short-term personal goals. Unless each member of an organization is making progress and feeling empowered, an uncomfortable dissonance is created. Keep a staff "library" shelf in the lounge where inspirational books and videos can be borrowed. Offer "Learning-to-Learn" workshops or "Learning for Life" seminars for staff and faculty. Include personality profiles and learning modalities/styles assessments in these workshops. Become a great learner. As you role-model lifelong learning, others will be more likely to follow. If you believe it, live it.

5. Promote Team Learning

Make a commitment to group and partner learning. Set up your planning meetings with this in mind. Through discussion, reflection, and team activities, staff and faculty will provide each other with valuable feedback, while processing and sharing their knowledge. Encourage team members to view each other as valuable resources. When we restructure our learning organizations into "sideways," rather than vertical power structures, we increase participation and accountability at all levels by default. Foster cooperation and teamwork.

6. Systems Thinking is Everyone's Business

Seek to understand the key relationships that influence your organization. Partly this is a matter of trial and error; and partly it is a matter of asking the right questions frequently enough. It may feel like you're only slowly chipping away at a granite bolder, but creating systematic change takes time. Discover what key statistical indicators your school uses to assess quality of learning. Focus on individual policy changes—one at a time, until eventually critical mass is reached, and the organization's investments become aligned with brain-based practice. Keep the focus on how one person's actions can influence the whole.

7. Nourish the Dream

All the "seed planting" in the world will produce nothing unless you nourish the dream. "Kaizen" is a Japanese word that means never-ending improvement: Make this your school's ten-year theme. Be satisfied with incremental improvements. Create a "scorecard" for the organization so that team members can chart overall progress. Encourage team members to also create scorecards that reflect their own personal progress. Get people together often to reflect on mutual needs and concerns, share successes, and celebrate milestones.

> *The number one thing that successful
> learning organizations do well is
> support people to embrace change.*

To assess how brain-friendly your learning organization is, answer the following questions:

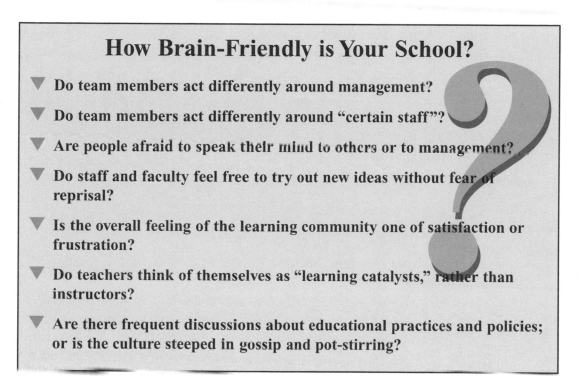

How Brain-Friendly is Your School?

▼ **Do team members act differently around management?**

▼ **Do team members act differently around "certain staff"?**

▼ **Are people afraid to speak their mind to others or to management?**

▼ **Do staff and faculty feel free to try out new ideas without fear of reprisal?**

▼ **Is the overall feeling of the learning community one of satisfaction or frustration?**

▼ **Do teachers think of themselves as "learning catalysts," rather than instructors?**

▼ **Are there frequent discussions about educational practices and policies; or is the culture steeped in gossip and pot-stirring?**

Your answers to these questions will shed light on the kind of learning climate that exists in your organization. In general, you'll know that your school is a learning organization when the following things are happening:

Your School is Brain-Friendly When:

▼ **The school's prevailing vision often emerges in discussions and policy revisions.**

▼ **Team members feel their work is meaningful and makes a difference.**

▼ **Team members work together frequently and well; they don't drag each other down or make unilateral decisions without regard for the rest of the group.**

▼ Team members feel free to share their successes, concerns, and setbacks with others in a regularly scheduled support meeting.

▼ Team members are encouraged to inquire further when they feel an action is unjust or out of line with the organization's vision. There are very few (if any) "sacred cows" (topics off limits for discussion).

▼ There's a great respect for differences: Personal experiences, diverse opinions, and individuality are valued, rather than squelched or feared.

▼ The focus is on continued growth and desired change: The majority of school members are committed to improving themselves and the organizational climate. The emphasis is on becoming the best learning organization possible.

▼ As you walk around campus, students appear to be enjoying themselves.

▼ Learners regularly do extra work on their own; and they meet in groups outside of class.

▼ Students bring things from home to share at school, even when it's not assigned.

▼ Tardies and absences are minimal.

▼ Teachers are highly regarded and spoken well of by students in private.

Learning organizations will succeed well into the twenty-first century, *not* because they are better at predicting *what change* will be necessary, but because they are better at *changing* when necessary. Even if we could predict the future, we would still not always agree on how to interpret it, react to it, or prepare for it. Any learning organization worth its salt will be made up of individuals with varying value systems; and conflict among these is natural. A learning organization, however, that is experienced in working with diverse opinions and value judgments, will be more efficient at coming to consensus. The infrastructure will be in place and the team members well versed in the process. The learning organization has established a culture of *learning their way into the future*.

Assessing the Learning Community

Is it really possible to measure to what degree a school is brain-based? The answer is yes and no. Like an automotive engine, a school can have many things wrong with it and still work; just as it can have many things right about it and still not work. Brain-based learning communities are not perfect; rather we ought to view ourselves on a continuum with "brain-based practices *always* implemented" on one side and "brain-based practices *never* implemented" on the other. The reality is, most of us will fall somewhere in-between. The deep-seeded problems educational systems are facing won't simply fall away once we've declared ourselves a brain-based school. It is an ongoing process. If a school declares it has reached brain-based *perfection*, it is likely off base. The model, itself, is rather one of continuous improvement and a recognition of the need for constant vigilance. Much of the true quality of a brain-based learning organization is in the process itself. To sum it up, brain-based schools *maintain brain-friendly practices most of the time.*

Figure 25.1
Implementation

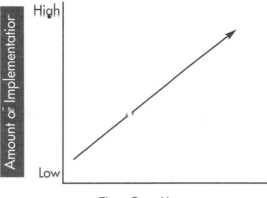

> ### *If you don't "live it" you don't believe it.*

What This Means to You

To discover the interest level among others at your school, start a conversation about brain-based learning during lunch or prep times. Keep a list of good suggestions that come to you. Even if only a few others show interest at first, organize a regular time for information-sharing. Support from others will grow exponentially as awareness increases. Meanwhile, implement positive changes in your own classroom and watch for progress. You have little to lose and much to gain. Schools around the world are incorporating the strategies outlined above. If you can't find support for your efforts immediately *inside* your organization, you can find it *outside*. Utilize your resources. There are many good Web sites available, numerous trainings (including the author's), and a huge array of good books on the subject (see appendix). A monthly brain research newsletter **(www.learningbrain.com)** offers practical applications based on the latest research.

Becoming a Local Expert

There's no better place to start than with ourselves. Learn as much about the subject as you can; try out some applications; integrate what works, and throw out what doesn't. Before you know it, you'll be teaching others. Expand your contacts and associations. Relate your learning beyond yourself and your students to the larger community. Making connections on a larger scale is often referred to as "natural knowledge." Form support groups, hold meetings, sponsor activities, write newsletters, and participate in a brain-based training network.

Speak on the topic at your school, in your district, and in the community. Make sure you role-model the principles you're advocating. You would be surprised how many people *lecture* on brain-based learning for a lengthy period of time, never realizing they are *doing* exactly what they are *saying* doesn't work. Create materials you can share with others. Include your name, phone number, email, and references so that interested individuals can follow up and learn more.

It's not easy, but it's simple. Take the first step and start walking. Get support and turn your good ideas into a movement. Learning can work for everyone: And it can begin with you. Take action, right now. You're in good company.

Reflection Questions

1. What from this chapter was novel, fresh, or new to you? What was familiar or "old hat"?

2. In what ways, do you already apply the information in this chapter?

3. What three questions might you now generate about this material?

4. How did you react emotionally to the information in this chapter?

5. How did you react cognitively to the information? Do you agree or disagree with the author's point of view? Why?

6. In what ways might you translate the principles presented in this chapter into practical everyday useful ideas?

7. If these things are, in fact, true about the brain, what should we do differently? What resources of time, people, and money could be redirected? In what ways might you suggest we start doing this?

8. What were the most interesting insights you gained from this material?

9. If you were to plan your next step for making your curriculum more brain-based, what would that be?

10. What obstacles might you encounter? How might you realistically deal with them?

Appendix

Bibliography

Ackerman, Herman; D. Wildgruber; I. Daum; and W. Grodd. 1998. Does the cerebellum contribute to cognitive aspects of speech production? A functional magnetic resonance imaging study in humans. *Neuroscience Letters*. Vol. 247(2), 187.

Allen, L. S. and R. A. Gorski. 1991. Sexual dimorphism of the anterior commissure and massa inter media of the human brain. *Journal of Comparative Neurology*, 312: 97-104.

Altman, Joseph. 1993. Timetables of neurogenesis in the human brain based on experimentally deter mined patterns in the rat. *Neurotoxicology*. Vol. 14(1), 83.

Amabile, Teresa. 1989. *Growing Up Creative*. New York, NY: Crown Publishing.

Amabile, Teresa and C. Rovee-Collier. 1991. Contextual variation and memory retrieval at six months. *Child Development*, Oct., 1155-66.

Anderson, R. C.; and P. D Pearson. 1984. A schema-theoretic view of basic processes in reading comprehension. In *Handbook of Reading Research*. (Pearson, Ed.) New York, NY: Longman.

Ankey, C. D. 1992. Sex differences in relative brain size: The mismeasure of woman, too? *Intelligence*, 16: 329-336.

Arenson, K. 1998. Test gap between sexes narrows. *Toronto Globe and Mail*, 15 January: A-15.

Asbjornsen A.; K. Hugdahl, and O. W. Hynd. 1990. The effects of head and eye turns on the right ear advantage in dichotic listening. *Brain and Language*. 39.3, 447-58.

Asher, James. 1986. *Learning Another Language through Actions*. Expanded Third Edition, Los Gatos, CA: Sky Oaks Productions.

Bandler, Richard. 1988. *Learning Strategies: Acquisition and Conviction*. (Videotape). Boulder, CO: NLP Comprehensive.

Barden, R. C. and M. E. Ford. 1990. *Optimal Performance in Golf*. Minneapolis, MN: Optimal Performance Systems.

Baumeister, Roy F. 1984. Choking under pressure: Self-consciousness and paradoxical effects of incentives on skillful performance. *Journal of Personality and Social Psychology* 46, 610-20.

Bennett, E. L.; M. C. Diamond; D. Krech; and M. Rosenzweig 1964. Chemical and Anatomical Plasticity of the Brain. *Science*, 146, 610-619.

Benton, D; and G. Roberts. 1988. Effect of vitamin and mineral supplementation on intelligence of a sample of schoolchildren. *The Lancet*, 140-143.

Bergland, Richard. 1986. *The Fabric of Mind*. Harmondsworth Middlesex, England: Viking.

Bever, T. G. and R. J. Chiarello. 1974. Cerebral dominance in musicians and non-musicians. *Science*. 185, 537-539.

Black, J. E. 1989. Effects of complex experience on somatic growth and organ development in rats." *Developmental Psychobiology* 22.7, 727-52.

Blackman, Derek, et. al. 1982. Cognitive styles and learning disabilities. *Journal of Learning Disabilities*. n2 15, 106-115.

Boller, K. and C. Rovee-Collier. 1992. Contextual coding and recoding of infant's memories. *Journal of Experimental Child Psychology* 53.1, 1-23.

Bower, Gordon and T. Mann. 1992. Improving recall by recoding interfering material at the time of retrieval. *Journal of Experimental Psychology* 18.6, 1310-20.

Bower, Gordon; T. D. Mann; and G. Morrow. 1990. Mental models in narrative comprehension. *Science* 247.4938, 44-8.

Brewer, Chris; and Don Campbell. 1991. *Rhythms of Learning*. Tucson, AZ: Zephyr Press.

Briggs-Meyers, Isabel. 1995. *Gifts Differing: Understanding Personality Type*. Palo Alto, CA: Davies-Black.

Burton, L. A.; and J. Levy. 1989.. Sex differences in the lateralized processing of facial emotion. *Brain and Cognition*. 11.2, 210-28.

Caine, Geoffrey and Renate Caine (Eds.) 1994. *Making Connections: Teaching and the Human Brain*. Menlo Park, CA: Addison-Wesley.

Caine, Geoffrey and Renate Caine. 1990. Downshifting: A hidden condition that frustrates learning and change *Instructional Leader* VI 3, 1-3, 12.

Caine, Geoffrey; Renate Caine; and Sam Crowell. 1994. *Mindshifts*. Tuscon, AZ: Zephyr Press.

Calvin, William. 1996. *How Brains Think*. New York, NY: Basic Books.

Calvin, William and George Ojemann. 1994. *Conversations with Neil's Brain*. Reading, MA: Addison-Wesley Publishing Co.

Campbell, Don. 1997. *The Mozart Effect*. Avon: New York.

Campbell, Don.(Ed.) 1992. *Music and Miracles*. Wheaton, IL: Quest Books.

_____1992. *100 Ways to Improve Your Teaching Using Your Voice & Music*. Tucson, AZ: Zephyr Press.

_____1983. *Introduction to The Musical Brain*. St. Louis, MO: Magnamusic.

Carbo, M.; R. Dunn; and K. Dunn. 1986. *Teaching Students to Read Through their Individual Learning Styles*. Englewood Cliffs, NJ: Prentice-Hall.

Casolini, P.; M. Kabbaja; and F. Leprat. 1993. Basal and stress induced corticosterone secretion is decreased by lesion of mesencephalic dopaminergic neurons. *Brain Research*. Vol 622(1-2) Sept, 311- 314.

Clynes, Manfred (Ed.) 1982. *Music, Mind and Brain*. New York, NY: Plenum Press.

Coles, Michael; E. Donchin; and Stephen Porges (eds). 1986. *Psychophysiology: Systems, Processes, and Applications*. New York, NY: Guilford Press.

Coren, Stanley. 1992. *The Left-Hander Syndrome: The Causes and Consequences*. New York, NY: Free Press.

Coulter, Dee. 1993. *Movement, Meaning and the Mind*. Keynote Address, Seventh Annual Educational Kinesiology Foundation Gathering (July), Greeley, CO.

Cousins, Norman. 1981. Anatomy of an Illness as Perceived by the Patient: Reflections of Healing and Regeneration. New York, NY: Bantam Books.

Crick, Francis. 1994.*The Astonishing Hypothesis: The Scientific Search for the Soul*. New York, NY: Charles Scribner and Sons.

Csikszentmihalyi, M; and Isabella Csikszentmihalyi. 1990. *Flow: The Psychology of Optimal Experience*. New York, NY: Harper & Row.

Czeisler, C. A. 1986. Arousal cycles can be reset. *Science* 233, 667-71.

Damasio, Antonio. 1994. *Descartes' Error: Emotion, Reason, and the Human Brain*. New York, NY: Putnam and Sons.

Dardis, Deborah J. Athas. 1999. A comparative study on the effect of student and instructor cognitive mapping on student achievement and attitudes. *Dissertation Abstracts International*. 59(7-A), 2 340.

Dartigues, Jean-Francois. 1994. Use it or lose it. *Omni*. Feb. p. 34.

DeBono, Edward. 1970. *Lateral Thinking*. New York, NY: Harper & Row.

Deci, Edward. L. and R. M. Ryan. 1987. The support of autonomy and the control of behavior. *Journal of Personality and Social Psychology*. Vol. 53, 6.

Della Valle, J., et al. 1986. The effects of matching and mismatching student's mobility preferences on recognition and memory tasks. *Journal of Educational Research* 79.5, 267-72.

Della Valle, J. 1984. An experimental investigation of the relationship(s) between preference for mobility and the word recognition scores of seventh grade students to provide supervisory and administrative guidelines for the organization of effective instructional environments. Dissertation. St. John's University.

DePorter, Bobbi; Mark Reardon; and Sarah Singer-Nourie. 1999. *Quantum Teaching*. Needham Heights, MA: Allyn & Bacon.

Diamond, Marian. 1988. *Enriching Heredity: The Impact of the Environment on the Brain*. New York, NY: Free Press.

Diamond, Marian and Janet Hopson. 1998. *Magic Trees of the Mind*. New York, NY: Dutton.

_____1999. Magic trees of the mind: How to nurture your child's intelligence, creativity, and healthy emotions from birth through adolescence. *Adolescence*. Vol. 34(133), 244.

Dienstbier, Richard. 1989. Periodic adrenaline arousal boosts health, coping. Brain/Mind Bulletin Collections. *New Sense Bulletin*. (Los Angeles, CA), 14.9A.

Doman, Glenn. 1965. *Teach Your Baby to Read: The Gentle Revolution*. London, England: J. Cape Publications.

_____1994. *How to Teach Your Baby to Read*. Garden City Park, NY: Avery Publishing Group.

Drake, Susan. 1996. Guided imagery and education: Theory, practice, and experience. *Journal of Mental Imagery*. Vol. 20: 1-64.

Drevets, Wayne. C. and Marcus E. Raichle. 1998. Reciprocal suppression of regional cerebral blood flow during emotional versus higher cognitive processes: Implications for interactions between emotion and cognition. *Cognition & Emotion*. Vol 12(3) May, 353-385.

Driesen, N. R. and N. Raz. 1995. The influence of sex, age, and handedness on corpus callosum morphology: A meta-analysis. *Psychobiology*, 23: 240-247.

Dryden, Gordon and Jeanette Vos. 1994. *The Learning Revolution*. Rolling Hills, CA: Jalmar Press.

Dunn, Kenneth and Rita Dunn. 1992. *Bringing Out the Giftedness in Your Child*. New York, NY: John Wiley.

Dunn, Rita, et al. 1985. Light up their lives: A review of research on the effects of lighting on children's achievement and behavior. *The Reading Teacher* 38.9, 863-69.

Dunn, Rita and Kenneth Dunn. 1978. *Teaching Students Through their Individual Learning Styles: A Practical Approach*. Reston, VA: Reston Publishing Co.

Dustman, Robert E. 1990. Age and fitness effects of EEG, ERP's, visual sensitivity and cognition. *Neurobiology of Aging*. Vol. 11(3), 193.

Easterbrook, M. A.; B. S. Kisilevsky; D. W. Muir; and D. P. Laplante. 1999. Newborns discriminate schematic faces from scrambled faces. Canadian *Journal of Experimental Psychology*. 53(3), 231-241.

Edelman, G. 1992. *Bright Air, Brilliant Fire*. New York, NY: Basic Books.

Educational Testing Services Annual College Board Statistics. 1999. Educational Testing Services. www.ets.org/

Eriksson, P. S.; E. Perfilieva; T. Bjork-Eriksson; A. M. Alborn; C. Nordborg; D. A. Peterson; and F. H. Gage. 1998. Neurogenesis in the adult human hippocampus. *Nature Medicine*. Nov: 4(11): 1313-7.

Farley, Frank and A. P. Grant. 1976. Arousal and cognition: Memory for color vs. black and white multimedia presentation. *Journal of Psychology*; Sep 94(1):147-150.

Felix, Uschi. 1993. The contribution of background music to the enhancement of learning in suggestopedia: A critical review of the literature. *Journal of the Society for Accelerative Learning and Teaching* 18.3-4, 277-303.

Fiske, S. T. and S. E. Taylor. 1984. *Social Cognition*. Reading, MA: Addison-Wesley.

Ford, Martin. 1992. *Motivating Humans*. Newbury Park, CA: Sage Publications.

Frank, Jerome D. 1985. Further thought on the anti-demoralization hypothesis of psychotherapeutic effectiveness. *Interpractice Psychiatry*. 3(1), 17-20.

Freeman, Walter. 1995. *Societies of the Brains: A Study in the Neurosciences of Love and Hate*. Hillsdale, NJ: Lawrence Erlbaum & Assoc.

Fry, William. 1997. Spanish humor: A hypotheory, a report on initiation of research. *Humor: International Journal of Humor Research*. Vol. 10(2), 165-172.

Fuchs, J. L.; M. Montemayor; and W. T. Greenough. 1990. Effect of environmental complexity on the size of superior colliculus. *Behavioral and Neural Biology* 54.2, 198-203.

Gage, Fred H. 1999. Running enhances neurogenesis, learning and long-term potential for mice. *Proceedings of the National Academy of Science of the USA*. Vol. 96(23), 13427.

Gardner, Howard. 1993. Open windows, open doors. *Museum News*. Vol. 72(1)Jan, 34.

Gazzaniga, Michael. 1998. *The Mind's Past*. Berkeley, CA: University of California Press.

_____ 1992. *Nature's Mind*. New York, NY: Basic Books.

_____1972. One brain-Two minds? *American Scientist*. 60(3), 311-317.

Glasser, William. 1999. *Choice Theory: A New Psychology of Personal Freedom*. New York, NY: Harper Collins.

Goleman, Daniel. 1995. *Emotional Intelligence*. New York, NY: Bantam Books.

Gordon, H. W. 1978. Left-hemisphere dominance for rhythmic elements in dichotically presented melodies. *Cortex* 14, 58-76.

Gratton, G.; M. G. Coles; and E. Donchin. 1992. Optimizing the Use of Information: Strategic Control of Activation of Responses. *Journal of Experimental Psychology* 121.4, 480-506.

Greenough, W. T. and B. J. Anderson. 1991. Cerebellar synaptic plasticity: Relation to learning versus neural activity. *Annals of the New York Academy of Science* 627, 231-47.

Greenough, W. T.; G. Withers; and B. Anderson. 1992. Experience-dependent synaptogenesis as a plausible memory mechanism. *Learning and Memory: The Behavioral and Biological Substrates*. (Gormezano, I. & Wasserman, E., Eds.) Hillsdale, NJ: Erlbaum & Associates. pp. 209-29.

Gregorc, A. F. 1979. Learning/teaching styles: Their nature and effects. In *Student Learning Styles*. Reston, VA: National Association of Secondary School Principals.

Grinder, Michael. 1989. *Righting the Educational Conveyor Belt*. Portland, OR: Metamorphous Press.

_____ 1993. *Envoy*. Battle Ground, WA: Michael Grinder & Associates.

Halpern, Steven. 1985. *Sound Health*. New York, NY: Harper & Row.

_____1999. Web site: www.musica.uci.edu.

Hampson, Edward. 1990. Variations in sex-related cognitive abilities across the menstrual cycle. *Brain & Cognition*. 14, 26-43.

Hannaford, Carla . 1995. *Smart Moves*. Arlington, VA: Great Ocean Publishing.

Harmon, D. B. 1991. *The Coordinated Classroom* [In Liberman, Jacob, Light: Medicine of The Future] Santa Fe, NM: Bear & Co. Publishing.

Hart, Leslie. 1983. *Human Brain and Human Learning*. White Plains, NY: Longman Publishing.

Harter, S. 1982. A Developmental Perspective on Some Paremeters of Self-Regulation in Children. *Self-Management and Behavior Change: From Theory to Practice*. (Karoly, P. and F. H. Kanfer, Eds.) New York, NY: Pergammon Press.

Hayne, H.; C. Rovee-Collier; and M. A. Borza. 1991. Infant memory for place information. *Memory and Cognition* 19.4, 378-86.

Healy, Jane. 1990. *Endangered Minds:Why Our Children Can't Think*. New York, NY: Simon and Schuster.

_____1987.*Your Child's Growing Mind*. New York, NY: Doubleday.

Herrmann, Ned. 1988. *The Creative Brain*. Lake Lure, NC: Brain Books.

Hirsch, Alan. 1993. Floral odor increases learning ability. Presentation at annual conference of American Academy of Neurological and Orthopedic Surgery. Contact: Allan Hirsch, Smell and Taste Treatment Foundation, Chicago, IL.

Hobson, J. Allan. 1989. *Sleep*. New York, NY: W. H. Freeman.

Hodges, H. 1985. An Analysis of the Relationships Among Preferences for a Formal/Informal Design, One Element of Learning Style, Academic Achievement, and Attitudes of Seventh and Eighth Grade Students in Remedial Mathematics Classes in a New York City Alternative Junior High school. *Dissertation*. St.John's University.

Houston, Jean. 1982. *The Possible Human: A Course in Enhancing Your Physical, Mental and Creative Abilities*. Los Angeles, CA: Jeremy Tarcher.

Howard, Pierce. 1994. *Owners Manual for the Brain*. Austin, Texas: Leornian Press.

Iaccino, James. 1993. *Left Brain-Right Brain Differences: Inquiries, Evidence, and New Approaches*. Hillsdale, NJ: Lawrence Erlbaum & Associates.

Isaacs, K. R., et al. 1992. Exercise and the Brain: Angiogenesis in the Adult Rat Cerebellum After Vigorous Physical Activity and Motor Skill Learning. *Journal of Cerebral Blood Flow and Metabolism* 12.1, 110-9.

Jacobs, Bob; M. Schall; and A. B. Scheibel. 1993. A quantitative dendritic analysis of Wernicke's Area in humans: Gender, hemispheric and environmental factors. *Journal of Comparative Neurology* 327(1), 83-111.

Johnson, David and R. T. Johnson. 1994. *The New Circles of Learning: Cooperation in the Classroom and School.* Alexandria, VA: Association for Supervision and Curriculum Development.

Johnston-Brooks, C. H.; M. A. Lewis; G. Evans; and C. K. Whalen. 1998. Chronic stress and illness in children: The role of allostatic load. *Psychsomatic Medicine.* Vol 60(5)Sept-Oct., 597-603.

Kagan, Jerome M. 1990. How Schools Alienate Students at Risk: A Model for Examining Proximal Classroom Variables. *Educational Psychologist* 25, 105-25.

Kazdin, Alan E. 1977. *The Token Economy: A Review and Evaluation.* New York, NY: Plenum Press.

Kandel, M. and E. Kandel. 1994. Flights of memory, *Discover Magazine*, May, pp. 32-38.

Kandel, E. and R. Hawkins. 1992. The biological basis of learning and individuality. *Scientific American* Sept., pp. 79-86.

Kendel, E. R.; Y. Lu; and R. D. Hawkins. 1999. Cellular/molecular nitric oxide signaling contributes to late phase LTP and CREB phosphorylation in the hippocampus. *Journal of Neuroscience: The Official Journal of the Society for Neuroscience.* Vol 19(23), 10250.

Khalsa, D.; M. Ziegler; and B. Kennedy. 1986. Body sides switch dominance. *Life Sciences.* 38, 1203-14.

Kimura, Doreen. 1999. *Sex and Cognition.* Boston, MA: Bradford Publishing.

_____ 1992. Sex differences in the brain. *Scientific American*, Sept., 119-25.

_____ 1989. Monthly fluctuations in sex hormones affect women's cognitive skills. *Psychology Today.* Nov., 63-66.

Kimura, D.; and E. Hampson. 1990. Neural and hormonal mechanisms mediating sex differences in cognition. *Research Bulletin/* April, 689. Dept. of Psych. University of Ontario, London, Canada.

King, Jeff. 1991. Comparing Alpha Induction Differences Between Two Music Samples. Abstract from the Center for Research on Learning and Cognition, University of North Texas, TX.

Klein, R.; and R. Armitage. 1979. Brainwave cycle fluctuations. *Science* 204, 1326-28.

Klutky, N. 1990. Sex differences in memory performance for odors, on sequences and colors. Zeitscrift fur Experimentelle und Angewandte *Psychologie* 37.3, 437-46.

Kohn, Alfie. 1993. *Punished by Rewards.* New York, NY: Houghton Mifflin Co.

_____ 1987. *No Contest: The Case Against Competition.* New York, NY: Houghton Mifflin Co.

Koulack, D. 1997. Recognition memory, circadian rhythms, and sleep. *Perceptual Motor Skills*, Aug., 85(1): 99-104.

Kroon, D. 1985. An Experimental Investigation of the Effects on Academic Achievement and the Resultant Administrative Implications of Instruction Congruent and Incongruent with Secondary Industrial Arts Student's Learning Style Perceptual Preferences. *Dissertation.* St. John's University.

Kuhn, Thomas. *The Structure of Scientific Revolutions.* 1996, 3rd. Edition. Chicago, IL: University of Chicago Press.

Kushner, Saville. 1996. The research assessment exercise versus development: A response to Richard Pring. *British Journal of Educational Studies.* Vol. 44(1), 5.

LaRue, A.; K. M. Koehler; S. J. Wayne; and S. J. Chiulli. 1997. Nutritional status and cognitive functioning in a normally aging sample: A 6-year reassessment. *American Journal of Clinical Nutrition;* Jan; 65(1): 20-29.

Lavabre, Marcel. 1990. *Aromatherapy Workbook.* Rochester, VT: Healing Arts Press.

Lazarus, Richard S. 1984. Puzzles in the study of daily hassles. *Journal of Behavioral Medicine.* 7(4) Dec, 375-389.

LeDoux, Joseph. 1996. *The Emotional Brain.* New York, NY: Simon and Schuster.

Leff, Herb and Ann Levin. 1994. *Turning Learning Inside Out: A Guide for Using Any Subject to Life and Creativity.* Tuscon, AZ: Zephyr Press.

Leiner, Henrietta and Alan Leiner. 1993. Cognitive and language functions of the human cerebellum. *Trends in Neuroscience.* Vol. 16911, 444.

Levin, Henry M. 1996. *Innovations in Learning: New Environments for Education.* Mahway, NJ: Lawerance Erlbaum Associates, Inc.

Levinthal, C. 1988. *Messengers of Paradise: Opiates and the Brain.* New York, NY: Doubleday.

Levy, Jerry. 1985. Right brain, left brain: Fact and fiction. *Psychology Today.* May, p. 38.

_____1983. Research synthesis on right and left hemispheres: We think with both sides of the brain. *Educational Leadership* 40.4, 66-71.

Liberman, Jacob. 1991. *Light: Medicine of the Future.* Santa Fe, NM: Bear & Co. Publishing.

Locke, E. A; and G. P. Latham. 1990. Work motivation and satisfaction: Light at the end of the tunnel. *Psychological Science* 1, 240-46.

London, Wayne. 1988. Brain/Mind Bulletin Collections. *New Sense Bulletin.* (Los Angeles, CA.) Vol. 13, April, 7c.

Lozanov, Georgi. 1991. On some problems of the anatomy, physiology and biochemistry of cerebral activities in the global-artistic approach in modern suggestopedagogic training. *The Journal of the Society for Accelerative Learning and Teaching* 16.2, 101-16.

_____1979. *Suggestology and Outlines of Suggestopedia.* New York, NY: Gordon and Breach.

Luiten, J.; W. Ames; and G. Ackerson. 1980. A meta-analysis of the effects of advance organizers on learning and retention. *American Educational Research Journal.* 17, 211-18.

MacLean, Paul. 1990. *The Triune Brain in Education.* New York, NY: Plenum Press.

_____1978. A mind of three minds: Educating the triune brain. In the *77th Yearbook of the National Society for the Study of Education.* Chicago, IL: University of Chicago Press. pp. 308-42.

Maguire, Jack. 1990. *Guide to your Gray Matter: Care and Feeding of the Brain.* New York, NY: Doubleday.

Malloy, John. 1975. *Dress for Success.* New York, NY: P.H. Wyden

May, Cynthia; L. Hasher; and Ellen Stoltzfus. 1993. Optimal time of day and the magnitude of age differences in memory. *Psychological Science.* Vol 4 (5) Sept. 517-525.

McCarthy, Bernice. 1990. Using the 4-MAT system to bring learning styles to schools. *Educational Leadership* 48.2, 31-37.

McGaugh J. L. 1989. Dissociating learning and performance: Drug and hormone enhancement of memory storage. *Brain Research Bulletin* 23.4-5, 339-45.

McGaugh J. L., et al. 1990. Involvement of the amygdaloid complex in neuromodulatory influences on memory storage. *Neuroscience and Biobehavioral Reviews* 14.4, 425-31.

McGuiness, D. 1985. *When Children Don't Learn.* New York, NY: Basic Books.

————-1976. Sex Differences in Organization, Perception and Cognition. in *Exploring Sex Differences.* (Lloyd, B., & J. Archer, Eds.) London, England: Academic Press.

Meece, J. L.; A. Wigfield; and J. S. Eccles. 1990. Predictors of math anxiety and its influence on young adolescents' course enrollment intentions and performance in mathematics. *Journal of Educational Psychology.* 82, 6070.

Mills, L. and G. B. Rollman. 1980. Hemisphereic asymmetry for auditory perception of temporal order. *Neuropsychologia,* 18, 41-47.

Mills, R. C. 1987. Relationship between school motivational climate, presenter attitudes, student mental health, school failure, and health damaging behavior. Paper at Annual Conference of the American Educational Research Association. April. Washington, DC.

Minninger, J. 1984. *Total Recall: How to Boost Your Memory Power.* Emmaus, PA: Rodale Press.

Miura, I. T. 1987. A multivariate study of school-aged children's computer interest and use. (Ford, M. E., & D. H. Ford, eds.). In *Humans As Self-Constructing Living Systems: Putting the Framework to Work.* Hillsdale, NJ: Lawrence Erlbaum & Assoc.

Murphy, M. and S. Donovan. 1988. *The Physical and Psychological Effects of Meditation.* San Rafael, CA: Esalen Institute.

Murrain, P. G. 1983. Administrative determinations concerning facilities utilization and instructional grouping: An analysis of the relationship(s) between selected thermal environments and preferences for temperature, an element of learning style. *Dissertation.* St. John's University.

Nadel, L.; K. Kein; and K. Putnam. 1999. Episodic memory: It's about time (& space). *The Behavioral & Brain Sciences.* Vol 22(3), 463.

Oakhill, J. 1988. Time of day affects aspects of memory. *Applied Cognitive Psychology.* 2, 203-12.

O'Keefe, J. and L. Nadel. 1978. *The Hippocampus as a Cognitive Map.* Oxford, England: Clarendon Press.

O'Leary, Dennis M. 1997. *The Lifespan Development of Individuals: Behavioral Neurobiological and Psychosocial Perspectives.* New York, NY: Cambridge University Press.

Orlock, Carol. 1998. *Know Your Body Clock.* New York, NY: Barnes & Noble.

_____1993. *Inner Time.* New York, NY: Birch Lane Press, Carol Publishing.

Ornstein, Robert. 1991. *The Evolution of Consciousness*. New York, NY: Simon & Schuster.
_____1984. *The Amazing Brain*. Boston, MA: Houghton-Mifflin.

Ostrander, Sheila and Lynn Schroeder. 1991. *Super Memory*. New York, NY: Carroll & Graf Publishers.

Palmer, Lyelle and J. McDonald. 1990. Monocular and binocular measurements of smooth eye pursuit by rural children in kindergarten and grade 2. *Perceptual & Motor Skills*. Vol. 70(2) April, 608.

Pakenberg, B.; and H. J. G. Gundersen. 1997. Neocortical neuron number in humans: Effect of sex and age. *Journal of Comparative Neurology*, 384: 312-320.

Parker, Kenneth. 1982. Effects of subliminal symbiotic stimulation on academic performance: Further evidence on the adaptation-enhancing effects of oneness fantasies. *Journal of Counseling Psychology*, Vol. 29 (1).

Penny, T. B.; M. D. Holder; and W. H. Meck. 1996. Clonidine-induced antagonism of norepinephrine modulates the attentional processes involved on peak -interval timing. *Experimental & Clinical Psychopharmacology*. Vol. 4(1), 82-92.

Pert, Candace. 1997. *Molecules of Emotion*, New York, NY: Scribner.

Pogrow, Stanley. 1994. Helping students who just don't understand. Educational Leadership: *Journal of Depart of Supervision & Curriculum Development*, N.E.A. Vol. 52(30), 62.

Popper, Karl. 1972. *Objective Knowledge*. Oxford, England: Oxford University Press.

Pribram, Karl. 1986. *Toward a Science of Consciousness: The First Tucson Discussion and Debates*. Cambridge, MA: MIT Press.
_____1979. Behaviourism, phenomenology and holism in psychology: A scientific analysis. *Journal of Social and Biological Structures*. 2:65-72.
_____1971. *Languages of the Brain: Experimental Paradoxes and Principles in Neuropsychology*. Monterey, CA: Brooks/Cole Publishing Co.

Posner, Michael and R. Badgaiyan. Time course of cortical activations in implicit and explicit recall. *Journal of Neuroscience*. 17(12), 4904-4913.

Ramakrishna, T. 1999. Vitamins and brain development. *Physiology Research*; 48(3): 175-87.

Ramachandran, V. S. and Sandra Blakeslee. 1998. *Phantoms in the Brain*. New York, NY: William Morrow and Co.

Ramey, Craig. 1992. High risk children and IQ: Altering intergenerational patterns. *Intelligence*. Vol. 16(2) April, 239.

Ramon y Cajal, Santiago. 1988. *History of Neuroscience*. New York, NY: Oxford University Press.

Ramon y Cajal, Santiago. 1980. Cajal on the cerebral cortex: An annotated translation of the complete writings. New York, NY: Oxford University Press.

Rauscher, F. H.; G. L. Shaw; L. J. Levine; E. L. Wright; W. R. Dennis; and R. L. Newcomb. 1997. Preschool keyboarding practice enhances long-term spatial temporal reasoning. *Neurological Research*, Feb. Vol 19.

Rauscher, F. H.; G. L. Shaw; L. J. Levine; K. N. Ky; and E. L. Wright. 1993. Music and spatial task performance. *Nature*, 365: 611.

Reis, Sally; and Eva Diaz. 1999. Economically disadvantaged urban female students who achieve in schools. *Urban Review*; March, 31(1): 31-54.

Restak, R. 1994. *The Modular Brain*. New York, NY: Charles Scribner's Sons.

Riggs, Karen; A. Spiro; K. Tucker; and D. Rush. 1996. Relations of vitamin B-12, vitamin B-6, folate, and homocysteine to cognitive performance in the normative age study. *American Journal of Clinical Nutrition*; Mar; 63(3): 306-14.

Rosenthal, R.; and L. Jacobsen. 1968. *Pygmalion in the Classroom*. New York, NY: Rinehart & Winston.

Rosenzweig, M. R.; W. Love; and E. L. Bennett. 1968. Effects of a few hours a day of enriched experience on brain chemistry and brain weights. *Physiology and Behavior* 3:819-825.

Rosenzweig, M. R.; D. Krech; E. L. Bennett; and M. C. Diamond. 1962. Effects of environmental complexity and training on brain chemistry and anatomy. *Journal of Comparative Physiological Psychology* 55(4): 429-437.

Rossi, A. S. and P. E. Rossi. 1980. Body time and social time: Mood patterns by cycle phase and day of the week. *The Psychobiology of Sex Differences and Sex Roles*. (Parsons, J. E., Ed.) London, England: Hemisphere.

Rossi, E. L. and D. Nimmons. 1991. *The 20-Minute Break: Using the New Science of Ultradian Rhythms.* Los Angeles, CA: Tarcher Press.

Rozanski, Alan. 1988, April 21). Mental Stress and the Induction of Silent Ischmia in Patients with Coronary Artery Disease. *New England Journal of Medicine* Vol 318, 16. pp.1005-12.

Russell, J. 1984. Effects of lecture information density on medical student achievement. *Journal of Medical Education.* 59: 881-889.

Samples, Bob. 1987. Open Mind/Whole Mind. Rolling Hills, CA: Jalmar Press.

Sampson, Amy; S. Dixit; A. Meyers; and R. Houser. 1995. The nutritional impact of breakfast consumption on the diets of inner-city African-American elementary school children. *Journal of the American Medical Association*; March; 87(3): 195-202.

Sapolsky, Robert. 1999. Stress and your brain—Trauma survivors can lose more than peace of mind: They may also lose some gray matter. *Discover*, March, p. 116.

_____1996. Why stress is bad for your brain. *Science.* Vol. 273, 749-750.

_____1992. *Stress, the Aging Brain, and the Mechanisms of Neuron Death.* Cambridge, MA: MIT Press.

Schacter, Daniel. 1996. *Searching for Memory: The Brain, the Mind and the Past.* New York, NY: Basic Books.

Scheibel, Arnold. 1994. You can continuously improve your mind and your memory. *Bottom Line Personal* (15) 21: Nov. 1, 9-10.

Schwartz, J. and P. Tallal. 1980. Rate of acoustic change may underlie hemispheric specialization for speech perception. *Science* 207, 1380-1381.

Shaffer, D. W. and M. Resnick. 1999. "Thick" authenticity: New media and authentic learning. *Journal of Interactive Learning Research.* 10(2), 195-215.

Shaw, Jenny. 1995. *Gender and Society: Feminist Perspectives on the Past and Present.* London, England: Taylor & Francis.

Shea, T. C. 1983. An Investigation of the Relationship Among Preferences for the Learning Style Element of Design, Selected Instructional Environments, and Reading Achievement of Ninth Grade Students to Improve Administrative Determinations Concerning Effective Educational Facilities. *Dissertation.*

Sheridan, S. and M. Henning-Stout. 1994. Consulting with teachers about girls and boys. *Journal of Educational & Psychological Consultation.* Vol. 5(2), 93-113.

Slavin, Robert. 1990. *Cooperative Learning Theory, Research, and Practice.* Englewood Cliffs, NJ: Prentice-Hall.

Sperry, Roger. 1968. Hemisphere disconnection and unity in conscious awareness. *American Psychologist* 23, 723-33.

Squire, Larry. 1992. Memory and the hippocampus: A synthesis from findings with rats, monkeys and humans. *Psychological Review.* 99.2, 195-231.

_____1987. *Memory and Brain.* New York, NY: Oxford University Press.

Squire, Larry and S. Zola. 1998. Episodic memory, semantic memory and amnesia. *Hippocampus.* Vol. 8(3), 205.

Sternberg, Robert J. 1997. Styles of thinking and learning. *Canadian Journal of School Psychology.* Vol 13(2), 15-40.

_____1994. Intelligence is more than IQ: The practical side of intelligence. *Journal of Cooperative Education.* Vol. 28(2), 6.

Stickgold, Bob. 1997. Video: *Pieces of Mind.* New York, NY: Scientific American.

Stone, Arthur. A.; D. S. Cox; and H. Valdimarsdottir. 1987. Evidence that secretory IgA antibody is associated with daily mood. *Journal of Personality & Social Psychology.* Vol. 52.2.

Strick, Peter. 1995. Introducing. *The Psychologist.* Vol. 38(6), 288.

Sullivan, R. M.; J. L. McGaugh; and M. Leon. 1991. Norepinephrine-induced plasticity and one-trial olfactory learning in neonatal rats. *Brain Research* 60.2, 219-28.

Sutter, Alice. 1991. VDT Noise Causes Stress. *Issues in Human Resources.* Jan.

Schwartz, J. and P. Tallal. 1980. Rate of acoustic change may underlie hemispheric specialization for speech perception. *Science.* 207, 1380-1381.

Sylwester, Robert. 1995. *A Celebration of Neurons.* Alexandria, VA: ASCD.

Taylor, E. 1988. *Subliminal Learning.* Salt Lake City, UT: Just Another Reality Publishing.

Taylor, H. L. and J. Orlansky, J. 1993. The effects of wearing protective chemical warfare combat clothing on human performance. *Aviation Space and Environmental Medicine* 64.2, A1-41.

Thayer, R. 1989. *The Biopsychology of Mood and Arousal*. New York, NY: Oxford University Press.

Tomatis, Alfred. 1983. Brain/Mind Bulletin Collections. *New Sense Bulletin*. (Los Angeles, CA.) Jan. 24, Vol. 8, #4A

Tonegawa, Susumu. 1995. Mammalian learning and memory studied by gene targeting. *Annals of the New York Academy of Sciences*. Vol 758, 213.

Torrance, P. and O. Ball. 1978. Intensive approach alters learning styles in gifted. *Journal of Creative Behavior*. 12, 248-52.

Turkington, Carol. 1996. *The Brain Encyclopedia*. New York, NY: Facts On File, Inc.

Urban, M. J. 1992. Auditory subliminal stimulation: A re-examination. *Perceptual and Motor Skills* 74.2, 515-41.

van Praag, Henriette; G. Kempermann; and F.H. Gage. 1999. Running increases cell proliferation and neurogenesis in the adult mouse dendate gyrus. *Nature Neuroscience*. March: 2(3): 266-70.

Velle, Weiert. 1992. The Nature of the Sexes: The Sociobiology of Sex Differences and the "Battle of the Sexes." Groningen, Netherlands: Origin Press.

Vincent, J. D. 1990. *The Biology of Emotions*. Cambridge, MA: Basil Blackwell.

Vuontela, V.; A. Reamae; H. Aronen; and S. Carlson. 1999. Selective dissociation between memory for location and color. Neuroreport: An International Journal for the Rapid Communication of Research in Neuroscience. Aug., 10, 2235-40.

Wallin, N; B. Merker; and S. Brown. 1999. *The Origins of Music*. Cambridge, MA: A Bradford Book.

Walker, Morton. 1991. *The Power of Color*. Garden City Park, NY: Avery Publishing.

Webb, W. B. 1982. *Biological Rhythms, Sleep and Performance*. Chichester, England: Wiley Press.

Webb, D; and T. Webb. 1990. *Accelerated Learning with Music*. Norcross, GA: Accelerated Learning Systems.

Weil, M. O.; J. Murphy. 1982. Instructional processes. In *Encyclopedia of Educational Research*. (Mitzel, H.E., Ed.) New York, NY: The Free Press.

Weinberger, Norman. 1995. Non musical outcomes of music education. *Musical Journal*. Fall: II(2): 6.

Weiner, Edith and Arnold Brown. 1993. Office Biology. New York, NY: Master Media Ltd.

Weinstein, C. E and R. E. Mayer. 1986. The teaching of learning strategies. In *Handbook of Research on Teaching*. (Wittrock, M.C. Ed.) 3rd edition. New York, NY: Macmillian Publishing.

Wenger, Win. 1992. *Beyond Teaching & Learning*. Singapore: Project Renaissance.

Williams, J. M. and M. B. Anderson. 1997. Psychosocial influences on central and peripheral vision and reaction time during demanding tasks. Behavioral Medicine. Vol 22(4), 160-167.

Witelson, Sandra; Debra Kigar; and Thomas Harvey. 1999. The exceptional brain of Albert Einstein. *The Lancet*, June 19, vol. 353: 2149-2153.

Wlodkowski, R. 1985. *Enhancing Adult Motivation to Learn*. San Francisco, CA: Josey-Bass.

Wolverton, B. C. 1996. How to Grow Fresh Air. New York, NY. Penguin Books.

Wurtman, Judith. 1986. *Managing Your Mind and Mood through Food*. New York: Harper & Row Publishers.

Yahnke, Beverly. 1989. The effects of functional brain asymmetry upon subliminal perception. *Imagination, Cognition & Personality*. Vol. 8(2), 121-139.

Yin, Jerry; J. Wallach, E. Wilder; J. Klingenshmith; D. Dang; N. Perrimon; H. Zhou; T. Tully; and W. Quinn. 1995. A drosophila CREB/CREM homolog encodes multiple isoforms, including cyclic AMP-dependent protein kinase responsive transcriptional activator and antagonist. *Molecular & Cellular Biology*. Vol 15(9), 5123.

Zatorre, Robert. 1997. Hemispheric specialization of human auditory processing: Perception of speech and musical sounds. *Advances in Psychology*. 123, 299.

About the Author

A former teacher and current member of the International Society for Neuroscience, **Eric Jensen, MA** has taught at all education levels, from elementary through university. In 1981 Jensen co-founded SuperCamp, the nation's first and largest brain-compatible learning program for teens, which now claims more than 25,000 graduates. He is currently President of Jensen Learning, Inc. in San Diego, California. His other books include: *The Great Memory Book, Teaching with the Brain in Mind, Brain-Compatible Strategies, Sizzle and Substance: Presenting With the Brain in Mind, Trainer's Bonanza, Completing the Puzzle,* and *Super Teaching.* He's listed in Who's Who Worldwide and remains deeply committed to making a positive, significant, and lasting difference in the way the world learns. Jensen is a sought-after conference speaker who consults and trains educators in the U.S. and abroad. **E-mail: jlcbrain@connectnet.com.**

Brain-Based Resources

The Great Memory Book by Karen Markowitz & Eric Jensen
The Great Memory Book balances current research with practical tips for optimal memory fitness. From its primer on brain biology to in-depth discussions on neuronutrients and mnemonics, this book is a great tool for anyone wanting to achieve memory excellence.

Completing the Puzzle by Eric Jensen
The newest brain-based learning book for presenters and administrators. Quick reading; cuts right to the heart of the matter; specific and highly practical.

ITI: The Model by Susan Kovalik
The best book out on brain-based curriculum. Effortlessly weaves brain research with curriculum and environments. Practical and complete.

The Learning Brain by Eric Jensen
Key brain research on nutrition, states, attention, music, gender, motivation, activity, environments, color, thinking, intelligences, prenatal, toxins, plants, aging, and memory.

Smart Moves by Carla Hannaford
An excellent overview of the body-mind relationship. Easy to understand and written for all levels, especially the introductory level. Best book on educational kinesiology.

Owner's Manual for the Brain by Pierce Howard
Here's a practical guide to everything you wanted to know about your brain. Especially strong in gender differences, stress, attention and memory. A must for all brain-owners.

Super Teaching by Eric Jensen
Over 1,000 practical strategies for energizers, discipline, openings, closings, environments, multiple intelligences, and brain research. Enough ideas for 3 years!

Bright-Brain Video Program
Learning readiness stimulators for children ages 4-8. Develop the proper neural patterning necessary for a bright brain. This video series builds a foundation for learning that will last a lifetime. You get 2 videos, a detailed instruction manual and a full color poster.

Order any of the above from The Brain Store. Call (800) 325-4769 or fax (858) 546-7560. Free catalog included. Unconditional satisfaction or money-back guarantee. Shop our website at: http://www.thebrainstore.com

Index

Notes

Notes

Please remember that this is a library book,
and that it belongs only temporarily to each
person who uses it. Be considerate. Do
not write in this, or any, library book.